THOMAS BRADWARDINE

A VIEW OF TIME AND A VISION OF ETERNITY
IN FOURTEENTH-CENTURY THOUGHT

STUDIES IN THE HISTORY
OF
CHRISTIAN THOUGHT

EDITED BY

HEIKO A. OBERMAN, Tucson, Arizona

IN COOPERATION WITH

HENRY CHADWICK, Cambridge
JAROSLAV PELIKAN, New Haven, Connecticut
BRIAN TIERNEY, Ithaka, New York
ARJO VANDERJAGT, Groningen

VOLUME LXV

EDITH WILKS DOLNIKOWSKI

THOMAS BRADWARDINE

A VIEW OF TIME AND A VISION OF ETERNITY
IN FOURTEENTH-CENTURY THOUGHT

THOMAS BRADWARDINE

A VIEW OF TIME AND A VISION OF ETERNITY IN FOURTEENTH-CENTURY THOUGHT

BY

EDITH WILKS DOLNIKOWSKI

E.J. BRILL

LEIDEN · NEW YORK · KÖLN

1995

The paper in this book meets the guidelines for permanence and durability of the Committee on Production Guidelines for Book Longevity of the Council on Library Resources.

Library of Congress Cataloging-in-Publication Data

Dolnikowski, Edith Wilks.
   Thomas Bradwardine: a view of time and a vision of eternity in
fourteenth-century thought / by Edith Wilks Dolnikowski.
     p.   cm. — (Studies in the history of Christian thought, ISSN
0081-8607 ; v. 65)
   Includes bibliographical references and indexes.
   ISBN 9004102264 (alk. paper)
   1. Bradwardine, Thomas, 1290?-1349—Contributions in concept of
time.   2. Time—Religious aspects—Christianity—History
of doctrines—Middle Ages, 600-1500.   I. Title.   II. Series.
B765.B774D65   1995
115'.092—dc20   95-2091
                                               CIP

Die Deutsche Bibliothek - CIP-Einheitsaufnahme

Dolnikowski, Edith Wilks:
Thomas Bradwardine: a study of time and a vision of eternity in
fourteenth-century thought / by Edith Wilks Dolnikowski. - Leiden ;
New York ; Köln : Brill, 1995
   (Studies in the history of Christian thought ; Vol. 65)
   ISBN 90-04-10226-4
NE: GT

ISSN   0081-8607
ISBN   90 04 10226 4

PRINTED IN THE NETHERLANDS

CONTENTS

ACKNOWLEDGMENTS

I would like to acknowledge the guidance, encouragement and support I have received from mentors, colleagues and friends as I have gone about the work of preparing this manuscript for publication. Because of the generosity of the Fulbright Commission, I was able to conduct much of my research in England. I particularly wish to thank Richard E. Sullivan and Emily Z. Tabuteau of Michigan State University for guiding me through the initial stages of research and writing. I am grateful for the assistance given to me by Jeremy I. Catto, who served as my adviser during my year of research at Oxford University. I also thank William J. Courtenay of the University of Wisconsin and Katherine H. Tachau of the University of Iowa, who have provided invaluable assistance over the last seven years through their critical evaluation of my work in its various stages of development. I am, of course, deeply honored that Professor Heiko Oberman has accepted this study of Bradwardine's views of time for publication in the *Studies in the History of Christian Thought* series. Professor Oberman's pioneering work on Bradwardine has served as a foundation for my own. I am most grateful for his encouragement of my research from its earliest stages.

I am also deeply indebted to my family and to my friends at the Episcopal Divinity School for their encouragement of my work. David Siegenthaler and Fredrica Harris Thompsett have consistently affirmed and supported my historical research amid all of the distractions of my course of study here. Patricia Panek not only offered friendship and support throughout the project but also diligently proofread my manuscript. My greatest gratitude, however, goes to my husband, Gregory, whose unfailing kindness and sense of humor have made the years spent working on this project both a happy and a productive time.

The Episcopal Divinity School
Cambridge, Massachusetts
August 26, 1994

ABBREVIATIONS

AHDLMA	*Archives d'histoire doctrinaire et littéraire du moyen âge.*
Barnes	*The Complete Works of Aristotle: The Revised Oxford Translation,* Volume I. Ed. Jonathan Barnes. Princeton: Princeton University Press, 1984.
CHLMP	*Cambridge History of Later Medieval Philosophy.* Eds. Norman Kretzmann, Anthony Kenny and Jan Pinborg. Cambridge: Cambridge University Press, 1982.
De causa Dei	Thomas Bradwardine. *De causa Dei contra Pelagium, et de virtute causarum ad suos Mertonenses, libri tres.* Ed. Henry Saville. London: Ex Officina Nortoniana apud Ioannem Billium, 1618.
De continuo	Thomas Bradwardine. *Tractatus de continuo.* Ed. John Emery Murdoch. In "Geometry and the Continuum in the Fourteenth Century: A Philosophical Analysis of Thomas Bradwardine's 'Tractatus de Continuo.'" Diss. University of Toronto, 1957.
De futuris	Thomas Bradwardine. *Tractatus de futuris contingentibus.* Ed. M. Jean-François Genest. *Recherches augustiniennes,* 14 (1979), pp. 249-336.
De incipit	Thomas Bradwardine. *Tractatus de incipit et desinit.* Ed. Lauge Olaf Nielsen. In "Thomas Bradwardine's Treatise on 'incipit' and 'desinit': Edition and Introduction." *Cahiers de l'Institute du moyen âge grec et latin,* 42 (1982), pp. 1-83.
De proportionibus	Thomas Bradwardine. *Tractatus de proportionibus.* Ed. H. Lamar Crosby. In *Thomas of Bradwardine, His Tractatus de Proportionibus: Its Significance for the Development of Mathematical Physics.* Madison, Wisconsin: University of Wisconsin Press, 1976.
MTSM	*Motion and Time, Space and Matter: Interrelations in the History of Philosophy and Science.* Eds. Peter K. Machamer and Robert G. Turnbull. Columbus, Ohio: Ohio University Press, 1976.
SMPSL	Moody, Ernest A. *Studies in Medieval Philosophy, Science and Logic: Collected Papers, 1933-1969.* London: University of California Press, 1975.
RTAM	*Recherches de théologie ancienne et médiévale.*

CHAPTER ONE

INTRODUCTION

Thomas Bradwardine is generally regarded as one of the most influential English philosophers and theologians in the early fourteenth century. His accomplishments in the fields of logic, mathematics, physics and theology, outstanding in their own right, account for only part of his fame. His abilities attracted the attention of a powerful patron, Bishop Richard of Bury, who helped him to attain high public office. As chancellor of St. Paul's and confessor to Edward III, Bradwardine demonstrated great skill in mastering the demands of ecclesiastical and civil service and was rewarded with the see of Canterbury in 1349. Yet in spite of his importance in fourteenth-century England and the survival of a relatively large portion of his writings, many important aspects of his thought remain unstudied.

Bradwardine lived and built his distinguished career in an age of intense scholarly debate. The earliest studies of Bradwardine's writings attempted to place him in the theological controversies of the thirteenth and fourteenth centuries, which resulted in a somewhat narrow view of his interests and beliefs. Current historical research on Bradwardine is directed more toward integrating his philosophical and scientific ideas with his theological convictions. As we come to see with greater clarity the academic environment in which Bradwardine worked, we seek to understand his views in the context of his relationships with other scholars. The difficulty of establishing this context is, of course, compounded by the multidisciplinary nature of his texts. Because of their highly technical nature and the wide range of topics which they embrace, Bradwardine's treatises present serious challenges to even the most skillful researchers. It is not surprising, therefore, that most studies of his work consist of critical editions and commentaries on single texts rather than investigations of concepts which emerge in various forms throughout his writings. Taken together, however, existing studies constitute a fairly complete record of Bradwardine's academic work and provide essential resources for a more synthetic approach to his thought. The recent growth of interest in some of Bradwardine's less well-known contemporaries, the men to and for whom he wrote, has created a substantial body of supplemental material which can be applied with good effect to an analysis of Bradwardine's theological and philosophical views.

This study traces the mathematical and philosophical foundations of Bradwardine's theology by considering his view of time, an issue which interested almost all natural philosophers and theologians in the late middle ages and which emerged in various contexts in all of Bradwardine's major treatises. Although infinity, continuity, contingency and other aspects of the problem of time seem to be primarily philosophical, fourteenth-century thinkers regularly considered these subjects in conjunction with more recognizably theological topics such as eternity, divine foreknowledge and free will.[1] In many cases, in fact, it is impossible to separate philosophical concerns from purely theological ones in late medieval discussions of time. Like many of his colleagues and his thirteenth-century predecessors, Bradwardine tried to accommodate both Aristotelian physics and Augustinian theology in his view of time. The distinctiveness of Bradwardine's approach to time resulted from his habit of treating almost all intellectual inquiries, both physical and theological, from the perspective of Euclidean mathematics. Bradwardine's view of time therefore provides an exceptionally clear example of the tendency among fourteenth-century thinkers to examine theological truths from mathematical and philosophical perspectives.

The specific aims of this research are to describe the classical and medieval treatments of time which Bradwardine inherited; to identify his responses to the problems of time in his early academic writings; and to determine the relative influences of Euclid, Aristotle, Augustine and Boethius on the view of time he proposed in his monumental theological work, the *De causa Dei*, first published in 1344.[2] The purpose of this study is not just to show how one prominent fourteenth-century thinker approached a long-standing philosophical problem; it also seeks to examine Bradwardine's interaction with predecessors and contemporaries by focusing on a issue which incorporates the methods and principles of several disciplines within the broad intellectual categories of natural

---

[1] For a good general discussion of late medieval attitudes to time see Jean Leclercq, "The Experience of Time and its Interpretation in the Late Middle Ages," *Studies in Medieval Culture*, 8-9 (1976), pp. 137-50.

[2] Full references to this and all subsequent texts by Bradwardine can be found under Thomas Bradwardine in the Bibliography. Citations to the most frequently used texts are included in the Abbreviations. Basic bibliographical works on Bradwardine are cited in this chapter. For a comprehensive list of Bradwardine's writings see James A. Weisheipl, "Repertorium Mertonense," *Mediaeval Studies*, 31 (1969), pp. 174-224.

philosophy and theology. This assessment of Bradwardine's view of time will help both to establish the main lines of controversy in four-teenth-century debates about time and also to assess Bradwardine's par-ticular role in those debates.

Despite reliable evidence that Bradwardine enjoyed a varied and suc-cessful career, he remains, like most fourteenth-century personalities, a mysterious figure. What little is known about his life comes primarily from his own writings and scattered references to his activities at Oxford or in the service of Edward III. Unfortunately, a purely textual approach to the biography of such an obscure figure as Bradwardine can give a distorted image of his character. According to Gordon Leff, an uncrit-ical reading of Bradwardine's treatises might lead one to describe him as "an inhumane genius" who "can hardly be called lovable."[3] Such a view hardly accords with the facts we have about Bradwardine's life. For all the apparent narrowness of his beliefs, he was obviously capable of earning and keeping the respect of several patrons who promoted him to the highest ecclesiastical office in England. His rise to prominence as a mathematician and theologian at Oxford in the 1320s and 1330s sug-gests an ability to engage his colleagues and students in conversation about the most controversial issues of his day. Though he expressed some of his opinions in terms strident enough to cause offense, he man-aged to escape personal censure in an age marked by sometimes bitter antagonisms. As to estimating Bradwardine's general reputation in late medieval England, he was sufficiently well known for Chaucer to men-tion him by name, along with Augustine and Boethius, as one of the few thinkers who could make sense of contemporary arguments about predestination.[4]

When considering such indirect evidence of Bradwardine's character, one must regret that no historian has yet been able to construct a

---

[3] Gordon Leff, *Bradwardine and the Pelagians*, Cambridge Studies in Medieval Life and Thought, Series 2, Number 5 (Cambridge: Cambridge University Press, 1957), pp. 18-19.

[4] "The Nun's Priest's Tale," in *The Riverside Chaucer*, ed. Larry D. Benson, 3rd ed. (Boston, Massachusetts: Houghton Mifflin, 1987), pp. 258-59, ll. 3240-50: "But I ne kan nat bulte it to the bren/ As kan the hooly doctour Augustyn,/ Or Boece, or the Biss-hop Bradwardyn,/ Wheither that Goddes worthy forwityng/ Streyneth me nedely for to doon a thyng—/ 'Nedely' clepe I symple necessitee—/ Or elles, if free choys be graunted me/ To do that same thyng, or do it nought,/ Though God forwoot it er that I was wroght;/ Or if his wityng streyneth never a deel/ But by necessitee condicioneel." In *Archbishop Thomas Bradwardine, A Fourteenth-Century Augustinian: A Study of his Theology in its Historical Context* (Utrecht: Kemink and Zoon, 1957), pp. 186-87, Heiko A. Oberman discusses the significance of this reference and suggests that Chau-cer's interest in Wyclif might have prompted him to cite Bradwardine in this way.

biography for him which is as full, for example, as the one which
Katherine Walsh has been able to produce for his slightly older
contemporary, Richard FitzRalph.[5] It is possible, however, to offer a
brief outline of his academic and political career. Historians have
estimated that Bradwardine was born some time during the last two
decades of the thirteenth century, probably in the early 1290s. There is
no evidence of his birthplace but an oblique reference in the *De causa
Dei* to his father as living in Chichester suggests that he might have
come from Hertfield or Heathfield in Sussex.[6] According to Oxford
University records, Bradwardine resided at Balliol College, where he
was a fellow from 1321 to 1323. In 1323 he accepted another fellowship
at Merton and spent the next three years completing his regency in the
arts. Sometime during this period he became the proctor of Merton;
afterwards he served as Chancellor of the University.[7] While at Merton
Bradwardine was introduced to the brilliant circle of mathematicians,
logicians, physicists and astronomers whose work contributed to the
outstanding reputation for natural philosophy which Oxford University
enjoyed in the first half of the fourteenth century. Bradwardine's early
work in mathematics and philosophy clearly indicates that he flourished
in this stimulating academic setting. Within a decade of his arrival at
Merton he had composed several important treatises on a wide range of
scientific and logical topics, including velocity, proportionality, continuity, contingency, memory and signification. His achievements in
these fields alone have led historians to call him a "mathematical
genius"[8] and to compare his works in physics favorably to those
of Galileo.[9] As a consequence of this remarkable productivity,
Bradwardine attracted the patronage of Richard of Bury, Bishop of

---

[5] Katherine Walsh, *A Fourteenth-Century Scholar and Primate: Richard FitzRalph in Oxford, Avignon and Armagh* (Oxford: Clarendon Press, 1981). Even for FitzRalph, whose career is remarkably well-documented, it is impossible to fix the details of his birth, early life and death (*ibid.*, pp. 1-15, 445-50).

[6] Leff, p. 2.

[7] Walsh, p. 28.

[8] James A. Weisheipl and Heiko A. Oberman, "The *Sermo Epinicius* Ascribed to Thomas Bradwardine (1346)," *AHDLMA*, 26 (1958), p. 295. For some useful remarks on Bradwardine's contribution to fourteenth-century mathematics and logic see J. M. M. H. Thijssen, "Burdian on Mathematics," *Vivarium*, 23 (1985), pp. 55-78 and Paul Vincent Spade, "*Insolubilia* and Bradwardine's Theory of Signification," *Annuaire de l'école pratique des hautes études*, 85 (1977-78), pp. 391-93.

[9] Anneliese Maier, "Zwei Recensionen," in *Ausgehendes Mittelalter: Gesammelte Aufsätze zur Geistesgeschichte des 14. Jahrhunderts*, 2 vols. (Rome: Storia e letteratura, 1967), II: 458.

Durham, who was instrumental in encouraging scientific inquiry of all kinds during the second quarter of the fourteenth century and was a particular patron of the fellows of Merton College.[10]   When he was invited to join Bishop Bury's household in 1335, Bradwardine entered a group of some of the most talented natural philosophers of the mid-fourteenth century.   The dedication of his monumental theological work, the *De causa Dei*, to his colleagues at Merton confirms both his recognition of the prestige associated with his former college and also his sincere affection for it.

Bradwardine's ecclesiastical career was equally distinguished, thanks again, in part, to Bury's influence.   About two years after entering into Bury's service, Bradwardine became Chancellor of St. Paul's in London. In 1339 he took on the additional responsibility of serving as Edward III's chaplain and confessor.   In fulfilling this office, Bradwardine was called upon to travel extensively with the king both at home and on campaigns and missions abroad.   According to J. A. Weisheipl and Heiko A. Oberman, who have analyzed the text of the *Sermo epinicius* ascribed to Bradwardine, he almost certainly accompanied Edward III on his French campaign of 1346 and witnessed the battle at Crécy on August 26.[11]   Bradwardine's appointment as a diplomatic envoy on October 22, 1346 suggests that he participated in subsequent negotiations for peace with France.[12]   During the late 1330s and 1340s Bradwardine came to be regarded through his preaching, lecturing and writing as one of England's most gifted academic theologians.   The culmination of his ecclesiastical career occurred in July of 1349, when he was consecrated as Archbishop of Canterbury at Avignon.[13]   Originally elected to this office by the monks of Canterbury in 1348, Bradwardine had been unable to take up the office earlier, owing to the king's resentment that the monks had acted without first consulting him.   Edward III's candidate, John Ufford, filled the office instead; but, when Ufford died shortly thereafter from the plague, the king acknowledged Bradwardine's election.   Unfortunately, Bradwardine himself soon fell victim to the plague and died on August 26, only one month after his consecration.

In spite of his remarkable achievements as a natural philosopher and public servant, Bradwardine's reputation in the twentieth century is

---

[10] William Abel Pantin, *The English Church in the Fourteenth Century* (Cambridge: Cambridge University Press, 1955), p. 159; Walsh, p. 28.

[11] Weisheipl and Oberman, p. 299.

[12] *Ibid.*, p. 300.

[13] Leff, p. 3.

based on his theological works, the interpretation of which has generated considerable controversy. The source of this controversy is the long-established strain in the historical literature which connects Bradwardine's predestinarian thought with that of John Wyclif. Whatever the true nature of his influence on Wyclif's theology, however, it is clear that Bradwardine arrived at his conclusions about God in a way which was altogether different from Wyclif's. As J. A. Robson has observed, Wyclif's theology evolved in the course of his philosophical studies, whereas Bradwardine's was the product of a deeply spiritual conversion which occurred while he was still studying in the arts faculty.[14]

The often-quoted autobiographical account of this conversion experience in the *De causa Dei* tells of Bradwardine's sudden disillusionment with the discussions of grace and free will which he often heard as a student of philosophy. He laments his early attraction to the "Pelagian" notion, which pervaded philosophical speculation at Oxford, "that we are the masters of our own free acts, and that it stands in our power to do either good or evil, to be either virtuous or vicious."[15] It was not sophisticated arguments or even faithful contemplation which transformed his opinion. Rather, he says:

> . . . before I had become a student of theology, the truth before mentioned struck upon me like a beam of grace, and it seemed to me as if I beheld in the distance, under a transparent image of truth, the grace of God as it is prevenient both in time and nature to all good deeds—that is to say, the gracious will of God which precedently wills, that he who merits salvation shall be saved, and precedently works this merit of it in him, God in truth being in all movement the primary Mover.[16]

This revelation inspired Bradwardine thereafter to devote his considerable energy and talent to refuting any arguments, whether ancient or contemporary, which called into question God's absolute omniscience or omnipotence. His opinions about grace and free will matured throughout his academic career. He refined his views both by engaging in debates with his peers and by incorporating his ideas into

---

[14] *Wyclif and the Oxford Schools* (Cambridge: Cambridge University Press, 1961), p. 39.

[15] Quoted in Gotthard Lechler, *John Wycliffe and his English Precursors*, trans. P. Lorimer (London: The Religious Tract Society, 1878), p. 66. See *De causa Dei*, I, 35, p. 308, C-E.

[16] *Ibid.*

his sermons after 1335. The *De causa Dei* itself presented a scathing attack on the views of Bradwardine's adversaries. Far from being an open-ended speculative treatise of the type which abounded generally in the 1320s and 1330s, this work was consciously polemical. In it Bradwardine applied the full vigor of his exceptionally analytical mind to the vindication of the absolute necessity of God's will as first cause in every human act. Bradwardine so forcefully defended his conclusions that readers of the *De causa Dei*, from the fourteenth century to the present, have objected to his apparently rigid determinism. Fourteenth-century critics simply complained that his conception of God's relationship to humanity unnecessarily restricted human free choice. They tried to refute his claims by attacking Bradwardine's definitions of time, eternity and contingency and so emphasized, as Bradwardine himself had done, the interconnection of natural philosophy and theology.

After the Reformation, however, the fourteenth-century critique of Bradwardine's theology was all but abandoned in favor of an approach which stressed his advocacy of an Augustinian form of predestination. Thus Bradwardine came to be regarded as a precursor to the Reformation. In the nineteenth and early twentieth centuries, historians saw Bradwardine primarily as a theologian and made almost no attempt to investigate the philosophical principles which influenced his religious thought. Even now, studies of Bradwardine's theology have not been entirely freed from such concepts as "nominalism," "Ockhamism" and "determinism," which have influenced the interpretation of fourteenth-century theology since the late nineteenth century. Bradwardine has emerged, therefore, as a fascinating but enigmatic figure whose philosophical interests seemingly bore little relation to his theological concerns. Historians investigating some of Bradwardine's contemporaries have begun recently to challenge the assumptions of the traditional interpretation of fourteenth-century intellectual life by closely examining the philosophical foundations of late medieval theology.[17]

---

[17] William J. Courtenay, "Recent Work on Fourteenth-Century Oxford Thought," *History of Education Quarterly*, Spring-Summer, 1985, pp. 227-32. In addition to the works cited in Courtenay's review article, most of the citations in this study dating from the past decade or so reflect the trend of integrating philosophy and theology. A representative but by no means exhaustive list of such works would include: *The Cambridge History of Later Medieval Philosophy*, eds. Norman Kretzman, Anthony Kenny and Jan Pinborg (Cambridge: Cambridge University Press, 1982); *From Ockham to Wyclif*, Studies in Church History, Subsidia 5, eds. Anne Hudson and Michael Wilks (Oxford: Basil Blackwell, 1987); and Katherine H. Tachau, *Vision and Certitude in the Age of Ockham: Optics, Epistemology and the Foundation of Semantics 1250-1345* (New

Bradwardine's provocative ideas about the relationship of natural philosophy to theology also deserve to be reconsidered in this way.

Since the late nineteenth century, Bradwardine's reputation as a scholar has rested on his supposed contributions to two distinct intellectual movements: early modern science (through Galileo to Newton) and Protestant Reformation theology (through Wyclif to Luther). Bradwardine's treatments of geometry and physics are well-known to specialists in the history of science. His theological works have received even broader recognition because of his supposed influence on Wyclif. Historians such as Sebastian Hahn, Gotthardt Lechler, Herbert Workman and J. F. Laun, who pioneered the study of Bradwardine's writings at the turn of the century, stressed the connection between Bradwardine's and Wyclif's approaches to predestination.[18] Aside from Wyclif's role in exposing some of Bradwardine's theological views, however, this association with Wyclif has actively harmed his reputation, not so much by implicating him in the Wycliffite heresy as by distorting his views in order to force them into forms which are recognizable components of Wyclif's thought.

Some of the problems of this traditional approach have been corrected in two major studies of the *De causa Dei*: Gordon Leff's *Bradwardine and the Pelagians* (1957) and Heiko A. Oberman's *Archbishop Thomas Bradwardine, A Fourteenth-Century Augustinian* (1958).[19] Because they concentrate only on the theological content of a

York: E. J. Brill, 1988). See also Richard C. Dales, *Medieval Discussions of the Eternity of the World* (New York: E. J. Brill, 1990), which traces the debate about eternity from antiquity to fourteenth-century Oxford and Paris; and the accompanying volume of primary sources, *Medieval Latin Texts on the Eternity of the World*, eds. Richard C. Dales and Omar Argerame (New York: E. J. Brill, 1991).

[18] Sebastian Hahn, *Thomas Bradwardine und seine Lehre von der menschlichen Willensfreiheit* (Münster: Aschendorff, 1904); Herbert Workman, *John Wyclif: A Study of the English Medieval Church* (Oxford: Clarendon Press, 1926); Justin Ferdinand Laun, "Die Prädestination bei Wiclif und Bradwardin," in *Imago Dei*, ed. H. Bornkamm (Giessen: Alfred Töpelmann, 1923), pp. 63-84; and Laun, "Thomas von Bradwardin, der Schüler Augustins und Lehrer Wiclifs," *Zeitschrift für Kirchengeschichte*, 47 (New Series 10) (1928), pp. 333-56. See also Laun, "Recherches sur Thomas Bradwardin, précurseur de Wyclif," *Revue d'histoire et de philosophie religieuse*, 9 (1929), pp. 217-33, which briefly summarizes the contents of the previous article and provides a useful appendix on texts.

[19] See also Oberman's "Thomas Bradwardine: un précurseur de Luther?," *Revue d'histoire et de philosophie religieuse*, 40 (1960), pp. 146-51 for a brief analysis of Bradwardine's place in the Reformation tradition. For a critical appraisal of Oberman's view see Alistair E. McGrath, "Forerunners of the Reformation," *Harvard Theological Report*, 7 (1982), pp. 219-42.

single work, the *De causa Dei*, neither historian does full justice to Bradwardine's wide-ranging contributions to fourteenth-century philosophy. Nevertheless, their profound disagreement over Bradwardine's theological determinism continues to shape historical discussions of his thought. Their differences of opinion arise less from variations in their reading of Bradwardine than from their assessments of his position in fourteenth- and fifteenth-century scholarly debate. Leff presents Bradwardine as a theological radical whose determinism struck at the heart of the prevailing philosophical attitude of the early fourteenth century. Oberman, by contrast, portrays Bradwardine as a conservative Augustinian who merely attempted to defend a moderate, orthodox view concerning God's prescience and will against nominalist or Ockhamist attacks. These variations in interpretation arise fundamentally from divergent views of the intellectual climate of the early fourteenth century. The differences between Leff's and Oberman's approaches to Bradwardine suggest that there is still room for discussion of such topics as Bradwardine's purpose in writing the *De causa Dei*, the nature of his audience, the selection of his sources and the impact of his work on his contemporaries and successors. One of the central aims of this study, therefore, is to resolve some of the questions suggested by the debate between Leff and Oberman by considering those questions from the perspective of Bradwardine's view of time.

Bradwardine's work in natural philosophy had also begun to receive attention by the mid-twentieth century. If the commentators on the *De causa Dei* rarely mention his scientific achievements, the historians who have examined his writings on physics and mathematics have been just as disinclined to discuss his theology. Apart from some critical editions, moreover, there have been no full-length studies of Bradwardine's scientific work comparable to the monographs of Leff and Oberman. Anneliese Maier, Marshall Clagett, James Weisheipl and John Emery Murdoch have made the greatest contributions to our knowledge of Bradwardine's scientific work through their specialized studies of his writings. None of these, however, has explored either the full range of his scientific thought or the relationship between his conception of natural philosophy and his theology.

Fortunately, interest in Bradwardine has remained strong in the last three decades, and, despite the absence of fresh attempts to examine his thought as a whole, he still attracts the attention of historians of late medieval intellectual and religious life. The major thrust of current research is to determine as accurately as possible what Bradwardine said and did between 1325 and 1349. To achieve precision in dating Brad-wardine's career, historians have tried to examine the entire corpus of his writings as well as the works of contemporaries with whom he con-versed. Lauge Olaf Nielsen, Hüner Gillmeister, Niels-Jorgen Green-Pedersen, Jean-François Genest and Katherine H. Tachau have enlarged the body of printed material on Bradwardine with their editions of some of his less known texts.[20] Zenon Kaluza and Katherine Walsh have made good use of this fundamental research and have succeeded in cor-recting errors about Bradwardine's position in the schools at the begin-ning of the fourteenth century.[21] Because the purpose of their research is to discern Bradwardine's relationships with contemporary scholars such as William of Ockham, Adam Wodeham, Thomas Buckingham and Nicholas Aston, these historians tend to emphasize common philosophi-cal and theological concerns, rather than to highlight Bradwardine's particular contributions to late medieval natural philosophy.

Though many historians have remarked, for example, on the mathe-matical structure and geometric precision of his arguments in the *De*

---

[20] For an excellent overview of the earlist phase of Bradwardine's academic career, see Genest and Tachau, "La lecture de Thomas Bradwardine sur les Sentences," *AHDLMA*, 56 (1990), pp. 301-306, which describes a possible fragment of Bradwardine's commentary on the Sentences—a work which up to now has been considered entirely lost. The editions produced by Nielsen and Genest will be discussed extensively in later chapters. Hüner Gillmeister has edited a very short treatise by Bradwardine on mnemonic devices in "An Intriguing Fourteenth-Century Document: Thomas Bradwardine's *De arte memorativa*," *Archiv für das Studium des neueren Sprachen und Literaturen*, 220 (1983), pp. 111-14. See also Beryl Rowland, "Bishop Bradwardine on the Artificial Memory," *Journal of the Warburg and Courtauld Institutes*, 41 (1978), pp. 307-12. Niels Jorgen Green-Pedersen discusses an anonymous text which has been attributed to Bradwardine in "Bradwardine (?) on Ockham's Doctrine of Consequences: An Edition, "*Cahiers de l'Institute du moyen âge grec et latin*, 42 (1982), pp. 85-150. Because evidence for the identification of the text is inconclusive and the subject of the treatise is unrelated to the issue of time, it will not be considered here.

[21] For some examples of recent work connecting Bradwardine with his contemporaries on issues not directly related to the subject of this study see Kaluza, "La prétendu discussion parisienne de Thomas de Bradwardine avec Thomas de Buckingham: témoinage de Thomas de Cracovie," *RTAM*, 43 (1976), pp. 209-36; Kaluza, "Le problème du 'Deum non esse' chez Étienne du Chaumont, Nicolas Aston et Thomas Bradwardine," *Mediaevalia Philosophia Polonorum*, 24 (1979), pp. 3-19; Kaluza, "L'oeuvre théologique de Nicolas Aston," *AHDLMA*, 45 (1978), pp. 45-82; Leonard Kennedy, "Oxford Philosophers and the Existence of God," *RTAM*, 52 (1985), pp. 194-208; and M. L. Rouré, "La problématique des proportions insolubles au XIIIe siècle—William Shyreswood, Walter Burleigh et Thomas Bradwardine," *AHDLMA*, 37 (1970-71), pp. 205-326.

causa Dei, none has yet examined this text from the perspective of his previous writings on mathematics and philosophy. A fundamental concept in many of Bradwardine's works is his definition of time, both in theological and in natural terms. By exploring his approach to time throughout a range of texts and by comparing his opinions with those of his contemporaries, I hope to establish the context for his assertions about time, contingency, divine foreknowledge and predestination as he presented them in the *De causa Dei*. Central to the interpretation of this treatise are the following questions: 1) To what extent did Bradwardine's understanding of time as a physical phenomenon influence his theological determinism? 2) How did he attempt to reconcile his appreciation of Aristotelian physics with his reverence for Augustinian theology? 3) Is there any correspondence between Bradwardine's approach to time and the approaches of the colleagues he referred to as "modern Pelagians," and, if so, what is the significance of that correspondence? 4) How does Bradwardine's view of time fit into his theological and scientific thought as a whole? Through a systematic analysis of Bradwardine's writing about time, I shall describe the close relationship between natural philosophy and theology in fourteenth-century academic discussions using a wider spectrum of Bradwardine's responses to these discussions than has commonly been applied to that purpose.

This analysis will proceed in three parts. Chapters Two and Three summarize the medieval debate about time and issues related to time from Peripatetic discussions in the fifth century B. C. E. to Bradwardine's immediate thirteenth-century predecessors. These chapters emphasize the importance of the legacy of classical approaches to medieval discussions of time. Although a long-standing tension between Plato's metaphysical and Aristotle's more physical approaches to time lay at the heart of the medieval debate, many other thinkers were drawn to the problem of time and made significant original contributions. By the fourteenth century, a rich and varied literature on time and subjects relating to time had become the foundation of the arts curriculum, and no trained philosopher or theologian could escape its influence. Time was one of the many concepts which emerged in philosophical and theological debates in the schools. Discussions of such topics as contingency, continuity, infinity and motion all depended on explicit or implicit definitions of time and thus assured frequent reference to the various aspects of time. To understand Bradwardine's positions on these issues it is necessary to establish the character of academic debates about time at Oxford on the eve of his arrival.

Chapters Four, Five and Six present a systematic examination of four of Bradwardine's treatises written in the 1320s which reveal the major elements of his approach to time. The tracts *De proportionibus* and *De continuo*, both dating from the late 1320s, are examples of Bradwardine's contribution to Oxford's achievements in the physical sciences in the late middle ages. Bradwardine's reputation as a mathematician rests on his innovative solutions to problems in classical physics involving motion, velocity and infinity. Because all of these topics demand specific reference to time, the *De proportionibus* and the *De continuo* define Bradwardine's view of time as a physical concept. Both treatises set out to endorse Aristotle's natural philosophy, but Bradwardine's penetrating mathematical analysis of velocity and continuity completely transforms Aristotle's original positions. In the former text, Bradwardine appears to accept Aristotle's definition of time but reshapes the physical description of motion which underlay it. In the latter text, Bradwardine uses time to illustrate how one might apply the characteristics of purely mathematical continua to physical continua, both permanent and successive.

Bradwardine's *De incipit et desinit* and his *De futuris contingentibus* are primarily philosophical works which address two different aspects of the question of foreknowledge. In the *De incipit et desinit*, Bradwardine argues that the future must be considered contingent because the human mind cannot predict with certainty any future event. In the *De futuris contingentibus*, however, he maintains that the future is not really contingent, because God, who exists outside of time, knows all of his creation in a single eternal present. These texts represent Bradwardine's earliest attempts to work out the contradictions between human and divine perspectives on time, eternity and knowledge.

Chapter Seven investigates Bradwardine's mathematical and philo-sophical approach to time as he defined it in the *De causa Dei*. This analysis indicates that he did not see any significant contradiction be-tween his modified Aristotelian conception of the physical universe and his passionate advocacy of Augustinian theology. A close examination of his conception of the role of time in creation, sin and grace will dem-onstrate that it is impossible to evaluate Bradwardine's theology without reference to his natural philosophy and will consider why many previous studies of the *De causa Dei* have not approached the treatise in this way. Bradwardine's unique method for synthesizing the two rather distinct views of time which came out of these traditions reflects an intellectual outlook which links him at once with such predecessors as Thomas

Aquinas, Anselm and Robert Grosseteste, and contemporaries such as William of Ockham, Thomas Buckingham and Robert Holcot. To look at the *De causa Dei* from the perspective of the single issue of time and in light of his earlier considerations of the same problem is a novel and fruitful method for studying not only this significant text but also Bradwardine's thought as a whole.

Throughout my investigation of Bradwardine's view of time, I shall try, wherever possible, to point out the connections between Bradwardine and Ockham, who, despite their frequent portrayal as antagonists, actually shared many common assumptions about natural philosophy and theology and together helped to give the early fourteenth century its distinctive intellectual character. A concluding chapter briefly traces the influence of Bradwardine's and Ockham's views of time among a wider circle of scholars, including Robert Holcot and Thomas Buckingham, in order to show how ideas were disseminated in the mid-fourteenth century, a period of unusually vigorous philosophical and theological speculation. These scholars, usually identified as "Ockhamists" and hence as Bradwardine's adversaries, actually had a much more complicated relationship with each other: they sometimes rejected aspects of Ockham's metaphysical approach to time in favor of Bradwardine's views and they were equally engaged in the attempt which dominated fourteenth-century academic life to reconcile theology with new discoveries in natural philosophy.[22] Discussions about time between the younger and the more established scholars reflect, therefore, the wide range of debate in the first half of the fourteenth century over the most effective way to relate natural philosophy and logic to theology in an age of expanding scientific knowledge. More important, however, the ideas of these thinkers provide the best possible context for evaluating Bradwardine's attempt to promote his geometrical synthesis of Aristotle and Augustine at a time of substantial reevaluation of all ancient authorities.

---

[22] In "Interfaculty Disputes in Late Medieval Oxford," *From Ockham to Wyclif*, pp. 331-42, John M. Fletcher outlines the political ramifications of these philosophical debates both within the university and beyond.

CHAPTER TWO

CLASSICAL AND EARLY MEDIEVAL VIEWS OF TIME

Bradwardine's views about time, like those of most other medieval thinkers, were influenced by classical discussions of the subject. In fact, Bradwardine and his contemporaries were thoroughly familiar with the full range of classical treatments of time and were aware that most medieval approaches to time relied on definitions or concepts derived from the natural philosophies of several ancient writers. Plato and Aristotle were the principal contributors. Classical philosophers engendered in their medieval counterparts a twofold interest in the problem of time by encouraging them both to master the practical difficulties of measuring time and also to discern time's larger cosmological significance. Through their debates about the nature of time, classical philosophers produced a rich technical vocabulary for analyzing time which has been used extensively throughout the centuries but was especially important in shaping late medieval approaches to natural philosophy.

Before attempting to assess late medieval approaches to time in general and Bradwardine's view in particular, it is necessary to establish the characteristics of the classical and early medieval discussions of time. While the analysis which follows is not intended to be comprehensive, it will serve to underscore the arguments about time which most influenced medieval discussions. We begin, therefore, with a short assessment of thought about time among the pre-Socratic philosophers, followed by a more thorough analysis of the ideas of Plato, Aristotle and Plotinus, each of whose concepts made tangible contributions to late medieval debates. Next comes a synopsis of Augustine's approach to time, which, because of its original and highly compelling synthesis of classical and Christian traditions, became a foundation for discussions of time throughout the middle ages. Finally, we shall consider briefly Boethius' view of time. Boethius enriched Augustine's approach by broadening the range of questions which Christian thinkers should consider in their speculations about time and inspired Bradwardine as he developed his own positions on time and eternity.

The earliest attempts to understand time arose, quite naturally, out of curiosity over astronomical phenomena. Long before natural philosophers had begun to regard time as a metaphysical entity, human societies had become skilled in reckoning time through lunar, solar or planetary cycles. Evidence from the earliest cultures suggests that people did not initially think of time as a concept distinct from individual events. In his analysis of views of time in the ancient world, for example, P. E. Ariotti describes the "multiple times" of the Egyptians, Babylonians and Hebrews, in which chronologies were marked by changes in natural phenomena. According to Ariotti, ancient Greek poetry provides the first suggestion that time might be understood more broadly as a single neutral frame of reference for establishing sequences of events.[1] The poets envisioned time as a distinct natural force and embodied its characteristics in a god, Chronos.[2] This deification of time prompted discussions about the effects of time in the natural world. Some Greek thinkers eventually rejected the notion of deified or personified time and began to regard time, along with such features of the natural order as space and motion, simply as abstract cosmological principles. As these early natural philosophers took on the difficult logical task of distinguishing time from space and motion, they provided the

---

[1] P. E. Ariotti, "The Concept of Time in Western Antiquity," in *The Study of Time*, ed. J. T. Fraser and N. Lawrence (New York: Springer-Verlag, 1975), II: 69-70. Ariotti points out, however, that the earliest Greek writers also conceived of time as the accumulation of "multiple times" (e.g., astronomical and seasonal cycles), rather than as a single entity. The poet Hesiod, for example, referred to several of these cycles in *Works and Days*. Says Ariotti (p. 69): "Natural events were used for timing important activities. The arrival of cranes in ancient Greece, Hesiod noted, marks the time for planting, the return of the swallows the end of preening. . . . Hesiod noted the setting of the Pleiades as marking the time for hauling the fragile ships of the Greeks up on dry land, and the summer solstice for safe seafaring."

[2] *Ibid.* Ariotti suggests that these artists (e.g., Pherecydes, Aeschylus, Sophocles, Solon) might have been influenced by Iranian sources. In *Studies in Iconology* (New York: Harper and Row, 1939), pp. 70-75, Erwin Panofsky discusses the mythological tradition of the god Chronos. Although there was no god of time in the earliest Greek pantheon, the similarity between the Greek word for time, *chronos*, and the name of the oldest Greek Titan, *Kronos* (Saturn, in Roman mythology), caused poets and philosophers to begin to associate the symbols of Kronos with concepts of time. Thus by the fourth century B.C.E. *Kronos'* name had been changed to *Chronos* and he was widely considered to be both a Titan and the god of time. Panofsky suggests, moreover, that the deification of time, though based on a linguistic coincidence, reflects a significant change in ancient Greek cosmology: "When religious worship gradually disintegrated and was finally supplanted by philosophical speculation, the fortuitous similarity between the words Chronos and Kronos was adduced as proof of the actual identity of the two concepts which really had some features in common" (p. 73). The association of Chronos with Kronos has had considerable influence on artistic expressions of time in western Art. Panofsky observes that Father Time is usually depicted as an old man with a scythe because Kronos, originally a god of agriculture, had those characteristics.

foundation for more sophisticated studies of time which were to follow.[3]

Some of the most persistent theories about time in the western philo-sophical tradition can be traced to two pre-Socratic philosophers, Heraclitus of Ephesus and Parmenides of Elea. Heraclitus' main contri-bution to the debates about time, besides his suggestion that the natural order was not created or influenced by anthropomorphic gods, was his observation that natural occurrences are both cyclical and linear:[4] while nature follows repeatable cycles, such as seasons, the changes which take place in the course of these cycles are nevertheless permanent and real.[5] The Pythagoreans adopted this principle of cycles and, in their attempts to analyze every aspect of nature in terms of number, gave time a mathematical definition. The most concise expression of the Pythago-rean view of time is Archytas of Tarentum's statement that time is "the number of a certain movement, or also, in general, the proper interval of the nature of the universe."[6] According to Zygmunt Zawirski, some modern commentators assume incorrectly that Archytas' understanding of "number" corresponds to Aristotle's more precise use of that term and therefore try to interpret Archytas' statements from an Aristotelian point of view when, in fact, it is more accurate to see Archytas' definition of time as representative of a completely separate Pythagorean approach to time.[7] Archytas' contribution to the discussion of time lies not in his direct influence on Aristotle but in his introducing into the western philosophical tradition the concepts of mathematical and absolute time.[8]

In contrast to Heraclitus, Parmenides and his followers doubted that time and the changes which time seems to engender existed at all. Parmenides himself argued that both motion and time are unreal because they lack permanence.[9] The cornerstone of his philosophy was the rejection of all multiplicity and change. His student, Zeno, the best-

---

[3] D. Corish, "The Beginning of the Beginning in Western Thought," in *The Study of Time*, IV, p. 36. For a good brief introduction to the cosmological aspects of classical temporal theory see also William Calvert Kneale, "Time and Eternity in Theology," *Proceedings of the Aristotelian Society*, 60 (1960-61), pp. 87-108.

[4] Ariotti, p. 72.

[5] J. Alexander Gunn, *The Problem of Time: An Historical and Critical Study* (London: Allen and Unwin, 1929), p. 18.

[6] Quoted by the Neoplatonist Simplicius in *In Aristotelis Categorias Commentarii*, ed. Carolus Kalbfleish (Berlin: G. Reimeri, 1907), p. 350. Trans. Ariotti, p. 72. See note 53 below for additional information on the Neoplatonists.

[7] Zygmunt Zawirski, *L'Évolution de la notion du temps* (Cracow: Libraire Gebethner et Wolff, 1936), pp. 8-10.

[8] Ariotti, p. 72.

[9] Gunn, p. 18.

known adherent of the Eleatic system, tried to prove that motion and time cannot exist with his four arguments against movement, or "paradoxes." All four paradoxes hinge on the apparent contradiction that motion, time and space can be conceived either as infinitely divisible and continuous or as indivisible and therefore discontinuous. Although his proofs of the unreality of motion, time and space are contrary to the evidence of sensory observation, his objections to contemporary definitions of time raised important philosophical questions which subsequent thinkers had to address. Ariotti points to the irony that a person who denied time's very existence should have prompted major advances in temporal theory.[10]   Nevertheless, the Eleatic studies of infinity and continuity provided a philosophical starting-point for the mathematical analysis of time, which was a particularly strong feature of late medieval natural philosophy.[11]

Medieval views about time were influenced more directly by Zeno's contemporary Plato, who synthesized elements of both Parmenides and Heraclitus in his own philosophical system. Like Parmenides, Plato believed that reality could be found only in what was eternal and unchanging. Along with Heraclitus, however, Plato acknowledged that the changes which human beings constantly experience are significant and have an aspect of reality about them which must be accounted for in any study of nature. Plato tried to resolve this dilemma by distinguishing the flux, succession and sensibility of changing human experience from the eternal forms, ideas and values which guide human perception.[12] In his cosmology, Plato identifies two kinds of being. Eternal being is perfect, limitless in time and space and therefore is the most real. Created beings, by contrast, are physically and temporally limited; they are imperfect both because they pass in and out of existence and because they change continually throughout their lives. The reality of created beings depends, therefore, on the eternal being which encompasses them. Although they can never approach the perfection of the eternal creator, the "becoming" of these creatures is analogous to the "being" of the creator, just as the time in which creatures experience this "becoming" resembles the creator's eternity. If creatures could share directly in the perfect being of the creator, argued Plato, there would be no time.[13]

---

[10] Ariotti, p. 72.
[11] Zawirski, pp. 11-12.
[12] Gunn, p. 22.
[13] Ibid., pp. 21-22.

Plato's consideration of the relationship between time and eternity often led him to speculate on the specific characteristics of time and eternity. These treatments proved to be highly influential both in the classical period and throughout the middle ages. His most concise statements about the nature of time appear in his early dialogue, the *Timaeus*, an allegorical poem about creation, in which the protagonist, Timaeus, asserts that time was created along with the rest of the universe and its existence depends on the existence of the universe: "Time came into being with the Heaven, in order that, as they were brought into being together, so they might be dissolved together, if their dissolution should come to pass. . . ."[14] When asked why the creator (God) had made the universe in the first place, Timaeus answers that God had wanted to bring order and harmony out of the primordial chaos. Because God is good and desires only the good for his creation, ". . . he fashioned reason within soul and soul within body, to the end that the work he accomplished might be by nature as excellent and perfect as possible."[15] The mind and soul of the universe are discerned in the regularity of its motion: whatever order and harmony exist in the universe are due to the intelligence which God has imparted to it. Because it possesses the characteristics of mind and soul, the universe is an animal, a complete animal in which all other intelligible animals and visible creatures are contained.[16]

Pleased at his creation of a living, moving universe, God wished to perfect it further by making it even more like the divine model of an animal. Because the model animal is eternal, however, and something created can never be eternal, God made "a moving likeness of eternity; and at the same time that he ordered the Heaven, he made, of eternity that abides in it as unity, an eternal image proceeding according to number."[17] This likeness or image of eternity is time. The things which we use to measure time, such as days, seasons and years, did not exist

---

[14] *Timaeus*, 38B, trans. Francis MacDonald Cornford in *Plato's Cosmology: The Timaeus of Plato Translated with a Running Commentary* (New York: Humanities Press, 1952), p. 99.

[15] John F. Callahan, *Four Views of Time in Ancient Philosophy* (Cambridge, Massachusetts: Harvard University Press, 1948), p. 6.

[16] Callahan, pp. 6-7.

[17] Callahan, p. 16, paraphrases *Timaeus*, 37D, which Cornford, pp. 97-98, translates as follows: "Now the nature of that Living Being (i.e., the universe) was eternal, and this character it was impossible to confer in full completeness on the generated thing. But the god took thought to make, as it were, a moving likeness of eternity; and, at the same time that he ordered the Heaven, he made of eternity, that abides in unity, an everlasting likeness moving according to number—that to which we have given the name Time."

before the universe was created but came into existence when and because the earth was made. The parts of time which we call past and future are therefore created forms of time which are not eternal. Eternal being simply is and does not become younger or older because of time, just as the cycles and processes of change which we observe in sensible objects do not occur in eternal being. Because time is patterned after eternity, however, we can understand at least something of the nature of eternity by studying its image in time.[18]

As "an image proceeding according to number," time depends for its existence on the orderly, measurable motions of created bodies. In the *Timaeus*, Plato suggests that the regular movements of the sun, moon, stars and planets determine and preserve the "numbers of time." These orderly celestial motions allow us to measure time with mathematical precision. In contrast to the ancient Greek religious tradition, which, for example, conceived of a year as a progression of seasons, Plato defines the year much more precisely as the amount of time it takes for the sun to leave and return to its position at the winter solstice. Similarly, a month is defined by the time it takes for the moon to complete its phases.[19] Thus time and motion are completely interrelated and are measures of each other. Like a clock, the heavenly bodies moving through space provide an absolute standard of time which is independent of human perception.[20]

The conception of time which Plato presents in the *Timaeus* is precise, thoughtful and appealing. It gracefully reconciles the Eleatic demand for attributing reality only to changeless being with Pythagorean observations about the connections among motion, time and space. By making time coterminous with the universe, it gives time, theoretically at least, a definite beginning and end. It establishes the characteristics of time in such a way that one can observe and comprehend them. Unfortunately, the *Timaeus* not only fails to resolve many of the problems which Plato's predecessors had identified in the study of time but it also raises some entirely new ones. As John F. Callahan notes, certain difficulties arise simply from the metaphysical language which Plato uses in the *Timaeus*. Such words as "God," "creation" and "goodness," which function perfectly well in Timaeus' allegorical explanations for the natural order, also have explicit religious connotations

---

[18] *Timaeus*, 37E-38B. See Callahan's paraphrase, p. 17.

[19] Robert E. Cushman, "Greek and Christian Views of Time," *Journal of Religion*, 33 (1953), p. 256.

[20] *Ibid.*, p. 257.

which Plato almost certainly does not intend. Moreover, he consciously
chooses his metaphors not to render a scientifically accurate account of
creation but "to awaken in the soul of the reader an insight into the nature of
the universe and its motions that could be produced . . . in no other way."[21]
Literal interpretations of Plato's specific remarks about motion and time can
lead to serious misunderstanding of his real intentions, as the subsequent
discussion of Aristotle's criticism of Plato will illustrate.

The problem of misinterpreting Plato's view of time is not confined,
however, to his contemporaries or to those who take his metaphors too
literally. Sometimes confusion arises from the reader's unwillingness to
admit that inconsistencies in Plato's account of creation could be the result of Plato's own mistakes, especially when those readers have been
trained to use a philosophical vocabulary which insists on precise definitions for every term. D. Corish observes, for example, that many
readers refuse "to believe that when Plato speaks in the *Timaeus* of a
situation before time existed he is merely contradicting himself. Plato
must be deliberately using the fanciful language of the myth here . . . because [as Plato himself admits] 'no sane man' could believe that there
was anything before time."[22] Corish attributes this contradiction, rather,
to Plato's being "not quite used to the full logical demands of temporal
theory."[23] Whether or not the contradiction was deliberate, it is still true
that many commentaries on Plato's view of time from the classical
period to the present involve the sorting out of Plato's seemingly ambiguous positions on "time before time" and eternity.

The most philosophically significant source of confusion over Plato's
ideas about time, however, is his failure to consider all of the temporal
ramifications of his cosmological system. Although he discussed
various aspects of continuity and divisibility in the *Timaeus* and other
works, he offered no consistent treatment of these concepts, which were
at the heart of the conflict between the Eleatic and the Pythagorean
views of time. In addition, his cosmology almost completely neglected
the role of human observation and thus sidestepped many important
questions concerning time's objectivity or subjectivity. More important
still, Plato did not resolve the paradox that time depends on the uniform
and continuous motion of the heavenly bodies, when, in fact, these bodies, as
created beings, can never attain perfect continuity and uniformity. He
openly admitted in the *Republic* that the heavenly bodies are incapable of

---

[21] Callahan, p. 189.
[22] Corish, p. 37.
[23] *Ibid.*

providing a perfect order for time when he stated: "The genuine astronomer . . . will think it absurd to believe that these visible material things go on forever without change or the slightest deviation . . . ."[24] Plato's failure or unwillingness to account fully for the discrepancies in his description of creation stimulated his colleagues and successors to pursue their own studies of time, motion and space in order to clarify, circumvent or apologize for Plato's conclusions. Despite all its deficiencies, however, Plato's conception of time stands as a remarkable intellectual achievement which attempted for the first time to articulate the precise relationship which exists between eternal being and the created, sensible world.

Advances on Plato's conception of time followed quickly in the work of his student Aristotle. Although he neglected openly to acknowledge his indebtedness to his teacher, Aristotle based his natural philosophy firmly on the foundation of Platonic theory. Indeed, Aristotle's systematic reevaluation of Plato's work and his powerful insights into the problems of time which Plato had posed without resolving make his comments on time extremely important in their own right.[25] More significant still, for our purposes, Aristotle profoundly influenced almost all areas of medieval thought, including semantics, natural philosophy, logic and theology. Through his imaginative synthesis of classical natural philosophy from the pre-Socratic age to his own, medieval thinkers acquired both a large body of practical information about the natural world and also a sophisticated theoretical system for analyzing it. Thus any study of medieval conceptions of time requires some account of Aristotle's contributions to the subject.

Aristotle's principal discussion of time is found in Book IV of his *Physics*. In chapters 10 to 14 of this book, Aristotle addressed such problems as the nature of the present, the reality of time and the relations among time, space and motion.[26] Like Plato, Aristotle assumed the inseparability of time and change and defined time as the number or measure of motion.[27] In developing these theories, however, Aristotle

---

[24] *Republic*, 528E-530C, trans. Francis MacDonald Cornford in *The Republic of Plato* (Oxford: Clarendon Press, 1961), p. 243.

[25] Cushman, p. 258.

[26] G. E. L. Owen, "Aristotle on Time," in *MTSM*, p. 3.

[27] Aristotle makes this observation in many places throughout the text. See, for example, *Physica*, IV, 12.221b2-3, in *Physica: translatio vetus*, eds. Fernand Bossier and Jozef Brams, in *Aristoteles latinus*, VII 1, *Fasciculus secundus, Corpus philosophorum medii aevi* (Leiden: E. J. Brill, 1990), p. 182: "Corruptionis enim causa per se tempus est; numerus enim motus est, motum autem distare facit quod est." Also *Physica*, IV,

demonstrated a much more comprehensive understanding of motion and other physical concepts than Plato had shown in the *Timaeus*. Aristotle was prepared to accept Plato's assertion that time depends on the regular movement of the heavenly bodies and so is coterminous with the universe but he was troubled by Plato's apparent willingness to define time solely in terms of celestial motion. Moreover, because Aristotle saw time as an integral part of nature, and the reality of nature was paramount in his philosophy, he could not conceive of time as unreal, as Plato had done.

Because Aristotle intended in the *Physics* to examine natural phenomena as sensible objects, not to provide a cosmological explanation for them, he was concerned with space, motion and time as features of observable reality. He did not begin his analysis of time with the kind of creation myth which appears in the *Timaeus*; his arguments move in the other direction, from precise definitions of sensible phenomena to more general principles concerning natural processes. Throughout his analysis of time Aristotle implied that Plato's account of time lacked scientific foundation in that it did not consider fully enough the physical realities of change in time and space. While Aristotle frequently reaffirmed his teacher's conclusions, his different interpretation of fundamental concepts and his more analytical approach to natural phenomena produced a conception of time which was quite distinct from Plato's.[28]

Aristotle's fascination with the physical world led him to study change and, consequently, time, as the medium in which change occurs. Although Aristotle believed time to be real in itself, he recognized that we cannot perceive time without detecting some physical change or motion. Thus he observed, " . . . when the state of our minds does not change at all, or we have not noticed its changing, we do not think that time has elapsed."[29] The paradox of time is that, while the perception of time requires some sort of change, time cannot be defined solely in terms of change: change happens within things, often at irregular rates;

14.223a30-33, p. 189: "Dubitabit autem aliquis et qualis motus tempus numerus est, aut cuiuslibet. Et namque fit in tempore et augmentatur et alteratur in tempore et fertur; secundum igitur quod motus est, sic est uniuscuiusque motus numerus." All subsequent citations to Aristotle's *Physica* refer to the *translatio vetus* edition of the Latin text:

[28] Cushman, pp. 258-59.

[29] *Physica*, IV, 11.218b21-24, p. 173: ". . . cum enim nichil ipsi [tempora] mutamus secundum intelligentiam aut latet transmutantes, non videtur nobis fieri tempus. . . ." Trans. Jonathan Barnes, in *The Complete Works of Aristotle: The Revised Oxford Translation*, Volume I (Princeton, New Jersy: Princeton University Press, 1985), p. 371.

but time itself is always uniform, distinct from objects and universal.[30]
Aristotle tried to resolve this dilemma by defining time as a kind of
number, but not the discrete arithmetic numbers which the Pythagoreans
and Plato had applied to celestial measurement. Unlike ordinary
mathematical units, units of time do not have a minimum value. In other
words, time is not a number in the sense that it is composed of distinct,
indivisible units which we can count as if we were counting objects.
Instead, a unit of time is a measurable segment of the continuum of time
in which a motion occurs. As such, a unit of time can vary in duration
according to the motion being measured, unlike arithmetic units which
must all be of identical value.

Therefore, Aristotle concludes that "time is not a movement, but only
a movement in so far as it admits of enumeration." Furthermore, because "we discriminate the more or the less [of things] by number, but
more or less movement by time," time is a kind of number.[31] In other
words, Aristotle conceives of time as a magnitude consisting of a succession of connected parts. Because it has no minimum, it can be
divided infinitely and proceed, through addition, without end. As a continuous entity, it cannot have a beginning or an end; and, because the
world is eternal, time must be also: ". . . there was never a time when
there was not motion, and will never be a time when there will not be
motion."[32]

After attempting to define time as an aspect of motion, Aristotle goes
on to consider its attributes, making use of an analogy between time and
a line. The now of time can be seen to represent a point on a line; the
infinite distances on either side of the point represent past and future
respectively. Like a point on a line, the now of time both connects past
and future and also serves as a limit to each. Although Aristotle
contends that the now functions simultaneously in these two ways, he is
careful to note that these functions are essentially different. The major
problem with the line analogy is that a point on a line is stationary,
whereas the now is continually moving from past to future.[33] According
to Aristotle, alluding again to the complementarity of time and motion,

---

[30] Ariotti, p. 75.

[31] *Physica*, IV, 11.219b3-5, p. 175: "Non ergo motus tempus est sed secundum quod
numerum habet motus. Signum autem est: plus quidem enim et minus iudicamus numero, motum autem plurem et minorem tempore; numerus itaque quidam tempus."
Trans. Barnes, p. 372.

[32] *Physica*, VIII, 1.252b5, p. 284: "Quod quidem igitur nullum tempus erat neque erit
quando motus non erat aut non erit, tanta dicta sunt." Trans. Barnes, p 421.

[33] Callahan, pp. 70-71, offers a useful analysis of this problem.

the now is more like a point moving along a line. Aristotle is careful, however, not to pursue this analogy too far. The motion of a moving point is absolutely dependent on sequential movement in any direction. Time, however, is continuous and must always move forward from past to future. Thus Robert Cushman observes: "Aristotle insists that the 'before-and-afterness' of time is conceptually separable from motion, but in the actuality of physical change it is not so separable."[34]

In addition to his more careful evaluation of the physics of time, Aristotle's greater awareness of the role of human perception in defining time represents an advance over Plato's conception of time. Aristotle never went so far as to say that time is in any way subjective or that its existence depends on human observation of motion. Still, Aristotle's dissatisfaction with Plato's remote, objectified, celestial time led him to consider the relationship between absolute time and the human perception of it. In his analysis of the now, for example, Aristotle took the trouble to examine the morphology of time. He was interested in how such expressions as "suddenly," "presently," "long ago" and "lately" help to illustrate the function of time in the process of change.[35] On other occasions, as we have seen, he considered whether time could exist without consciousness; and, although he failed to explore this question in any depth, he identified an important teleological problem about time which others, most notably Augustine, would later develop more fully.[36] Because Aristotle generally preferred to concentrate on the physical characteristics of time, he never reached a firm position on this confusing issue. His contribution was mainly to point out that the issue of consciousness was a valid consideration in any philosophical treatment of time.

It is easy to see how Plato's conception of time might be misunderstood if one were to approach it from the perspective of Aristotle's definitions of motion, number and measurement. The vocabularies of the two philosophers are similar enough to cause confusion, and commentators have struggled with ambiguities of terminology from classical times to the present. Despite this confusion, indeed to some extent because of it, Plato's and Aristotle's views about time have exerted tremendous influence on almost all subsequent approaches.

Following Aristotle, there were few major advances in classical temporal theory until the third century C. E., when the philosopher Plotinus

---

[34] Cushman, p. 260.
[35] Callahan, pp. 72-73.
[36] Cushman, p. 260.

tried to rehabilitate Plato's cosmological system. In his treatise "On Eternity and Time," Plotinus enlarged his predecessors' conceptions of time by giving time a moral dimension. Plotinus' cosmology, while largely dependent on Plato's, also reflected the influence of Aristotle's methods of systematic analysis. Plotinus' investigation of the problem of time proceeded according to a well-organized critical review of all previous efforts to describe the distinction between time and eternity and revealed his unwillingness to accept without question what Plato and Aristotle had said about time. After refuting both non-Aristotelian and Aristotelian theories of time, Plotinus went on to develop his own approach which integrated many of his predecessors' views into a substantially new perspective on the problem of time.[37] His aim was to demonstrate that time is not merely a created and therefore imperfect measure of the universe, as Plato had claimed. Plotinus thought instead that time belongs to a higher order than that of the created universe and has a special relationship to eternity. His philosophical system, in which time and eternity played a major part, attracted a wide circle of students who were known as the Neoplatonists due to their adherence to many of Plato's fundamental definitions and assumptions. While Plotinus' view of time is well worth exploring in its own right, his Neoplatonist followers also contributed substantially to late classical discussions of time because of their imaginative elaborations on various elements of Plotinus' temporal theory. Through Augustine, moreover, the Neoplatonists had an undisputed influence on early Christian and medieval views of time.[38]

As the title of his treatise suggests, Plotinus recognized the interdependence of time and eternity as a profound metaphysical truth. His initial descriptions of these two concepts varied little from Plato's: time relates to the "sphere of becoming and the sensible universe," while eternity relates to the "everlasting nature."[39] According to Plotinus, the superficial understanding of "becoming" and the "sensible universe" which we can achieve through intuition breaks down when we try to investigate these ideas more with more cognitive rigor. Although he felt assured that the "ancients of happy memory" had found answers to the

---

[37] Callahan, p. 88. "On Eternity and Time" is the seventh treatise of the third book of Plotinus' *Ennead*. For a standard edition and English translation of this text see *Plotinus*, Volume III, ed. and trans. Arthur Hilary Armstrong (London: Heinemann, 1967), pp. 293-355. In the following discussion I quote from excerpts of this treatise which have been translated by Callahan in his chapter on Plotinus, pp. 88-148.

[38] Gordon H. Clark, "The Theory of Time in Plotinus," *Philosophical Review*, 53 (1944), p. 337.

[39] *Ennead*, III.7.1, trans. Callahan, pp. 88-89.

paradoxes of eternity and time, Plotinus wanted to make his own inquiry
so that he could discover the truth for himself. He thought this inquiry
should begin with eternity rather than time, "for if we know what the
unchanging model is, perhaps we can thereby arrive at a knowledge of
its image, which we call time."[40]

After considering various definitions of eternity, Plotinus concludes
that eternity encompasses every feature of the intelligible world, including motion and rest, difference and identity. Eternity, says Plotinus, is

> the life that is forever unchanging and possesses all its reality in the pre-
> sent. There is no succession involved in this life, since nothing has passed
> and nothing is to come, but whatever it is it is always . . . . Since there is
> nothing that it can come to possess that it does not already possess and
> nothing that it loses of what it possesses, we cannot say of it that it was, or
> will be, but only that it is. Thus we find that eternity is the life of being in
> its very being, at once whole, complete and entirely without succession.[41]

Relying on Plato's assumption that the eternal nature is bound up with
unchanging being, Plotinus calls the unity of the eternal nature with unchanging being the "One." Then he enlarges Plato's cosmology by
inserting another level between the One and the sensible world. He
makes the One, which has neither being nor real knowledge, the source
of all unity and goodness. Eternity, by contrast, rests in the intermediate stage of "intelligible essence . . . which may be thought of as an
unmoving circle which has the One or the Good as its center, and it is
this proximity to the very source of all unity that gives to the intelligible
essence the kind of life we call eternity."[42]

Turning now to time itself, Plotinus claims that time exists on the next
step below eternity in a series of states which link the sensible world
with the One. He begins his analysis of time with a review of three
categories of theories about time's relationship to motion. First, he
challenges the thesis that time is identical with motion on the grounds
that motion is *in* time and must therefore be distinct from it. Motion,
moreover, can be sporadic and cease, while time remains continuous.[43]
His arguments against this thesis depend heavily on Aristotle's assertion
that all things moving or at rest are in time. In spite of a few minor
discrepancies, Plotinus largely accepts Aristotle's definition of time as

---

[40] *Ibid.*, p. 89.
[41] *Ennead*, III.7.3, trans. Callahan, pp. 90-91.
[42] Callahan, p. 93.
[43] *Ennead*, III.7.8, discussed by Callahan, p. 98.

the measure of motion but transforms it through his investigation of the relationship between the sensible world and the One.[44]

Plotinus then criticizes a second theory of time which denies time any existence apart from that of the moving sphere. Like Aristotle, Plotinus dismisses this theory as untenable, though his method of refuting it is different from Aristotle's.[45] Finally, Plotinus refutes the theory that time is an extension of motion on the grounds that the extensions of all of the many kinds of motion are too irregular to account for the uniformity of time.[46] Nor can Plotinus wholly accept Aristotle's argument that time is the number or measure of motion. Time certainly is not the measure of particular motions; rather, time is a reflection of the uniform and continuous unfolding of the life of the soul:

> [F]or if eternity is life at rest, unchanging and identical and already unbounded, [time is] an image of unity, that which is one in continuity; and instead of a complete unbounded whole, a continuous unbounded succession, and instead of a whole altogether, a whole which is, and always will be, going to come into being part by part.[47]

Thus Plotinus emphasizes the motion of time as the agent of change within creation.

Viewed superficially, this argument seems simply to qualify Aristotle's position without actually contradicting it. Another of Plotinus' criticisms of Aristotle is more serious, however, because it calls into question the validity of Aristotle's technique for defining time. To describe time in terms of motion can help one to visualize the relationship between time and motion, says Plotinus, but this approach cannot tell anyone what time actually is.[48] Like Plato, Plotinus seeks a more complete metaphysical explanation of time which takes into account the relationship between time and eternity.

Because he finds Plato's cosmological system too simplistic, however, Plotinus modifies Plato's two-fold division between perfect eternal

---

[44] Callahan, p. 101.

[45] *Ibid.*, p. 102. Whereas Aristotle based his rejection of this second theory on an argument from natural philosophy (time is the measure of heavenly bodies so it cannot be equated with them), Plotinus used a more metaphysical approach by placing time in a different coeval from the material sphere of heavenly bodies.

[46] *Ennead*, III.7.8.

[47] *Ennead*, III.7.11, trans. Armstrong, pp. 340-43.

[48] According to Callahan, in *Ennead*, III.7.12-13, Plotinus considers many of the problems involved in measuring time through astronomical phenomena such as the sun rising and setting. He concludes that human beings find this kind of measurement particularly problematic because we lack an independent frame of reference from which to observe the change that marks off a segment of time. See Callahan, p. 111.

being and the "becoming" of the sensible world into a hierarchy of
levels of existence.   Within this hierarchy Plotinus places the inter-
mediary of "soul" between eternity and time: "Soul must precede time
because we understand time to be related somehow to the motion of the
universe that is the product of soul; and time must precede motion, in the
order of nature, because we say that motion is in time."[49] Plotinus' view
of time, according to Callahan, clearly echoes Plato's approach and can
be summarized as follows:

> Time is an image of eternity, therefore, as life on a lower level of perfec-
> tion. Its striving to be as like eternity as possible is the reason for its
> constant progress, in order that it may be a whole in succession as eternity
> is a perfect whole without succession. This striving explains why time will
> never end, for its complete fulfillment is always beyond it. Time does not
> proceed according to number because ideal number is fixed at a higher
> level, and to think that the soul produces in accordance with number con-
> flicts with the infinity of time.[50]

Plotinus' conclusions about time, then, though undeniably influenced by
Aristotelian natural philosophy, comes out of a cosmological system
which depends in large measure on Platonic metaphysics.

Indeed, Plotinus sought to enhance Plato's metaphysics by clarifying
the Platonic dichotomy between eternal and created being. According to
Plotinus, there is a continuum of being which can be described as a
succession from lower to higher orders of existence. Whereas Plato
regarded time as a true image of eternity and a source of order and
harmony on which one could model one's moral life, Plotinus perceived
time as only one stage in a long series of states of being which link the
individual to eternity.[51] Plotinus attracted many disciples who embraced
both the moral tone and the emphasis on metaphysical levels which
characterize Plotinus' philosophy.   In fact, the Neoplatonists after
Plotinus increased the number of spheres in the hierarchy, even to the
point of dividing time itself into spheres, which resulted in many subtle
variations in Neoplatonic approaches to time.[52]   Modern philosophers
have dismissed these approaches to time as too complicated and
untenable. Historians, theologians and philologists, on the other hand,
have recognized the need to understand the Neoplatonists, who exerted

---

[49] Callahan, p. 122, paraphrasing *Ennead*, III.7.11, lines 40-60, Armstrong, pp. 340-43.
[50] Callahan, p. 123.
[51] *Ibid.*, pp. 197-98.
[52] Samuel Sambursky and Shlomo Pines, *The Concept of Time in Late Neo-Platonism*
(Jerusalem: The Israel Academy of Sciences and Humanities, 1971), pp. 12-13.

tremendous influence on Christian and Islamic thought in the early middle ages.[53] Neoplatonic ideas are particularly important in any discussion of medieval views of time because early Christian thinkers drew heavily on Neoplatonism when they wished to provide a philosophical basis for their theological insights into time and eternity. Both the moral outlook of the Neoplatonists and their intense scrutiny of the relationship of time and eternity strongly affected two of Bradwardine's most important sources, Augustine and Boethius.

While the ancient Greeks and the Neoplatonists gave the problem of time a special philosophical significance, Augustine transformed it into a theological problem as well. His most thorough and concise treatment of time appears in Book XI of his *Confessions*, in which he presents time as a quality which arose out of creation. Although he based his arguments firmly on the words of Genesis, and in addressing the problem of time, desired only to arouse in himself and others greater love of God,[54] his analysis of time reflects the influence of his classical education. Augustine's contribution to the study of time is important not just because he invested time with theological significance: his attempt to solve the problem of time was also highly original. Indeed, his "psychological" solution to the problem of time has influenced discussions of time from the fourth century to the present.

Augustine's view of time has received, therefore, considerable attention from modern theologians, historians and philosophers. Their chief concerns have been to explain what Augustine had to say about time and such related issues as eternity, memory, creation, free will and contingency; but they also regard the question of Augustine's indebtedness to his predecessors as a crucial one. Those who emphasize the continuity between classical views of time and Augustine's view focus on his special reliance on Neoplatonism, which he had followed before his

---

[53] Richard Sorabji thoroughly discusses the temporal theory of the late Neoplatonists in *Time, Creation and the Continuum: Theories in Antiquity and the Early Middle Ages* (London: Duckworth, 1983). For a good general introduction to the late Neoplatonists see A. C. Lloyd, "The Later Neoplatonists," in *The Cambridge History of Later Greek and Early Christian Philosophy*, ed. Arthur Hilary Armstrong (Cambridge: Cambridge University Press, 1967), pp. 272-32; see also R. T. Wallis, *Neo-Platonism* (London: Duckworth, 1972); and Philip Merlan, *From Platonism to Neoplatonism* (The Hague: Martinus Nijhoff, 1975).

[54] ". . . et olim inardesco meditari in lege tua et in ea tibi confiteri scientiam et inperitiam meam." *Confessions*, X.II.2, p. 194 of *Sancti Augustini confessionum libri XII*, ed. Lucas Verheijen, Volume 27 of *Sancti Augustini opera in corpus christianorum series latina* (Turnholti: Brepols, 1981). Citations to the *Confessions* refer to this critical edition. For a discussion of this passage see Callahan, p. 149.

conversion to Christianity. Others, who wish to stress Augustine's originality, argue that many accounts of Augustine's dependence on the Neoplatonists are exaggerated.[55]

It is undeniable, however, that Augustine's conception of time depended on certain elements which he borrowed, consciously or unconsciously, from the Greek philosophical tradition which formed the basis of his education. Like Plato's *Timaeus*, Augustine's essays on time in the *Confessions* and the *City of God* have a strikingly poetic quality: they both rely on symbolism and imagery rather than on logical deduction to convey the mystery of creation. Nevertheless, Augustine's conclusions about time also echo Aristotelian themes. Augustine claimed that time is the measure of motion and that nothing exists of time except the present, which is indivisible. Augustine shared with classical philosophers the tendency to analyze time according to its parts: past, present and future. He concurred with his predecessors that time came into existence only with creation and had a counterpart in eternity. Augustine's main divergence from Plato and Aristotle was that, while they were content to describe or explain time (a characteristic feature of Greek philosophy), he wanted to discover the meaning of time in both its human and divine contexts.[56] His fascination with the mysterious elusiveness of time and its effect on the sensible world led him to ask a broader range of questions than Plato and Aristotle had done. Augustine's originality stemmed from his insight: "Few men," observes Herman Hausheer, "have been as intensely sensitive to the pathos of mutability, of the rapidity, transitoriness, and irreversibility of time."[57]

Whether or not Augustine's conception of time was truly dependent on Neoplatonism, his general philosophical outlook was at least greatly enhanced by his study of the Neoplatonists. According to Richard Sorabji, Plotinus was the source of many of Augustine's mystical impulses towards time and eternity. Sorabji cites Augustine's discussion with his mother about the eternal life of the saints as an example of Augustine's dependence on Plotinus' concept of "the life which is wisdom." Augustine writes:

> Life is that Wisdom by which all these things that we know are made, all things that ever have been and all that are yet to be. But that Wisdom is

---

[55] Clark, p. 358. See also Hugh M. Lacey, "Empiricism and Augustine's Problems about Time," in *Augustine: A Collection of Critical Essays*, ed. Robert Austin Markus (New York: Doubleday, 1972), pp. 280-308.

[56] Herman Hausheer, "St. Augustine's Conception of Time," *Philosophical Review*, 46 (1937), p. 512.

[57] *Ibid.*, p. 503.

not made: it is as it has always been and as it will be for ever—or rather, I should not say that it *has been* or *will be*, for it simply *is*, because eternity is not in the past or in the future. And while we spoke of the eternal Wisdom, longing for it and straining for it with all the strength of our hearts, for one fleeting instant we reached out and touched it. Then with a sigh, leaving *our spiritual harvest* [Rom. 8:23] bound to it, we returned to the sound of our own speech, in which each word has a beginning and an ending—far, far different from your Word, our Lord, who abides in himself for ever, yet never grows old and gives new life to all things.[58]

Augustine's image of the soul striving beyond simple understanding to attain a higher spiritual state and his association of that experience with feelings of passion and shock are strikingly reminiscent of Plotinus' writings about striving towards the One.[59]

Sorabji warns, however, of the danger of reading too much of Neoplatonic philosophy into Augustine's conception of time and eternity. Just because Augustine was familiar with Neoplatonism and often seemed to express his ideas in Neoplatonic terms does not mean that he accepted Neoplatonism uncritically. More often than not in his direct references to the Neoplatonists, Augustine portrayed their ideas as uninformed, imperfect versions of Christian truths: their assertion that God's mind contains the ideal forms was an implicit acknowledgement of God as creator of all being; their recognition of three levels of reality, the One, the World Intellect and the World Soul, reflected their acceptance of the Trinity.[60] Thus Sorabji concludes that Augustine's relationship to the Neoplatonists was a complex one of "initial acceptance and of subsequent borrowing, adapting, distancing himself and urging them to follow."[61]

Augustine begins his discussion of time in the *Confessions* with an exclamation of frustration, which sets the tone for his own uniquely psychological approach to time: "if no one asks me [what time is], I know; if I try to explain it to someone, I do not know."[62] His investigations into the nature of time start with an account of creation, which, like Plato's creation story in the *Timaeus*, emphasizes the non existence of time before creation

---

[58] *Ibid.*, p. 503.

[59] Sorabji, pp. 164-165.

[60] *Ibid.*, pp. 304-305.

[61] *Ibid.*, p. 304.

[62] *Confessions*, IX.X.24, p. 202: "[Q]uid est ergo tempus? Si nemo ex me quaerat, scio; si quaerenti explicare uelim, nescio." C.f. Plotinus, *Ennead* III.7.1, where he discusses the difficulty of explaining time. See also *Saint Augustine's Confessions*, trans. Henry Chadwick (New York: Oxford University Press, 1991), pp. 230-31, n. 19.

and posits a divine goodness as the motive for creation. Augustine departs
from Plato in insisting that God created the universe not out of pre-existing
chaos but out of nothing. Paying particular attention to the text from Genesis
"In the beginning God created heaven and earth," Augustine argues that
scripture attributes a beginning to every creature. Because time involves
change, it also is a creature, and so has a definite beginning. Therefore
neither time nor the world is eternal. Augustine has no patience with people
like the Manicheans, who impertinently ask what God was doing before the
moment of creation.[63] In his view, scripture clearly tells us that there was
nothing before creation: one cannot even say that God was before creation
because, perfect and immutable, God has no before and after. God simply is
in a motionless eternity.[64] Augustine is not speaking here, however, of any
kind of eternity that human beings, bound in time, can comprehend or
experience. In fact, Augustine sharply opposes Plato's and Aristotle's
arguments in favor of the eternity of the world. Because the world, and thus
time, had a definite beginning in the event of creation and will continue
according to principles established by God, it is neither eternal, nor does it
share in any way in God's capacity for everlasting being.[65]

Augustine was not satisfied simply with refuting the opinions of his
predecessors or with determining the characteristics which time does not
have. His real goal was to discover what time really is like, to the extent
that a human being can actually recognize its features. His treatment of
time in the *Confessions* involves, therefore, a transition from an
ontological discussion of the origins of time to a psychological analysis
of the effects of time on the soul.[66] In fact, from Augustine's point of
view, human experience, subjective as it is, must be paramount in any

---

[63] In response to people who asked what God was doing before creation, Augustine
said that God was creating Hell for those impertinent enough to ask such a question. See
Confessions, X.XII.14, p. 201: "Ecce respondeo dicenti: 'quid faciebat deus antequam
faceret caelum et terram?' Respondeo non illud, quod quidam respondisse perhibetur
ioculariter eludens quaestionis uiolentiam: 'Alta,' inquit, 'scrutantibus gehennas para-
bat.'" See also Sorabji, p. 233.

[64] *Confessions*, XI.XXXI.41, pp. 215-15: "Domine deus meus, . . . [n]eque enim sicut
nota cantantis notumue canticum audientis exceptione uocum futurarum et memoria
praeteritarum uariatur affectus sensusque distenditur, ita tibi aliquid accidit incommu-
tabiliter aeterno, hoc est vera aeterno creatori mentium. Sicut ergo nostri in principio
caelum et terram sine uarietate notitiae tuae, ita fecisti in principio caelum et terram sine
distentione actionis tuae."

[65] J. de Blic, "Les arguments de saint Augustin contre l'éternité du monde," *Mélanges
de science religieuse*, 2 (1945), pp. 43-44.

[66] Jules Chaix-Ruy, "Le problème du temps dans les 'Confessions' et dans 'La cité de
Dieu,'" *Giornale di metafisica*, 9 (1954), pp. 468-69.

discussion of time because, although time could still exist in a created world without people, in the world which God actually created, it is people who measure time in their minds. Like all other creatures, humans live and change in time; but, because they have souls, they can transcend, in certain respects, the limitations of creation. Their souls make them more like God and make God's eternity more accessible to them. Thus humanity stands between time and eternity and the soul is the tool for measuring and interpreting time.[67]

Augustine's ultimate conception of time is based on his observations that time seems to have three parts, past, present and future; that it proceeds in a single, irreversible direction; and that it consists of a succession of segments which are easily perceived but are extremely difficult to examine rigorously. These observations raise serious problems about the nature of time because they seem to present contradictory evidence. Of the three "parts" of time, only the present seems actually to exist, because the past is "no more" and the future is "not yet"; but if the present is always moving forward, how can we determine exactly where the present is? Moreover, we can think of past times as having long or short duration, but can one really measure something that no longer exists? Indeed, we cannot even measure the present, for every duration of time has its own sequence of past, present and future.[68] Augustine points out that even the hour

> is made of fleeing moments; so much of the hour as has fled away is past, what still remains is future. If we conceive of some point of time which cannot be divided into even the minutest parts of moments, that is the only point which can be called the present; and that point flees at such lightning speed from being future to being past, that it has no extent of duration at all. For if it were so extended, it would be divisible into past and future; the present has no length.[69]

Nevertheless, says Augustine, we cannot deny that we think of the world in terms of the concepts of past, present and future, despite our inability to develop a standard for determining when the present actually is. The present remains a crucial concept because it distinguishes past and

---

[67] *Confessions*, XI.XV.19, p. 203: "Videamus ergo, anima humana, utrum praesens tempus possit esse longum: datum enim tibi est sentire moras atque metiri." For a discussion of this passage see Rudolph Berlinger, "Le temps et l'homme chez saint Augustin," *L'année théologique augustinienne*, 13 (1953), pp. 278-79.

[68] James McEvoy, "St. Augustine's Account of Time and Wittgenstein's Criticisms," *Review of Metaphysics*, 37 (1984), p. 555.

[69] *Confessions*, XI.XV.20, p. 204, translated by McEvoy, pp. 555-56.

future. Its function in making this distinction depends, however, not on
some objective continuum such as the motion of heavenly bodies but on
the mind itself. Augustine concludes his speculations on the relationship
of the present to past and future with the suggestion that

> perhaps it would be more correct to say: there are three times, a present of
> things past, a present of things present, a present of things future. For
> these three exist in the mind, and I find them nowhere else: the present of
> things past is memory, the present of things present is immediate intuition
> (*contuitus*), the present of things future is expectation. . . . By all means
> continue to say that there are three times, past, present and future; for
> though it is incorrect, custom allows it.[70]

Augustine's approach to time, then, is consciously subjective, at least to
the degree that he believes that the parts of time are realized and measured within the mind.   This emphasis on the mind emerges from
Augustine's acceptance of an Aristotelian description of time as successive, continuous and infinitely divisible. Augustine wanted to protect
the eternity of God from anything changeable[71] without sacrificing his
belief that the human mind is capable of understanding God's activity in
the world. Therefore he had to place the human capacity to understand
time in the soul.

   If the present has no extension, and past and future do not exist, how
then do we measure time? Augustine answers that we measure time in
the memory. Through the power of our minds we can create and measure segments of time which bear no resemblance to the actual succession
of individual moments. The memory is a spiritual power which allows
images in the soul to be measured: as such, it can stop the course of
time and stabilize it.[72] Using the example of the recitation of a poem,
Augustine describes how the memory not only makes the various aspects of time accessible to human experience but also represents the
unity of parts and whole in every aspect of human life:

> Suppose that I am about to recite a psalm that I know. Before I begin, my
> expectation is directed to the whole of it; but when I have begun, so much
> of it as I pluck off and drop away into the past becomes the matter for my
> memory; and the whole life of the action is stretched out between my
> memory, in regard to what I have said, and my expectation, in regard to
> what I am still to say. But there is a present act of attention, by which what

---

[70] *Confessions*, XI.XX.26, pp. 206-7, translated by McEvoy, p. 557.

[71] Jules Chaix-Ruy, *Saint Augustin: temps et histoire* (Paris: Études augustiniennes,
1956), p. 15.

[72] M. Moreau, "Mémoire et durée," *Revue des études augustiniennes*, 1 (1955), p. 244.

was future passes on its way to becoming past. The further I go in my recitation, the more my expectation is diminished and my memory lengthened, until the whole of my expectation is used up, when the action is completed and has passed wholly into my memory. And what happens in the case of the whole psalm happens for each part of the whole, and for each syllable; and likewise for any longer action, of which the canticle may be only a part: indeed, it is the same for the whole life of man, of which all man's actions are parts; and likewise for the whole history of the human race, of which all the lives of all men are parts.[73]

Augustine recognizes previous definitions which associate time with motion as valid insofar as motion occurs in time—we might even use the motion of an object to measure time—but the act of measurement takes place entirely within the soul. Observations of individual motions become images which the mind uses to determine intervals. Augustine's emphasis on the mind as an active agent in defining time had bearing on many of his other theological positions which involved the soul's activity, particularly in regard to the Trinity.[74] By stressing the connection between time and the soul Augustine offers a psychological answer to a metaphysical problem, or, as many commentators would argue, he transforms the metaphysical problem of time into a psychological one.

This transformation had consequences in all areas of Augustine's theological system but it was especially important in those discussions which involved some explanation of God's understanding of human activities. Here Augustine had to address the paradox that God, omniscient and outside of time, allows his creatures to act freely within time. Augustine readily admitted that he had trouble in resolving this problem but he ultimately concluded along Platonic lines that God created time so that his creatures, in all of their limitation and imperfection, could exercise their wills under divine guidance. It was the spiritual contrast between the finiteness of human experience and the infinity of God, not the physical contrast between time and eternity, which most fascinated Augustine. According to Robert Jordan, "Augustine's investigation of time is a study in contingency, finiteness, creatureliness, dependency, incompleteness, imperfection—a study of the limitations of being that characterize *any* finite entity, that entity which *is*, but which is not He Who Is. Time exists because there are

---

[73] *Confessions*, XI.XXVIII.38, p. 214, translated by McEvoy, p. 562.

[74] Joseph Maréchal, "Lettres sur le problème du temps chez saint Augustin et sur le problème de la philosophie catholique," *Mélanges Joseph Maréchal*, 2 Vols. (Paris: Desclée, de Brouwer et Cie, 1950), I, p. 263.

existent things in the universe which are just so much reality, but no more. The existence of only one of these things is of genuinely intimate concern to man—himself."[75] Thus, Jordan asserts, for Augustine time becomes more than a cosmological problem: it is a problem of moral philosophy, bound up with the religious life of humanity.[76]

The fundamental problems of time arose, therefore, not only in Augustine's formal discussions of time in Book XI of the *Confessions* but also explicitly or implicitly in many other contexts. Most notably, he approached the whole problem of God's foreknowledge and human free will from the perspective that God's knowledge in his timeless present that a person will sin does not compel that person, living in earthly time, to sin. In Augustine's opinion, God's eternal foreknowledge actually safeguards the freedom of the human will since will is a divinely created gift. Indeed, he remarked in the *City of God*:

> Our wills are ours and it is our wills that affect all that we do by willing, and which would not have happened if we had not willed. But when anyone has something done to him against his will, here, again, the effective power is will, not his own but another's. But the power of achievement comes from God. . . . Therefore, let us never dream of denying his foreknowledge in the interests of our freedom, for it is with his help that we are, or shall be, free.[77]

Although in this case divine knowledge, not time, was the central issue, Augustine's definition of the relationship between time and eternity provided the basis of his solution to a difficult cosmological and theological dilemma.

Because Augustine's theology made such a lasting impression on medieval theological discussions of all sorts, it is not surprising that his ideas about time appear repeatedly in the works of his successors. Comparisons between Augustinian and Greek philosophies of time

---

[75] Robert Jordan, "Time and Contingency in St. Augustine," *Review of Metaphysics*, 8 (1955), p. 395.

[76] *Ibid.*, p. 394.

[77] *De civitate Dei*, V.10, trans. Henry Bettensen, in *Concerning the City of God against the Pagans*, (Harmondsworth, Middlesex, England: Penguin, 1972), p. 195. For a critical edition of this text see *Sancti Aurelii Augustini episcopi de civitate dei libri XXII recognoverunt Bernardus Dombart et Alphonsus Kalb*, in *Bibliotheca scriptorum Graecorum et Romanorum Teubneriana*, Vol. I (Stuttgart: Teubner, 1981), p. 209. For a complete discussion of this topic see William L. Rowe, "Augustine on Foreknowledge and Free Will," and John M. Rist, "Augustine on Free Will and Predestination," in *Augustine: A Collection of Critical Essays*, ed. Robert Austin Markus (New York: Doubleday, 1972), pp. 209-17 and 218-52.

reflect both his dependence on an established vocabulary and list of concerns and also his remarkable originality. Augustine's analysis of time is important because it introduced later thinkers to principles of classical philosophy which retained many of their original features in spite of Augustine's reinterpretation of them. Moreover, because Augustine's writings soon came to be considered theologically central, his philosophical treatment of problems such as time legitimized not only a philosophical approach to theology but also an acceptance of ideas whose origins were in a non-Hebraic pre-Christian tradition.

Augustine's psychological view of time and eternity is closely related to that of Boethius, whose speculations on the nature of eternity greatly influenced discussions about time throughout the middle ages. Although Boethius was not interested in time as such, his definition of eternity hinged on the contrast between human temporal existence and the non-temporal existence of God. Boethius was a scholar of considerable skill who composed several original works on logic, theology and natural philosophy. He also embarked on the ambitious task of translating all the writings of Plato and Aristotle into Latin. Even in the small number of translations he actually completed, Boethius gave medieval scholars direct access to many classical theories and analytical methods. Unlike Augustine, whose philosophical impulses were always directed towards theological ends and whose assimilation of classical ideas was almost subconscious, Boethius openly advocated the study of philosophy, particularly ancient Greek philosophy, for its own sake. In addition to his contribution to the debate about time and eternity, Boethius added to the medieval literary tradition Aristotle's logical system of categories. He also suggested a method for organizing the disciplines of learning which formed the basis of the medieval academic curriculum. His best-known work, the *Consolation of Philosophy*, is an allegorical account of his conversion to the belief that philosophy, defined as the love of wisdom, the pursuit of wisdom or the quest for God, is the highest human aspiration.[78]

---

[78] There is a vast bibliogrpahy on Boethius, most of which is only tangentially related to this study. A good summary of nineteenth- and early twentieth-century scholarship on Boethius may be found in Étienne Gilson's *History of Christian Philosophy in the Middle Ages* (London: Sheed and Ward, 1955), p. 97. Two recent comprehensive works on Boethius' life and writing include Henry Chadwick's *The Consolations of Music, Logic, Theology and Philosophy* (Oxford: Clarendon Press, 1981) and a collection of scholarly articles entitled *Boethius: His Life, Thought and Influence*, ed. Margaret Gibson (Oxford: Basil Blackwell, 1981). There is no consensus among historians as to whether Boethius was a professed Christian. Because he consciously approached

It is not surprising, therefore, that Boethius' conception of time bears
the mark of his study of the ancient Greeks, the Neoplatonists and
Augustine. Boethius shares with Augustine a psychological view of
time and eternity: both see the problem of the relationship of time and
eternity as a matter of interaction between God and the human soul,
rather than simply as an explanation of a phenomenon of nature. Some
modern commentators judge Boethius' treatment of these problems
superior to Augustine's because of Boethius' special philosophical
training.[79] His approach to eternity in the *Consolation of Philosophy* involves an attempt to prove a theological assumption about the eternity of
God using philosophical means without reference to scripture. To this
end Boethius states:

> That God is eternal, then, is the common judgement of all who live by
> reason. Let us therefore consider what eternity is, for this makes plain to
> us both the divine nature and knowledge. Eternity, then, is the complete
> possession all at once of illimitable life. This becomes clearer by compar-
> ison with temporal things. For whatever lives in time proceeds as
> something present from the past into the future, and there is nothing placed
> in time that can embrace the whole extent of its life equally. Indeed, on the
> contrary, it does not yet grasp tomorrow but yesterday it has already lost;
> and even in the life of today you live no more fully than in a mobile, trans-
> itory moment. . . . Therefore, whatever includes and possesses the whole
> fullness of illimitable life at once and is such that nothing future is absent
> from it and nothing past has flowed away, this is rightly judged to be eter-
> nal and of this it is necessary both that being in full possession of itself it
> be always present to itself and that it have the infinity of mobile time
> present [to it].[80]

---

cosmological questions from the perspective of classical natural philosophy rather than
Christian theology, his writings do not indicate the specific nature of his religious views.
In the biography *Boethius* (Boston, Massachusetts: Twayne, 1982), Edmund Reiss
argues convincingly from indirect evidence of Boethius' career that he was probably a
practicing Christian at least at some point in his life. In any event, virtually all medieval
writers, including Bradwardine, considered Boethius' philosophy to be esentially
Christian. Therefore, my treatment of Boethius assumes that he sought a philosophical
understanding of creation which at least would not openly contradict Christian doctrine.

[79] Sorabji, p. 256. Unlike Augustine, who applied philosophical techniques to
theology, Boethius was a trained, practicing philosopher. Moreover, his translations of
Plato and Aristotle gave Boethius greater mastery of these materials than Augustine had.

[80] *Consolation of Philosophy*, 5:6, ed. Edward Kennard Rand, in Hugh Fraser
Stewart, Edward Kennard Rand and S. J. Tester eds., *Boethius: The Theological
Tractates and the Consolation of Philosophy* (London: Heinemann, 1973). Translated
by Eleonore Stump and Norman Kretzmann, in "Eternity," *Journal of Philosophy*, 78
(1981), p. 430. For a critical edition of the Latin text see *Anicii Manlii Severini Boethii*

Boethius' argument that eternity is completely distinct from the sequential character of human time is entirely in keeping with Augustine's view because it emphasizes both the divine nature of eternity and the difficulty human beings have in grasping either time or eternity.

Recognizing this difficulty, Boethius explores the implications of his assertion that eternity is "the complete possession all at once of illimitable life." He agrees with his predecessors that eternity is neither simply a limitless duration of time nor a condition of static atemporality.[81] His analysis of the misunderstanding of eternity in his treatise *On the Trinity* offers a remarkably clear rendering of the classical conception of eternity. Boethius thus contends:

> What is said of God, [namely, that] he is always, indeed signifies a unity, as if he had been in all the past, is in all the present—however that might be—[and] will be in all the future. That can be said, according to the philosophers, of the heaven and of the imperishable bodies; but it cannot be said of God in the same way. For he is always in that for him *always* has to do with the present time. And there is this great difference between the present of our affairs, which is *now*, and that of the divine: our now makes time and sempiternity, as if it were running along; but the divine now, remaining and not moving, and standing still, makes eternity. If you add '*semper*' to 'eternity' you get sempiternity, the perpetual running resulting from the flowing, tireless now.[82]

For Boethius, then, eternity is not a sterile condition which removes God from the temporal reality of his creation, however hard it might be for us to understand how this can be so. Boethius' God transcends time: indeed, as Anthony Kenny observes, God might be pictured "as surveying the battle-ground of human existence from a high tower above, with past, present, and future as different parts of the field open to divine vision."[83]

Boethius, like Augustine, also tries to define how his conception of divine eternity relates to human experience. First, he addresses the question of whether the world is eternal. As a natural philosopher, Boethius preferred not to rely, as Augustine had, primarily on the

---

philosophiae consolatio, ed. Ludouicus Bieler in *Corpus christianorum, series latina*, Vol. 94 (Turnholti: Typographi Brepols Editores Pontifici, 1957).

[81] Stump and Kretzmann, p. 430. See Dales, *Medieval Discussions of the Eternity of the World*, pp. 13-17.

[82] *De trinitate*, 20.64-22.77, ed. Rand. Translated by Stump and Kretzmann, pp. 430-431. For a standard edition of this work see *Corpus christianorum series latina*, Vol. 94.

[83] Anthony Kenny, *The God of the Philosophers* (Oxford: Clarendon Press, 1979), p. 107.

authority of scripture. Instead Boethius looked to Plato and Aristotle to discover methods for analyzing the nature of eternity. Although his evaluation of Platonic and Aristotelian arguments affirms the truths of each, Boethius shows a clear preference for Plato's overall approach:

> So what is subject to the condition of time is not yet such as rightly to be judged eternal, even if, as Aristotle believed of the world, it never began to exist, and does not cease, but has its life stretched out with the eternity of time. For even if its life is infinite, it does not include and embrace the whole extent of that life all together, since it does not yet possess the future and already lacks the past. . . . Hence those are not right who hear that Plato thought this world had no beginning in time and will have no end, and who conclude that the created world is in this way made co-eternal with the creator. For it is one thing to be drawn through an endless life, which is what Plato attributed to the world, and another to have embraced equally the whole presence of a life which cannot end, which is clearly the special characteristic of the divine mind. Nor should God be thought older than created things by some amount of time, but rather by the peculiarity of his nature which is simple. . . . Thus if we want to apply names appropriate to things, let us say, following Plato, that God indeed is eternal, but the world perpetual.[84]

Boethius' argument that the world is not eternal because it was created and exists under the influence of time corresponds to Augustine's assertion that time had its origin in creation. While Boethius does not deny creation, he is not prepared to go so far as Augustine in claiming that creation has a definite beginning and end. He prefers Plato's designation of the world as perpetual, which suggests that worldly time, though not identical with eternity, bears some relation to it. This opinion, though hardly orthodox in the Augustinian sense, nevertheless came to be considered theologically valid, due to the widespread influence of Boethius' writings throughout the middle ages.[85]

Boethius' ideas are more in keeping with Augustine's on a second aspect of the problem of time's relation to eternity, that of God's foreknowledge. We have already seen that Augustine proposed the solution that God sees all human action at once and that his knowledge that a person will act in a particular way does not constitute coercion. Boethius clarifies this position by shifting attention away from the human experience of time toward a consideration of how God perceives

---

[84] *Consolation of Philosophy*, 5:6, trans. Sorabji, pp. 119-20.
[85] De Blic, p. 42.

human activity.[86] God can know the future without manipulating it, he argues, because God exists in a state of eternal presentness: "Embracing the infinite lengths of past and future, [God] considers everything as if it were going on now in a simple mode of awareness."[87]

The appeal of Boethius' conception of eternity lies in its comprehensibility and simplicity. He defines God's relationship to the temporal world in such a way as to free human will from the necessity of God's foreknowledge, without denying that God indeed knows every possible human act in his eternal present. From the Augustinian perspective, however, this conception is incomplete because it fails to take into account evidence from scripture of God's intervention in the world. Boethius' philosophical account of divine knowledge concedes the mystery of God's transcendent power but makes no provision for God's active participation in the lives of his creatures through grace. Although Augustine agrees with Boethius that God can be omniscient yet ensure the freedom of his creation, Augustine, as a theologian, cannot avoid the elements of Christian revelation which complicate the discussion.

Taken together, then, Augustine and Boethius offered their medieval successors a variety of philosophical and theological approaches to the study of time. Through their particular references to classical authors and scriptural texts, they provided rich resources for contemplating the relationship between time and eternity. The persistence of both Augustinian and Boethian traditions throughout the middle ages indicates the compelling nature of this relationship for medieval thinkers. Even Boethius, who usually eschewed theology, captivated medieval theologians because he consciously introduced classical philosophical approaches to theological topics. His influence was perhaps most crucial in the eleventh and twelfth centuries, when such theologians as Anselm and Peter Abelard attempted to discern a philosophical framework for their theological understanding of time and eternity.[88]

Anselm, for example, often referred in his writings to the philosophical and theological problems which arise from studying time and eternity. Historians have long recognized that Anselm's views of time were shaped by Augustine's, even though Anselm apparently did

---

[86] Sorabji, p. 256.

[87] *Consolation of Philosophy*, 5:6, trans. Sorabji, p. 256. See below, Chapter 6.

[88] For a good general introduction to Boethian influences on early medieval natural philosophy see William A. Wallace, "The Philosophical Setting of Medieval Science," in *Science in the Middle Ages*, ed. David C. Lindberg (Chicago: University of Chicago, 1978), pp. 91-119.

not have access to the *Confessions*. According to Gillian Evans, what is not often considered is that Anselm also knew of Boethius' views on time as they were set forth in his commentaries on Aristotle's *Categories*.[89] Although it is difficult to ascertain the exact source of influence, it is clear that Anselm's treatment of time involves geometrical definitions which bear a greater resemblance to a classical tradition than to an Augustinian one. Not only did Anselm, like Plato and Aristotle, use mathematical terminology to describe the nature of time and eternity, but he also held the Aristotelian opinion that eternity differs from time because, unlike time, eternity cannot be measured. Anselm argued that the distinction between time and eternity rests on the fact that time is a sequence of parts, while eternity is whole, without parts and dimensionless.[90] In order to emphasize this point, he compared the unity of eternity with the unity of the Trinity: "We do not think of God as having grades of different standing, for He is one; nor, when we show how the Son is 'of' the Father, or the Holy Spirit of Father and Son, do we construct intervals in eternity which is beyond all time."[91]

While one might describe Anselm's view of time as mathematical, Abelard and his contemporary Garlandus Compotista treated time as a grammatical or dialectical problem. Drawing on both Greek sources and Augustine's discussions of the ambiguities of tenses in language, Garlandus showed that grammatical limitations can interfere with an adequate metaphysical definition of time.[92] Abelard also discussed the

---

[89] Gillian R. Evans, "Time and Eternity: Boethian and Augustinian Sources of Thought in the Late Eleventh and Early Twelfth Centuries," *Classical Folia*, 31 (1977), p. 105. In "Anselm on Future Contingencies: A Critical Analysis of the *De concordia*," *Anselm Studies*, 1 (1983), pp. 165-73, Paul A. Streveler explores the logical principles which undergird Aristotle's position on eternity and emphasizes Anselm's dependence on Aristotle, Augustine and Boethius in developing his own approach to eternity. Anselm's knowledge of Aristotle and Boethius, as well as his theological convictions about God's absolute power, made him an important authority for Bradwardine, who regularly cited Anselm's works in his theological treatises. For additional information about Anselm's life, career and theological outlook, see especially: G. Stanley Kane, *Anselm's Doctrine of Freedom and the Will* (New York: Edwin Mellen, 1981); G. R. Evans, *Anselm* (Wilton, Connecticut: Morehouse-Barlow, 1989); and R. W. Southern, *Saint Anselm: A Portrait in a Landscape* (Cambridge: Cambridge University Press, 1990).

[90] Evans, pp. 107-8.

[91] *De Processione Spiritu Sancti*, 52.200.1-2, from *Sancti Anselmi Opera Omnia*, ed. Franciscus Salesius Schmitt (Rome: 1938), quoted and translated by Evans, p. 108.

[92] Evans, "Time and Eternity," pp. 109-10, cites and translates a passage from Garlandus Compotista's *Dialecta*, ed. Lambertus Maria De Rijk (Assen: Van Gorcum, 1959), pp. 25-27.

grammatical problems associated with time, but he went beyond these to address some of the underlying philosophical and theological roots of these problems. He pointed out, as Augustine had done, that the simplest way to teach students about time is to direct them to the revolutions of planets and stars; but, as Evans observes, Abelard agreed with Augustine that this approach is theoretically incorrect because the existence of time "must be independent of any one means of measuring it."[93] Abelard also recognized the difficulty in describing durations of time which consist of continuous series of points, saying: "time is either indivisible, like the present moment which we call an instant, or it is composite, like an hour, a day, a week, a month, a year, which is made up of different instants following one another in succession, past, present and future."[94]

Anselm, Garlandus and Abelard, therefore, all focused on the practical problems of measuring and describing time which were central features of ancient Greek discussions of time. Although they obviously drew on classical treatments, their approaches also reflect their own particular logical and philosophical interests. Augustine and Boethius helped to direct these later discussions not so much by dictating the course that investigations about the nature of time should take, as by providing access to the rich and varied history of the subject in an age of scarce literary resources.

This brief survey of the origins of medieval discussions about time identifies several important themes. First, the problem of time had been the subject of rigorous philosophical speculation in the western tradition from the patristic age and cannot be understood in isolation from pre-Christian philosophical speculation. Second, discussions of time are intimately bound up with, and must be viewed in terms of, a variety of larger cosmological concerns including creation, God and eternity. Third, as the main contributors to the discussion addressed the views of their predecessors, the debate about the nature of time became increasingly complex and approaches to the problem more varied. By the time of Boethius, philosophers and theologians could draw on Pythagorean, Platonic, Aristotelian, Neoplatonic and Christian explanations of time; they could conceive of time mathematically, astronomically, metaphysically or psychologically; and they often used more than one approach to explain the anomalies of time.

---

[93] Evans, p. 111.

[94] Evans, p. 112, cites and translates a passage from Abelard's *Dialectica* in *Peter Abaelards philosophische Schriften*, ed. Bernhard Geyer (Münster: Aschendorff, 1933), p. 184.34-6.

This ongoing debate about the nature of time was formative for both later medieval philosophy and theology. Each generation to approach the subject of time brought its own concerns to the discussion as well as the accumulated wisdom of the past. One can hardly begin to evaluate the emergence of time as a philosophical and theological topic in the late middle ages without acknowledging the inheritance medieval thinkers received from Plato, Aristotle, Plotinus, Augustine and Boethius. Indeed, it is a testament to their perspicacity that philosophers and theologians still refer to their treatments of time.

CHAPTER THREE

THIRTEENTH-CENTURY APPROACHES TO TIME

During the century and a half before Bradwardine, the problem of time
emerged as a specific component in the general discussions of Aristotelian
philosophy in the western universities. A major stimulus to these discussions was the increased accessibility of Aristotle's writings through new
translations from Arabic into Latin. Most of the translations were done in
Spain, where Muslim, Jewish and Christian thinkers worked together in a
relatively cooperative intellectual community. By the mid-twelfth century,
Muslim scholars had not only translated a large number of Greek
philosophical texts into Arabic but had also produced an impressive array of
commentaries, especially on Aristotle's writing, which reevaluated classical
philosophy from the perspective of Islamic theology. Although some
scholars in Spain and Northern Europe rejected non-Christian natural
philosophy and tried to resist its influence, many more welcomed
translations of Aristotle's writings on physics, astronomy, biology and
cosmology which had not been readily available for study in the early
middle ages.[1] The influence of these translated texts on western theology
and natural philosophy was considerable and so had direct bearing on
subsequent discussions of time in the thirteenth and fourteenth centuries.

The appeal of this new body of literature lay in the information it
provided about the natural order. For all of the theological richness of

---

[1] For additional information about the introduction of Aristotelian philosophy into the
medieval west see especially David C. Lindberg, "The Transmission of Greek and Arabic
Learning in the West," in *Science in the Middle Ages*, pp. 52-90; Marie Thérèse
d'Alverny, "Translations and Translators," in *Renaissance and Renewal in the Twelfth
Century*, eds. Robert E. Benson and Giles Constable (Oxford: Clarendon Press, 1982),
pp. 421-62; "The Entry of the 'New' Aristotle," Part IV of *A History of Twelfth-Century
Western Philosophy*, ed. Peter Dronke (Cambridge: Cambridge University Press, 1988);
and "Aristotle in the Middle Ages," Part II of *CHLMP*. For an account of and
bibliography for the reception of Aristotelian and Muslim learning in the twelfth through
fourteenth centuries see John Marenbon, *Later Medieval Philosophy (1150-1350): An
Introduction* (New York: Routledge and Kegan Paul, 1987). For an excellent survey of
medieval science see Lindberg, *The Beginnings of Western Science: The European Scientific Tradition in Philosophical, Religious and Institutional Context, 600 B.C. to A.D.
1450* (Chicago: University of Chicago Press, 1992).

Christian scripture and doctrine, these sources did not provide medieval scholars with adequate answers to their questions about the natural world. By the thirteenth century, western thinkers had become interested in many topics which pertained more to natural philosophy than to theology. Classical works on physics, biology, astronomy and mathematics, along with the Muslim commentaries, excited their curiosity both by suggesting new questions which one might ask about the natural world and by conveying information about particular natural phenomena.

As David Lindberg observes, however, these writings arrived in the west sporadically because scholars usually translated only the passages of longer works that pertained directly to their specific research interests. The quality of the translations also varied considerably according to the translator's linguistic proficiency and knowledge of the subject matter.[2] This haphazard introduction of classical material stimulated scholarly discussions on a wide range of new topics but did not encourage comprehensive treatments of any single issue.

Western readings of these texts were also complicated by the failure of both Aristotle and the Muslim scholars who commented on his writings to distinguish their theories about the natural world from their religious beliefs. Many Christian thinkers in the thirteenth century were alarmed by the rapid spread of "pagan" philosophies which appeared to obscure, when they did not actually contradict, accounts of creation found in scripture. In the first half of the thirteenth century, some theological masters tried unsuccessfully to abolish the teaching of Aristotle at the universities, or at least to restrict Aristotelian studies to his works on logic. A more typical response was to try to reconcile Aristotelian principles with Christian theology, although few accomplished this task convincingly. In spite of strong efforts to forestall it, Aristotle's scientific and metaphysical thought was firmly established in the university curriculum by the end of the thirteenth century and young scholars turned with vigor to classical problems of cosmology which they encountered in their studies of the Aristotelian corpus.

To understand the philosophical and theological dimensions of late medieval discussions of time, therefore, it is essential to examine late twelfth- and thirteenth-century treatments of time in light of this rediscovery of classical natural philosophy. By trying to integrate empirical, philosophical and theological evidence into their responses to metaphysical questions, thirteenth-century thinkers mastered a variety of

---

[2] Lindberg, *Science in the Middle Ages*, pp. 75-6.

interrelated disciplines. The study of time, as we have already seen, naturally invites multidisciplinary investigation; indeed, one could argue that a successful study of time is impossible without such an approach. In the twelfth century the Muslim philosopher Averroes and the Jewish philosopher Moses Maimonides reinterpreted Aristotelian views of time and eternity from the perspectives of classical philosophy and monotheistic theology. Their work provided an important legacy for such influential western scholars such as Robert Grosseteste, Albertus Magnus, Thomas Aquinas and John Duns Scotus, who tried in various ways to reconcile theological doctrine with the concepts and methods of Aristotelian natural philosophy. Although these thinkers did not exert equal influence on Bradwardine, and their individual conclusions about time often varied substantially from each other, their common struggle to understand time offers valuable insights into the unsettled intellectual climate into which Bradwardine entered early in the fourteenth century.

Any discussion of the revival of Aristotelian natural philosophy in the Christian west must consider the important contributions of Averroes. An active participant in the vibrant, international academic community of twelfth-century Spain, his studies included theology, jurisprudence, medicine, mathematics and philosophy. He was best known in northern Europe, however, for his commentaries on Aristotle.[3] As an ardent proponent of Aristotelian natural philosophy in an ideologically conservative culture, Averroes found himself in the same sort of conflict with Islamic authorities that western thinkers experienced with their Christian counterparts.[4] Because Muslim thinkers hesitated to accept ideas which did not originate from sacred texts, Averroes tried to steer a middle course between Aristotelian philosophy and the religious doctrine revealed through the Koran. Not wishing to stray too far from orthodoxy, he openly acknowledged the miraculous nature of the Koran, which brought truth to all people whatever their capacity to receive it.

---

[3] As is the case for Boethius, there is a vast bibliography on the life, works and philosophy of Averroes. References here are to works particularly useful in tracing Aristotelian influences on Latin scholars. In addition to citations in note 1 above, see especially the following: René Antonin Gauthier, "Notes sur les débuts (1225-1240) du premier 'averroisme,'" *Revue des sciences philosophiques et théologiques*, 66 (1982), pp. 321-74; Gauthier, *Ibn Rochd (Averroes)* (Paris: Presses Universitaires de France, 1948); Majid Fakhry, *A History of Islamic Philosophy* (New York: Columbia University Press, 1970), pp. 302-25; and Oliver Leaman, *An Introduction to Medieval Islamic Philosophy* (Cambridge: Cambridge University Press, 1985), pp. 42-57, 92-104. Leaman's book provides an excellent recent bibliography of secondary works concerning Averroes' influence in nonwestern settings.

[4] Leaman, pp. 5-6.

He nevertheless considered Islam to be a rational faith whose truths cannot be fully comprehended without some sort of rigorous intellectual training. Philosophy, he argued, was not a substitute for revelation but a method for discovering how religious truths are revealed in the world. Therefore, anyone capable of philosophical analysis of scripture should take advantage of the insights of Aristotle, who provided both an explanation for the natural order and a method for investigating it.[5] In fact, Averroes went so far as to proclaim: "The doctrine of Aristotle is the supreme truth because his intellect was the zenith of human intellect. It is therefore rightly said that he was created and given to us by divine providence, so that we might know all that can be known."[6] Although few Christian thinkers were prepared to regard Aristotle as the zenith of the human intellect, Averroes' powerful portrayal of his understanding of the natural order encouraged Latin scholars to read Aristotle's writings as well.[7]

Averroes' commentary on Aristotle's view of time reflects both his profound respect for his teacher and his own preoccupation with philosophical problems. Averroes was troubled by Aristotle's definition of time as the number of motion because it did not adequately distinguish time from motion. Thus Averroes proceeded to examine the source of Aristotle's dilemma without openly criticizing any of Aristotle's statements. In his analysis of Aristotle's view of time Averroes included several insights on the nature of time which Avicenna had advanced in his own commentary on Aristotle, although he did not acknowledge his indebtedness.[8] Averroes' main complaint was that, by linking the concepts of time and motion too closely, Aristotle seemed to imply that one had to observe motion to experience time. This theory presented many difficulties, not the least of which is the anomaly that the heavenly bodies continue to measure time even under conditions

---

[5] *Ibid.*, pp. 145-46.   Leaman devotes special attention to Averroes' defense of Aristotelian natural philosophy in Part II of his book, titled "Practical Philosophy."

[6] "Aristotelis doctrina est summa veritas, quoniam eius intellectus fuit finis humani intellectus. Quare bene dicitur quod fuit creatus et datus nobis divina providentia, ut sciremus quidquid potest scire."   Quoted and translated by Gilson, my translation adapted, p. 220. See also Gilson, p. 642, note 17, for additional references to Averroes' praise of Aristotle.

[7] A concise appraisal of this influence can be found in Wallace, "The Philosophical Setting of Medieval Science," *Science in the Middle Ages*, pp. 103-7.

[8] Augustin Mansion, "La théorie aristotélicienne du temps chez les péripateticiens médiévaux: Averroès, Albert le Grand, Thomas d'Aquin," *Revue néo-scholastique,* 32 (1934), p. 280.

which prevent human observation of their motion.[9] To resolve this dilemma, Averroes suggested that the experience of time is not related to the individual perception of earthly or celestial motion: our capacity to sense change is inadequate to the task of accounting for the regular and continuous passage of time.[10] Although, like Augustine, Averroes seemed at first to stress the importance of perception in assessing the nature of time, his approach was not a psychological one. While the occasion of a motion might allow us to perceive time, Averroes argued, time itself does not depend merely on our observation of motion. Because we are always both in a state of change (*in esse moto*) or in a state which anticipates our essential capacity for change, we perceive time subjectively. The objective, ordered passage of time is assured, however, by the circular motion of the celestial sphere: all movement and change depend on its motion, which continues in an orderly fashion whether or not we can comprehend its course. Without departing from Aristotelian principles, therefore, Averroes nevertheless reconsidered and refined Aristotle's problem of explaining the interrelationship of time and motion.[11]

Averroes' most original contribution to the medieval debate about time, and his chief advance over Aristotle, arose from his insistence that time is a fundamental feature of material being, which must possess the capacity to move and change. Averroes developed this theme by distinguishing between our perception of time based on direct experience of local motion and our universal acknowledgement of a uniform temporal order which applies whether or not we observe change. According to Averroes, the latter position best expresses Aristotle's position because it is based on his teaching about the uniform motion of the heavenly

---

[9] Averroes, Commentary 98 on Aristotle's *Physics*, quoted from Volume IV of *Aristotelis Opera cum Averrois Commentarius* (Venice: Juntas, 1562-74) by Mansion, p. 281: "Si tempus non sequitur aliquem motum existentem extra animam, . . . quomodo igitur dicit Aristoteles post, ipsum sequi motum corporis caelestis ? Et etiam si sequitur motum corporis caelestis, continget ut caecus non percipiat tempus, quia numquam percepit motum caeli. Et etiam, si sequitur omnem motum, continget etiam ut tempus multipliciter per multiplicationem motuum. Aut sequetur unum motum, et sic qui non sentit illum motum non sentit tempus, quod est impossibile."

[10] *Ibid.*, quoted by Mansion, p. 282: "Et manifestum est quod nos non sentimus nos esse in esse transmutatabili, nisi transmutatione caeli. Et, si esse possible ipsum quiescere, esset possible nos esse in esse non transmutabili. Sed hoc est impossibile. Ergo necesse est ut sentiat hunc motum qui non sentit motum corporis caelestis, scilicet per visum."

[11] Mansion, pp. 282-83; Leaman, pp. 42-46; Sorabji, p. 97.

bodies.[12] After examining the main principles of Aristotle's temporal theory, Averroes concluded that when Aristotle defined time as the number of motion, he was talking not about any observable or measurable motion but about the particular motion of the celestial sphere.[13] Averroes thus clarified Aristotle's position to the point of over-simplification in order to protect Aristotle from the criticism that his theory of time is ambiguous.

Through this reevaluation of Aristotle, Averroes succeeded in defining time as both a philosophical and a physical problem in terms which were comprehensible to medieval scholars. Because it made no reference to theological truth, many Muslim and Christian thinkers refused to accept completely Averroes' interpretation of Aristotle's temporal theory. Nevertheless, they searched his commentaries for practical information about the interrelationship of motion, time and space.[14] Their fascination with Aristotle's methods for studying the natural world accounts for the wide circulation and influence of Averroes' commentaries, which made those methods more accessible to northern European scholars in the thirteenth and fourteenth centuries.

Averroes' contemporary, Moses Maimonides, also helped to introduce Aristotelian natural philosophy to Latin scholars. Throughout his life Maimonides was an active participant in the diverse and

---

[12] Averroes, Commentary 98, quoted by Mansion, p. 284: " . . . quarum *una* est, quod nos non percipimus tempus, nisi quando fuerimus moti in anima nostra; et hoc existimavit Galenus, et est corrupta per se. *Secunda* autem est, quod nos non percipimus tempus, nisi cum perceperimus aliquem motum quicumque sit, et hoc est percipere per accidens. *Tertia* vero est, quod nos non percipimus motum neque tempus, nisi cum percipimus nos transmutari, quia sumus in esse transmutabili; et ista perceptio est perceptio quam sequitur tempus essentialiter, et non accidet ei aliqua quaestio. Et verba Aristotelis manifesta sunt secundum hanc intentionem . . . et secundum hunc modum possumus ponere tempus sequi motum corporis caelestis, et quod sentiet tempus qui numquam sensit corpus caeleste. Et ideo omnes conveniunt in hoc quod tempus sequitur motum caeli."

[13] *Ibid.*, quoted by Mansion, p. 288: ". . . quia unaquaeque rerum numeratur per aliquod suae speciei, . . . necesse est ut tempus etiam numeretur per aliquod tempus notum et terminatum naturaliter. Et *dixit* (*scil.* Aristoteles) *in praecedenti* quod hic est motus translationis et circularis; quoniam, cum fuerit positum quod tempus est numerus cuiuslibet motus, et fuerit positum quod hic est prior motus caeteris motibus, sequitur ut tempus istius motus sit prius caeteris temporibus, et numerans illa."

[14] Leaman's first chapter on the cultural context of Averroes' natural philosophy offers an excellent analysis of the responses from within the Muslim intellectual community. Northern European responses to Averroes' natural philosophy are best traced through studies of such western Aristotelians as Albertus Magnus, Thomas Aquinas and Thomas Bradwardine, whom Averroes chiefly influenced.

cosmopolitan intellectual communities in Spain and Egypt. While he shared Averroes' general interests in law, medicine, natural philosophy and theology, he did not share Averroes' Aristotelian philosophical outlook. His writings indicate a more eclectic philosophy which incorporated Platonic, Neoplatonic and Aristotelian approaches as well as Jewish theological traditions.[15] Unlike Averroes, Maimonides believed that faith was a prerequisite for seeking philosophical truth.

The centrality of faith to philosophical discourse was the premise of his most widely read book, the *Guide of the Perplexed*. Maimonides modified Averroes' argument that the highest form of intellectual activity involved the study of Aristotelian metaphysics. He accomplished this task by presenting divine law and philosophy as two equally valid areas of inquiry, both of which are necessary for establishing a rational confirmation of faith.[16] Maimonides hoped to show that it was possible for an educated, perceptive person to reconcile observed physical realities with the literal meaning of the scriptures. While he felt in no way compelled to accept the theological implications of Aristotelian natural philosophy, he acknowledged the utility of Aristotle's methods for describing natural phenomena. Maimonides' critical approach to Aristotelian physics and his firm attachment to the Hebrew Bible made the *Guide of the Perplexed* a valuable resource for

---

[15] Maimonides was born and received his early education in Spain but spent his professional life in Egypt, where he worked as a jurist, philosopher, teacher and physician. For an analysis of Maimonides' scholarly context see *Studies in Maimonides and Saint Thomas Aquinas*, ed. Jacob I. Dienstag (New York: KTAV, 1975), especially Dienstag's introductory chapter, "The Relationship of Maimonides to his Non-Jewish Predecessors: An Alphabetical Survey," pp. xiii-lix. For a good general introduction to his life, philosophical interests and career, see Colette Sirat, *La philosophie juive au moyen âge selon les textes manuscrit et imprimés* (Paris: Editions de Centre National de la Recherche Scientifique, 1983), pp. 179-232. For accounts of Maimonides' intellectual interests, the following collections of essays are helpful: *Perspectives on Maimonides*, ed. Joel L. Kraemer (New York: Oxford University Press, 1991), in which see especially Alfred I. Ivry's essay, "Neoplatonic Currents in Maimonides' Thought," pp. 115-40; and *Maimonides and Philosophy*, eds. Shlomo Pines and Yirmiyahu Yovel (Boston, Massachusetts: Martinus Nijhoff, 1986). Good additional secondary accounts of Maimonides are Georges Vajda, "Moïse ben Maïmon," in *Introduction à la pensée juive du moyen âge* (Paris: J. Vrin, 1974), pp. 129-51; *Essays on Maimonides: An Octocentennial Volume*, ed. Salo Wittmayer Baron (New York: Columbia University Press, 1941); and Abraham Joshua Heschel, *Maimonides: A Biography*, trans. Joachim Neugroschel (New York: Farrar, Strauss, Giroux, 1982).

[16] In "Rationality and Revelation in Maimonides' Thought" (*Maimonides and Philosophy*, pp. 15-23), Eliezer Goldman explores Maimonides' efforts to reconcile his commitments to Aristotelian natural philosophy, Neoplatonic metaphysics and Jewish theology in the *Guide of the Perplexed*.

Christian scholars, because it demonstrated that a faithful person could make good use of Aristotelian concepts in his inquiries without being enslaved by them.

In addition to his general influence on medieval western theology, Maimonides contributed specifically to the discussion of time through his comments on the eternity of the world. Although he accepted many aspects of Aristotle's physical theory, he could not accept Aristotle's argument that the world had had no beginning in creation. Because he could find nothing in Aristotle's writings to prove that the world had not been created by God, Maimonides felt justified in rejecting this particular element of Aristotelian natural philosophy in favor of the scriptural doctrine of creation in time. On the other hand, he admitted that creation in time cannot be proved. Therefore, Maimonides implied, the belief in creation in time cannot serve as a philosophical principle for defining such theological truths as the existence of God.[17]

Maimonides based his proof of God's existence on an entirely different kind of argument: being is necessary and requires a primary mover or cause, which is God. According to this argument, God exists as the primary agent of creation, whether he made the world from nothing in time or it existed from all eternity. Indeed, Maimonides asserted that all created being exists as a unified whole as a consequence of God's will:

> [W]e contend that God brought the world as a whole into existence after nonexistence and formed it until it achieved perfection as you see it. . . . And its Creator may, if He wishes to do so, render it entirely and absolutely nonexistent.[18]

In subsequent discussions of motion, space and time, all using Aristotelian terminology and based on Aristotelian physical theory, Maimonides refused to concede the point that the world began through God's creation of it in time. Though he could find no satisfactory way of refuting Aristotle's position on the eternity of the world philosophically, he remained steadfastly faithful to the scriptural account of creation.

The importance of Maimonides' discussion about eternity in the medieval debate about time, then, does not rest in any clarifying remarks

---

[17] Jonathan W. Malino, "Aristotle on Eternity: Does Maimonides Have a Reply?" in *Maimonides and Philosophy*, pp. 53-4; 59.

[18] *The Guide of the Perplexed*, II:17, trans. Shlomo Pines (Chicago: University of Chicago Press, 1963), pp. 296-97; cited by Malino, pp. 57-8. For an analysis of the philosophical and theological implications of Maimonides' view of creation, see Joseph Puig, "Maimonides and Averroes on the First Mover," in *Maimonides and Philosophy*, pp. 213-23.

that he made about time itself. As Jonathan Malino observes, Maimonides was guilty of both misconstruing Aristotelian principles and of expressing his own views of time in such a contradictory way that his readers had difficulty making sense of them.[19] Still, Maimonides contributed substantially to medieval discussions about time because he tried to redefine Aristotelian natural philosophy within the theological parameters of Hebrew scripture. It was his conviction that biblical tenets could be defended without physical proof, rather than any specific conclusions about time and eternity, that caught the attention of Christian thinkers of the thirteenth century.[20] Like Averroes, Maimonides suggested to medieval Christian thinkers how one might try to solve a cosmological problem by considering both philosophical and theological evidence. In their treatments of the problems of time and eternity both Averroes and Maimonides emphasized the inadequacy of approaching time exclusively either from a theological or a philosophical perspective and offered Aristotelian natural philosophy as a useful tool for evaluating conflicting accounts of creation in time.

As welcome as these new insights were for some scholars, many religious leaders perceived them as threats to traditional learning and tried to suppress them. Just as Averroes drew criticism from Muslim authorities for embracing Aristotelian natural philosophy, western thinkers also faced opposition for their enthusiastic study of such non-Christian writers as Averroes and Maimonides. In the west, lines of conflict were fairly clearly drawn between advocates of Aristotelianism as it was interpreted by Averroes and ecclesiastical leaders who feared pagan influences on the university curriculum. One of the main issues of debate, which Maimonides had raised in his attempts to accommodate Aristotelian perspectives in his reading of Hebrew scripture, was the role of reason in defining truth.[21] The "Latin Averroists," as they are often called, tended to favor philosophical methods rather than revelation through scripture or faith as a means of discerning truth, particularly truth about the natural world.[22] Siger of Brabant and Boethius of Dacia, two of the most articulate followers of Averroes in the west, helped to accelerate the spread of Aristotelianism by making Aristotle's natural

---

[19] Malino, pp. 60-1.

[20] For an account of Maimonides' influence on twelfth- and thirteenth-century western philosophy, see Wolfgang Kluxen, "Maimonides and Latin Scholasticism," in *Maimonides and Philosophy*, pp. 224-32.

[21] Pearl Kibre and Nancy G. Siraisi, "The Institutional Setting: The Universities," in *Science in the Middle Ages*, pp. 103-7.

[22] *Ibid.*, p. 104.

philosophy a subject of controversy at European universities. In the process, they refocused scholarly attention on the age-old problems of time and eternity.

True to their Aristotelian leanings, the Latin Averroists acknowledged Aristotle's assertion that the world did not begin in creation and is eternal.[23] As Richard Dales has, shown, however, even so ardent a proponent of Aristotle as Boethius of Dacia did not accept Aristotle's conception of time and eternity uncritically. Indeed, when he set about to write his own account of the eternity of the world, Boethius of Dacia's main source was neither Aristotle nor Averroes, but Maimonides.[24] Boethius chose the complex problem of eternity to illustrate his thesis that there is no conflict between Christian faith and classical philosophy. His argument rested on his belief that natural philosophy—the observation of the world as it actually is—has no connection with speculation about the possibility of supernatural creation. Like Maimonides, Boethius believed that neither the eternity of the world nor its creation in time could be proven through demonstrable arguments, although he showed a greater willingness than Maimonides to accept the possibility of an eternal world.[25] In an attempt to correct the misconceptions of his predecessors, however, Boethius followed an argument proposed by Maimonides to demonstrate that Aristotle had not successfully proven the eternity of the world.[26] Preoccupied as he was with the thirteenth-century debates concerning the relationship of faith to reason, Boethius felt compelled to find a way of balancing his own deep commitment to philosophy with the religious concerns which dominated his age. His reading of Maimonides aided him in envisioning the problem of eternity as a significant but abstract problem which the methods of neither theology nor natural philosophy could solve.[27] His conclusion that faith and reason should not be forced to compete in the search for truth is an approach which was not regularly taken in the middle ages. Nevertheless, his atypical approach focused attention on the struggle between faith and reason which influenced all medieval discussions of

---

[23] The Latin Averroists' views on the eternity of the world are briefly sketched by Sorabji, pp. 195-6; p. 243 and Leaman, p. 165.

[24] Dales, "Maimonides and Boethius of Dacia on the Eternity of the World," *The New Scholasticism*, 56 (1982), p. 306. A strong advocate of Averroes, Boethius of Dacia relied on the criticism developed by Maimonides in the *Guide of the Perplexed* to refute Aristotle's and Averroes' notion that the world had no beginning in creation.

[25] *Ibid.*, pp. 309-312.

[26] *Ibid.*, p. 315.

[27] *Ibid.*, p. 319.

time.[28]   As we shall see, those fourteenth-century theologians who
eventually tried tentatively to separate faith from reason were profoundly disturbed by the implications their predecessors' speculations
had for both theology and natural philosophy.

More common in the thirteenth century than Boethius of Dacia's
separation of faith and reason was the attempt to integrate natural
philosophy and scripture into a consistent cosmology.   Some western
natural philosophers tried to synthesize Greco-Arabic and Christian
traditions into a single philosophy.   Others, such as the Dominican
scholar Albertus Magnus, used Greco-Arabic philosophy to supplement
an essentially Christian outlook. Albertus, who is perhaps best known as
the teacher of Thomas Aquinas between 1245 and 1248, was a prominent churchman and a gifted student of philosophy in his own right.
His many writings, translations and commentaries span an extremely
wide range of topics, reflecting both his varied interests and his encyclopedic knowledge.   Albertus regarded logic, metaphysics and natural
philosophy as valuable tools for enriching theological understanding.[29]
Though he was aware that Greco-Arabic learning sometimes conflicted
with the western Christian tradition, Albertus believed that the truths of
one tradition could be applied usefully to intellectual enquiries in another. He therefore encouraged his students to master as much scientific
and philosophical material as possible, regardless of its origin. Albertus
was not apparently concerned about building his own philosophical or
theological system out of the information which he accumulated in his
studies. For this reason, Albertus is often identified as a scholar in the
general sense rather than as a theologian or a philosopher.[30]

It is not surprising, then, that Albertus' view of time is a composite of
several theories which were available for him to consider. His reading
of classical works and the commentaries of the Muslim philosophers

---

[28] Edward Grant, "Cosmology," in *Science in the Middle Ages*, p. 269.

[29] See Weisheipl, *Friar Thomas d'Aquino: His Life, Thought and Works* (Oxford:
Basil Blackwell, 1975), pp. 272-9.

[30] For a full discussion of Albertus' broad scientific and philosophical interests see
Albertus Magnus and the Sciences: Commemorative Essays 1980, ed. Weisheipl
(Toronto: Pontifical Institute of Mediaeval Studies, 1980); see especially Edward A.
Synan's introduction, pp. 1-12, and Weisheipl's "The Life and Works of St. Albert the
Great," pp. 13-52. Most accounts of Albertus' life are found in materials concerning
Thomas Aquinas.   For a good brief introduction to Albertus' life and career, see
Weisheipl, *Friar Thomas d'Aquino*, especially pp. 38-51. See also the collection of es-
says entitled *Albert the Great*, eds. Francis J. Kovach and Robert W. Shahan (Norman,
Oklahoma: Univeristy of Oklahoma Press, 1980); the biographical material in the intro-
duction to this volume, pp. vii-xix, is particularly helpful.

gave him a good introduction to Greco-Arabic approaches to time, while his knowledge of Augustine and the other Church Fathers provided him with information concerning the biblical doctrines of time and eternity. Albertus' specific theories concerning time and eternity combined passages from scripture with classical descriptions of creation and Aristotelian natural philosophy. In one of his earliest treatises, the *Summa de creaturis*, Albertus borrowed from Aristotelian and Augustinian vocabulary to describe the metaphysical significance of God's acts of creation. According to Albertus, God established the fundamental features of the created world by making four coevals: matter, the empyrean heaven, the angelic nature and time.[31] After characterizing the various kinds of matter which God created, Albertus discussed the distinctions between the philosophical and the theological approaches to matter. For theologians, matter is the single substance out of which God fashioned the universe in six days; for philosophers, most notably Aristotle, matter is the subject of change, and, because there are many kinds of change, there must be many kinds of matter.[32] Albertus accepted both positions, claiming that it is not a contradiction to admit that all matter shares a common source in God's creation, while acknowledging the varieties of forms God has given matter in the natural world.[33] Albertus' fascination with the observable changes in these forms is evident in his enthusiastic study of all the natural sciences, including (among others) astronomy, alchemy, metallurgy, psychology, physiology and biology.[34]

Although Albertus, as a Christian thinker, recognized that time and eternity were significant theological issues, he was much more intrigued by the nature of time as an indicator of physical change. His treatments of time depend, therefore, on Aristotle's definition of time as the measure of motion or change.[35] In the *Summa de creaturis*, for example, Albertus incorporated Aristotelian views of time even into sections of the treatise which were devoted to the issue of eternity. Albertus, referring to Boethius, defined eternity as perfect, simple and infinite.

---

[31] Leo Sweeney, "The Meaning of *Esse* in Albert the Great's Texts on Creation in *Summa de creaturis* and *Scripta super sententias*," in *Albert the Great*, pp. 72-3.

[32] Summary of *Summa de creaturis*, Tract I, Quaestio 2 (De materia), in Volume XXXIV of *Alberti Magni Opera Omnia*, ed. A. Borgnet (Paris: L. Vivès, 1890-99), pp. 320-27.

[33] *De creaturis*, I:2, p. 327.

[34] See Weisheipl, "Albert's Works on Natural Science (*libri naturales*)," Appendix I of *Albertus Magnus and the Sciences*, pp. 565-77.

[35] John M. Quinn, "The Concept of Time in Albert the Great," in *Albert the Great*, pp. 28-9.

Time, by contrast, belongs to the realm of corruptible being and so is defined as the measure of motion or change.[36] Albertus agreed with Augustine that human beings use their imaginations to comprehend time but his main concern was to evaluate time as an agent of real physical change in the natural world.[37] Albertus' approach to time included a critical evaluation of Platonic, Aristotelian, Augustinian and Boethian arguments ranging from the relationship between time and the motion of heavenly bodies to the divisibility of time and the progression of time from past to future. In his assessment of Albertus' view of time, John Quinn has admitted that Albertus often overstated or misrepresented the views of others in order to clarify his own positions, which were not always especially lucid themselves. Quinn ends his study, however, by praising rather than dismissing Albertus for the intensity he brought to the study of "the cosmic accident, always easily employable in practice yet frequently exasperatingly baffling in theory, that is physical time."[38]

Albertus' greatest contribution to the thirteenth-century discussion of time, of course, was not that he solved the philosophical problem it entails but that he helped to legitimate the use of non-Christian philosophies in considering topics of interest to Christian thinkers. Although he most carefully followed Averroes in his treatments of time and eternity, he referred to many other writers, including Avicenna, Themistius, Alexander of Aphrodosias, Theophrastus and Porphyry.[39] Like Averroes, Albertus wanted to prove that the various times which creatures experience really constitute a single unified time: if they did not, it would be impossible to measure time at all. It is the uniform motion of the heavens which provides a fundamental reference by which all other motions and times are numbered.[40] Albertus' active role in the medieval discussion of time, then, was not one of original insight, but

---

[36] *De creaturis*, II:3, p. 347. See also Quinn, p. 43. Throughout this essay, Quinn notes the similarity between Albertus' early treatise *De creaturis* and his later *Physica*, indicating that Albertus' attraction to the Aristotelian conception of time was fairly constant throughout his career.

[37] *De creaturis*, II:3, p. 365.

[38] Quinn, p. 47.

[39] Mansion, pp. 289-90.

[40] From Albertus' commentary on Aristotle's *Physics* in Borgnet, Volume III, p. 341; quoted by Mansion, p. 295: "Cum autem dicimus suum (*scil.* circulationis primae) tempus esse mensuram aliorum temporum, non intelligimus plura esse tempora, sed unum diversimode referri ad multa. Refertur enim tempus ad primam mobile et ad motum ejus sicut ad subjectum et numeratum, ad alios autem motus sicut numerus extrinsecus ad numerata solum et in illis non est sicut in subjecto: et ideo non multiplicatur multiplicatione eorum."

instead one of informed commentary. He concluded that philosophical and theological approaches to matter and time do not contradict each other. This approach cannot legitimately be called a synthesis because he made no further effort to bring them together. On the other hand, as an active proponent of both kinds of knowledge, Albertus would have opposed any claim that there are certain questions which either faith or science alone can answer. Both his specific views about time and his opinions about knowledge in general had bearing on subsequent discussions of the problem of time.

Albertus' student, Thomas Aquinas, is credited with the effort to achieve an actual synthesis between Christian doctrine and Greco-Arabic learning. While Aquinas did not attempt to master Albertus' encyclopedic knowledge of the natural world, his writing demonstrates a much greater sensitivity to metaphysical and cosmological concerns. Because one of the main objectives of Albertus' ministry was to encourage theologians, especially those in the Dominican Order, to have a thorough understanding of classical philosophy, Aquinas, as Albertus' student, was exposed to a wide range of philosophical traditions. During three years of study under Albertus, Aquinas heard him lecture on moral philosophy and on the Bible. Albertus' published lectures on Psalms, Jeremiah and Daniel date from the period of Aquinas' study with him. At the same time Albertus was preparing a paraphrase of Aristotle, a commentary on Book IV of Peter Lombard's *Sentences* and lectures on the Apocalypse and Gospels.[41]

The young Aquinas took seriously his teacher's devotion to classical learning and soon became familiar both with Aristotle and with the Arabic commentaries, particularly those of Averroes. Unlike Albertus, however, Aquinas was not satisfied with acquiring and assimilating many sources of learning to support the broadly based, eclectic sort of theological speculation which is characteristic of Albertus. Aquinas' special gift was for philosophical analysis. Thus his aim was to produce a more conscious synthesis of scripture, patristic writings and classical philosophy than Albertus had ever attempted to achieve. For this reason, Aquinas' writings have almost as much significance in the field of philosophy as they have in theology, which was, in Aquinas' view, the more important discipline.

---

[41] Weisheipl, *Friar Thomas d'Aquino*, pp. 46-7. For additional information about Aquinas' education and philosophical and theological interests see especially Marie Dominique Chenu, *St. Thomas d'Aquin et la théologie* (Bourges: L'imprimerie Tardy, 1959) and Frederick Charles Copelston, *Aquinas* (Hammondsworth, Middlesex, England: Penguin, 1965).

In light of debates about time and eternity which encouraged the use of non-Christian sources in the thirteenth century and considering the nature of his training and his interest in philosophy, it is not surprising that Aquinas frequently mentioned aspects of time in his own writing. As a Christian philosopher, he often found it necessary to examine time both as a spiritual and as a physical phenomenon. On the one hand, he had to take into account the biblical explanation of time as a part of creation, as well as Augustine's psychological approach, which emphasized the function of the soul in defining time. On the other hand, he wanted to affirm the Aristotelian approach to time, which provided a more objective explanation of time's relationship to space and motion. When he set out to discuss the nature of eternity, moreover, Aquinas was well aware of the long debate over time's relationship to eternity which dated from Plato's treatment of this issue.

Aquinas' own views on time are scattered throughout several of his works, including his commentaries on Lombard's *Sentences* and on Aristotle's *Physics* as well as his own *Summa theologica*. Hence, Aquinas' references to time arise in many different contexts. In every instance, however, he approached the problem of time in a way which demonstrates both a good understanding of the Aristotelian position and a respect for Christian authority. He carefully combined Platonic, Aristotelian and patristic positions to produce his own view, which, though not unique, provided a reasonable guideline for reconciling contradictory traditions. His work of synthesis, which his contemporaries and followers read avidly, helped to transform old ideas into new subjects for debate. Aquinas' writings about time are important, therefore, not so much for their originality but for their role in reintroducing the problems of time and eternity to scholars whose expertise in classical physics was becoming increasingly mature.

A useful way of beginning a review of Aquinas' view of time is to examine what he had to say about eternity, for, like many of his predecessors, he thought that these two concepts were interrelated. Aquinas accepted the standard distinction between the eternity of God, who is perfect and unchanging, and the transitory existence of created being. Like Augustine, Aquinas stressed not only God's all-encompassing nature but also his active participation in everything he creates. Thus Aquinas states in the *Summa theologica* that God "is infinite and comprehends within himself the plenitude of all perfection of all being," whereas every creature is mutable.[42]

---

[42] *Summa Theologica*, Ia.ix.1-2, quoted in *St. Thomas Aquinas: Philosophical Texts*, trans. Thomas Gilby (London: Oxford University Press, 1951), p. 82.

Aquinas then proposes the distinction between God's complete perfection and the mutability of creation as the principle for distinguishing time from eternity:

> Some seize on this as the difference between time and eternity, that time has a beginning and an end, but eternity not. This difference, however, is quite incidental and not essential; for even granting that time always was and always will be, there remains this difference between them, that eternity is simultaneously whole, whereas time is not. Eternity is the measure of permanence; time the measure of change.[43]

Aquinas' view of time and eternity reflects the influence of both Augustine's platonic notion that time is a function of creation, and the Aristotelian position that time is a function of change.

Much of Aquinas' discussion about time and eternity can also be seen as a modification of Augustine's psychological view of time. In Aquinas' opinion, the distinction between time and eternity is important not simply because it allows the memory to separate past and future but also because it facilitates the attainment of different kinds of knowledge:

> The higher reason and the lower reason, of which Augustine speaks, are in no wise distinct faculties. For he says that by the former a man is intent on things eternal, contemplating them in themselves and consulting them for his rule of conduct, while by the latter he is intent on things temporal. Now these two, namely eternity and time, are so related that one is the medium in which the other is known. For in the order of discovery, we come to the knowledge of things eternal through things temporal, according to the words of St. Paul, *the things of God are clearly seen, being understood by the things that are made.* On the other hand, in the order of interpretation, we judge of temporal things in light of eternity and dispose of temporal matters according to eternal laws. The higher and the lower reason, then, are one and the same faculty, distinguished only by different habits and active functions. Wisdom is attributed to the higher reason, scientific knowledge to the lower.[44]

Aquinas also observes that Augustine's conception of memory underestimates the complexity of the relationship between the intellect and time. "Pastness," for example, can be applied either to an object or to an act of knowing an object in the past. In the case of an object, its being in the past, present or future is incidental; but in the second case, "the pastness of an act can be essential to the intellect, for our act of

---

[43] *Summa Theologica*, Ia.x.4, trans. Gilby, p. 83.
[44] *Summa Theologica*, Ia.lxxix.9, trans. Gilby, p. 26.

understanding is a particular activity at a certain time."[45] In Aquinas' more highly developed ideas about sense, intellect and knowledge, it is not accurate to confine the conception of past, present or future to the mind alone. Aquinas therefore advocates a broader approach to time which also includes Aristotelian observations about motion and change.

How, then, does Aquinas define the human experience of time? First of all, he emphasizes that time has both intellectual and physical dimensions and is a state which affects only created beings:

> Because our knowledge is enclosed in the order of time, either directly or indirectly, the time-factor enters into our calculations, and our knowledge reckons things as past, present, or future. Past, in memory; present, in experience; future, by anticipation in present causes. Future events are either certainties, when they are wholly determined in their causes, or conjectures, when they can usually be forecast, or unknown, when their causes are not yet committed to action. God, however, is entirely above the order of time. He is at the peak of eternity, surmounting everything all at once. Thence the stream of time can be seen in one simple glance.[46]

Aquinas thus concurs with Augustine and Boethius that God, being above time, sees all creation as a totality, whereas his creatures must experience existence as a continuous succession of nows; this notion has important implications for subsequent discussions of human will and contingency.[47] Moreover, although God actively participates in his creation, he does so in a way that does not change him: "Since God is outside the whole scheme of creatures, though all of them are ordered to him, and not conversely, it is clear that while creatures are really related to God, in God there is no real relation to creatures, but only a logical one."[48] The two main features of Aquinas' view of time, therefore, are that God created time for a specific purpose along with the rest of the universe and, ultimately, that the measure of time is the divine will, which is eternal. It is pointless to ask precisely when God created time because such a question implies that there was time before creation by which one could measure the event and this is impossible.[49]

---

[45] *Summa Theologica*, Ia.lixxix.6, trans. Gilby, pp. 250-51.

[46] Commentary, I *Perihermenias*, lect. 14, trans. Gilby, pp. 84-5.

[47] See Anthony Kenny, "Divine Foreknowledge and Human Freedom," in *Aquinas: A Collection of Critical Essays*, ed. Anthony Kenny (London: Macmillan, 1969), pp. 255-70.

[48] *Summa Theologica*, Ia.xiii.7, trans. Gilby, p. 95.

[49] For an analysis of Aquinas' treatment of time before time, see James F. Anderson, "Time and Possibility of an Eternal World," *Thomist*, 15 (1932), pp. 144-7. See also *The Eternity of the World in the Thought of Thomas Aquinas and his Contemporaries*, ed. J.

Second, Aquinas acknowledges that our perception of time depends to some extent on motion. In fact, much of his language about time reflects his dependence on the Aristotelian tradition: time is *aliquis motus*, an aspect of motion; time is a continuum; time is a number which arises from the division of motion; time is an image of motion.[50] Just as he refuses to accept Augustine's view of time uncritically, so Aquinas also draws out of Aristotle the themes which best support his own view while dismissing what he thinks is incorrect. Although he discusses time in terms of motion according to the Aristotelian tradition, for example, Aquinas recognizes that the concept of motion itself poses serious difficulties for the natural philosopher. In his commentary on Aristotle's *Physics* he prefers to describe the relationship between time and change, rather than time and motion, because "any process is a kind of change and [even] what happens suddenly is temporal, for it is what happens in a moment of time. Time itself is defined in terms of change."[51] Nor can Aquinas accept what he considers Aristotle's rather primitive assertion that time and motion are essentially different aspects of the same phenomenon. In his commentary on Aristotle's *Metaphysics*, Aquinas asserts that "Aristotle was convinced that motion was everlasting, and time likewise. But his arguments [in the eighth book of the *Physics*] are probable and not cogent, except perhaps as disproofs of some early physical theories about the inception of motion."[52]

This criticism of Aristotle rests on the distinction which Aquinas often made between eternal and created being: "For time itself is contained in the universe, and therefore when we speak about creation we should not inquire at what time it happened."[53] The only appropriate context for the question whether the world existed before time is a purely logical one in which one can consider "an instant before any other instant."[54] So, although Aquinas was fascinated by the philosophical implications of time and eternity for creation and made repeated references to this topic in his commentaries on Aristotle, his theological impulse was to accept Augustine's conception of time and

---

B. M. Wissink (New York: E. J. Brill, 1990), which describes the reception of Aquinas' views on eternity in the late thirteenth- and early fourteenth-century universities.

[50] John M. Quinn, *The Doctrine of Time in St. Thomas: Some Aspects and Applications. An Abstract of a Dissertation* (Washington, D. C.: The Catholic University of America Press, 1960), pp. 17-23.

[51] Commentary, *III Physics*, lect. 2, trans. Gilby, p. 51.

[52] Commentary, *XII Metaphysics*, lect. 5, trans. Gilby, p. 53.

[53] Disputations, *III de Potentia*, 17, trans. Gilby, p. 138.

[54] Disputations, *III de Potentia*, 17 ad 5, trans. Gilby, p. 138.

matter as created and not eternal. Aquinas' willingness to discuss the question of the eternity of the world and even to suggest ways of treating it without contradicting scripture nevertheless reflects his strong desire to reconcile Christian and Greco-Arabic traditions.[55]

Aquinas also demonstrated his capacity for synthesis in his analysis of time as a continuum. Although we think of time as a succession of before and after, we cannot grasp the now which is fleeting and insubstantial. Neither is it a simple matter to measure time by observing change for change has the same characteristic as time: both "have potentiality mingled with actuality."[56] The now of time shares certain features with a point on a line, in that it represents part of a continuous sequence; but unlike points which make up a line, nows do not produce measurable substance. The now is like a point mainly in its capacity to connect past to future.[57] Because the now is dimensionless and has no substance, it cannot have number in the conventional sense: number is impossible without substance, continuum or quality.[58] To the extent that time can be measured, therefore, it must be measured in respect of the continuous succession of nows and not on the basis of the duration of a single now. Aquinas thus was forced to consider the same sorts of problems about time which his predecessors had faced, and his attempt at synthesis led him to accept both a modified psychological view of time as far as perception is concerned and a modified statement of Aristotelian physics regarding the measurement of time.

Clearly, Aquinas' view of time is a composite of several traditions. Modern commentators generally concede that his views were mostly in keeping with Aristotle and that Averroes' reevaluation of Aristotle strongly influenced him.[59] It has been suggested, however, that, unlike Aristotle or his teacher Albertus, Aquinas thought of time less as a factor in scientific inquiry than as a subject for philosophical inquiry because he did not consider time, space or motion to be subsistent things.[60] Although he did not contribute much to the solution of problems

---

[55] For a discussion of Aquinas' opinions about the eternity of the world, see Anderson, pp. 137-144, and Wissink.

[56] *Summa Theologica*, Ia.vii.3, trans. Gilby, p. 140.

[57] Vincent Edward Smith, *St. Thomas on the Object of Geometry* (Milwaukee, Wisconsin: Marquette University Press, 1954), pp. 54-55.

[58] "Ohne Dinge, ohne Qualität, ohne Kontinuum ist keine Zahl möglich." See Ewald Bodewig, "Zahl und Kontinuum in der Philosophie des hl. Thomas," *Divus Thomas*, 13 (1935), p. 63.

[59] Anderson, p. 144; Mansion, pp. 297-98.

[60] Copelston, *Aquinas*, p. 79.

involving the physical manifestations of time, he took the original step
of isolating some aspects of the problem of time from physical,
theological and psychological considerations and so proposed a distinctly philosophical approach to time.

The type of intellectual activity which Albertus had tried to instill in
Aquinas and other continental scholars had a counterpart in England. In
some respects, the study of natural philosophy as an adjunct of theology
became by the end of the thirteenth century an even stronger feature of
the curriculum at Oxford than it was at Paris. For Bradwardine, the importance of this trend was two-fold. Like many other students, he
benefited enormously from the vibrant interactions of logicians, natural
philosophers and theologians who were active at Oxford at the turn of
the fourteenth century. First, as the reputation of Oxford became identified increasingly with the physical and mathematical studies of such
men as Robert Grosseteste, the arts curriculum at Oxford began to favor
such disciplines as astronomy, mathematics and optics. Second, because
Oxford continued to promote theology as most worthy of advanced
study, the best arts students were encouraged to suspend their studies of
natural philosophy in order to take advanced degrees in theology, with
the result that many young scholars left their "scientific" pursuits just
when they were beginning the most productive stages of their intellectual development.[61]

Of the several thirteenth-century English thinkers who shaped
intellectual life at Oxford, Robert Grosseteste and John Duns Scotus
most influenced fourteenth-century approaches to time. While Scotus'
work was fundamentally philosophical and theological in nature and
therefore speculative rather than empirical, Grosseteste's achievements
are usually associated with his dedication to experimental science. Like
Albertus, Grosseteste is noted for the breadth of his interests in natural
philosophy and theology. Born in 1175, he studied at Paris and at
Oxford, where he became a master of theology, and later served as the
chancellor of Oxford.[62] He reached the height of his ecclesiastical career
when he was elected bishop of Lincoln in 1235, an office which he held

---

[61] There was, of course, significant intercourse of ideas among thirteenth- and
fourteenth-century universities, especially between Oxford and Paris, as scholars moved
from place to place. The English natural philosopher Roger Bacon, for example, studied
at Oxford but produced his most influential treatises in Paris. In *Vision and Certitude*,
Tachau provides a thorough account of such intercourse; for Roger Bacon, see especially
pp. 3-26.

[62] Daniel A. Callus, "Robert Grosseteste as Scholar," in *Robert Grosseteste, Scholar
and Bishop*, ed. D. A. Callus (Oxford: Clarendon Press, 1955), pp. 6-9.

until his death in 1253. During his lifetime, he was not only an active church administrator but also a productive author of treatises on natural philosophy and theology. Before his election to the see at Lincoln he composed commentaries on the Bible and on Aristotle. After 1235 he was engaged in translating Aristotle's writings from Greek to Latin. Throughout this entire period he regularly composed original treatises on a variety of topics in natural philosophy, including logic, mathematics and optics, for which he is best known.[63]

The source of the view that Grosseteste advocated a kind of experimental science is his commentary on Aristotle's *Posterior Analytics*. In this treatise Grosseteste explored Aristotle's claim that the purpose of natural philosophy is to acquire demonstrable knowledge of observable phenomena. A. C. Crombie develops the thesis that Grosseteste derived from Aristotle the notion that "scientific knowledge, properly speaking, was the demonstrative knowledge of things through their causes, and its instrument was the demonstrative syllogism, which established the connexion between premises and conclusions, or causes and their effects, through the middle term."[64] In his commentary on the *Posterior Analytics* Grosseteste seemed to envision science as an intellectual activity which applied observation and mathematical precision to the examination of matter. Indeed, he claimed that real science is "the comprehension of the truth of those things which always behave in a given manner, and in mathematics both the premises and conclusions are known in this way . . . . Therefore, to know simply and most appropriately is to understand the unchanging cause of a thing in itself, . . . and this knowledge is the most special goal of this [metaphysical] science and is acquired by demonstration most properly so called."[65] On the basis of this and other passages from Grosseteste's writings, Crombie argues that Grosseteste devised a theory of scientific investigation which became the foundation of modern empirical science. Grosseteste's extensive commentaries on many topics in natural philosophy

---

[63] *Ibid.*, pp. 12-13. For additional information on Grosseteste see Richard William Southern, *Robert Grosseteste: The Growth of an English Mind in Medieval Europe* (Oxford: Clarendon Press, 1986); and James McEvoy, *The Philosophy of Robert Grosseteste* (Oxford: Clarendon Press, 1982).

[64] *Robert Grosseteste and the Origins of Experimental Science* (Oxford: Clarendon Press, 1953), pp. 52-53.

[65] Commentary on the *Posterior Analytics*, i.2, f. 2vb, quoted in Crombie, pp. 58-59. For the critical edition of this work see *Commentarius in Posteriorum analyticorum libros*, ed. Pietro Rossi, Unione Accademica Nazionale Corpus Philosophorum Medii Aevi, Testi e Studi, II (Florence: L. S. Olschki, 1981).

and his praise of mathematical applications to physics lend support to Crombie's interpretation.

More recently, this view has been questioned. Eileen F. Serene suggests, for example, that Crombie has placed too much emphasis on Grosseteste's and Aristotle's concern for demonstration, since they were primarily concerned not with empirical but rather with logical verification of natural phenomena. Furthermore, Grosseteste's philosophy was so heavily influenced by Augustinian Neoplatonism that it is misleading to overemphasize the connections among Aristotelian physics, Grosseteste's methods of inquiry and modern science.[66]   Nevertheless, Grosseteste's belief that certainty comes as a result of divine illumination which only clarifies what already exists in the mind, encouraged natural philosophers to make careful observations and to interpret them in reasonable ways.[67]   The most intriguing aspect of his philosophy, therefore, was not his experimental method but his conviction that questions about God and about the human capacity to understand the physical universe are fundamentally related.   To the extent that Bradwardine shared the same conviction, he was undeniably one of Grosseteste's most successful followers.

The research of James McEvoy supports Serene's thesis that Grosseteste's philosophy displays a subtle blend of Aristotelian and Augustinian elements. McEvoy identifies Grosseteste's cosmology as essentially Aristotelian; but by carefully comparing Grosseteste's views to Aristotle's, he has discovered significant deviations. While Grosseteste readily accepted Aristotle's treatment of the physical aspects of time, for example, he, like many of his contemporaries, rejected Aristotle's belief in the eternity of the world. Instead, Grosseteste advocated a cosmology which acknowledged the world's creation in time. Moreover, Grosseteste's enthusiasm for describing nature mathematically has no counterpart in Aristotle.[68]   In his treatise *Concerning Lines, Angles and Figures*, Grosseteste claims that there is a recognizable mathematical component in all natural phenomena: "all causes of natural effects can be discovered by lines, angles and figures, and in no other way can the reason of their action possibly be known."[69] According to McEvoy,

---

[66] "Robert Grosseteste on Induction and Demonstrative Science," *Synthese*, 40 (1979), p. 97.

[67] *Ibid.*, p. 113.

[68] McEvoy, p. 168.

[69] Translated by McEvoy, p. 168, from *Die philosophischen Werke des Robert Grosseteste, Bischof von Lincoln*, ed. Ludwig Baur, Volume XV of *Beiträge zur Geschichte der Philosophie und Theologie des Mittelalters* (Münster: Aschendorff, 1912), pp. 59-60.

this notion emerges with even greater force from his *Notes on Physics*, in which Grosseteste "describes God as a mathematician who established the basic indivisible units of space and time from which the whole extension of the material world is effected."[70]

Grosseteste also considered the validity of Aristotle's definition of time as a measure of motion, concluding that Aristotle had failed to demonstrate concretely the reality of time. In his own explanation of time, Grosseteste used the well-documented comparison between time and a line, arguing that, because both the line and time have a single infinite dimension, exact numerical measurement of either puts one "in an area of such difficulty that it lies almost beyond the scope of the human mind."[71] Nevertheless, although Grosseteste admitted that time defies accurate measurement, he believed, according to McEvoy, that there is "an ultimate foundation of the extension of space and time, a final unit and measure which determines their nature."[72] The human mind is incapable of comprehending the infinity of time and space, which consists of an extension of infinite points. Only God, who possesses wisdom "without number," can perceive and measure time and space accurately: for God an infinite number is as finite as the number two is for us.[73] Although Grosseteste did not go on to develop possibilities for coping with the difficulty of measuring time, his conception of time as the creation of a mathematical God helped to transform the problem of time into a geometrical one, a change which had an obvious impact on Bradwardine's thinking about time, space and motion.

The contribution of John Duns Scotus to the medieval discussion of time is more philosophical than scientific. Scotus was born in Scotland in 1266, a little more than a decade after Grosseteste's death. He was a Franciscan who studied and taught in Cambridge, Oxford, Paris and Cologne. Before his death in 1308 he composed an extensive array of philosophical works, including commentaries on Aristotle's metaphysical works, commentaries

---

[70] McEvoy, pp. 175-76.

[71] Translated by McEvoy, p. 176, from Annaliese Maier's transcription of the Venice Bibl. Marciana MS Lat. VI, 222, printed in her *Zwischen Philosophie und Mechanik: Studien zur Naturphilosophie der Spätscholastik* (Rome: Storia e letteratura, 1958), pp. 24n.-25n.

[72] McEvoy, p. 176.

[73] Quoted by McEvoy, p. 177, from Maier's transcription: "Sicut enim que vere in se finita sunt, nobis sunt infinita, sic que vere se sunt infinita, illi sunt finita. Iste autem omnia creavit in numero, pondere et mensura, et isti est mensurator primus et certissimus. Isti numeris infinitis, sibi finitis, mensuravit lineas quas creavit. Numero aliquo infinito sibi certo et finito mensuravit et numeravit lineam cubilem, et numero infinito duplo lineam bicubilem et numero infinito subduplo lineam semicubilem."

on the *Sentences* and several original treatises. His most important work, the *Ordinatio*, appears to be a written compilation of the course which he gave at Oxford, but it contains his most mature reflections on many philosophical and theological problems and so has been called his "definitive work and masterpiece."[74] Even as a young student Scotus showed a remarkable talent for metaphysical speculation which his teachers recognized and helped him to develop. Later he earned the title of Subtle Doctor, which attests to the respect which he received from his students and peers.[75] Scotus' thought deserves to be considered because he proposed original solutions to a wide range of philosophical problems which attracted a large following at Oxford and Paris.

Scotus' philosophy must be seen in the context of the debate which raged in his day over the relative merits of Augustinian and Aristotelian metaphysics. Both sides accepted "the strict metaphysical transcendence of God over creatures" but they disagreed about defining the precise relationship of God to his creation.[76] In response to the burst of interest in Aristotelian philosophy in the second half of the thirteenth century, many conservatives complained that Christian interpreters of Aristotle, particularly Aquinas, stressed God's transcendence too much and urged instead a more Augustinian approach which did not depend on such a rigid separation of God and creation. Threatened by the radical Aristotelianism espoused by certain followers of Averroes, theologians from many schools, including some Dominican masters, raised opposition

---

[74] Efrem Bettoni, *Duns Scotus: The Basic Principles of his Philosophy*, Bernardine Bonansea, ed. and trans. (Westport, Connecticut: Greenwood, 1978), p. 10. Although Bettoni calls this work the *Opus Oxoniensis*, it is more commonly known as the *Ordinatio*. See Marilyn McCord Adams' introduction to Allan Bernard Wolter, *The Philosophy of John Duns Scotus*, ed. Adams (Ithaca, New York: Cornell University Press, 1990), pp. 1-2. Wolter's essays trace Scotus' influence in the universities where he studied and taught. In this context, see also the references to Scotus in *Vision and Certitude*. For additional information on Scotus see Hermann Schwamm, *Das göttliche Vorherwissen bei Duns Scotus und seinen ersten Anhängern*, Volume V of *Philosophie und Grenzwissenschaften* (Innsbruck: Felizan Rauch, 1934) and Étienne Gilson, *Jean Duns Scot* (Paris: J. Vrin, 1952). See also the introduction to the critical edition of Scotus' works, ed. Charles Balic, *Opera omnia, iussu et auctoritate Pacifici M. Perantoni. Studio et cura commissionis Scotisticae as fidem codicum edita* (Civitas Vatican: Typis Polyglottis Vaticanis, 1950-66), 17 volumes.

[75] Bettoni, pp. 13-14, points out that Scotus had received relatively little scholarly attention in this century and observes that the lack of current studies on Scotus can give the wrong impression that he was a minor figure in the medieval universities; in fact, the numerous references to Scotus in works of his contemporaries indicate that his views were quite influential.

[76] *Ibid.*, p. 15.

even to the moderate Aristotelianism of Albertus and Aquinas. The most vocal opponents of Aristotelian philosophy, however, were the Franciscans.[77] As a Franciscan, Scotus responded to the dispute not by taking a side but by trying to synthesize a new philosophical system which preserved the best features of both approaches. To achieve such a synthesis, he criticized both traditions with great skill and insight.[78] His comments on time and space particularly reflect his subtle reconsideration of both Aristotelian and Augustinian metaphysical theory.

In his analysis of time as a phenomenon of nature, Scotus readily accepted Aristotle's definition of time as the measure of motion. In the *De rerum principio* Scotus confirmed Aristotle's assertion that motion and time are different aspects of the same thing.[79] Scotus also maintained the validity of Augustine's view that the human experience of time is subjective because time consists of a continuum of unanalyzable nows. To support his synthesis of the two positions, he recounted Aristotle's story of the sleepers of Sardis which illustrates how our sense of time comes from the subjective experience of before and after, rather than from the objective observation of motion. When the sleepers awoke they failed to realize that any time had passed because the last now of their former consciousness was linked to the first now of their waking; thus the intervening time was essentially lost to them. Scotus then related Aristotle's story to the common experience of falling asleep and awakening in a dark place: usually we cannot tell what time it is without referring to an external source of information.[80]

---

[77] *Ibid.*, pp. 16-17.

[78] *Ibid.*, p. 21. For a comprehensive analysis of Scotus' philosophical outlook, see Part III of Wolter's collected essays on philosophical theology (ed. Adams), which contains "Duns Scotus and the Existence and Nature of God," (pp. 254-77) and "Scotus' Paris Lectures on God's Knowledge of Future Events," (pp. 285-333). For Scotus' interactions with other scholars, see also the following series of essays and editions of related texts: Stephen Dumont, "The Univocity of the Concept of Being in the Fourteenth Century: John Duns Scotus and William of Alnwick," *Mediaeval Studies*, 49 (1987), pp. 1-75; Dumont, "The Univocity of the Concept of Being in the Fourteenth Century, II: The *De ente* of Peter Thomae," *Mediaeval Studies*, 50 (1988), pp. 186-256; and Stephen F. Brown and Dumont, "The Univocity of the Concept of Being in the Fourteenth Century, III: An Early Scotist," *Mediaeval Studies*, 51 (1989), pp. 1-129.

[79] *De rerum principio*, q. xviii, art. I, n. 4, quoted by Charles Reginald Schiller Harris in *Duns Scotus*, 2 vols. (New York: Humanities Press, 1959), II.129-30: ". . . motus et tempus non dicunt diversas res absolutas sicut quantitas et qualitas inhaerens, sed omnino dicunt eandem secundum diversas rationes denominatam aliquando tempus, aliquando motus." For a standard edition of this work see John Duns Scotus, *Opera Omnia*, ed. Luke Wadding (Paris: L. Vivès, 1891-95).

[80] *De rerum principio*, q. xviii, n. 6 (Commentary on Aristotle's *Physics*, Book IV, Cap. xi), quoted by Harris, p. 131: "Aristoteles videtur suadere tempus extra animam

This is not to say that there is no objective basis for time, but merely
that we cannot easily recognize it. Our perception of time relies on our
perception of the sequence of past, present and future, which has nothing
to do with motion itself, though it does involve change.[81] Scotus warns
us not to confuse his acknowledgement of the difficulty of measuring
time with an acceptance of Augustine's position. In Scotus' opinion
Augustine erred by conceiving of time purely subjectively and by failing
to "consider it a property of real things."[82] Nor does Scotus entirely accept Aquinas' objective conception of time, which identifies the unity of
time with "the unity of the first heaven, by which all motion is
measured."[83]

Because he wished to preserve some features of Augustinian
subjectivity while retaining the basic objectivity of Aquinas' view,
Scotus attempted to reconcile the two approaches. Thus he proposed
that "time and motion are objectively (*in re*) identical, but conceptually
(*formali ratione*) diverse. According to its *esse materiale*, time exists in
things; according to its *esse formale*, in virtue of which it is to be called
time in the truest sense, it depends on the mind and exists in the mind."[84]
Scotus insisted that his view was in keeping with Aristotle and Averroes,
both of whom stressed that time has a universal nature as the number of
motion and a subjective nature, because the number of time is
determined by the mind.[85] Although time is the objective measure of

---

nihil esse . . . . Si ergo ipsum est aliquid, est ab actione animae . . . . Hanc autem rationem videtur Philosophus deducere 'quia cum nihil ipsi mutamur secundum
intellegentiam aut latet nos mutari, non videtur nobis fieri tempus sicut neque his qui in
Sardo fabulantur dormire apud Heroas, cum expergis cuntur. Copulant enim primum
nunc posteriori nunc, et unum faciunt removentis proper insensibilitatem medium.'
Putabant enim esse numero tempus quo dormire coeperant et in quo evigilabant . . . .
Unde etiam dormientes in obscuro loco, non perpendentis aliquid se motu coeli per
lucem solis, quando evigilant quaerunt tempus, nec scimus quae hora sit certitudinaliter,
nisi referemus nos ad alia signa."

[81] Harris, pp. 131-32.

[82] *De rerum principio*, q. xviii, n. 13, quoted and translated by Harris, p. 134: "Patet
ergo quod haec fuit ejus opinio, tempus habere esse in conceptu animae non extra."

[83] Harris, p. 136.

[84] *De rerum principio*, q. xviii, n. 16, quoted by Harris, p. 136: "Alii dicunt magis
realiter, ut credo quod tempus sit idem in re quod motus, differens formali ratione, per
quam rationem vocatur vere tempus: secundum suum esse materiale est in rebus extra,
secundum suam vero rationem formalem est ab anima et est in ea."

[85] *De rerum principio*, q. xviii, n. 16, quoted by Harris, p. 136: "Et huius opinionis
videtur fuisse Commentator . . . . Et ista est doctrina Aristotelis . . . ubi vult quod tempus
inest omnibus rebus per motum in terra, in mare et in coelo, cum sit passio et mensura
motus, nec possint ab invicem separari. Motus autem est aliquid reale praeter actionem

motion, we perceive time subjectively as a continuum of past, present and future.

Scotus next suggested that the real problem with previous efforts to understand time lay in the tendency of some of his predecessors to identify time with motion when, in fact, they are significantly different:

> Motion, therefore, taken in its strictest sense, does not include in its notion the concepts of before and after, except potentially, in so far as these may be added to it by thought. But time includes them formally in its concept and is therefore partially subjective, being a measure of motion. It is plain, then, that from the standpoint of the objective world motion is more real than time, for motion is in its essence the continuous flux whose being is not derived from thought, but quite independent of it. Time, consequently, has a feebler being than motion, and is less real.[86]

The relationship between time and eternity rests on this concept of time's weakness compared to motion. Time is the measure of change in corruptible being; eternity, because it is completely removed from time and is a feature of God's perfect, unchanging being, cannot be measured. Between time and eternity is the aevum, which governs such created beings as angels and heavenly bodies which have a beginning in time, but only potentially an end, because they do not pass in and out of existence as earthly creatures do.[87]

Scotus' synthetic view of time was essentially a reconsideration of his predecessors' distinction between time and motion from the perspective of their distinction between time and eternity. In forging this synthesis, Scotus was especially indebted to Aquinas' own efforts to reconcile Aristotelian and Augustinian views of time. Like Aquinas, Scotus ultimately failed to provide a solution to the problem of measuring duration when time is defined as having both objective and subjective characteristics. Scotus admitted that there must be some principle which explains time, aevum and eternity in terms of each other but he was unable to propose either a mathematical or a philosophical principle which determined precisely how they coexist.[88] Thus he was caught up in the same dilemma over time which had frustrated natural philosophers and theologians for many centuries.

---

et conceptum animae. Quod autem habet aliquem motum essendi habeat ab anima immediate concedit, arguens quod tempus est numerans; ergo numerans; hoc autem est anima."

[86] *De rerum principio*, q. xviii, n. 32, translated by Harris, pp. 139-40.

[87] Harris, pp. 141-45.

[88] *Ibid.*, p. 145.

In many respects, one might conclude, temporal theory itself did not develop much in the late twelfth and thirteenth centuries, except to the extent that Christian thinkers learned to apply Greco-Arabic methods to their studies of time. Naturally, their prevailing tendency either to correct the Aristotelian position or to integrate Aristotelian and Augustinian principles was not confined to the problem of time, which was only one of many philosophical and theological problems under discussion in this period. The real achievement of thinkers like Albertus, Aquinas, Grosseteste and Scotus was not that they solved any of these problems but that they embraced new ways of seeking the truth about the connection between natural phenomena and God's plan for creation. The foundation of these accomplishments was the body of scientific and philosophical material which had become available at the end of the twelfth century. By the end of the thirteenth century the energetic interplay between advocates for Greco-Arabic learning and their conservative critics had given way to a more serious debate about the possibility of reconciling the two traditions. It was during this troubled phase of speculation that Bradwardine entered Oxford as a young student in the early fourteenth century.

CHAPTER FOUR

MATHEMATICS, PROPORTIONALITY AND TIME

If the thirteenth century was the age of Aristotelian revival in the medieval universities, the early fourteenth century was a period of great diversification in the application of classical philosophical methods to problems of contemporary interest. The basic tools of propositional logic and Euclidean mathematics which accompanied the Aristotelian revival allowed fourteenth-century thinkers to develop a variety of new approaches to long-standing philosophical dilemmas about complex issues such as time. The expansion of the curriculum in natural philosophy, especially at Oxford, encouraged students to conceive of old problems, even theological ones, in new ways.[1] This movement has been called the "mathematization" of theology because fourteenth-century theologians not only discussed theological questions in physical and mathematical terms but in some cases adopted the axiomatic model of Euclidean geometry to present their theological arguments.[2]

Bradwardine's academic work provides an excellent illustration of this tendency towards "mathematical" theology. His mastery of Euclidean geometry and Aristotelian physics is a central feature of all of his major treatises. Indeed, Bradwardine achieved such a high standard of mathematical logic that he was able, both in philosophical and theological texts, to launch devastating intellectual challenges to his opponents'

---

[1] For a concise account of the development of the natural philosophy curriculum in the medieval universities see Edward Grant, "Science and the Medieval University," in *Rebirth, Reform and Resilience: Universities in Transition, 1300-1700*, ed. James M. Kittelson and Pamela J. Transue (Columbus, Ohio: Ohio State University Press, 1984), pp. 68-102. In the same collection of essays Courtenay traces the influence of Oxford on continental universities, especially Paris, in "The Role of English Thought in the Transformation of University Education in the Late Middle Ages," pp. 103-62. See also Jürgen Sarnowsky, "Natural Philosophy at Oxford and Paris in the Mid-Fourteenth Century," in *From Ockham to Wyclif*, pp. 125-34.

[2] William J. Courtenay, *Schools and Scholars in Fourteenth-Century England* (Princeton, New Jersey: Princeton University Press, 1987), pp. 262-63. Courtenay's book presents a thorough study of fourteenth-century academic life in England. For a good brief review of the theological trends in fourteenth-century universities, see Paul Vignaux, "La philosophie médiévale dans 'Le temp de l'église,'" in his *De saint Anselm à Luther* (Paris: J. Vrin, 1976), pp. 69-75.

positions.   Unlike most of his contemporaries, who composed lengthy
and exhaustive refutations of their opponents' views, Bradwardine took
a much more subtle approach: he criticized his opponents by isolating
the principles which underlay their primary assertions and then systematically exposed their weaknesses using the axiomatic methods of
Euclidean geometry.[3] The next three chapters trace the development of
Bradwardine's critical method through an examination of his treatments
of time as a physical phenomenon and a philosophical problem.

Because Bradwardine's reputation rested, in his own age and for several centuries to follow, on his mathematical works, it is appropriate to
begin to explore his views about time by reflecting on one of his early
scientific treatises.   The *De proportionibus*[4] clearly demonstrates the
capacity for mathematical reasoning which characterizes all of Bradwardine's works, including those devoted exclusively to philosophical or
theological topics.   Written in 1328, when Bradwardine was just em-
barking on his theological studies, the *De proportionibus* proposed a
more precise mathematical language for describing various kinds of
motion than had been available previously.   His colleagues at Merton
not only received it enthusiastically themselves but, by their frequent
references to it in their own treatises, helped to ensure its circulation
among all the European universities.   Indeed, by the end of the fourteenth century, the *De proportionibus* had become standard academic
reading and its principles profoundly influenced physical speculation of
all sorts for at least another century.[5]

---

[3] For an illustration of Bradwardine's method of argumentation see John Emery Murdoch, "Atomism and Motion in the Fourteenth Century," in *Transformation and Tradition in the Sciences: Essays in Honor of I. Bernard Cohen*, ed. Everett Mendelsohn
(Cambridge: Cambridge University Press, 1984), pp. 45-66.

[4] Some notes on the name of this work are found in Weisheipl, "Ockham and Some
Mertonians," *Mediaeval Studies*, 30 (1968), p. 191. Marshall Clagett has published and
discussed sections from an abbreviated version of the *De proportionibus* entitled *Tractatus brevis proportionum* in Chapter 7 of *The Science of Mechanics in the Middle Ages*
(Madison, Wisconsin: University of Wisconsin Press, 1959), pp. 421-44, 465-84. The
edition of the *De proportionibus* which will be used in this study is *Thomas Bradwardine, His Tractatus de Proportionibus: Its Significance for the Development of
Mathematical Physics*, ed. H. Lamar Crosby (Madison, Wisconsin: University of Wisconsin Press, 1961). Hereafter, citations to Bradwardine's text will appear in the notes as
De proportionibus and references to Crosby's introduction will be noted as "Crosby."

[5] Weisheipl, "Ockham and Some Mertonians," p. 189.   Some studies of medieval
commentaries on the *De proportionibus* include Anne Harrison, "Blasius of Parma's Critique
of Bradwardine's 'Tractatus de proportionibus,'" *Scienza e filosofia all'Università di Padova
nel Quattrocento*, Centro per storia dell'Università di Padova I (Trieste: Edizione Lint, 1983),
pp. 19-69; Michael McVaugh, "Arnold of Villanova and Bradwardine's Law," *Isis*, 58 (1967),

The significance of Bradwardine's mathematical approach to natural philosophy goes well beyond his attempt to discuss motion, space, time and other physical phenomena in terms of a well-ordered geometrical system. Bradwardine was certainly not original in his zeal for applying mathematics to physics, nor were many of his observations about motion entirely correct, at least if judged by modern standards. In her study of late medieval physical theory, Anneliese Maier portrays Bradwardine as a precocious thinker handicapped by the rudimentary level of mathematical knowledge in the early fourteenth century. Referring to the depth of his mathematical insight, Maier comments: "One might almost say that Bradwardine would have wanted to write the *Principia mathematica philosophiae naturalis* of his century,"[6] but she goes on to demonstrate why he was unable to do so. Bradwardine's generation lacked the knowledge of certain aspects of higher mathematics such as logarithms and the calculus which are necessary for developing a comprehensive mathematical description of the problems which interested them. Moreover, when Bradwardine left Oxford a few years after writing the *De proportionibus*, his concentration on natural philosophy in an academic setting came to an end. In spite of these obstacles, however, Bradwardine produced in the *De proportionibus* a mathematical approach to physics which stimulated interest in natural philosophy for several generations. The *De proportionibus* is also an important historical text. Through it, the historian can discover how scientific information passed from scholar to scholar and how thinkers like Bradwardine responded to the views of their predecessors. The obvious sources for Bradwardine's speculations about motion are Aristotle's *Physics* and Euclid's works on geometry but medieval thinkers such as Robert Grosseteste and Roger Bacon offered precedents for applying mathematics to physics which also influenced Bradwardine's scientific works.[7]

The purpose of this chapter is to analyze the *De proportionibus*: first, as a text of general interest in the history of late medieval science; second, as an extension of Bradwardine's mathematical thought which

---

pp. 56-64; and Graziella Frederice Viscovini, "Due commenti anonimi al 'Tractatus proportionum' di Tommaso Bradwardine," *Rinascimento*, Series 2, 19 (1979), pp. 231-33.

[6] *Die Vorläufer Galileis im 14. Jahrhundert*, 2nd edition (Rome: Storia e letteratura, 1966), p. 86, note 10. See also Edward Grant, "Bradwardine and Galileo: Equality of Velocities in the Void," *Archive for the History of Exact Sciences*, 2 (1965), pp. 344-64; and Edith Sylla, "Compounding Ratios: Bradwardine, Oresme, and the First Edition of Newton's *Principia*," in *Transformation and Tradition in the Sciences*, pp. 11-43.

[7] Weisheipl, p. 198. See also Crosby, p. 4.

originated in his short treatise, the *Geometria speculativa*; and third, as an illustration of his analytical approach to time. Although the *De proportionibus* is not specifically devoted to the problem of time, but only treats time as an incidental feature of motion, it helps to clarify Bradwardine's conception of the relationship between time and motion. This discussion of the *De proportionibus* will suggest that Bradwardine's scientific thought was firmly rooted in an Aristotelian tradition and that, despite his willingness occasionally to correct or modify Aristotelian definitions, he largely adopted Aristotle's description of the physical universe. The novelty of Bradwardine's work lay in his attempt to use geometry to reconcile contradictions in traditional physics which previous Aristotelians such as Avicenna and Averroes had been unable to resolve because they did not supplement their philosophical approaches to physics with mathematical analysis.

A review of the main themes and structure of the *De proportionibus* emphasizes the significance of this work in early fourteenth-century scientific thought. In his introductory remarks, Bradwardine set out both his intentions for the treatise and also his general views about the applicability of mathematics to the study of physics:

> Since each successive motion is proportionable to another with respect to speed, natural philosophy, which studies motion, ought not to ignore the proportion of motions and their speeds, and, because an understanding of this is both necessary and extremely difficult, nor has as yet been treated fully in any branch of philosophy, we have accordingly composed the following work on the subject. Since, moreover (as Boethius points out in Book I of his *Arithmetic*), it is agreed that whoever omits mathematical studies has destroyed the whole of philosophic knowledge, we have commenced by setting forth the mathematics needed for the task in hand, in order to make the subject easier and more accessible to the student.[8]

Following this preface, Bradwardine spelled out in four chapters precisely how he proposed to establish Aristotle's thesis concerning the proportionality of motion, proceeding from general definitions and properties of proportions, to criticism of four attempted revisions of Aristotle, to a discussion of the relationship between force and resistance and, finally, to an analysis of the principles of circular motion, which was commonly held to be the most regular and perfect kind of motion. Bradwardine defined the problems surrounding motion according to Euclidian suppositions. This mathematical approach set his analysis

---

[8] *De proportionibus*, pp. 64-65.

apart from those of his predecessors, who had not appreciated the advantages of approaching studies of motion in this way.

Beyond the insights which this introduction provides into Bradwardine's purpose in the *De proportionibus*, it reflects his commitment both to the Aristotelian tradition, which identified the study of nature with the study of motion, and to the Platonic tradition, which emphasized mathematics as the appropriate language for philosophical and scientific discourse. The rest of the *De proportionibus* reveals, however, that Bradwardine did not wish to use mathematics in a purely Platonic way, that is, as a description of a natural order which could be perceived through philosophical speculation. Nor was he content with an Aristotelian approach to motion, which did not take into account sufficiently the axiomatic principles of mathematics.

The *De proportionibus* not only incorporated features of these ancient schools of thought, both of which had been widely pursued in the thirteenth century, but it also presented a novel approach to natural philosophy based on a mathematical view of nature. Bradwardine's work on the proportionality of motion helped to push discussions of natural philosophy in new directions and to encourage speculation among his peers, principally his colleagues at Merton, the Oxford "Calculators." It is useful, therefore, to look at the antecedents of his mathematical thought, both in the ancient sources of Plato, Aristotle, Euclid and Boethius and among his more immediate predecessors. Only then can his views be seen in the appropriate context and the themes which have particular significance for his view of time be adequately isolated and evaluated.

Bradwardine's convictions about the applicability of mathematics to nature stemmed from a long debate which dated from the classical period. As we have seen, some classical philosophers regarded time as a physical force and described time mathematically, whereas others concentrated on the metaphysical problem of the relationship between time and eternity. Judeo-Christian notions of creation provided the impetus to study time both philosophically and theologically, using the mathematical theories of Plato and Aristotle. These theories deserve special attention in any study of medieval views of time because many of the advances in late medieval natural philosophy resulted from this interplay between classical mathematics and Judeo-Christian theology.[9]

---

[9] For the following discussion I am dependent on Lindberg, "On the Applicability of Mathematics to Nature: Roger Bacon and his Predecessors," *British Journal for the History of Science*, 15 (1982), pp. 3-25. For additional material on late medieval applications of

The disagreement between Plato and Aristotle over the role of mathematics in natural philosophy was fundamentally cosmological. Plato's view of the material world rested on his belief that being is composed of four elements—earth, air, fire and water—each particle of which has a definite, regular geometrical shape. The unity of the universe and the course it takes in its development come from the mathematical rule of geometric proportion.[10] Thus one cannot attain complete knowledge of the sensible world without comprehending the mathematical framework which determines its forms. According to Plato, therefore, the pursuit of natural philosophy demands the contemplation and the analysis of mathematical laws which govern the form of matter, not the observation of natural phenomena as such.[11]

Although Aristotle considered mathematics an extremely useful tool for scientific investigation, he completely rejected the notion that all knowledge of the world must be expressed in the abstract terminology of mathematics. Plato's approach would make it impossible to consider such sensible qualities as color, taste or temperature which were at the heart of his exploration of the natural world but which he had no means to quantify or express mathematically. Thus Aristotle remarked in the *Metaphysics*:

> . . . in his investigations [the mathematician] first abstracts everything that is sensible, such as weight and lightness, hardness and its contrary, and also heat and cold and all other sensible contrarieties, leaving only quantity and continuity—sometimes in one, sometimes in two and sometimes in three dimensions—and their affections *qua* quantitative and continuous, and does not study them with respect to any other thing.[12]

The mathematician shares in the process of scientific investigation by evaluating information but he does not dominate it. In the discipline of astronomy, for example, " . . . it is the business of the empirical observer to know the fact, of the mathematician to know the reason for the fact."[13]

---

mathematics to natural philosophy see *MTSM*; Ernest Moody, "Laws of Motion in Medieval Physics," *SMPSL*, pp. 189-201; and James A. Weisheipl, "Matter in Fourteenth-Century Science," in *The Concept of Matter in Greek and Medieval Philosophy*, ed. Ernan McMullin (Notre Dame, Indiana: University of Notre Dame Press, 1965), pp. 147-69.

[10] Robert P. Multhauf, "The Science of Matter," in *Science in the Middle Ages*, p. 370.

[11] Multhauf, pp. 382-83, contrasts "[t]he Good in the prototype of forms in which Plato based his analysis of nature, [with] Aristotle, to whom mathematics and metaphysics were immaterial entities. . . ."

[12] *Metaphysics*, xi.3.1061a30-35, trans. Hugh Tredennik (London, 1935), quoted by Lindberg, p. 7.

[13] *Posterior Analytics*, i.13.78b34-79a3, quoted and translated by Lindberg, p. 7.

Without denying the advantages of mathematics as a scientific resource, Aristotle minimized its position in natural philosophy because, in his opinion, mathematics could offer only vague and incomplete descriptions of observable phenomena.

Both sides in this dispute found their way into early medieval philosophy. Augustine and Boethius focused on the Platonic concept of the mathematical order of nature and asserted that creation proceeds according to numerical principles in the mind of God. At the same time, however, Boethius encouraged the application of mathematics to empirical observation by establishing the medieval classification of disciplines along Aristotelian lines.[14] His writings clearly demonstrated the validity of mathematical analysis in both metaphysics and physics.

After Boethius, such thinkers as Hugh of St. Victor, Thierry of Chartres, Gilbert of Porrée, William of Conches and Clarembaud of Arras tried to distinguish between the mathematics of metaphysics and the mathematics of physics. While they recognized the practical benefits of mathematics in scientific inquiry, they generally emphasized the transcendent power of mathematics to define the order of the natural world. In his *Didascalicon*, for example, Hugh of St. Victor accepted aspects of both Aristotelian and Platonic approaches to mathematics. On the one hand, his conception of scientific disciplines was rooted in Aristotle's notion of sensible entities. He contrasted mathematics, which treats abstract things such as lines and surfaces, with physics, which concerns real things. Thus mathematics "has its business in the consideration of things which, though actually fused, are rationally separated by it. . . . The business of physics, however, is to analyze the compounded actualities of things into their elements."[15] In his treatment of the soul, however, Hugh accorded to the study of numbers a metaphysical reality far greater than Aristotle had ever acknowledged. In fact, for Hugh "number itself teaches us the nature of the going out and the return of the soul."[16]

Bradwardine's immediate predecessors in the thirteenth century wrestled with the same ambiguity about the proper role of mathematics in natural philosophy. Robert Grosseteste, for example, devoted much attention to the problem of integrating physics and metaphysics along

---

[14] Lindberg, pp. 7-8.

[15] Jerome Taylor, ed. and trans., *The Didascalicon of Hugh of Saint Victor: A Medieval Guide to the Arts* (New York: Columbia University Press, 1961), p. 72, quoted by Lindberg, p. 9.

[16] Taylor, p. 64, quoted by Lindberg, p. 9.

mathematical lines. Grosseteste is best known for his development of
the "metaphysics of light," a system which sought to define the function
of light in the creation of the universe. He did not confine his speculations to natural philosophy, however; theology, epistemology and
metaphysics also contributed to his synthesis. Although his use of light
to explain the creative forces of the universe had Platonic origins, many
of his concrete statements about mathematics and physics were more in
keeping with Aristotelian principles of natural philosophy. Grosseteste
might have been attracted to Neoplatonic discussions of light because of
his interest in giving natural phenomena mathematical explanations. His
consideration of the Neoplatonists and the Muslim philosopher Al-kindi
led him to develop a "metaphysics of light" based on geometrical optics,
which he hoped could be verified experimentally.[17] Basing his system
both on the geometrical concepts of Neoplatonism and on Aristotle's
scheme of four elementary spheres, Grosseteste tried to accommodate
the ideas of both traditions in a single physical system which was also
thoroughly in harmony with his Christian theology.

In his commentary on Aristotle's *Physics*, Grosseteste expressed a
view concerning the proper relationship between mathematics and time
which was later adopted by Bradwardine. Grosseteste asserted that
mathematics and physics

> have much common ground and because of this a physicist can easily make the
> mistake of thinking that mathematical being is physical being and that physical
> being is mathematical being; and so that he [Aristotle] himself will not in this
> science [physics] suppose something purely mathematical to be a
> demonstration on the assumption that it is physical, or omit something physical
> on the ground that it is mathematical, he subtly shows the difference between
> physics and mathematics so that it may be possible to distinguish what belongs
> to this science and what not. And so I say that there are three things, namely,
> physical body, magnitudes which belong to physical bodies, and accidents of
> bodies purely speaking. Mathematicians abstract magnitudes from motion and
> matter and have as subjects abstract magnitudes, and from these they
> demonstrate accidents which are *per se* accidents of magnitudes. But the
> physicist does not demonstrate *per se* accidents of magnitudes as belonging
> simply to magnitudes, but he demonstrates the figured magnitudes of physical
> bodies as belonging to physical bodies in so far as they are physical.[18]

---

[17] Crombie, *Grosseteste*, pp. 105-6. See also material on Grosseteste in Lindberg,
Theories of Vision from Al-kindi to Kepler (Chicago: University of Chicago Press,
1976), especially pp. 94-102; and James McEvoy, "La connaissance intellectuelle selon
Robert Grosseteste," *Revue philosophique de Louvain*, 75 (1977), pp. 26-29.

[18] *Commentarius in VIII Libros Physicorum Aristotelis*, trans. Crombie, p. 94. For a

Thus Grosseteste affirmed Aristotle's distinction between the abstract analysis of the mathematician and the observation of sensible qualities which is the proper task of the natural philosopher.

In his geometrical treatise, *Concerning Lines, Angles and Figures*, Grosseteste emphasized the essential place that mathematics holds in physical investigations. According to Grosseteste, the mathematician helps the physicist to elucidate the structure of things by providing a system for describing natural phenomena.[19] In a continuation of this treatise entitled *De natura locorum*, Grosseteste stressed the necessity of mathematical analysis in the study of light. As a conclusion to his discussion of reflection and refraction of light, for example, he claimed:

> These rules, foundations, and fundamentals having been given by the power of geometry, the diligent investigator of natural things can in this manner specify the causes of all natural effects. And he can do this in no other way, as has already been shown in general, since every natural action is varied in strength and weakness according to the variation of lines, angles and figures.[20]

Through this study of light and his commentaries on Aristotle, Grosseteste achieved a balance between Platonic and Aristotelian views which gave mathematics a prominent place in late medieval natural philosophy while preserving the integrity of investigation based on the observation of sensible qualities. In Grosseteste's view, the world is not composed of mathematical entities, but it exists in patterns which mathematics can explain and describe once observations have been made.

Another thirteenth-century thinker who stressed the importance of mathematics to scientific inquiry was Roger Bacon. In his *Opus maius* Bacon argues that Aristotle himself placed the highest value on mathematics as a method for determining the causes of things:

> But only cause leads to true knowledge (*scientia*), or at least it does so far better than effect, since Aristotle says in the *Posterior Analytics*, book I,

---

critical edition of this text, see *Commentarius in VIII Physicorum Aristotelis; fontibus manu scriptes nunc primum in lucem*, ed. Richard C. Dales, *Studies in Medieval Thought* (Boulder, Colorado: University of Colorado Press, 1963).

[19] See Lindberg's edition and translation of the text, *Concerning Lines, Angles, and Figures*, in *Sourcebook in Medieval Science*, ed. Edward Grant (Cambridge, Massachusetts: Harvard University Press, 1974), p. 385; also quoted by Lindberg in "Applicability," p. 12.

[20] *De natura locorum* in *Die philosophischen Werke des Robert Grosseteste*, ed. Ludwig Baur, in *Beiträge zur Geschichte der Philosophie des Mittelalters*, ix (Münster: Aschendorff, 1912), pp. 59-60; translated and quoted by Lindberg, p. 12.

that we think we know when we know the causes. Therefore, since demonstration, as he says in the same place, is a syllogism causing us to know, demonstration by cause is necessarily far more powerful than demonstration by effect. . . . Therefore, since in natural things demonstration by cause is obtained by means of mathematics, and demonstration by effect is obtained through natural philosophy, the mathematician is better able to obtain true knowledge of natural things than is the natural philosopher.[21]

Mathematics maintains this advantage over natural philosophy because it can be used to create an internally consistent and self-verifying argument. Bacon contrasts science, which, "full of doubts and sprinkled with opinions and obscurities, cannot be verified except through other sciences," with mathematics, which "remains certain and verified to the limits of verification."[22] It is the philosophical rigor of mathematics, whose principles can be mastered by any educated person, which makes it indispensable for any advanced study of nature.

Bacon was certain, therefore, that mathematics could enrich the full range of human inquiry, including theology, not by reducing all subjects to numerical or geometrical forms, but by providing a precise vocabulary for describing those subjects.[23] Like Grosseteste, moreover, Bacon believed that knowledge of God and the scriptures depended on the scientific investigation, aided by mathematics, of all natural phenomena: "the theologian must know the things of this world if he wishes to understand the sacred text."[24] This progression of mathematics from a simple tool to a necessary language for natural philosophy and finally to a component in theological speculation underlay all discussions of mathematics in the early fourteenth century and must be taken into account in any investigation of Bradwardine's use of mathematics in his philosophical and theological studies.[25]

---

[21] *The Opus Major of Roger Bacon*, Volume I, ed. John Henry Bridges (Oxford: Clarendon Press, 1897-1900), pp. 168-69; translated by Lindberg, p. 18.

[22] Bridges, p. 107; translated by Lindberg, p. 18.

[23] Tachau notes, for example, in "The Problem of *species in medio* at Oxford in the Generation after Ockham," *Mediaeval Studies*, 44 (1982), pp. 441-42, that Bacon, like Grosseteste, advocated mathematics as a way for theologians to understand how grace is transmitted to the created world through the metaphysics of light.

[24] Bridges, p. 175; translated by Lindberg, p. 19. For an edition of the *Geometria speculativa* see A. G. Molland, ed., "The *Geometria speculativa* of Thomas Bradwardine: Text with Critical Edition," Dissertation, University of Cambridge, 1967.

[25] In *Vision and Certitude*, p. 312, Tachau emphasizes the importance of metaphysics, especially light metaphysics, in the natural philosophy of Bradwardine and his colleagues.

Bradwardine's position on the role of mathematics in philosophical inquiry, as it emerged in the *De proportionibus* and even more fully in the *De continuo*, developed out of his early studies in elementary geometry. Because geometrical analysis is the hallmark of Bradwardine's work, it is worthwhile to look briefly at one of his earliest treatises, the *Geometria speculativa*.[26] More a notebook than a treatise, the *Geometria speculativa* represents Bradwardine's attempt to organize all of the material on geometry which he had heard in the lectures required for the master of arts degree. His success in accomplishing this task is evident in the wide circulation of the text among students at Oxford and other European universities. The major sources for the *Geometria speculativa* were the mathematical writings of Euclid and Aristotle, although Bradwardine also referred at appropriate points to Boethius' *Arithmetica* and the Arabic commentaries on Aristotle.[27] The contents of the *Geometria speculativa* covered all the major topics of elementary geometry, including the definitions of points, lines and angles; Euclidean theorems regarding these definitions; an analysis of polygons and circles; an examination of ratios; and a study of regular solids and spheres.[28] Because Bradwardine intended his treatise to be a systematic review of what he had learned in the lectures rather than a work of original research, he generally chose not to advance his own opinions about controversial issues. His arrangement and treatment of standard topics nevertheless reflect his own style of mathematical thinking and reveal many of his philosophical assumptions.

Throughout the *Geometria speculativa*, for example, Bradwardine suggested that the discipline of geometry, and mathematics generally, could be useful in the investigation of natural phenomena. In making this claim, Bradwardine placed himself firmly on the side of the Aristotelians in the debate over of how best to use mathematics in the pursuit of natural philosophy. As we have already seen, some medieval mathematicians, following the Platonic tradition, argued that mathematics was a fundamentally conceptual activity; that is, they stressed the abstract qualities of mathematics and preferred to concentrate on abstract problems which were removed from any reference to physical reality. Others, who were more sympathetic with the Aristotelian approach to physics, tried to make mathematics conform to sensible qualities and so have been called realists.

---

[26] Molland discusses the dating and authenticity of this treatise in "An Examination of Bradwardine's Geometry," *Archive for the History of Exact Sciences*, 19 (1978), pp. 115-20.

[27] *Ibid.*, p. 121.

[28] Molland provides an informative synopsis of the contents, pp. 122-31.

In the discipline of geometry, each side could claim to hold the ideologically stronger position. The conceptualists, being aware of the abstract nature of geometrical definitions and manipulations and comforted by the traditions of Platonism and Neoplatonism, argued quite convincingly that an understanding of geometry could reveal the mathematical basis of nature without any reference to the sensible world. The realists, on the other hand, claimed that geometry would be an empty discipline if it were not used to explore the physical world which directed and shaped human existence. Both sides encountered problems in defining the proper scope of geometrical studies. As A. G. Molland points out, "the realist may have had difficulties in adapting his geometry to the physical world, but the conceptualist could not easily find grounding for a mathematical natural science."[29] According to Molland, who has studied the *Geometria speculativa* at considerable length, Bradwardine's early position in this debate placed him near the realists. Bradwardine's analysis of geometrical subjects in this text routinely involved a statement of relevant Aristotelian principles, an exposition of the problems which these principles generated and a brief consideration of possible solutions. Thus, students found the *Geometria speculativa* more helpful as an Aristotelian manual, "gathering together all the geometrical conclusions which are most needed by students of arts and the philosophy of Aristotle,"[30] than as a general work on geometry.

Certainly the *Geometria speculativa* indicates Bradwardine's interest in applying the principles of geometry to problems in natural philosophy. It is here, for example, that Bradwardine first addressed the dilemma of infinity, a necessary concept in Euclidian geometry which directly contradicts Aristotle's assertion that the world is finite.[31] By raising this issue at all, Bradwardine showed that he was already thinking about the convergence of metaphysics and physics in the study of mathematics. Bradwardine's consideration of such topics as Aristotle's definition of space and the problems involved in measurement is further evidence of his growing fascination with Aristotelian natural philosophy, which blossomed later in the *De proportionibus* and the *De continuo*.[32]

---

[29] *Ibid.*, p. 131.

[30] Pedro Sanchez Cirvelo, first editor of the *Geometria speculativa*, on the title page (Paris: 1495); quoted in A. G. Molland, "The Geometrical Background to the 'Merton School': An Exploration into the Application of Mathematics to Natural Philosophy," *British Journal for the History of Science*, 4 (1968), p. 112.

[31] Molland, "Examination," pp. 170-72.

[32] *Ibid.*, p. 174.

In the context of the *De proportionibus*, the most interesting section of the *Geometria speculativa* is the one which deals with ratio theory. Bradwardine first distinguishes between arithmetic ratios and the much wider range of geometric ratios and then devises a definition which would apply to both types. Thus he states:

> Because the intention of 'ratio' is extended and applied to almost all things that are mutually comparable according to greater and less, it can be defined in accord with this general concept: A ratio is a certain habitude of some things that are mutually comparable one to the other. For example, of a number to a number, a magnitude to a magnitude, a sound to a sound, a time to a time, a motion to a motion, a humour to a humour, a heat to a heat, a taste to a taste. But geometry ascribes the intention of 'ratio' to magnitude and has it to be defined thus: A ratio is a certain habitude of two qualities of the same genus, one to the other. I say 'of the same genus' because only such are mutually comparable.[33]

quantities

Bradwardine goes on to distinguish between rational and irrational ratios along the lines of Book V of Euclid's *Elements*:

> Ratio is divided into two species which are received in comparison with proportionally diverse quantities. For some quantities are communicating or commensurable, some incommunicating and incommensurable. Commensurable quantities are those for which there is a common quantity measuring them. One quantity is said to number another if when taken according to a certain number [taken a certain number of times] it produces it [the second quantity], as a foot line [produces] a two-foot line and a three-foot line. Therefore, a two-foot line and a three-foot line are communicating quantities which a foot line numbers by Two and Three. But quantities for which there is no common quantity numbering them are called incommensurable. Of this kind are the diagonal and side of a square. According to this, therefore, there are two species of ratios, namely rational and irrational. A rational ratio is found (*debetur*) in commensurable quantities, and it is the only one that is found in numbers. But an irrational one fits incommensurable quantities, but in nowise numbers. Whence it is manifest that the whole consideration of ratio concerns geometry, because every ratio is of magnitude, but not every ratio is numerable.[34]

Bradwardine's explanation of ratios rests initially, then, on the logical distinction between things which have a common denominator and those which do not. He was not primarily interested, however, in demonstrating

---

[33] *Geometria speculativa*, translated by Molland in "Examination," pp. 150-51.
[34] *Ibid.*, p. 151.

this distinction mathematically. In evaluating this feature of Bradwardine's ratio theory, Molland suggests that Bradwardine's flexibility on this point helped him to develop his broader theories of ratios in series, or, in other words, his theory of proportions.[35]

Central to Bradwardine's theory of proportions is the concept of denomination, that is, the quantity or quality by which two commensurable things can be compared. He points out that both rational and irrational ratios can be denominated, though, of course, in different ways:

> A rational ratio therefore is immediately denominated by some certain number, for, since it is of commensurable quantities, it is necessary that the lesser or some part of the lesser should number the greater according to some number, on account of which Euclid says that of any two commensurable quantities the ratio of one to the other is that of a number to a number, and this will be clearer below. This species is divided in every mode, in which ratio is divided in arithmetic. For one is a ratio of equality, another of inequality. . . . An irrational ratio is not in this way immediately denominated by some number or by some numerical ratio, because it is not possible that some part of the lesser should number the greater according to some number. But it turns out that an irrational ratio may be mediately denominated by number. For example, the ratio of the diagonal [of a square] to the side is half of a double ratio, and so other species of this ratio receive denominations by number.[36]

Bradwardine's logical analysis of irrational ratios continues with a further distinction, first introduced by Euclid, between ratios of lines which are commensurable in length only and ratios of lines which are commensurable in respect of both length and power. He provides a method for producing an infinite series of irrational ratios by manipulating terms of previous ratios through division:

> Each species can be divided into as many species as there are ways for lines to be thus or thus incommensurable, for not only can lines be incommensurable in length only when they are as diagonal and square, but in other ways perhaps infinite [in number]. I speak similarly of lines incommensurable in length and power, because they are not only those that are taken as means between side and diagonal, and the means between the mean and them, and further the means between these and those, and so on indefinitely, but also many others.[37]

---

[35] Molland, "Examination," p. 154.

[36] *Geometria speculativa*, translated by Molland in "Examination," pp. 154-55. "Double ratio" in this context means a squared ratio. Fourteenth-century mathematicians did not have two separate expressions to distinguish $2x$ from x^2.

[37] *Ibid.*, p. 157.

Although it is expressed primarily in abstract terms in the *Geometria speculativa*, this logical framework of ratio theory is the starting point in the *De proportionibus* for further consideration of motion as a physical phenomenon.

When Bradwardine returned later to the problem of ratio and proportionality, his intentions were more specific; and the resulting work was much more original. He nevertheless drew on a large body of commentary whose contributors spanned the classical and medieval periods. As the *Geometria speculativa* indicates, proportional theory was widely discussed among Latin and Arabic mathematicians and was applied to the problems of arithmetic, algebra and geometry. Bradwardine expanded the scope of proportional theory in the *De proportionibus* by applying it to physics as well.[38] It was at this stage that his tendency towards realism, first suggested in the *Geometria speculativa*, emerged fully and his dedication to an Aristotelian physical theory became firmly established.

Bradwardine's originality lay not so much in his support for the idea that mathematics should be at the disposal of natural philosophy for, as we have seen, he was not the first to make this claim. His reputation as an innovator rests instead on his application of proportional theory to a mechanical problem which had previously defied mathematical analysis. Bradwardine did not, of course, come close to articulating the principles of advanced mathematics which later allowed Newton to explain the properties of motion more elegantly and, in a modern sense, more accurately; but his recognition that elementary geometry and algebra are inadequate for describing such concepts as force, velocity and resistance had a profound effect on future scientific investigation. Bradwardine's insight that the medieval natural philosopher required a better mathematical language, coupled with his conviction that natural philosophy could not be well understood without mathematics, explains why historians associate Bradwardine with Galileo and other formulators of modern scientific thought.

In the *De proportionibus* Bradwardine was chiefly concerned with demonstrating how the theory of proportions could be applied to the

---

[38] John Emery Murdoch, "The Medieval Language of Proportions: Elements of the Interaction with Greek Foundations and the Development of New Mathematical Techniques," in *Scientific Change*, ed. A. C. Crombie (London: Heinemann, 1961), p. 265. See also Murdoch, "From Social to Intellectual Factors: An Aspect of the Unitary Character of Late Medieval Learning," in *The Cultural Context of Medieval Learning*, ed. Murdoch and Edith Dudley Sylla (Boston, Massachusetts: D. Reidel, 1975), pp. 280-89, in which Murdoch describes the application of proportion theory to a wide variety of logical problems in the early fourteenth century.

study of velocity so as to defend Aristotle's laws concerning natural motion.[39] According to Aristotle, the universe is finite, and the change which occurs within it is successive and takes place within time. Aristotle went on to define change as a kind of motion: change takes place as motion overcomes natural resistance in a successive, though not necessarily uniform, manner. Change, then, requires space, time and the superiority of a moving force over a resisting force. Yet Aristotle also admitted that some kinds of change do not appear to fit this definition. He affirmed, for example, that the heavenly bodies move even though they are not subject to any resistance; and although the heavenly bodies cannot be equated with time, an observer can measure time by marking their movements.

As we have already seen in the discussion of Averroes' criticism of Aristotle's view of time, Aristotle himself neither resolved this problem nor provided enough information for his successors to do so on his behalf. Medieval Aristotelians were willing to accept that a distinction had to be made between the two kinds of natural motion, that is, motion against resistance along straight lines as experienced on earth (rectilinear motion) and the free motion in the celestial sphere. They nevertheless believed that both kinds of motion should conform to the same laws.[40] The search for these laws within the framework of Aristotelian physics as it was understood in the thirteenth and fourteenth centuries provides the context for Bradwardine's thesis about proportions.

In the thirteenth century, considerations of the nature of motion focused on the differing explanations of two Muslim thinkers, Avempace and Averroes. Avempace's approach to the problem of the relationship of resistance to force in motion, based as it was on logical definitions of the celestial sphere, was essentially Platonic. He argued that, because heavenly bodies move at a steady rate and do not appear to encounter any resistance, the resistance which affects sublunary motion must be impeding a force which would otherwise move at a steady, absolute speed.[41] In other words, all motion would proceed at a determinate rate both in heaven and on earth if resistance were eliminated. Avempace reduced this theory to a simple arithmetic equation: v=f-r, that is, the velocity of an object is equal to the amount

---

[39] Crosby, p. 13. For a thorough discussion of treatments of motion by medieval philosophers and theologians, see John Murdoch and Edith Sylla, "The Science of Motion," in *Science in the Middle Ages*, pp. 206-64.

[40] Crosby, p. 14.

[41] *Ibid.*, p. 15.

of force which overcomes the resistance which impedes it. This theory ✗
was in conflict with Aristotelian principles because it was based on a
narrower definition of motion than Aristotle would have accepted.
Avempace assumed that all motion is fundamentally regular, orderly,
and consistent, which directly contradicted Aristotle's observation that
motion is a kind of change. According to Aristotle, many motions, such
as the motion of fire or that of a growing plant, are too irregular and
complex to be described accurately with a simple mathematical
construct such as Avempace's equation.

Admittedly, Aristotle and his followers failed to provide an alternative theory. Averroes in particular struggled with this problem without
producing a coherent solution. His suggestion, for example, that the
heavenly bodies actually do encounter resistance, on the grounds that
resistance is a necessary cause of the successive nature of motion, led
him to conclusions which contradicted other Aristotelian positions and
did not shed much light on the problem of comparing different types of
motion.[42] Nevertheless, Averroes' criticism of Avempace's theory of
motion focused attention on the weaknesses of classical physics and
stimulated discussions of those weaknesses throughout the thirteenth
century. In spite of Averroes' objections, however, the simplicity of
Avempace's explanation of force made it appear the more reasonable
approach, and it won adherents even among those who sympathized
most with Aristotle. H. Lamar Crosby observes that Thomas Aquinas,
Roger Bacon, Pierre Jean Olivi and John Duns Scotus were all influenced to some extent by Avempace's view.[43]

Bradwardine's contribution to this debate involved his mathematical
insight into the rather vague use of the concept "ratio" within the
Aristotelian tradition. Aristotle's law of motion states that the speed
(velocity) of a moving object depends on the *ratio* of its motive power
(force) and its resistance: $v = f/r$; but his analysis of the relationship
between force and resistance suggests that he had no rule in mind for
calculating the force of any particular moving object. When Averroes
turned to the same problem, he restated Aristotle's position without
making it clear whether he believed that the ratio between force and
resistance was a simple proportion or, if so, how such a simple
proportion could explain changing rates of speed or irregular motions.
Averroes simply declared, in opposition to Avempace, that "it is
necessary that between the mover and the thing moved there be a

---

[42] *Ibid.*, p. 14.
[43] *Ibid.*, p. 15.

resistance. . . . [Therefore,] every motion will be according to the excess of the potency of the mover over the thing moved, and the diversity of motions in speed and slowness is according to this proportion which is between the two potencies and these resistances."[44]

What came to interest Bradwardine was the notion of "diversity of motions in speed and slowness." He was not satisfied simply to know that such a diversity had to exist whenever motion varied according to speed and slowness. He wanted to be able to calculate this diversity mathematically. Thus, after giving an extensive review of the mathematics of ratio in the *De proportionibus*, he turned in the second chapter to a refutation of common assumptions about the nature of motion. Bradwardine's first target was Avempace, whose theory he challenged on Aristotelian lines:

> Having looked into these introductory matters, let us now proceed with the undertaking which was proposed at the outset. At first, after the manner of Aristotle, let us criticize erroneous theories so that the truth may be the more apparent. There are four false theories to be proposed as relevant to our investigation, the first of which holds that: *the proportion between the speeds with which motions take place varies as the difference whereby the power of the mover exceeds the resistance offered by the thing moved.*[45]

Bradwardine based his criticism of Avempace on the observation (mathematical, of course, not experimental) that the halving or doubling of a force does not result directly in the halving or doubling of velocity. The relationship between force and resistance is proportional, so the change in velocity must proceed geometrically (that is, exponentially), not arithmetically:[46]

> . . . it follows from [Avempace's] theory that, given two movers moving two *mobilia* through equal distances in equal times, the two movers, conjoined, would not move the two *mobilia*, conjoined, through an exactly equal distance in an equal time, but, instead, through double that distance. This consequence follows necessarily because the excess of the two movers, taken together, is twice the excess of each of them over its own *mobile*; for, just as anything having a value of 2 exceeds unity by 1, so two such '2's' (which make 4) exceed two '1's' (which make 2) by 2, which is

[44] *Opera Aristotelis cum Averrois commentariis*, Volume IV, fol. 132v (Venice: 1560), translated by Ernest A. Moody in "Galileo and Avempace," *Journal of the History of Ideas*, 12 (1951), p. 191.

[45] *De proportionibus*, pp. 86-87.

[46] See Murdoch and Sylla's evaluation of Bradwardine's use of proportional theory to transform Aristotle's defintion of motion in "The Science of Motion," pp. 224-31.

twice the excess of 2 over 1. The foregoing holds in all cases in which two subtrahends are equally exceeded by two minuends. That the above consequence is false is evident from the foregoing argument in Aristotle, in Book VII of his *Physics*, where he demonstrates the following conclusion: 'If two powers move two *mobilia* separately, through equal distances in equal times, those powers conjoined, will move the two *mobilia* conjoined, through an equal distance in a time equal to the former one.' This argument of Aristotle is sufficient proof that the relationship between a single mover and its *mobile*, and a compound mover and its *mobilia*, is a proportional one.[47]

Bradwardine defended both Aristotle and Averroes from the charge that they perceived the diversity of motions as a matter of simple proportions:

> Nor can it be legitimately maintained that, in the passages cited, Aristotle and Averroes understand by the words 'proportion' and 'analogy,' arithmetic proportionality (that is, equality of differences), as some have claimed. Indeed, in book VII of the *Physics*, Aristotle proves this conclusion: 'If a given power moves a given *mobile* through a given distance in a given time, half of that power will move half the *mobile* through an equal distance in an equal time, because, "analogically," the relation of half the mover to half the *mobile* is similar to that of the whole mover to the whole *mobile*.' Such a statement, interpreted as referring to arithmetic proportionality, is discernibly false (as has already been made sufficiently clear in the first argument raised against the present theory). Moreover, regarding the same passage, Averroes says that the proportion will be the same 'in the sense that geometricians universally employ in demonstrations.'[48]

Even as Bradwardine defended the Aristotelian position, however, he enhanced it to make it conform to his own more sophisticated understanding of ratio theory. He similarly dismissed the next three theories, which relate to particular aspects of Avempace's original assertion. Throughout this discussion, Bradwardine repeatedly vindicated Aristotle and Averroes against the misjudgments of Avempace and his followers.

In his third chapter, Bradwardine suspended his criticism of others and offered a more positive approach to the problem of proportional motion, declaring confidently: "Now that these fogs of ignorance, these winds of demonstration, have been put to flight, it remains for the light of knowledge and of truth to shine forth. For true knowledge possesses a fifth theory which states that the proportion of the speeds of motions

---

[47] *Ibid.*, pp. 86-89.
[48] *Ibid.*, pp. 88-89.

varies in accordance with the proportion of power of the mover to the power of the thing moved."[49]   Arguing again that this proposition was thoroughly in keeping with the ideas of Aristotle and Averroes, Bradwardine actually suggested here a much more complex principle than any of his predecessors had ever stated either explicitly or implicitly.

Bradwardine's theory of the "proportionality of proportions," as it later came to be called, was based on his rejection of the traditional formulation of Aristotle's law of motion which claimed that velocity could be doubled either by doubling the force or halving the resistance. In the first place, although this particular ratio of force to resistance might be true in some cases, it could not be applied to all motion: most motions do not conform to a strict two-to-one ratio. Second, Bradwardine believed that a simplistic interpretation of Aristotle's law would suggest that any force can move any object, when in fact motion only takes place when force exceeds resistance. What was required instead was a new interpretation of the laws of motion which took into account the exponential character of force: to double a velocity, Bradwardine concluded, one does not double the force but square it. Or, as Weisheipl explains,

> Bradwardine proposed a new law, maintaining that a double velocity must follow from the entire power-to-resistance ratio *duplata*, i.e., not multiplied by two, but squared, for twice a *proportio tripla* is one which contains the ratio 3:1 twice. But only the square of the ratio, i.e., only 9:1, contains twice the *proportio tripla*, for the ratio 9:1 is composed of 9/3·3/1. Thus only the ratio squared can give twice the velocity. Similarly, triple velocity follows from the ratio *triplata*, i.e., raised to the third power. Conversely, half the velocity would follow from the *medietas* of the ratio, that is, the square root of the ratio; one third of the velocity follows from the cube root, and so forth; thus the mover can never be less than the resistance. Bradwardine's exponential function was theoretically valid for all cases, and it eliminated the possibility of zero-velocity. Today the latter situation is taken care of by a logarithmic function.[50]

It is worth noting that, in spite of Bradwardine's originality in devising this fifth theory, neither he nor his contemporaries realized how great an advance he had made over his predecessors. Bradwardine, with abiding respect for Aristotle, merely assumed that he had discovered Aristotle's original intention; and his contemporaries responded to the fifth theory

---

    [49] *Ibid.*, pp. 110-11.
    [50] Weisheipl, *The Development of Physical Theory in the Middle Ages* (London: Sheed and Ward, 1959), p. 75.

not so much because they perceived it to be original as because it presented a plausible explanation of Aristotle's law of motion.[51]

In the final chapter of the *De proportionibus*, Bradwardine addressed the special problems of circular motion which Avempace's references to the celestial sphere had prompted. Bradwardine acknowledged that rectilinear and circular motion had different characteristics but insisted that both kinds of motion were subject to the same laws of proportionality. The purpose of the fourth chapter, therefore, was to demonstrate the influence of proportionality on the motions of geometrically different entities. His conclusion was, essentially, that proportional motion applies equally to a body moving in a circle or in a straight line. The speed of the moving body, not its path, was the most important factor for consideration.[52]

Thus Bradwardine united into one comprehensive rule the principles of linear and circular motion. His theory of proportionality could be used to explain both kinds of motion and to compare them to each other with a mathematical precision which had never before been possible. Because his system was purely descriptive and was based on no experimental evidence, Bradwardine did not realize that many of his specific claims do not actually correspond to the realities of motion. Nevertheless, his main purpose, to defend Aristotle from claims that his laws of motion were vague and self-contradictory, was well-fulfilled in the *De proportionibus*. More important for the history of science, his underlying assumption that acceleration involves geometrical proportionality was substantially correct and his presentation of that thesis stimulated more successful studies of the problem of motion. His greatest contribution, however, was his enthusiastic demonstration that mathematics could and should be applied to practical problems in natural philosophy.

What does the *De proportionibus* tell us about Bradwardine's view of time? In answering this question it is important to remember that Bradwardine does not discuss time as a distinct concept in this treatise but refers to it only in reference to other concepts, such as motion, velocity, distance and magnitude. Similarly, one must keep in mind the strong philosophical orientation of the treatise, which is heavily influenced by his interpretation of Aristotelian physics. We can assume, then, that, in the context of this treatise, Bradwardine accepts Aristotle's definition of time as the number or measure of motion. Bradwardine takes it for

---

[51] Stillman Drake, "Medieval Ratio Theory vs. Compound Medicines in the Origins of Bradwardine's Rule," *Isis*, 64 (1973), pp. 72-73.

[52] *De proportionibus*, pp. 130-31.

granted that the most efficient way of comparing two motions is to compare the amount of time it takes for the moving bodies to traverse a
given distance. Like Aristotle, moreover, he is always careful to include
the aspect of time in calculations involving change or motion.

In Bradwardine's more elaborate system for relating the factors
which influence motion, however, time becomes a more complex entity
than it was for Aristotle. Like distance or any other factor in the process
of motion, time can be measured and is subject to the same kind of proportional analysis. Bradwardine makes this point most succinctly in his
discussion of Aristotle's view of yet another factor in motion, the relative density of the medium through which an object moves.
Bradwardine believes that in both the *Physics* and the *De caelo* Aristotle
manifestly proves that time itself has a proportional character, that is,
times can be compared to each other in simple ratios, since "the proportion of the times measuring . . . motions varies also in accordance with
the proportion of the media (namely, that the longer time corresponds to
the motion through the denser medium and the shorter time through the
rarer medium)."[53] There is little doubt, therefore, that Bradwardine's
approach to time in the *De proportionibus* was based both on Aristotle's
concrete association of time with motion and also on his own more
specialized understanding of the proportionality of motion.

Weisheipl observes, "The aim of Bradwardine's treatise was to
determine a universal rule that would govern proportions between
moving power and resistance, on the one hand, and distance and time on
the other."[54] Implicit in Bradwardine's rule was the notion that time is a
measure of motion, because the time it takes for a motion to be
completed determines the "quantity" of motion, just as the intensity of a
motion determines its "quality."[55] This emphasis on time as a measure
of motion accounts for Bradwardine's frequent references to "equal
times" both in his quotations from Aristotle and in his own commentary.
Discussions of "equal times" in the *De proportionibus* give one the
impression, however, that Bradwardine, like Aristotle, was not
particularly interested in actually measuring motions. His acceptance of
Aristotle's definitions of time and motion and his own mathematical
instinct confirmed that time and distance were related to force and

---

[53] *Ibid.*, pp. 94-95. The meaning of "proportio" in this context is slightly different
from Bradwardine's use of this term in his treatment of velocity. Here Bradwardine uses
the word "proportio" to mean a simple ratio or comparison of two times or two distances.
[54] "Aristotle's Physics and the Science of Motion," *CHLMP*, p. 535.
[55] *Ibid.*, p. 534.

intensity in motion; moreover, Bradwardine realized that, for the sake of mathematical proofs, times and distances often have to be defined as equal, in spite of practical difficulties involved in making accurate measurements. Indeed, Bradwardine routinely ignored the empirical problem of measurement, preferring instead to prove his assertions through pure mathematical logic. His few attempts to support his assertions with empirical evidence amounted to the use of simple demonstrations from everyday experience, such as Aristotle himself had often given. Thus, for example, he ended his refutation of Avempace with the common observation that.

> if a given mover were to exceed its resistance by a greater amount than another mover exceeded its own resistance, the former motion would be faster. Then, since a strong man exceeds anything he moves by a greater excess of power than a weaker mover (such as a boy, or a fly, or something of that sort) exceeds what it moves, he should move it more rapidly. Experience, however, teaches us to the contrary, for we see that a fly carrying some small particle flies very rapidly, and that a boy also moves a small object rather rapidly. A strong man, on the other hand, moving some large object which he can scarcely budge, moves it very slowly, and even if there were added to what he moves a quantity larger than either the fly or the boy can move, the man will then move the whole not much more slowly than he did before.[56]

This appeal to common sense certainly involved no experimentation and hardly illustrates the problem of force and resistance in motion. As an item of proof, it was added merely to suggest a logical relationship between the "quality" and the "quantity" of motion.

The question now arises whether Bradwardine was aware, as he wrote the *De proportionibus*, of the philosophical implications of his new theory about motion for other scientific or theological topics, including time. Because he thought of the treatise as a clarification of what Aristotle had already said, we should not expect the *De proportionibus* to contain a self-conscious statement of its originality either as a scientific or as a philosophical text. Some historians regard the *De proportionibus* as an almost purely mathematical work which only indirectly addressed underlying philosophical issues. Thus Crosby says:

> Approaching the problem of establishing an adequate law of motion from the standpoint of a mathematician rather than that of a philosopher, it is the mathematical formulae which appear explicitly, and the philosophical

---

[56] *De proportionibus*, pp. 92-93.

theory on which they are ultimately grounded, that remains implicit. It is indeed, quite conceivable that Bradwardine might have been almost wholly unconcerned with the philosophical issues involved, but simply interested in demonstrating the mathematical fallacies implied in previous theories and in showing how a proper understanding of mathematics involved in the manipulation of exponential series could solve any objections against the classic notion that velocities are proportional to proportions of forces.[57]

In Crosby's view, then, Bradwardine perhaps unknowingly made philosophical assumptions that served his mathematics, but not the other way around.

Other historians have observed that Bradwardine's approach to the problem of motion, though we might label it mathematical, had a firm and conscious philosophical basis. They see works such as the *De proportionibus* as evidence of a general development in early fourteenth-century thought towards a new epistemology. In this context, Crombie remarks: "when Bradwardine rejected Avempace's 'laws of motion,' he made use of arguments similar to Ockham's, and it is difficult not to see a connexion in the common shift of the problem from the 'why' to the 'how' which Ockham made as a logician and Bradwardine as a mathematical physicist."[58] Crombie bases this statement on the observation that, in his *Expositio super libros physicorum*, Ockham not only repudiated Avempace's doctrine but did so by relying on the same concepts of space, time and magnitude which form the foundation of Bradwardine's theory.[59] This is not to say, of course, that Ockham's approach to this topic was structurally identical to Bradwardine's. Quite the contrary: Ockham relied on logical distinctions and definitions which he

---

[57] Crosby, p. 31.

[58] *Augustine to Galileo*, II, p. 79.

[59] *Ibid.* See, for example, Ockham's *De proprietatibus temporis*, lib. IV, cap. 24, of his *Expositio in libros I-III Physicorum Aristotelis*, eds. V. Richter and G. Liebold, in *Guillelmi de Ockham Opera philosophica et theologica ad fidem codicum manuscriptorum edita. Opera philosophica V* (St. Bonaventure, New York: Franciscan Institute of St. Bonaventure University, 1985), pp. 260-61: "Quod enim tempus determinet et mensuret motum, est manifestum, cum tempus sit numerus motus, sicut dictum est prius. . . . Quod etiam per motum inferiorem contingat mensurare motum primum et tempus patet etiam per hoc quod aliquis [sciens] quantitatem virtutis alicuius motivae, et sciens quantum spatium pertransiit, quamvis non considerasset de motu caeli, potest cognoscere quantum de motu caeli et de tempore pertransiit. . . . Et ex isto eodem posset patere quomodo per magnitudinem continget mensurare motum et tempus, quia ex hoc scitur quantum est spatium pertransitum a mobili moto a tanta virtute nota alicui, potest talis scire quod motus d̶u̶i̶/duravit, et per consequens quod tempus est longum, et ita per magnitudinem et virtutem motivam potest mensurare tam motum quam tempus."

expressed, for the most part, in a completely nonmathematical vocabulary, whereas, as we have seen, Bradwardine's logic was fundamentally a mathematical or geometrical exercise.[60] The convergence of Ockham's and Bradwardine's philosophy cannot be seen readily in the *De proportionibus* but it becomes strikingly apparent in other works in which Bradwardine addresses broader philosophical problems such as infinity, continuity and contingency. Here it is sufficient to note that Bradwardine's mathematical studies can be seen to have a philosophical origin.

One of the major questions about early fourteenth-century philosophy involves the extent to which thinkers were empiricists.[61] In pulling away from the debates about the "whys" of the physical world in favor of concentration on the "hows," fourteenth-century philosophers often had to leave the familiar ground of Aristotelian or Neoplatonic physics; and their success in making the transition to a new cosmology has often been questioned. In an attempt to defend late medieval philosophy from the complaint that the shift from metaphysical to empirical inquiry represents a decline, Ernest Moody argues that late medieval philosophy moved from a scholastic, theological orientation towards a more modern scientific outlook.[62] Moody sees the period in which Bradwardine lived and worked as a formative age when the cosmological and speculative philosophy of the Greeks became analytical, critical and modern.[63]

Moody's rather strong statement has been modified in recent years as further research on early fourteenth-century philosophy has uncovered more of the complexity of intellectual developments in this period. Thus John Murdoch has remarked that, if late medieval scholars seemed to turn away from traditional questions, it was not because they had lost interest in them but because they were searching for better ways of investigating them.[64] New analytical methods, the new language of proportions and new approaches to logic all advanced philosophical

---

[60] Weisheipl, *Development*, pp. 68-69.

[61] Throughout *Science in the Middle Ages*, one can find examples of medieval experimentation and observation techniques in a variety of disciplines. See especially Wallace, "The Philosophical Setting of Medieval Science," pp. 91-119; Charles H. Talbot, "Medicine," pp. 391-428; and Jerry Stannard, "Natural History," pp. 429-60.

[62] "Empiricism and Metaphysics in Medieval Philosophy," *SMPSL*, p. 301.

[63] *Ibid.*, p. 302.

[64] "The Analytic Character of Late Medieval Learning: Natural Philosophy Without Nature," in *Approaches to Nature in the Middle Ages*, ed. Lawrence D. Roberts (Binghamton, New York: Center for Medieval and Early Renaissance Studies, 1982), pp. 174-75.

thought and theological speculation. In the absence of effective
techniques for experimentation, investigators who wanted to apply these
philosophical innovations to physical problems were faced with the
knowledge that they could not easily explain the realities of nature.
Although their efforts to integrate philosophy and science were not
immediately fruitful, their work provided a foundation for continued
development in many branches of scientific and philosophical inquiry.

The contents and structure of the *De proportionibus* indicate that
Bradwardine did in fact have a clear philosophical orientation when he
wrote this work, even though his intention was not primarily to treat the
problem of motion philosophically. He approached Aristotle's law of
motion mathematically in the conviction that anything less than the
precision of a geometrical method could not adequately express what
Aristotle had meant. Bradwardine's geometrical language of proportions possesses its own order and logic, while the shape of its
arguments rests on his analysis of the propositions of Aristotle, Averroes
and their opponents. Crosby is correct, of course, in stating that in the
De proportionibus Bradwardine did not attempt to consider explicitly
the broader philosophical implications of his mathematical approach to
motion. Full discussions of time, space and continuity, all of which
have bearing on the problem of motion, are clearly absent. We should
not assume, however, that Bradwardine had no thoughts on these
matters, for he reflected upon them at length in other treatises. It is
possible that Bradwardine had only begun to work out his opinions on
these issues when he wrote the *De proportionibus*. In any event, the
clarity and orderliness of expression in this work serve to emphasize its
mathematical orientation. One can therefore understand Crosby's
identification of the text as one which, "through the introduction of
mathematical analysis, . . . sets the stage for the quantitative measurement of physical processes, and, hence, that typically modern physics
which was to appear with Galileo's wedding of mathematics and
experimental observation."[65]

Still, the richness of the *De proportionibus* goes well beyond the
mathematical concepts that it presents. The treatise establishes Bradwardine's Aristotelian inclinations as well as his capacity for revision of
his predecessors' ideas. More important for this study, the *De proportionibus* introduces us to Bradwardine's way of thinking about physical
problems such as time: although he shows a tendency towards realism
and empiricism, his acute grasp of abstract mathematics assures us that

---

[65] Crosby, p. 17.

he also learned much from the Platonic tradition. In fact, Bradwardine's treatment of time in the *De proportionibus* in light of Aristotelian and Platonic notions reflects his particular interest in a much larger medieval debate about the physical reality of time.[66] Eventually, as the conclusion of the *De proportionibus* suggests, Bradwardine would be prepared to consider as well the theological dimensions of his work on proportions:

> Thus comes to completion this work, concerning the proportion between the speeds with which motions take place, by the grace of that Mover—from whom all motions proceed and between Whom and the thing He moves there exists no proportion—to Whom be honor and glory as long as there is any motion. Amen.[67]

---

[66] See Anneliese Maier, "Die Subjectivierung der Zeit in der scholastichen Philosophie," *Philosophia Naturalis*, 1 (1951), pp. 361-98.

[67] *De proportionibus*, pp. 140-41.

CHAPTER FIVE

TIME AND CONTINUITY

While the *De proportionibus* offers the best general introduction to Bradwardine's mathematical method and his Aristotelian leanings in natural philosophy, his *Tractatus de continuo* gives much more specific indications of his view of time. Bradwardine had already touched on certain aspects of continuity as early as 1323 in a treatise on beginning and ceasing[1] but his most sophisticated treatment of continuity dates from the late 1320s, shortly after the composition of the *De proportionibus*. Similar to the *De proportionibus* in method and style, the *De continuo* surpassed Bradwardine's previous mathematical works to the extent that it directly confronted the fundamental problems surrounding infinity and continuity which underlay all medieval discussions of cosmology. In the *De continuo*, Bradwardine relied almost entirely on Euclidean geometry to prove that continuous entities are infinitely divisible.[2] Bradwardine's main achievement in this treatise was to establish a theoretical correspondence between such abstract mathematical continua as lines, planes and spheres and the physical continua of temperature, motion and time. In this way he transformed a previously philosophical problem into a physical one which could be analyzed mathematically. As in the *De proportionibus*, Bradwardine went far beyond Aristotle in rationalizing and mathematizing the natural philosopher's approach to motion and change without deviating from the basic principles of Aristotelian physics.

Unlike the *De proportionibus*, however, the *De continuo* was a polemical work directed against a vocal group of contemporary scholars who claimed that continua are composed of indivisible parts or atoms. Bradwardine, following Euclid and Aristotle, argued instead that all parts of a continuum must be infinitely divisible. By writing and publishing the *De continuo* Bradwardine entered into one of the most contentious philosophical and logical debates of the late middle ages.

---

[1] *De incipit.* For a full discussion of this text, see Chapter Six.

[2] References to the *De continuo* in this thesis are from John Emery Murdoch's edition of the text, which also includes a good introduction to the philosophical aspects of continuity in late medieval academic debates.

There has been confusion among twentieth-century historians over Bradwardine's position in this debate. Some, noting the significant differences between Bradwardine's and Ockham's approaches to Aristotelian physics, have assumed that Ockham was the principal target of the *De continuo*. Yet this interpretation fails to account for many similarities in their approaches to natural philosophy. In fact, Bradwardine and Ockham agreed on many Aristotelian concepts, including the definition of continuity and the characterization of time and motion as physical continua. They even shared, to some extent, a common method for analyzing continuity and other physical problems.[3] As Weisheipl has pointed out, Ockham and Bradwardine stood on the same side of the medieval debate about physics: Grosseteste, Walter Chatton and Henry of Harclay were the real targets of the *De continuo*, not Ockham.[4]

The topic of time provides a good focus for exploring the positions of both Ockham and Bradwardine in the larger debate over continuity which dominated thirteenth- and fourteenth-century studies of natural philosophy. Because they both regarded time as the continuum which defines all other mathematical and physical continua, Ockham and Bradwardine paid special attention to time in their discussions of continuity. Despite their agreement about the continuity of time, they

---

[3] See Tachau, "The Influence of Richard Campsall on Fourteenth-Century Thought," *From Ockham to Wyclif*, pp. 121-23. Here Tachau challenges the standard interpretation of late medieval academic debates which makes Ockham the instigator of "nominalist" philosophy, which some scholars wholeheartedly embraced and others attacked. According to Tachau, many of Ockham's supposed innovations can be traced back to Richard Campsall, who taught theology at Oxford while Ockham was a student there (pp. 109-10). This connection suggests, obviously, that late medieval philosophical debates were more complex and varied than is usually admitted. Hester Gelber concurs with Tachau in "The Fallacy of Accident and the *dictum de omni*: Late Medieval Controversy over a Reciprocal Pair," *Vivarium*, 25 (1987), pp. 114-15, that Campsall was an extremely innovative thinker, though overlooked even in his own century, whose ideas Ockham adopted and spread. Tachau believes that both Ockham and Bradwardine had access to Campsall's writings, possibly through a common source unknown to us. This information indicates that late medieval academic discussions had many participants whose contributions cannot be specifically identified. Thus it is misleading to assume direct influence between Ockham and Bradwardine, or any other medieval scholars, when ideas probably evolved in a more collegial environment.

[4] "The Interpretation of Aristotle's Physics and the Science of Motion," *CHLMP*, p. 523. Grosseteste's atomism came not from a rejection of Aristotelian physics but from his particular interpretation of Aristotle to support his metaphysics of light. Although Bradwardine was influenced by Grosseteste's use of mathematics, he did not consider atomism in the *De continuo* from the perspective of Grosseteste's metaphysical system. Therefore, Grosseteste's views will not be treated in this chapter. See McEvoy, *The Philosophy of Robert Grosseteste*, pp. 153-54.

disagreed profoundly about the nature of time's relationship to created matter. It is in this cosmological context that Ockham's rejection and Bradwardine's affirmation of Aristotelian physics must be seen.

The purpose of this chapter is to examine the late medieval debate about continuity in order to clarify the main features of Ockham's and Bradwardine's conceptions of time. The first part of this chapter reviews the thirteenth-century controversy over Aristotle's confusing writings about continuity, to which Bradwardine and his contemporaries responded early in the fourteenth century. A second section explores Ockham's strategy for reconciling his Aristotelian ideas about time with a distinctly non-Aristotelian metaphysical system. A final section considers Bradwardine's view of time, as he expressed it in the *De continuo*, in light of Ockham's position. These discussions will help to identify the source of conflict between Bradwardine's and Ockham's approaches to natural philosophy and to illustrate the centrality of temporal continuity in Bradwardine's own physical system.

Ockham's and Bradwardine's views about time were shaped by classical discussions which were revived by natural philosophers in the thirteenth century. All fourteenth-century studies of motion, change and time included some reference to the definitions of infinity and continuity which Aristotle had originally proposed in his treatments of these topics. Despite the tremendous variety of scientific subjects which late thirteenth- and fourteenth-century thinkers pursued, the questions Aristotle had raised about continuity and infinity were at the root of almost all of them.[5] Of course, late medieval natural philosophers did not accept Aristotle's definitions of continuity and infinity wholly or uncritically; instead, they generally saw those definitions as a starting point for their own scientific investigations into motion, time, light or other topics of contemporary interest.

It was Aristotle's portrayal of the interrelationship of continuity, motion and change, for example, that stimulated many of the innovations in late medieval physical theory. In his discussions of motion, Aristotle had always contended that all sorts of movement and change, even if discontinuous, could be observed and measured because all change

---

[5] Murdoch, "Infinity and Continuity," *CHLMP,* p. 564. For an introduction to the classical origins of the problems of infinity and continuity see Leo Sweeney, *Infinity in the Presocratics: A Bibliographical and Philosophical Study* (The Hague: Martinus Nijhoff, 1972); for discussions of various aspects of these problems from the classical period to the late middle ages see Norman Kretzmann, ed., *Infinity and Continuity in Ancient and Medieval Thought* (London: Cornell University Press, 1982).

occurs within the framework of continuous time. This theory, which
Aristotle developed most explicitly in his *Physics* and *De caelo*, is so
prevalent in the whole of his natural philosophy that his medieval successors could hardly have avoided some consideration of it.[6] At the
same time, as we have seen, Aristotle did not provide a particularly
strong mathematical system for measuring continuous change. He was
more concerned with establishing infinity and continuity as physical
realities underlying continuous change in the natural world.   Bradwardine and his contemporaries at Oxford were deeply influenced by the
Aristotelian preoccupation with infinity and continuity, though they
often differed on how apply Aristotle's theories to their own philosophical or theological investigations. Some preferred Aristotle's emphasis
on observation of natural phenomena, while others tried to reconcile the
Aristotelian understanding of infinity and continuity with the symbolic
mathematics of the Platonic tradition. This conflict over the philosophical parameters of these concepts led, predictably, to serious dis-
agreements among medieval natural philosophers.

The main controversy in the late medieval debate over continuity had
its origins in classical discussions of atomism. Aristotle, who devoted a
large portion of his writings on physics to refuting the atomists, developed a theory about the infinite divisibility of continua which enjoyed
wide acceptance in his own time and throughout the middle ages. Aristotle identified Democritus and Zeno as the chief proponents of the
atomist theory. According to Democritus, all being consists of distinct,
invisibly small atoms which are in perpetual motion in a void. Though
they are all made of the same substance, atoms come in many shapes
and sizes. The variety of objects which we observe in the material world
is the consequence of the interaction of the atoms as they collide in
space. All physical change results from the combination and recomb-
ination of these essential materials. Democritus also applied his atomic
theory to change in the immaterial world of the soul, claiming that even
human personality and intellect are composed of atoms. To support the
atomist theory Democritus devised an entire system of physical laws
which explained how atoms maintain the constant motion necessary for
growth and change to occur in a dynamic universe.[7]

Although Democritus' theory of atoms seemed to account for both
the variety and change of the sensible world, it was immediately

---

[6] Murdoch, "Infinity and Continuity," p. 565.

[7] Edwin Schrödinger, *Nature and the Greeks* (Cambridge: Cambridge University Press,
1954), pp. 74-77.

criticized for its emphasis on perpetual motion in a void: most ancient
Greek philosophers believed that both perpetual motion and the existence of a void were impossible. Aristotle disagreed with the notion that
atoms of matter could be isolated and indivisible and argued instead that
the physical world was whole, continuous and unified. Aristotle's criticism of Zeno took a slightly different form from his criticism of
Democritus. Whereas his objection to Democritus was essentially cosmological, he attacked Zeno primarily on logical grounds. Aristotle
would not accept the validity of Zeno's paradoxes which denied the reality of motion and change. Zeno was not in fact an atomist, but he
cleverly exploited certain logical features in the Euclidean definition of
continuity to the advantage of the atomists. Through his paradoxes Zeno
tried to defend Parmenides' assertion that only one thing exists by exposing the contradictions in seeing nature as many bodies in motion.
The essence of his argument was that, if every motion, time and distance
were infinitely divisible, it would be impossible to traverse any given
segment of a continuum: the runner of a race, for example, could never
reach the finish line, no matter how he close got to it, because his distance from it would remain infinitely divisible at every point. Thus
Zeno actually accepted the infinite divisibility of continua on the
grounds that this principle proved the impossibility of motion.

Of course, atomists, both classical and medieval, used the paradoxes
not to deny motion as such but to put the discussion of motion on a different footing. For them, motion of a body only made sense as a
reflection of the motions of the indivisible atoms which composed it.
Although they regarded Zeno's view of motion as absurd, the late medieval atomists skillfully used his analysis of continuity to discredit the
Euclidean position on infinite divisibility.[8] Through his elaborate refutation of Zeno, Aristotle unwittingly encouraged this alliance between
Zeno and the atomists by showing how the paradoxes could be used to
support the theory of atomism.[9]

---

[8] Sorabji, p. 321.

[9] See, for example, *De generatione et corruptione translatio vetus, Aristoteles latinus,*
IX, ed. Joanna Judycka (Leiden: E. J. Brill, 1986), I, 2.316b20-35, p. 14: "Omne
quidem igitur corpus sensibile esse divisibile secundum quodcumque signum et indivisibile, non inconveniens; hoc enim potestate, hoc autem entelechia existit. Esse autem
simul omnino divisibile potestate impossibile videbitur utique esse. Si enim possibile, et
fieret; non ut sit simul actu ambo, indivisibile et divisum, sed divisum secundum quodcumque signum. Nullam igitur erit reliquum et in incorporeum corruptum corpus, et
generabitur utique rursus aut ex punctis, aut omnio ex nichilo. Et hoc quomodo possibile? Sed quoniam dividitur in separabilia et semper in minores magnitudines et in

Aristotle's criticism of Zeno also inspired natural philosophers like Bradwardine, who accepted the Euclidean definition of continuity. At the heart of Aristotle's attack on Zeno was his refusal to accept Zeno's premise that the oneness of matter makes motion impossible. Aristotle also dismissed those philosophers who claimed that the universe is one and immovable because they could not explain change. Although their reasoning might be impeccable, their conclusions make no sense: "For indeed," says Aristotle, "no lunatic seems to be so far out of his senses as to suppose that fire and ice are one: it is only between what *is* right, and what *seems* right from habit, that some people are mad enough to see no difference."[10] The only sensible way to approach nature, Aristotle contended, was to accept that change exists and to try to characterize it.

In Book V of his *Physics*, Aristotle defined continuity in terms which would eventually allow him to characterize change, time, space and matter as continuous. His definitions of the adjectives "successive," "contiguous" and "continuous" imply that continuity is the most specialized of the three because it contains elements of all three in unity. Because Aristotle's definitions of these concepts prevailed throughout the medieval period, they are worth presenting in their original form:

> A thing is in succession when it is after the beginning in position or in form or in some other respect in which it is definitely so regarded, and when further there is nothing of the *same* kind as itself between it and that to which it is in succession, e.g. a line or lines if it is a line, a unit or units if it is a unit, a house if it is a house (there is nothing to prevent something of a *different* kind being between). For that which is in succession is in succession to a particular thing, and is something posterior; for one is not in succession to two, nor is the first day of the month to the second: in each case the later is in succession to the former. A thing that is in succession and touches is contiguous. The continuous is a subdivision of the contiguous: things are called continuous when the touching limits of each become one and the same and are, as the word implies, contained in each

---

semota et segregata, manifestum. Neque utique secundum partem dividenti erit infinita incisio, neque simul possible est dividere secundum omne signum (non enim possibile), sed usque ad quid. Necesse igitur indivisibiles existere magnitudines invisibiles, et aliter et si erit generatio et corruptio, hec quidem segregatione, hec autem congregatione." For an analysis of Aristotle's method of refuting Zeno see Sorabji, pp. 336-38.

[10] *De generatione et corruptione*, I, 8.325a17-23, pp. 40-41: "Amplius autem in sermone quidem videntur hec contingere, in rebus autem dementie simile opinari ita. Nullum enim dementium egredi in tantum, ut ignem unum existimet et glaciem, sed solum bona et apparentia propter assuetudinem hec quibusdam propter dementiam nichil videntur differre." Trans. Barnes, p. 531.

other: continuity is impossible if the extremities are two. This definition
makes it plain that continuity belongs to things that naturally in virtue of
their mutual contact form a unity. And in whatever way that which holds
them together is one, so too the whole will be one, e.g. by a rivet or glue or
contact or organic union.[11]

Aristotle then distinguished successive from continuous beings, borrowing from the language of geometry. Although points and units can both
be successive, only points can be continuous, since units represent distinct entities (e.g., whole numbers) but points do not: points can touch
each other and more points can exist between points, but no whole number can exist between the numbers one and two.[12]

These definitions provide the foundation of Aristotle's theory of
divisibility. According to Aristotle, nothing that is continuous can be
composed of indivisible parts because continuity requires each part to be
connected to another part. Therefore, each part possesses some aspect which
belongs to other elements in the series and some aspect which does not:

[A] line cannot be composed of points, the line being continuous and the
point indivisible. For the extremities of the two points can neither be *one*
(since of an indivisible there can be no extremity as distinct from some
other part) nor *together* (since that which has no parts can have no
extremity, the extremity and the thing of which it is the extremity being
distinct). . . . Nor, again, can a point be *in succession* to a point or a now
to a now in such a way that length can be composed of points or time of
nows; for things are in succession if there is nothing of their own kind
intermediate between them, whereas intermediate between points there is
always a line and between nows a period of time. . . . [Therefore,] everything
continuous is divisible into divisibles that are always divisible.[13]

Thus Aristotle concludes that time, magnitude and motion are all subject
to the same theoretical principles that govern continuity.

Indeed, for Aristotle, continuity is the universal concept which links
motion, time and space. In the case of magnitude, for example, the infinity of a line is equivalent to that of time and motion:

---

[11] *Physica*, V, 3.226b34-227a16, pp. 200-2; trans. Barnes, pp. 383-84.

[12] *Physica*, V, 3.227a27-227b2, pp. 202-3: "Quare si est punctum et unitas qualia
dicunt separata, non possibile est esse unitatem et punctum idem; his quidem enim (inest)
tangere, unitatibus autem consequenter; et horum quidem contingit esse medium; omnis
enim linea medium punctorum est; horum autem non est necesse; nullum enim medium
dualitatis est et unitatis. Quid quidem igitur est simul et extra, et quid tangere, et quid
medium, et quid consequenter, et quid habitum et continuum, et qualibus unumquodque
horum inest, dictum est." Trans. Barnes, p. 384.

[13] *Physica*, VI, 1.231a24-231b15, pp. 216-17, trans. Barnes, p. 391.

[S]ince every motion is in time and a motion may occupy any time, and the motion of everything that is in motion may be either quicker or slower, both quicker motion and slower motion may occupy any time: and this being so, it necessarily follows that time also is continuous. By continuous I mean that which is divisible into divisibles that are always divisible . . . . And at the same time it is clear that all magnitude is also continuous; for the divisions of which time and magnitude respectively are susceptible are the same and equal. . . . [Therefore] if time is infinite in respect of its extremities, length is also infinite in respect of its extremities; if time is infinite in respect of divisibility, length is also infinite in respect of divisibility; and if time is infinite in both respects, magnitude is also infinite in both respects.[14]

Moreover, because magnitude is continuous, movement along a magnitude is continuous, as is the time in which the movement occurs. So Aristotle remarks in Book IV of the *Physics*:

Now we perceive movement and time together; for even when it is dark and we are not being affected through the body, if any movement takes place in the mind we at once suppose that some time has indeed elapsed; and not only that but also, when some time is thought to have passed, some movement also along with it seems to have taken place. Hence time is either movement or something that belongs to movement. Since then it is not movement, it must be the other. But what is moved is moved from something to something, and all magnitude is continuous. Therefore the movement goes with the magnitude. Because the magnitude is continuous, the movement too is continuous, and if the movement, then the time; for the time that has passed away is always thought to be as great as the movement.[15]

Aristotle presents us, then, with a view of motion, time and space which depends on the inherent continuity of each quality. Because they are all related to each other, time cannot be atomic if magnitude is not: in proving that a line is not composed of a finite number of distinct points, one can suggest, by analogy, that time does not consist of indivisible instants.[16] In fact, although it is possible to conceive of an atomic theory of magnitude which does not require an atomic view of time, Aristotle so closely binds together time and motion that he is unable to see how the one could be atomic and the other not.[17]

---

[14] *Physica*, VI, 2.232b20-233a12; 233a18-21, pp. 222-24, trans. Barnes, p. 393.

[15] *Physica*, IV, 11.219a4-14, pp. 173-74, trans. Barnes, p. 371.

[16] F. D. Miller, "Aristotle against the Atomists," in *Infinity and Continuity in Ancient and Medieval Thought*, pp. 106-7.

[17] *Ibid.*, p. 109.

Medieval debates about continuity reflect the legacy of Aristotle's criticism of atomism and his alternative theory. The Muslim philosophers were keenly interested in continuity, and some of them responded to Aristotle and Zeno by advocating a modified form of classical atomism. Both Muslim atomism and the objections of certain Muslim philosophers to Greek atomism influenced Latin thinkers.[18] Classical philosophers had either confined their discussion of atomism entirely to the physical world or, like Democritus, left their speculations about the nonmaterial world largely undeveloped. Medieval thinkers, by contrast, took a wider approach to these topics. Of particular interest was the question of how infinity and continuity applied to God and his creation. Thirteenth- and early fourteenth-century scholars made the debate about infinity and continuity more complex by trying to analyze these concepts both as features of observable phenomena and as expressions of divine omnipotence. Thus Murdoch concludes: ". . . since God's absolute power extended to everything that did not include a contradiction, to invoke this power in examining infinity or continuity was to transfer one's analysis from the realm of the physically possible (within the confines of Aristotelian natural philosophy) to the broader realm of the logically possible."[19] This new way of thinking led to new formulations and innovative solutions for a problem which still retained its classical characteristics.

The late medieval discussions of continuity revolved around the classical debate over atoms or "indivisibles" but it was also fueled by a newer preoccupation with the definition of infinity. In Book III of the *Physics*, Aristotle had denied actual infinity on the grounds that the universe is finite. The only infinity Aristotle would admit was the potentially infinite divisibility of a continuum: "since no sensible magnitude is infinite, it is impossible to exceed every definite magnitude; for if it were possible, there would be something bigger than the heavens."[20] Medieval philosophers generally accepted Aristotle's authority concerning infinity in the physical world but they went on to consider the possibilities of the actual infinities which God might create. From this avenue of speculation came the "paradox of unequal

---

[18] Sorabji, p. 401.

[19] Murdoch, "Infinity and Continuity," p. 566.

[20] *Physica*, III, 7.207b16-21, p. 131: "In magnitudinibus autem contrarium est; dividitur quidem enim in infinita continuum, in maius autem non est infinitum. Quantum enim contingit potentia esse, et actu contingit tantum esse. Quare quoniam infinita nulla est magnitudo sensibilis, non contingit omnis excellentiam esse determinate magnitudinis; esset enim utique aliquid celo maius." Trans. Barnes, p. 353.

infinities" which Bonaventure helped to popularize in his discussion of the eternity of the world. Murdoch defines this paradox in this way: "if one allows the existence of actual infinities, then it appears that some infinities will clearly be greater than other infinities which are equally clearly part of the former; but it is axiomatic that all infinities are equal; therefore, in this instance a part is not less than, but equal to, its whole—which is absurd."[21] Bonaventure's use of this paradox in his treatment of eternity stimulated a wide range of commentary[22] and reinforced the link between infinity and time.

While some philosophers resolved the paradox simply by using it to prove the impossibility of actual infinities, others faced the problem more directly by analyzing the differences between actual and potential infinities. These investigations were directly concerned with continua because, by virtue of its composition from infinitely divisible elements, a continuum is potentially infinite. The characteristics of potential infinities were investigated from a variety of perspectives, but most studies began with mathematical analysis. Aristotle's observations about the general nature of continua and the continuous quality of physical forces shaped the conversation; but Euclid contributed an essential technical vocabulary for the study of infinity and so provided a mathematical framework for analyzing continua.[23]

Averroes' treatment of infinity, which was so influential in late medieval discussions of continuity, was based on just such a Euclidean framework for sorting out Aristotle's various comments about continua. In Book V of his commentary on Aristotle's *Physics*, for example, Averroes tried to simplify Aristotle's definition of the continuous as a special kind of contiguity. Averroes recognized that Aristotle had been correct to link continuity and contiguity in the case of physical entities but he pointed out how difficult it is to express this link with Euclidean mathematics. Two physical bodies must be contiguous for there to be any continuity between them; but, in abstract mathematics, it is not necessary to hold tightly to this definition. Instead, it is more convenient to say of mathematical entities (for example, lines, surfaces or solids) that, when two such bodies come together, their extremities

---

[21] Murdoch, "Infinity and Continuity," p. 569.

[22] *Ibid.*, pp. 569-70. Dales summarizes Bonaventure's position on the eternity of the world, as compared to that of Henry of Harclay in the introduction to his edition, "Henricus de Harclay. Quaestio 'utrum mundus potuit fuisse ab aeterno,'" *AHDLMA*, 50 (1983), pp. 224-28.

[23] Murdoch, "Medieval Language," p. 520.

are not contiguous but superimposed on each other: the extremities of each become one.[24]

Albertus Magnus helped to disseminate this notion of superposition in mathematical continua in the west by emphasizing superposition in his own commentary on Aristotle. By incorrectly attributing the idea to Euclid instead of Averroes, Albertus put the whole discussion of continuity into a form which stressed the geometrical nature rather than the philosophical significance of the continuum.[25] As far as Albertus was concerned, it was Euclid who had provided the necessary vocabulary for explaining the contiguous qualities of mathematical entities, so the supposition theory should be credited to him as well.[26] Although Averroes' ideas undoubtedly influenced Albertus' approach, Albertus preferred to stress Euclidean themes in his study of Aristotelian continuity. Albertus thus helped to legitimate a geometrical approach to natural philosophy by illustrating how Euclid's methods for analyzing abstract entities could be applied to mathematical continua, and, by analogy, to physical continua as well.

Other attempts to apply Euclidean geometry to the problem of continuity were considerably more controversial. Henry of Harclay, Chancellor of Oxford in 1312, believed, for example, that actual infinities could exist and that continua were composed of indivisibles. His solution to the infinity paradox rested on his acceptance of unequal infinities. Like Averroes and Albertus, Harclay used a Euclidean principle to distinguish between natural and mathematical continua. He agreed with Euclid's axiom that, in nature, every whole is greater than its parts. In abstract mathematics, however, a broader axiom could be exploited. Henry assumed that every infinity is whole in itself, even if it is a subset

---

[24] See Murdoch, "Superposition, Congruence and Continuity in the Middle Ages," in *L'Aventure de la science: Mélanges Alexandre Koyré*, I (*Histoire de la pensée*, XII) (Paris: *École pratique des hautes études*, 1964), p. 424. Here Murdoch quotes from commentary twenty-two of Averroes' Commentary on the *Physics*, Volume IV of *Aristotelis Opera cum Averrois Commentarius* (Venice: Juntas, 1562-74): "Deinde dixit: Et dico contingua et cetera, id est, et contigua sunt corpora quorum ultima, scilicet superficies, sunt simul ita quod inter illas non est corpus extraneum; et hec est contiguatio naturalis. Contiguatio vero mathematica est in magnitudinibus quorum ultima superponuntur. Si igitur fuerint corpora, superponuntur superficies eorum contigue; et si superficies, superponentur linee; et si linee, superponentur puncta, sicut dicitur punctus superponitur puncto. Set hic non intendit mathematica, quoniam in mathematicis duo ultima revertuntur in unum, et sic assimilantur continuo. In naturalibus vero duo ultima remanent duo demonstrata."

[25] Murdoch, "Superposition," pp. 428-29.

[26] Murdoch examines Albertus' approach to Euclid in "Superposition," pp. 428-29.

of another infinity: "that which (e.g., an infinite set) contains another thing (e.g., an infinite proper subset) and something else beyond it, or in addition to (*praeter*) it, is a whole with respect to the other thing."[27]

This assumption was soon criticized for its ambiguous interpretation of Euclid and its misrepresentation of Aristotle. The Franciscan William of Alnwick pointed out that Henry's distinction between infinities and their proper infinite subsets did not imply that the latter were smaller, because only finite things have quantity, the necessary prerequisite for comparison of size.[28] In his commentary on the *Sentences*, given in Paris in the academic year 1343-44, Gregory of Rimini enlarged on William's observation.[29] Himself an advocate of the existence of actual infinities, Gregory tried to explain how some infinities can exist as part of other infinities. In the sense that a whole is made up of parts, he argued, an infinite subset must be considered part of any infinity which includes it; but considered mathematically, those infinities become equal because each contains an infinite number of elements.[30] The approaches of William and Gregory to this problem reflect the medieval tendency in natural philosophy to distinguish physical continua from purely mathematical ones.

When Bradwardine set out to define his own view of continuity in the mid-1320s, he had to consider two major questions: how well did Aristotle's theory of infinite divisibility apply to physical and mathematical continua respectively; and how appropriate was geometrical analysis to the study of physical continua such as motion, time and temperature? His efforts to solve these problems show a striking similarity to those of Ockham. Both approached the subject of continuity along Aristotelian

---

[27] Henry of Harclay, *Quaestio de infinito et continuo* (MS Tortosa Cated. 88, 83v; MS Firenze Naz. II.II. 281, 95r), quoted and translated by Murdoch in "Infinity," p. 571: "Illud quod continet aliud et aliquid ultra illud vel praeter illud est totum respectu illius." See also, Dales, "Henry of Harclay on the Infinite," *Journal of the History of Ideas*, 45 (1984), pp. 295-301.

[28] Murdoch, "Infinity and Continuity," p. 572. For further information on Gregory of Rimini's philosophical outlook see Leff, *Gregory of Rimini: Tradition and Innovation in Fourteenth-Century Thought* (Manchester: Manchester University Press, 1961).

[29] For the dating of Gregory of Rimini's career, see Venicio Marcolino, "Der Augustinertheologie an der Universität Paris," in Heiko A. Oberman, ed. *Gregor von Rimini. Werk und Wirkung bis zur Reformation* (New York: W. de Gruyter, 1981), pp. 127-94, cited by Tachau in *Vision and Certitude*, p. 358. For a discussion of Gregory's treatments of time, motion and quantity, along with an assessment of his influence on William of Ockham, see Courtenay, "The Role of English Thought," *Rebirth, Reform and Resilience*, pp. 129-33.

[30] Murdoch, "Infinity and Continuity," p. 572.

lines: they largely accepted Aristotle's method for refuting the atomist position and explicitly acknowledged the continuous nature of time and motion. Moreover, both exhibited the same tendency to isolate the analysis of physical continua from larger metaphysical considerations. In their works of natural philosophy both Ockham and Bradwardine approached physical continua as particular mathematical or logical problems and rarely connected such discussions with considerations of the philosophical significance of continuity. In this sense, their views represent a more authentic Aristotelianism even than those of their great predecessor Thomas Aquinas, whose discussions of continuity always began with an analysis of being.[31]

The differences between Bradwardine and Ockham on this issue are equally remarkable, however. Bradwardine was a staunch defender of Aristotelian physics: his mathematical transformation of Aristotle's physical theory was done in a spirit of respect and acceptance. Ockham, on the other hand, openly criticized the philosophical basis of Aristotle's physical system, while admitting that many of Aristotle's observations concerning motion, time and space were substantially correct. Nor were the analytical methods of Bradwardine and Ockham entirely compatible. Bradwardine chose a mathematical method along the lines of Grosseteste, while Ockham preferred the more traditionally logical approach of Averroes and Aquinas. If Bradwardine and Ockham actually influenced each other, as textual evidence seems to suggest, it is important to examine Bradwardine's view of the continuity of time in the context of Ockham's own views and his criticism of Aristotle.

In spite of an interrupted academic career and political involvements which drew him farther and farther away from academic circles in the last two decades of his life, Ockham is generally regarded as "the most influential philosopher of the fourteenth century."[32] This does not mean,

---

[31] Aquinas' position on continuity is thoroughly discussed by Bodewig in "Zahl und Kontinuum." According to Bodewig, Aquinas' view of continuity was essentially Aristotelian except for a somewhat Platonic tendency to consider continuity in terms of being, that is, as a metaphysical problem not a physical or mathematical problem, and to emphasize the symbolic importance of number in his analysis. Of course, the context of this discussion included other medieval thinkers with expertise in both mathematics and metaphysics. For an assessment of influences on Ockham and Bradwardine in the specific area of continuity going back to Roger Bacon and John Duns Scotus, see J. M. M. H. Thijssen, "Roger Bacon (1214-1292/97): A Neglected Source in the Medieval Continuum Debate," *Archives internationales d'histoire des sciences*, 34 (1984), pp. 25-34.

[32] Ernest Moody, "William of Ockham," *SMPSL*, p. 409. As noted above (n. 3), however, Tachau and Gelber argue that Ockham's role was significant mostly as a promoter of philosophical innovations, some of which he derived from other sources.

of course, that he was immune from the influence of other thinkers or
that his ideas were revolutionary in every respect. Ockham's thought
was the product of a collegial academic environment in which scholars
received the same sort of education and pursued the same kinds of questions, applying the philosophical methods which most appealed to them:
some preferred propositional logic, others mathematics, still others
metaphysics; but all were conversant with a wide range of possible approaches to natural philosophy and understood that these approaches
could be interconnected. An accurate appraisal of Ockham's influence
must acknowledge both the conventional aspects of his philosophy and
the subtle ways in which his contemporaries modified his ideas to suit
their own arguments.[33]

Ockham's views about continuity and time illustrate the complexity
of the late medieval debate about natural philosophy, as well as
Ockham's formative position in it, for they reflect both hearty
acceptance and severe criticism of classical Aristotelianism. In addition
to establishing the main features of Bradwardine's conception of time,
the following comparison of Ockham and Bradwardine will help to
clarify Ockham's role as a participant in a much larger discussion
among thinkers of different talents and at various levels of experience.
Just as Bradwardine's views of time and continuity depend on an
evaluation of his mathematical thinking, Ockham's views cannot be
understood properly without reference to his metaphysical system.
Although Ockham's critics claimed that his conception of reality made
God a capricious and unfathomable force in the universe and thus
undermined faith, he always maintained that his primary goal was to
exalt the complete freedom and omnipotence of God's will and to
elevate faith above reason. In developing this thoroughly orthodox point
of view, Ockham drew heavily on Aristotle and Averroes and was also
deeply influenced by John Duns Scotus, despite his fundamental
disagreement with certain features of Scotist philosophy.[34] Ockham's

---

See, for example, Girard J. Etzkorn, "Codex Merton 284: Evidence of Ockham's Early
Influence at Oxford," in *From Ockham to Wyclif*, pp. 31-42.

[33] For a discussion of this problem see Courtenay, "The Reception of Ockham's
Thought in Fourteenth-Century England," in *From Ockham to Wyclif*, pp. 89-107.

[34] Weisheipl, "Ockham and the Mertonians," in *The Early Oxford Schools*, ed. Jeremy
I. Catto, Volume I of *The History of the University of Oxford*, ed. T. H. Aston (Oxford:
Clarendon Press, 1984), pp. 609-10. For an extensive treatment of Ockham's view of
reality and the sources thereof, see Marilyn McCord Adams, *William Ockham* (Notre
Dame, Indiana: University of Notre Dame Press, 1987), p. 495; pp. 547-50. See also
Vision and Certitude, especially the chapter on Ockham, pp. 113-53.

discussions with his fellow scholars mark a new stage in the long-standing debate about the relationship between faith and reason in a Christian society. Having benefitted from more than a century of scholarly criticism of Aristotle and Averroes, Ockham and his contemporaries had the expertise to challenge those authorities and attempt to devise their own understanding of the relationship of faith and reason.

Like almost every other thinker of his age, Ockham had to confront the contradictions in classical metaphysics before attempting to produce his own metaphysical system. Along with Thomas Aquinas and John Duns Scotus, Ockham wanted to reconcile Aristotelian philosophy and Christian doctrine but he was deeply dissatisfied with his predecessors' solutions. While Ockham rejected Aquinas' strong dependence on Aristotle, he also questioned the approach favored by Franciscans from Bonaventure to Scotus, which tried to moderate Aquinas' system through greater reference to Plato and Greek Neoplatonism.[35] Furthermore, Ockham could not accept the thirteenth-century attempts to reconcile philosophy and theology because they made use of the principle of realism, defined by Ernest Moody as "the metaphysical and epistemological doctrine . . . that the human intellect discovers the particulars apprehended by sense experience in an intelligible order of abstract essences and necessary relations ontologically prior to particular things and contingent events, and that from this order the intellect can demonstrate necessary truths concerning first causes and the being and attributes of God."[36] The realists, in keeping with both Platonic and Aristotelian metaphysics, believed that objects have sensible qualities, such as size, color, number and location, which have universal reality. A thorough analysis of an object would be impossible without reference to these universals, which have significance beyond the individual characteristics of that object. To the extent that every object has size, for example, all objects share a common nature with respect to that universal quality. Aristotle's entire system for observing matter involved close attention to this concept of universal qualities. His extensive analysis of qualities largely defined medieval investigations into both metaphysics and natural philosophy.

Ockham's main objection to realism was that it accorded to sensible qualities a reality beyond the reality of a particular thing. Ockham believed instead that the human mind could directly apprehend the qualities of an object. Weisheipl explains:

---

[35] *SMPSL*, pp. 412-13.
[36] *Ibid*, p. 413.

for Ockham, among the ten 'categories' of Aristotle, only individual 'substances' and individual 'qualities' were *res absolutae*, existing outside the human mind. All other things, such as quantity, motion, time, place, velocity and causality, were only terms (*termini*) or words (*nomina*) to stand for (*sup-ponere*) nothing but the individual under some consideration of connotation of the mind, and did not represent the apprehension of the mind of some objective reality distinct from individual substances or individual qualities.[37]

Ockham's insistence that descriptive qualities were inherent in objects and had no independent reality was not an entirely new idea: philosophers before Ockham had claimed, for example, that universal natures existed only as mental abstractions.[38] By the early fourteenth century, however, some natural philosophers were beginning to argue that the common natures which the mind can recognize in various objects have no reality, even potentially or incompletely, but are only mental terms (*intentiones animae*) which have logical functions in propositions.[39] The adherents of this position provided a new direction for late medieval philosophy because they openly and rigorously challenged Aristotle's teaching about qualities. In doing so, they went far beyond Ockham himself in their criticism of medieval realism and orthodox metaphysics.[40]

Even Ockham's more moderate views had a major influence on late medieval natural philosophy because he popularized new lines of philosophical and theological reasoning. His denial of the reality of universals outside the mind allowed him to reject the notion that God created individuals to conform with divine ideas: any similarities which exist between two individuals are the result of God's free choice and do not require an elaborate metaphysical explanation. Therefore the intellect, whether human or divine, should be directed towards comprehending the individual thing which exists.[41] Such a perspective can, on the one hand, call into question any intellectual activity which involves deduction from general principles. In this sense, Ockham's positions were at odds with the traditional Aristotelianism of medieval natural philosophy. In fact, Ockham used his new system of propositional logic to demonstrate that many of the principles which Aristotle had

---

[37] Weisheipl, "Ockham and the Mertonians," p. 611.

[38] *Ibid.*, p. 610.

[39] *Ibid.*

[40] For an analysis of Ockham's views about quality, see Adams, *Ockham*, pp. 277-85.

[41] Weisheipl, p. 612. For a philosophical analysis of this problem in the context of late medieval natural debates, see Adams, *Ockham*, Chapter 2: "Universals Are Not Things Other Than Names," pp. 13-69.

considered necessary and self-evident were not so.[42] Because Ockham offered no new cosmology to replace Aristotle's, one might say that he undermined late medieval science with his skepticism. On the other hand, Ockham's assertion that there might be several possible and equally valid explanations for a particular phenomenon, as well as his emphasis on the human capacity to analyze individual objects or events, had a stimulating effect on physical theory throughout the fourteenth century. Indeed, Moody goes so far as to say that Ockham's new approach to knowledge was instrumental in establishing "the intellectual environment in which later fourteenth-century philosophers explored new physical theories . . . [and so] laid the foundations for the scientific revolution of the seventeenth century."[43]

In his penetrating study of Ockham's physical theory, André Goddu provides a useful framework for understanding Ockham's opinions about continuity and time. According to Goddu, Ockham tried in his natural philosophy to maintain both the hypothetical necessity and the factual stability of the natural order, while at the same time defending God's omnipotence and freedom.[44] While Ockham applied his logical system to a wide variety of metaphysical, theological and physical questions and sought a comprehensive explanation of natural phenomena whenever possible, he realized that certain problems had to be treated in isolation from others. Goddu contends that Ockham borrowed Aristotle's methods of isolation and imagination experiments when he speculated about physical realities, though Ockham's own ideas about God's relationship to humanity affected his use of these methods. Instead of merely accepting the principles of Aristotelian physics, Ockham was more likely to use isolation and imagination experiments to disprove their logical necessity and to assert the contrary: that abstract concepts and connotative terms can be reduced to subjects and their absolute qualities.[45]

One of Ockham's main philosophical goals, therefore, was to disengage natural philosophy from metaphysics. By emphasizing that sensible

---

[42] Moody, "William of Ockham," p. 429.

[43] *Ibid.*, p. 430.

[44] André Goddu, *The Physics of William of Ockham* (Leiden: E. J. Brill, 1984), p. 83.

[45] *Ibid.*, p. 84. By "imagination experiment" Goddu simply means that Aristotle, Ockham (and Bradwardine) used a method for investigating physical problems which somewhat resembles modern scientific methods, in that it involved proposing hypotheses and devising specific procedures for testing their validity. Because these inquiries were conducted according to a precise methodology but were confined to purely mental speculation devoid of laboratory experimentation, Goddu calls them thought or "imagination" experiments.

qualities are inherent in and inseparable from matter, Ockham tried to undermine Aquinas' synthesis of Plato and Aristotle, which established a link between forms in the world and forms in the mind.[46] Although he obviously accepted many principles of Aristotelian physics, Ockham insisted that Aristotle's theories ought to be tested empirically, preferably by focusing on specific physical phenomena unhindered by metaphysical considerations. Bradwardine followed a similar analytical method by isolating physical problems in order to examine them geometrically. Goddu argues that Ockham's application of the principle of isolation to Aristotelian physics, together with other fourteenth-century criticisms of Aristotle, contributed to a growing movement to correct Aristotle's mistakes, which led ultimately to the complete rejection of Aristotelian natural philosophy by the seventeenth century. Because Ockham relied simply on propositional logic as his empirical technique, however, he was not able to progress very far on his own in designing a new physical theory to take the place of the one he so effectively dismantled.[47]

Ockham's accomplishment lay, rather, in his ability to discern problems in Aristotelian physics brought to light by late medieval discoveries in logic and metaphysics. When we turn to the question of Ockham's view of continuity, for example, we find that he did not believe in the existence of indivisibles, an opinion which contradicted both Aristotle and Euclid but was consistent with his own position on universals. Using the familiar illustration of points in a line, Ockham argued that one need not think of lines terminating with points: a finite line is simply a line of a particular length.[48] According to Ockham, it

---

[46] *Ibid.*, p. 110.

[47] *Ibid.*, p. 236.

[48] In "Infinity and Continuity," p. 573, Murdoch quotes the following text from Thomas Bruce Birch's edition of *The De Sacramento Altaris of William of Ockham* (Burlington, Iowa: The Lutheran Literacy Board, 1930), pp. 36-38: "Et si queratur quid est punctus, aut est res divisibilis, dicendum est quod, si sic dicendo 'punctus est aliquid' vel 'punctus est res' vel huiusmodi li 'punctus' supponat pro aliquo ita quod habeat precise vim nominis et non includat equivalenter unum complexum ex nomine et verbo vel aliquid consimile quod secundum proprietatem vocis potest reddere suppositum verbo, debet concedi quod punctus est aliquid et quod punctus est res; et hoc quia debet concedi quod punctus est linea et punctus est quantitas, quia tunc hoc nomen 'punctus' equivalet toti isti: 'Linea tante vel tante longitudinis' sive 'linea non ulterius protensa vel extensa' vel alicui toti composito ex adiectivo et substantivo vel alicui toti composito ex nomine et verbo mediante coniunctione vel adverbio vel hoc pronomine 'qui,' secundum quod placet dare diversas diffinitiones exprimentes quid nominis illius 'punctus.'"

was misleading to say that a line is made up of an infinite number of points because only individual, permanent points and lines are real.[49] Thus Ockham regarded Euclidean terminology as merely symbolic: words such as "point," "line" or "instant" are not things in themselves but terms which stand for more complex concepts in a proposition; similarly, "motion" and "time" are not physical entities distinct from things which move or exist in time.[50]

Whenever Ockham approached the problem of time, he used the traditional Aristotelian vocabulary of motion and change but his understanding of these concepts was considerably different from Aristotle's.[51] Ockham's reluctance to consider any aspect of change as distinct from the object undergoing change constituted a major break with Aristotelian physical theory, especially in regard to motion and time. Because Aristotle had argued that everything which moves is moved by something and that all change comes about as the result of some kind of motion, the Aristotelian concept of motion had great metaphysical significance: Aristotle and his followers took it for granted that motion had a reality and purpose prior to and distinct from any object experiencing change. Ockham's identification of qualities with individual objects seriously undermined these metaphysical distinctions.

By the thirteenth century, as we have seen, discussions about motion, time and continuity had become extremely sophisticated. Consequently, a debate ensued over whether motion (and, by analogy, time) was a flowing form (*forma fluens*), that is, a distinct, continuous entity, or a flux of form (*fluxus forme*), in which an object undergoes successive change.[52] In his effort to define motion as an inherent feature of a moving object rather than a separate force acting on the object, Ockham clearly sided with the second position.[53] As with other aspects of his philosophical system, Ockham did not abstract or analyze the characteristics of motion as general principles. He argued that the only way to understand motion is to examine the motion involved in particular cases.[54]

---

[49] See Adams' section on points, lines and surfaces in *Ockham*, pp. 201-12.

[50] Murdoch, "Infinity and Continuity," p. 574.

[51] Adams, *Ockham*, pp. 853-55. See also Adams' Chapter 20, "On Time," pp. 853-99.

[52] Herman Shapiro, *Motion, Time and Place According to William Ockham* (St. Bonaventure, New York: The Franciscan Institute, 1957), p. 36, n. 75. Also discussed in Gordon Leff, *William of Ockham: The Metamorphosis of Scholastic Discourse* (Manchester: Manchester University Press, 1975), p. 585.

[53] Adams, *Ockham*, pp. 811-27, carefully analyzes Ockham's thesis that "motion (motus) is not really a distinct thing."

[54] See Adams, *Ockham*, pp. 818-19; pp. 826-27. In the *Brevis summa libri*

Ockham emphasized the individual nature of change by describing change as a successive process of internal transformation.[55] His description of change as continuous followed Aristotle. His assertion that the form of the object undergoing change actually changes itself, however, was at odds with Aristotle's theory of forms. Ockham's explanation of successive transformation reduced motion and time to sensible characteristics of objects and stressed the absolute individuality of every instance of change. Thus Ockham could argue that broad explanations of natural phenomena based on Aristotle's theories of motion were inadequate. The implications of this approach for theology were even more striking: if God does not need to create according to pre-existing forms and can change individuals directly without applying external forces such as motion, his actions cannot be predicted or explained by the Aristotelian or any other metaphysical system.[56]

Ockham's view of time was consistent with his view of motion both in its Aristotelian origins and in its ultimate emphasis on individual experience. Throughout his *Tractatus de successivis*, a compilation of three short works, Ockham presented the thesis that motion, place and time are inseparable from objects which are in motion, space or time. This view, Ockham contended, was fully in keeping with Aristotelian physics.[57] In a sense, of course, Ockham's description of change did

---

physicorum, III.2 (*De motu*), ed. Stephanus Brown in Volume VI *Guillelmi de Ockham Opera philosophica et theologica*, p. 40, Ockham argues that Aristotle himself held the same view: "Secundo notandum quod motus non est aliqua res per se distincta quae possit definiri, sed si significat res non significat nisi res praesentes, praeteritas vel futuras. Quod probatur esse de mente Aristotelis primo per Commentatorem hic: dicit enim in solvendo quandam dubitationem quod Aristoteles in *Praedicamentis* ideo posuit motum in genere passionis tamquam [esset] res media et distincta, quia ibi induxit modum famosum sed falsum. Hic autem, quia loquitur de motu ex intentione, inducit proprium modum et verum: Quod motus non est aliquid distinctum vel aliqua res distincta praeter res ad quas est motus. Et est diligenter advertendum quod hoc dictum Commentatoris debet notari pro regula, quia quando Philosophus loquitur non ex intentione inducit modum communem loquendi sed falsum, ut 'scientiam esse de rebus' et 'universalia esse res,' et huiusmodi. Sed ubi loquitur ex intentione ibi inducit modum verum, et sic patet quod non omnia verba Philosophi debent intelligi sicut sonant."

[55] See Adams' analysis of Ockham's theory of intensification and reduction of forms, where he contrasts sudden and successive changes, in *Ockham*, pp. 697-740.

[56] Adams, *Ockham*, p. 994.

[57] In the introduction to his edition to *The Tractatus de Successivis Attributed to William of Ockham* (St. Bonaventure, New York: The Franciscan Institute, 1944), p. 30, Philotheus Boehner refers the reader to the following passage from Part I, chapter 44 of Ockham's *Summa logicae*: "Ideo est alia opinio de quantitate, quae mihi videtur esse de mente Aristotelis, sive sit haeretica sive catholica, quam volo nunc recitare, quamvis nolim eam asserere. Et ideo quando illam opinionem posui et scripsi super Philosophiam

concur with Aristotle's. It was widely accepted in the fourteenth century that change is continuous and can be observed only by examining the body undergoing change. Ockham suggested that his position made it easier to explain the difference between regular, cyclical motion (such as the movements of the heavenly bodies) and irregular change (such as the growth of a tree), which was a perennial problem for the Aristotelians. Nonetheless, Ockham firmly stated that his theory was sanctioned and even dictated by Aristotelian physics.

Ockham begins his discussion of time in the *Tractatus de successivis* by positing that time, like motion and place, "is not something in itself totally distinct from a permanent thing."[58] He goes on immediately to point out that, as Aristotle says, time is inextricably bound up with motion and is part of the process by which an object is changed.[59] Time and motion therefore share the characteristic of being intrinsic in a particular body; they do not exist apart from the reality of matter. This assertion does not contradict Aristotle, who acknowledged himself that one cannot observe time without observing change in some physical body. Ockham continues in his interpretation of Aristotle by developing the orthodox principle that time and motion are really different aspects of the same phenomenon.[60] Because time is the measure of change in a

---

[vz., the *Expositio aurea* and the *Expositio super libros Physicorum*], non scripsi eam tamquam meam, sed tamquam Aristotelis, quam exposui ut mihi videbatur; et eodem modo nunc sine assertione recitabo eam. Est autem ista opinio, quam etiam multi theologi tenent et tenuerunt, quod scilicet nulla quantitas est realiter distincta a substantia et qualitate, sive tales propositiones: substantia est quantitas, qualitas est quantitas, sin concedendae, sive non." For the entire chapter, see *Venerabilis Inceptoris Guillelmi de Ockham Summa logicae*, eds. Philotheus Boehner, Gedeon Gal and Stephanus Brown (St. Bonaventure, New York: The Franciscan Institute, 1974), pp. 132-39. See also Adams, *Ockham*, pp. 853-99, for an account of how Ockham's view of time accords with and differs from Aristotle's.

[58] Boehner, ed., *Tractatus de Successivis*, p. 96: " . . . tempus non est aliquid secundum se totum distincta a rebus permanentibus."

[59] *Tractatus de Successivis*, p. 97: "Dum motus durat, oportet necessario quod aliquid sit futurum, quod non habet esse extra animam, quamvis possit cognosci ab anima; et praeter illud est aliquid importatum realiter per hoc nomen motus, quod est est realiter extra animam; et ita si accipiatur quasi unum aggregatum ex omnibus, quae importantur per hoc nomen motus, oportet quod sit aliquid extra animam et aliquid quod non est extra animam, quamvis possit cognosci ab anima."

[60] *Ibid.*, pp. 98-99: "Verumtamen sciendum, quod aliquo modo magis dependet tempus ab anima quam motus, quia sicut declarabitur, tempus non est aliqua res distincta a motu. . . . Servando talem modum loquendi, isti aequivalent: motus est tempus, et: motus est motus, quo anima cognoscit, quantus est alius motus. Et ita cum illud praedicatum motus, quo aliquis cognoscit, quantus est motus alius, non possit competere alicui sine anima, ideo impossibile est, quod motus sit tempus nisi per animam; sicut

particular object, moreover, it has no meaning outside the context of the motion of a physical body.[61]

Although time is an observable phenomenon which accompanies motion, it is not its own substance and therefore cannot have parts. Ockham clarifies this Aristotelian language about time by arguing that time does not consist of the parts past, present and future; rather, time is divided into past or future with respect to the individual objects which endure.[62] By analogy, says Ockham, one could imagine that a length of time is like a line which, being a continuum, can be divided infinitely. In reality, however, neither lines nor times exist as an infinite series of atoms or parts.[63] Certainly no one could physically divide these entities into as many parts as is theoretically possible. Thus the infinite divisibility of a continuum is, as far as Ockham is concerned, a reasonable theoretical and logical definition but also, as Aristotle himself freely admits, an extremely difficult one for the human mind to comprehend.[64] Ockham therefore presents his thesis that time, motion and place are inherent in objects as a practical solution to the problem of recognizing infinities in physical matter.

In the case of instants, for example, Ockham argues that, in contrast to what contemporaries (*moderni*) claim, instants are inherent in real things and are not abstract, whether they can be divided infinitely or

---

impossibile, est quod motus sit illud, quo mensurat anima motum sine anima. Et ita patet, quod in definitione exprimente quid nominis temporis necessario ponitur operatio animae. Et propter hic dicit Commentator commento 88⁰, quod 'tempus est de numero entium, quorum actus completur per animam.'"

[61] *Ibid.*, p. 99: ". . . unde tempus potest esse motus sine anima, sed nullo modo tempus potest esse tempus sine anima."

[62] In *The Logic of William of Ockham* (New York: Russell and Russell, 1965), p. 147, Moody takes the following quotation from Ockham's *Expositio aurea et admodum utilis super artem veterem edita per venerabilem Guillelmi de Ockham cum quaestionibus Alberti parvi de Saxonia* Part II, f. 55r (Bononiae: 1496; reprinted 1965): "Praeterea quod tempus non est aliqua res talis alia ostendo, quia omnis res per se una habens partes distantes realiter, si sic accidens, est in aliquo subiective tam secundum se quam secundum partes suas. Sed tempus non est in aliquo subiective tanquam unum accidens ipsius, quia subiectum non est subiectum alicuius nisi quod actualiter existit, sed partes temporibus non existunt secundum istos. . . . Praeterea, nulla pars temporis est, quid nec praeterita nec futura, igitur nec ipsum tempus est aliqua res distincta totaliter ab aliis rebus."

[63] *Ibid.*, II, 78v; quoted in Moody, p. 171: ". . . quando non dicat rem talem aliam . . . quia sic necessario derelinquitur ex tempore in re, sed hoc est impossibile, nam tunc in illa re quae fuit infinitis instantibus esset tales res infinitate . . . ."

[64] Goddu, p. 167.

not.[65] Ockham does not see any contradiction in holding this view while
at the same time using Aristotle's own arguments for infinite divisibility
of instants to refute Zeno's half-distance paradox.[66] Yet, while he
willingly accepts the traditional position on the theoretical nature of the
divisibility of continua, Ockham is reluctant to minimize the integrity of
individual continuous entities. A continuum is not merely composed of
its divisible parts: a finite line is simply a line, not an infinite series of
points, just as a finite period of time is not a procession of individual
instants.[67]

This review of Ockham's position on continuity and time serves to
illustrate his ready acceptance of certain Aristotelian concepts and his
firm rejection of others. Ockham saw no difficulty in seeing time as the
measure of motion or as the number of motion according to before and
after.[68] He conceived of time as being both continuous and successive
and admitted that time is discrete because "the mind divides motion into
prior and posterior, and numbers the prior and posterior parts in
motion."[69] With Aristotle he affirmed that the circular movements of
the heavenly bodies provide a uniform standard by which one can
measure other times and motions.[70] In fact, Ockham's teaching on
continuity conformed to Aristotle's in every major respect with one
significant exception. For Ockham, time was not some relation distinct
from permanent things, as Aristotle had claimed, but was a relative or
connotative name.[71] To say "time is" is equivalent to saying "something

---

[65] *Tractatus de Successivis*, pp. 120-21: "Et quod instans non sit talis res raptim
transiens secundum se totum distincta ab omni re permanente, sicut moderni ponunt,
ostendo breviter sic: Tum quia aut est substantia aut accidens; non substantia, quia nec
materia nec forma nec compositum. Nec accidens, quia quaero de subiecto eius primo:
Aut est divisibile aut individibile. Non primum, quia quando subiectum primum est
divisibile; ipsum accidens existens in eo est divisibile. Si detur secundum, scilicet quod
subiectum primum est indivisibile tunc quaero de isto subiecto: Aut est substantia aut
accidens.   Non primum, quia nec substantia corporea nec incorporea, sicut patet
inductive. Nec accidens quia quaerendum est de subiecto eius primo, et sic in infinitum.
Tum quia in tempore finito esset res infinitae secundum se totas distinctae pertransitae.
Tum quia non possit dari, quomodo talis res possit corrumpi, quia nec per corruptionem
sui subiecti nec per inductionem contrarii nec per subtractionem causae conservantis vel
per eius absentiam, sicut patet inductive."
[66] Goddu develops this idea at length in his chapter on Ockham's view of place, pp. 112-36.
[67] Goddu, p. 32.
[68] *Ibid.*, p. 144.
[69] *Ibid.*, p. 46.
[70] *Ibid.*, pp. 141-42.
[71] See in *Ockham*, Adams' treatment of Ockham's views about names, especially
Chapter 3: "Names and Concepts," pp. 71-107.

is moved whence the mind measures how much another thing is moved."[72] This apparently minor distinction actually reflected the main thrust of Ockham's attack on Aristotelian metaphysics, which he pursued in several different contexts. In short, Ockham repeatedly showed his willingness to draw on Aristotle for explanations of certain natural phenomena but freely interpreted and revised Aristotle when Aristotle's ideas conflicted with his own logical principles.

In the *De continuo*, Bradwardine sought, like Ockham, to make the concept of continuity more comprehensible. Whereas Ockham had relied on propositional logic for this purpose, Bradwardine characteristically turned to geometry, even, at times, to the point of ignoring major logical problems which called into question his mathematical calculations.[73] Although both Bradwardine and Ockham conceived of continuity and time primarily in Aristotelian terms, Euclid's *Elements* provided the inspiration for Bradwardine's approach in the *De continuo*. As with the *De proportionibus*, Bradwardine emphasized in the *De continuo* the necessity of applying mathematics to the study of natural philosophy, remarking:

> No one studying physics can hope to succeed unless he uses mathematics and is helped by its aid and counsel, for it is a discipline which reveals every genuine truth, knows every hidden secret, and holds the key to every subtlety of letters; whoever, then, presumes to study physics while neglecting mathematics should know from the start that he will never make his entry through the portals of wisdom.[74]

Thus Bradwardine made use of a mathematical argument to try to disprove the atomist position that continua are composed of indivisibles. In the course of this analysis, Bradwardine encountered Ockham's problem

---

[72] Goddu, p. 139, cites *Quaestiones in libros physicorum*, MS Paris Bib. Nat. Lat. 17841, quaestio 39; and also quaestio 40, "tempus est motus quo anima cognoscit quantus alius motus."

[73] Goddu, p. 167, suggests, for example, a connection between Bradwardine's critique of atomism and his derivation of instantaneous velocities. Although Bradwardine did not support the atomist position, he often took advantage of atomist reasoning when it suited his mathematical analysis.

[74] *De continuo*, p. 63, ll. 3-7: "Nullus enim physico certamine se speret gavisurum triumpho nisi mathematice utatur, consilio et auxilio confortetur. Ipsa enim revelatrix omnis veritatis sincere, et novit omne secretum absconditum, ac omnium literarum subtilium clavem gerit. Quicumque igitur ipsa neglecta physicari presumpserit, sapientie ianuam se numquam ingressurum agnoscat." The last part of this translation is based on Weisheipl's translation in *The Development of Physical Theory in the Middle Ages*, p. 73. See also Murdoch's introduction to the *De continuo*, p. 59, hereafter cited as "Murdoch."

of explaining how the theoretically acceptable premise of infinite divisibility could be demonstrated in the physical world. Unlike Ockham, who had been content to define the problem without resolving it, Bradwardine attempted to devise a mathematical solution. In the *De continuo*, Bradwardine examined several kinds of continua, both physical and purely mathematical. In general, his analysis of mathematical continua was more successful than his treatments of various physical continua, although his application of mathematical models to the continuity of time proved to be extremely fruitful.[75]

Bradwardine tried in the *De continuo* to dismantle the atomists' position by demonstrating the absurdity of their main principles. Beginning with an extensive list of definitions, Bradwardine went on to develop one hundred and fifty-one propositions concerning continua, drawing primarily on geometrical arguments to establish his case against atomism. So mathematically meticulous was his procedure that he waited until Proposition 141 to state explicitly his thesis that a continuum cannot be composed of indivisibles.[76] This concept is implicit, however, throughout the work and it dominates his analysis of both geometrical and physical continua. In the *De continuo* Bradwardine not only borrowed freely from Aristotelian physical theory but also derived his own position in favor of infinite divisibility from Euclidean mathematics. Often, as in the *De proportionibus*, Bradwardine used Euclidian concepts to correct Aristotle's analysis of a physical problem. In the case of Bradwardine's theory of imposition, for example, he demonstrated geometrically that two continua could overlap to form one continuum in order to avoid Aristotle's ambiguous distinction between continuous and contiguous elements.[77] The advantage of this theory for natural philosophy was that Bradwardine could use it to prove that physical continua such as motion and time can have discrete parts or segments and still remain connected to the rest of the continuum.

---

[75] This interpretation is one of the major thrusts of Murdoch's research on the *De continuo* and is well borne out by reading his edition of Bradwardine's text. The following analysis of the *De continuo* is based on my reading of Bradwardine with appropriate reference to Murdoch's analysis.

[76] *De continuo*, p. 121, l. 5: "Nullam continuum ex athomis integrari." Here Bradwardine uses the term "athomis" to mean an individual "now" or instant of time which is itself infinitely divisible, as opposed to a time segment which consists of a series of consecutive instants. This use of the term "athomis" is consistent with Aristotelian physics and does not imply that an atom of time is indivisible.

[77] For a discussion of this problem see Murdoch, pp. 89-91.

Bradwardine's main targets in the *De continuo* were the advocates of immediate indivisibilism, who believed that continua are composed of a series of indivisible points between which there are no additional points. With the aid of Euclidean geometry, Bradwardine successfully refuted them. Realizing that geometry alone could not conclusively disprove immediate indivisibilism, he did not even attempt to refute the theory of mediate indivisibility, which posits that between any two indivisibles in a continuum there is always another indivisible.[78] Despite its relatively limited scope, however, the *De continuo* achieved its main aim of undermining mathematically the principle of indivisibility on which all atomist theories depend.

Bradwardine begins his refutation of atomism with an examination of several types of continua, both mathematical and physical, and in the process he explicitly delineates his view of time. At the outset of the *De continuo* Bradwardine introduces his conception of time as a continuum in a series of definitions pertaining to continuous substances. After defining the continuum itself as a quality whose parts are mutually connected (*ad invicem copulantur*), he proceeds to distinguish between permanent continua, whose parts exist simultaneously, and successive continua, whose parts, in the words of Aristotle, succeed according to before and after (*succedunt secundum prius et posterius*). In definitions four, five and six Bradwardine gives solids, planes and lines as examples of permanent continua. Definitions nine and eleven establish time and motion as successive continua. Definition ten defines an instant as an atom of time. In these definitions, Bradwardine emphasizes the connection between motion and time by defining motion as a successive continuum measured by time (*continuum successivum tempore mensuratum*). Time, on the other hand, is measured not by motion but by its own successiveness: *tempus est continuum successivum successionem mensurans*.[79]

In definitions seventeen to twenty-two Bradwardine explains how the terms past, present, future, beginning and ending should be applied to successive continua.[80] These definitions provide the foundation for

---

[78] Murdoch, p. 247.

[79] *De continuo*, p. 1, ll. 1-15.

[80] *Ibid.*, p. 2, l. 5 - p. 3 l. 2: "17. Aliquod post aliud esse, fuisse, vel fore est ipsum cum medio inter illa esse, fuisse, vel fore. 18. Aliquod immediate post aliud esse, fuisse, vel fore est ipsum sine medio esse, fuisse, vel fore. 19. Incipere esse per affirmationem de presenti et negationem de preterito est nunc esse et immediate ante hoc non fuisse. 20. Incipere esse per negationem de presenti et affirmationem de futuro est nunc non esse et immediate post hoc fore. 21. Destinere esse per negationem de presenti et

examining time by establishing that all successive continua are essentially temporal: they are not simultaneous but have some parts which exist before other parts. When one wishes to consider a successive thing or a particular segment of a successive continuum, says Bradwardine, one must determine the first and last instants of its existence. Definitions nineteen to twenty-two provide specific rules for making these determinations under various conditions.

In his propositions and corollaries Bradwardine was able to comment at greater length on the features of time which his definitions could only imply. Some aspects of time which Bradwardine considered in the treatise include the infinity of time, its relation to motion, its composition and the beginnings and endings of time segments. In pursuing these topics Bradwardine rarely strayed from an Aristotelian framework. His mathematical approach allowed him to focus on the physical and geometrical characteristics of time without reference to broader metaphysical or theological issues. In this way Bradwardine proved himself an advocate of Ockham's methods of isolation and imagination experiment. Bradwardine's analysis of infinity, for example, rested firmly on the classical Greek sources, particularly Aristotle's *Physics*.[81] Quite apart from any possible theological considerations, Bradwardine accepted the thesis that time is infinite in the Aristotelian sense, that is, time is infinitely divisible and moves in a forward direction. As a geometer, Bradwardine preferred to regard infinity as a fundamental concept uncomplicated by inappropriate logical concerns. He therefore pointed out the logical inconsistencies that could result from applying the concept of infinity to either singular or universal things. In the process of condemning a logical argument which confused universals with particular things, Bradwardine clearly categorized time and geometrical points as universal infinities; for although a mountain of gold, say, is continuous throughout, it has physical limits which time and geometrical entities do not.[82]

---

affirmationem de preterito est nunc non esse et immediate ante hoc fuisse. 22. Destinere esse per affirmationem de presenti et negationem de futuro est nunc esse immediate post hoc non fore." The implications of these definitions will be discussed at length in Chapter Six, which examines Bradwardine's view of contingency.

[81] *De continuo*, p. 4, l. 13: "Pro istis duabus diffinitionibus est sciendum, quod secundum Philosophum tertio *Physicorum*, ratio infiniti quantitati congruit."

[82] *Ibid.*, p. 9, l.6 - p. 10, l. 2: "Si autem dicatur quod est negativa, aut est universalis, aut particularis, indefinita, vel singularis. Singularis autem non est propter rationem predictam; nec est indefinita vel particularis, quia tunc ille essent vere: 'Infinitum est mundus,' 'Infinita puncta sunt duo puncta,' 'Infinita chymere currunt,' qui universales

It is the infinity of time, moreover, which makes it the measure of finity in motion and space. Bradwardine explicitly states the connection between motion, time and space in his first proposition concerning continua, which restates Aristotle's thesis that a continuous quality can be divided infinitely:

> 6. Every body, surface, line and point can be moved uniformly and continually. 7. In the case of two local motions which are continued in the same or equal times, the velocities and distances traversed by these [movements] are proportional, i.e., as one velocity is to the other, so the space traversed by the one is to the space traversed by the other. 8. In the case of two local motions traversing the same or equal spaces, the velocities are inversely proportional to time, i.e., as the first velocity is to the second, so the time of the second velocity is to the time of the first. 9. A [given] moving body can be moved at any speed whatsoever or a [given] space can be traversed by any [body] at all. 10. The being or non-being [of finite things] is measured in a certain time.[83]

In an argument strongly reminiscent of those in the *De proportionibus*, Bradwardine establishes here the Euclidean principles that geometrical entities can be moved continuously and that the speed and position of a moving object can be varied.

Bradwardine turns next to the theories of proportional velocity which he first developed in the *De proportionibus* to prove that his conclusions about continuous motion in geometrical entities can be applied equally well to observable motions. The notable difference between his

---

affirmative contradicentes eis sunt false, et alique illarum habent aliquas singulare veras ut: 'Hoc finitum non est mundus,' 'Hec puncta non sunt duo puncta.' Item, in sua exponente negation precedit totum, igitur est universalis negativa. Ideo, forte dicitur quod est universalis negativa, sed tunc sunt iste vere: 'Infinitum est mons aureus,' 'Infinita chymere currunt,' 'Infiniti mundi sunt,' quia particulares affirmative contradicientes eis sunt falsa. Et iste sunt false: 'Infinitum tempus est finitum,' et 'Infinita puncta sunt finita'; significent enim quod nullam tempus est finitum, et quod nulla puncta sunt finita; que tamen solent concedi et debent."

[83] *Ibid.*, p. 11, l. 13 - p. 12, l. 6: "6. Omne corpus, superficiem, lineam, acque punctum, uniformiter et continue posse moveri. 7. Omnium duorum motuum localium eodem tempore vel equalibus temporibus continuatorum velocitates et spacia illis pertransita eodem tempore proportionales existere. Id est, sicud una velocitatum ad aliam, ita spaciam per unam velocitatem pertransitum ad spacium per aliam pertransitum. 8. Omnium duorum motuum localium super idem spacium vel equalia deditorum, velocitates et tempora proportionales econtrario semper esse. Id est sicud velocitas prima ad secundam, ita tempus secunde velocitatis ad tempus prime. 9. Quacumque velocitate vel tarditate potest unum mobile moveri, vel unum spacium quodcumque pertransiri potest quocumque. 10. Esse vel non esse finitum certo tempore mensuratur." Suppositions 6-8, trans. Clagett, pp. 230-31. Suppositions 9 and 10, my translation.

treatment of this subject in the *De continuo* and similar ones found in the *De proportionibus* is Bradwardine's explicit recognition in the *De continuo* of the role of time in the process of measuring motion. Although he had accounted for time in his calculations in the *De proportionibus*, it is only in the *De continuo* that he defines time as the continuous, uniform standard by which velocities can be measured. Moreover, supposition ten accords the continuum of time an even larger cosmological significance, for, if the being or non-being of finite things is measured by time, every created thing is subject to temporal limits.[84]

Because he had no wish in the *De continuo* to explore the theological ramifications of his temporal theory, we should not be surprised to find him concentrating on the mathematical consequences of his characteristically Aristotelian approach to motion, time and space. The majority of subsequent propositions which mention time follow the pattern of the *De proportionibus*, in which time appears as a necessary constant in measuring motion. Bradwardine's technique in the *De continuo* was first to illustrate some feature of continuity in purely geometrical terms and then to show how this feature influenced a physical continuum such as time, motion or temperature. After describing the continuity of points in a circle, for example, Bradwardine turned in proposition twenty-four to an analysis of uniform circular motion in which time provides the test and measure of uniformity.[85] In making this transition Bradwardine implicitly acknowledged that geometrical successiveness is a kind of timeless motion. The reality of motion in the physical world, on the other hand, depends on temporal definition. Time, therefore, is a prerequisite for all physical continua whether successive, as with motion, or permanent, as with space.

Thus Bradwardine shows early in the *De continuo* that time is the central concept in his arguments that the continuity of proportional motion is equivalent to the continuity of a geometrical line and that motions, like lines, are infinitely divisible.[86] To demonstrate the divisibility of motion, Bradwardine once again begins with a purely geometrical proof. Propositions thirty-two through forty-two offer an elaborate Euclidean analysis of the divisibility of lines and angles, as

---

[84] Murdoch, pp. 96-97. In proposition 121 Bradwardine applies the same argument to the physical continuum of temperature (*De continuo*, p. 106, l. 15 - p. 107, l. 1).

[85] *De continuo*, p. 38, ll. 8-12. In a slightly different context, in proposition 124, Bradwardine makes a similar observation about the importance of time in other physical continua, again using temperature as an illustration.

[86] Murdoch, pp. 166-67.

well as a thorough discussion of the mediate divisibility of points. In the next eight propositions Bradwardine applies this analysis to motion. Rather than arguing positively that motion must be divisible, however, Bradwardine focuses on the absurdities of claiming, like the Pythagoreans and Henry of Harclay, that uniform motion and time are composed of indivisibles.[87] The actual form which this negative argument takes has little bearing on Bradwardine's view of time and offers no additional insight into it. Nevertheless, his constant repetition of the connection between the continua of time and motion reinforces the Aristotelian definitions of time which he presents at the beginning of the treatise.

Bradwardine's analysis of the composition of continua forced him to think about a more complicated problem, one which Aristotle himself had only partially solved. Bradwardine's Euclidean models depended on the axiom that geometrical entities can be divided and that these divisions occur at specific points. Although he could conceive of such points as atoms, he did not consider them indivisible, as his opponents did. In Bradwardine's view, physical continua are even less subject to an atomistic analysis than geometrical ones, which led him to declare in proposition 100: "It is manifest that no natural substance is composed of finite atoms."[88] There follows a geometric proof which demonstrates the equivalence of proportional velocities occurring in equal times. In fact, Bradwardine asserts, the opposite conclusion, that motions occurring in equal times are not proportional on account of their composition out of distinct indivisibles, is unreasonable and contrary to principles already proven in the De proportionibus.[89] As Murdoch observes, however, Bradwardine's distinction between the two conceptions of the physical composition of continua is not entirely convincing because it is based only on a negative argument.[90]

Bradwardine's strategy against the atomists was more successful when he avoided altogether the issue of indivisible atomism and

---

[87] De continuo, p. 52, ll. 7-11: "Si sic, motus uniformis per unum gradum velocior alio equali sibi in tempore acquirit plus illo, et per nullam divisibile sed per indivisibile tantum. Postquam reprobavit opiniones Pytagori et Henrici in quo conveniunt per rationes geometricas, hic incipit facere idem per rationes naturales."

[88] De continuo, p. 94, ll. 10-12: "Si sic de substantia, velocitatem in motibus proportionem motorum ad sua mota non sequi. Quare manifestum est: substantiam naturalem compositam ex finitis athomis non componi."

[89] De continuo, p. 94, l. 12 - p. 95, l. 14.

[90] Murdoch, pp. 50-52, outlines Bradwardine's method of establishing points through negative arguments, that is through proving that a proposition is untenable, and contrasts it with his more positive method of proving propositions through geometric analysis.

concentrated instead on the equivalence of continuity within motion. In proposition 105, for example, he drew on the principle of equal infinities to prove that equivalent continua have an equal number of components, whether those components are divisible or indivisible. Again, the continuum of time served as the necessary standard by which to measure this equivalence.[91]   Bradwardine restated this position even more strongly in proposition 120, in which he added the dimension of varying speeds of velocities. Here he implied that it is the divisible nature of time which makes it possible to compare the relative speed of motions.[92] These considerations about the continuity of motion eventually helped Bradwardine to dismiss the theory that continua can be composed of immediate indivisibles. His whole theory of imposition rested on his assumption that equivalent continua have the same number of components and so can be superimposed. In Bradwardine's view, then, time has the crucial function in natural philosophy of bridging the gap between the theoretical nature of geometrical continua and real, physical continua existing within a temporal framework.

In contrast to the *De proportionibus*, the *De continuo* provides a concrete definition of time according to Aristotelian principles. Bradwardine presents time as a successive continuum which can be divided infinitely into time-atoms or instants, which are themselves subject to further division. Time is the single continuum which governs all other physical continua including motion, space and temperature. For all that, Bradwardine does not invest time with any independent physical reality, nor does he consider in any depth how time can be used practically to measure other continua: time is a measure of motion, but motion is not a measure of time, according to Bradwardine's initial definitions. This vagueness actually helps Bradwardine to make time a pivotal concept for comparing geometrical and physical continua by means of Euclidean geometry.

---

[91] *De continuo*, p. 97, l. 19 - p. 98, l. 6: "Si sic, omnis motus similis speciei in velocitatibus adequari. Quia per quemlibet, in quolibet instanti temporibus mensurantis motum, acquiritur unum indivisibile tantum, ut patet per 26[am] et eius corollarium manifeste; igitur omnia illa indivisibilia acquisita sunt equalia illis instantibus tempori, igitur sunt equalis inter se, igitur per secundam, continua composita ex illis sunt equalia, ex quo patet propositum."

[92] *De continuo*, p. 116, ll. 3-10: "Si sic, omnes velocitates et tarditates motuum equale esse. Hec sequitur ex proxima. Ad item: per 26[am] et eius corollarium, per omnem motum semper in uno instanti acquiritur unum indivisibile tantum; igitur indivisibilia acquisita per quemcumque motum in aliquo tempore sunt equalia numero instantibus illius temporis, et per consequens quibuscumque indivisibilius acquisitis per motum in eodem tempore. Igitur, per 26[am], continua composita ex illis sunt equala. Igitur motus sunt equeveloces."

Bradwardine's view of time is thus both strikingly Aristotelian in its identification of time with motion and strikingly non-Aristotelian in its elevation of mathematical reasoning to a degree not found in any of his predecessors. In this respect, Bradwardine's isolation of the problems of time and continuity from other metaphysical considerations is similar to Ockham's; and, of course, on a theoretical level, both of them reach the same conclusions about the nature of permanent and successive continua. Bradwardine's implicit acknowledgment that geometrical figures do not represent real things indicates, for example, at least partial agreement with Ockham's criticism of Aristotelian physics. Both Bradwardine and Ockham realize that, by intermingling geometrical and physical continua, Aristotle failed to distinguish them adequately or to take into account the real usefulness of geometrical continua in the investigation of natural philosophy. In proposition 151, Bradwardine actually claims that "there are no surfaces, lines or points at all."[93] Of course, Bradwardine's denial of a separate reality for these entities does not amount to an affirmation of Ockham's thesis that these concepts have no reality apart from a real physical object. In the De continuo, Bradwardine simply wants to point out the practical difficulties of describing physical continua geometrically, so he consciously avoids broader metaphysical considerations. Nevertheless, proposition 151 clearly indicates Bradwardine's conviction that the proper goal of geometry is to study real solids,[94] a position with which Ockham would have concurred.

Furthermore, Bradwardine did not follow Ockham in defining motion as an inherent part of a moving object. Throughout the De continuo, Bradwardine maintained Aristotle's position that motion and time are categories of being and consequently failed to identify exactly how the continuity of space and time influences the continuity of motion.[95] Although Ockham's approach to the fundamental problem of time more directly challenged Aristotelian presuppositions, neither Ockham nor his immediate followers solved the problems presented by physical continua in a way that is more convincing than Bradwardine's. Still, in their studies of time and continuity, both Ockham and Bradwardine were able to suggest new methods for investigating an ancient problem and they successfully expanded for a more skeptical fourteenth-century audience the Aristotelian definitions of time and motion found in the writings of Averroes and Aquinas.

---

[93] De continuo, p. 132, l. 20: "Superficiem, lineam, sive punctum omnio non esse."
[94] Murdoch, p. 196.
[95] Murdoch, p. 173.

CHAPTER SIX

TIME AND CONTINGENCY

Closely related to continuity was the problem of contingency, which often concerns the predictability of continuous events. Unlike continuity, however, contingency did not easily lend itself to mathematical analysis. For this reason, discussions of contingency in the Aristotelian corpus and in the medieval treatments it prompted were primarily linguistic or logical in character. Still, Bradwardine's devotion to Aristotle, who had originally posed the problem of contingency in Book IX of his *De interpretatione,* and the general importance of this topic in late medieval scholarly debates stimulated Bradwardine's interest in contingency in spite of its fundamentally nonmathematical nature. Although geometry certainly influenced his view of contingency, Bradwardine was forced to employ other methods when he confronted the problem of contingency.

In the *De incipit et desinit* and the *De futuris contingentibus,* Bradwardine examined some of the logical and psychological aspects of time which a purely mathematical approach could not properly consider. These texts complement his scientific writing about time because they present an alternative, more metaphysical view of time based not on its relationship to motion but on its enigmatic capacity to link the past to the future. Bradwardine's early work on contingency reveals both a profound interest in the problem of time and also the origins of the mature opinions concerning predestination and divine foreknowledge which dominate the *De causa Dei.* It is in the *De incipit et desinit* and the *De futuris contingentibus,* moreover, that we find the clearest evidence of Bradwardine's early interaction with the most influential logicians of his day, particularly William of Ockham.

The wide variety of medieval discussions about contingency makes it necessary to restrict this analysis to aspects of the problem which specifically concern time as a successive continuum. The preceding examination of Bradwardine's concept of time in the *De proportionibus* and the *De continuo* has shown that he largely accepted Aristotle's definition of time as the number or measure of motion according to before and after. He also concurred with Aristotle that time, like motion, is successive and infinitely divisible. Thus time and motion cannot be considered as separate entities. These Aristotelian principles define a rational natural order which can be investigated through observation and mathematical analysis. Bradwardine found this notion of rationality very appealing. Unfortunately, even Aristotle recognized that his definitions were not entirely compatible with human perceptions of time. The ambivalence about time in Aristotle's natural philosophy encouraged discussions of contingency from the classical age through the middle ages. This chapter highlights the two aspects of contingency which have the greatest bearing on Bradwardine's view of time: prediction in the context of beginning and ceasing within a continuum, and the question of whether a future event can be both contingent and foreknown by God.

The problem of prediction which features so prominently in Bradwardine's view of contingency originated in Aristotle's physical theory. Bradwardine's interest in this problem grew out of his study of the attempts of some medieval logicians to use the principles of Aristotelian physics to make predictions. Although the subject of prediction has received relatively little attention from modern scholars, those who have studied it agree that medieval thinkers often saw prediction as a subject properly belonging to the discipline of physics, in that prediction involves assessing a change in the natural world; and, because Aristotle had defined change as a continuous process, prediction involved determining where a particular observed change actually began and ended. Hence, medieval thinkers produced a considerable number of treatises on the topic of beginning and ceasing in a continuum. Aristotle himself provided the starting-point for these discussions by suggesting that specific changes in a natural process could be measured against the universal continuum of time.[1] Having established that time, like the motion it measures, is an infinitely divisible continuum, Aristotle then had to explain how a change could begin or end in a point or now of time when a now is both divisible and singular. To do so, he adopted the Euclidean image of points on a line: if two things cannot occur in the same now, neither can the process of moving from a state of rest to a state of motion be described as occurring within a single now. Aristotle identified the difficulty of assigning a first moment of motion in Book V of the *Physics*:

---

[1] See Norman Kretzmann, "Incipit/Desinit," *MTSM*, p. 102. Sorabji reviews Aristotle's position and subsequent treatments of it through the early fourteenth century in Chapter 26 of *Time, Creation and the Continuum*, pp. 403-21.

And not only must that which is changing have changed, but that which has changed must also previously have been changing, since everything that has changed from something to something has changed in a period of time. For suppose that a thing has changed from A to B in a now. Now the now in which it has changed cannot be the same as that in which it is at A (since in that case it would be A and B at once); for we have shown above that that which has changed, when it has changed, is not in that from which it has changed. If, on the other hand, it is a different now, there will be a period of time intermediate between the two; for, as we saw, nows are not consecutive. Since, then, it has changed in a period of time, and all time is divisible, in half the time it will have completed another change, in a quarter another, and so on always; consequently it must have previously been changing.[2]

On the basis of this argument, Aristotle went on to show that these ambiguities surrounding beginning and ceasing resulted directly from his definition of continuity:

So it is evident also that that which has become must previously have been becoming, and that which is becoming must previously have become, everything (that is) that is divisible and continuous. . . . So, too, in the case of that which is perishing and that which has perished; for that which becomes and that which perishes must contain an element of infiniteness since they are continuous things. . . . It is evident, then, that what has become must previously have been becoming, and that which is becoming must previously have become; for all magnitudes and all periods are always divisible.[3]

---

[2] *Physica*, VI, 6.237a17-28, p. 240: "Non solum autem quod mutatur necesse est mutatum esse, sed et mutatum esse necesse est mutari prius; omne enim quod ex quodam in quiddam mutatum est, in tempore mutatum est. Sit enim in ipso nunc ex A in B mutatum esse. Ergo in eodem quidem nunc in quo est in ipso A, non mutatum est (simul enim esset in ipso A et B); quod enim mutatum est, quando mutatum est, quod non est in hoc, ostensum est prius; si vero in alio est, medio erit tempus; non enim coniuncta erant ipsa nunc. Quoniam igitur in tempore mutatum est, tempus autem omne divisibile est, in medio aliud erit mutatum, et iterum in illius medio aliud, et sic semper; quare mutabitur prius." Trans. Barnes, p. 400.

[3] *Physica*, VI, 6.237b10-22, pp. 241-42: "Manifestum igitur est quoniam et quod factum est necesse est fieri prius et quod fit factum esse, quecumque divisibilia et continua sunt, non tamen semper 'quod' fit, sed aliud aliquando, ut illius aliquid, sicut domus fundamentum. Similiter, autem est et in eo quod corrumpitur et quod corruptum est; mox enim inest ei quod fit et quod corrumpitur infinitum quoddam cum sit continuum, et non erit neque fieri non factum aliquod neque factum esse nisi fiat aliquid, similiter autem est et in corrumpi et in corrupto esse; semper enim erit ipso corrumpi corruptum esse prius, corrupto autem esse corrumpi. Manifestum igitur est quoniam et quod factum est necesse est fieri prius et quod fit factum esse; omnis enim magnitudo et omne tempus semper divisibilia sunt." Trans. Barnes, p. 401.

Thus Aristotle graphically described the dilemma endemic to all studies of continuity: the need to reconcile the simultaneous distinctiveness and connectedness of all parts of a continuum.

Aristotle recognized the frustration involved in sorting out this logical dilemma and admitted that this sort of analysis might thoroughly discourage the observer of an event from trying to determine its precise duration. On the other hand, his approach to continuity suggested that one could reconstruct the past and predict the future (in a limited way, of course) simply by examining a particular successive continuum in its present state. Although Aristotle's theory posed serious difficulties for medieval natural philosophers, who wished to measure events clearly and accurately, it promised tantalizing possibilities to logicians, who welcomed any method which might help to verify the truth of logical propositions. Much of the excitement over beginning and ceasing among medieval thinkers grew out of the philosophical implications of Aristotle's theory. Because Bradwardine was more interested in natural philosophy than in pure logic, he seemed to find the logical implications of beginning and ceasing somewhat confusing and bewildering.

Aristotle was too good an observer of nature to ignore the impracticality of his theory of beginning and ceasing. He knew from his own experience that the mind can discern the beginning and the ceasing of motions: to argue otherwise would be to support, implicitly or explicitly, Zeno's half-distance paradox. Aristotle thus needed to find a way of assigning the precise instant of initial motion without undermining his theory of continuity. His solution to the problem, as he outlined it in Book VIII of the *Physics*, involved the admission that logical considerations must precede physical ones in this case because it is impossible physically to isolate the first instant of a process's beginning or ceasing:

> It is also plain that unless we hold that the point of time that divides earlier from later always belongs only to the later so far as the thing is concerned, we shall be involved in the consequence that the same thing at the same moment is and is not, and that a thing is not at the moment when it has become. It is true that the point is common to both times, the earlier as well as the later, and that, while numerically one and the same, it is not so in definition, being the end of the one and the beginning of the other; but so far as the thing is concerned, it always belongs to the later affection.[4]

---

[4] *Physica*, VIII, 8.263b9-16, p. 325: "Manifestum autem est et quoniam nisi aliquis faciat temporis dividens signum prius et posterius semper posterioris re, erit simul idem esse et non esse, et quando fuit, non esse. Signum quidem igitur utrisque commune est, et primo et posteriori, et idem et unum numero, ratione autem non idem est (huius

If one can logically attribute only one state of being to a given now, Aristotle insisted that the emphasis should be placed on the first instant of being rather than on the last instant of non-being. Similarly, when the motion ceases, emphasis should be placed on the last instant of being instead of the first instant of non-being.[5]

Aristotle's solution generated several commentaries on beginning and ceasing in the middle ages. Lauge Olaf Nielsen suggests, however, that medieval philosophers usually failed to grasp Aristotle's exact position on this subject.[6] A likely source of confusion was Aristotle's own presentation of beginning and ceasing as a physical problem in some of his works and as a linguistic problem in others. Whether they derived their information about beginning and ceasing from Aristotle's *Physics* or from one of Aristotle's grammatical texts, it is certain that medieval thinkers framed their responses to this issue in classical terms. Indeed, as Norman Kretzmann has observed, early medieval thinkers considered beginning and ceasing to be a linguistic problem and regarded the verbs *incipere* and *desinere*, along with other particles of speech, as logically complex.[7] By the twelfth century, logicians had begun to include *incipere* and *desinere* in lists of syncategorematic words (prepositions, adverbs, conjunctions and quantifiers) because they also complicate logical propositions. After syncategorematic analysis, for example, the sentence "Socrates begins to be" becomes "Socrates is now and was not before," just as "Only man is capable of smiling" becomes "Man is capable of smiling and nothing that is not man is capable of smiling."[8] While the syncategorematic analysis of the problem of beginning and ceasing was primarily grammatical and logical, it still exposed the underlying concept of before and after which Aristotle stressed in all of his writings about time and continuity.

---

quidem enim finis, illius autem principium est); re autem semper posterioris passionis est." Trans. Barnes, p. 440.

[5] See Nielsen's discussion of Aristotle in the introduction to his "Thomas Bradwardine's Treatise on 'incipit' and 'desinit': Edition and Introduction," pp. 8-9, hereafter cited as "Nielsen." References to Bradwardine's text will be cited as *De incipit*.

[6] Nielsen, pp. 10-11.

[7] In "Incipit/Desinit," pp. 104-5, Kretzmann suggests that early medieval interest in these words was primarily grammatical and based on the rediscovery of Aristotle's *De sophisticis elenchis*. This is in contrast to Curtis Wilson's thesis, developed in *William Heytesbury: Medieval Logic and the Rise of Mathematical Physics* (Madison, Wisconsin: University of Wisconsin Press, 1960), that medieval logicians were inspired mostly by the passage from Aristotle's *Physics* quoted above.

[8] For discussions of syncategorematic words, see especially Wilson, pp. 11-12, and Nielsen, pp. 10-11.

In the introduction to his edition of Bradwardine's *De incipit et desinit*, Nielsen reviews both the grammatical and the physical approaches which thirteenth- and early fourteenth-century philosophers applied to the problem of beginning and ceasing. According to Nielsen, medieval logicians, having misunderstood what Aristotle had said about this issue, went in the opposite direction from Aristotle when they tried to assign temporal limits. Whereas Aristotle had always affirmed the first and last instants of being in permanent things, many medieval thinkers affirmed the first and last instants of non-being. While Aristotle would have expounded the sentence "Socrates begins to be" as "Socrates is now and was not before," the medieval logician usually expounded it as "Socrates is not now and will be immediately after this." The medieval logicians, therefore, "negated the present and affirmed the future."[9] By Bradwardine's day all discussions of beginning and ceasing stressed this grammatical aspect of the problem, though several scholars, including Bradwardine, also investigated some of its physical aspects.

Nielsen compares Bradwardine's position on beginning and ceasing to the views of his slightly older contemporaries, William Sherwood, Peter of Spain and Walter Burley, to show that a late medieval philosopher's view of time could influence his analysis of the problem as much as his assumptions about grammar.[10] According to Nielsen, Sherwood and Burley rejected both Aristotle's view of time and his solution to the problem of beginning and ceasing. In his *Treatise on Syncategorematic Words*, for example, Sherwood tried to refute a variety of current proposals for establishing limits for permanent and successive continua and for describing the transition from a permanent to a successive continuum. His most significant contribution to the general debate was his logical analysis of different kinds of transition. His thesis concerning beginning and ceasing depended on the presupposition that a point dividing a line cannot be common to two adjacent segments. In this way, Sherwood compromised Aristotle's assertion that time is continuous.[11]

---

[9] Nielsen, pp. 10-11.

[10] William Sherwood was an English master at the University of Paris in the first half of the thirteenth century who wrote extensively on syllogisms and dialectics. Peter of Spain (d. 1277), also a logician at Paris, wrote a number of very influential treatises on logic and physics. For details of their work see Gilson, *History of Christian Philosophy*, pp. 317-23. Walter Burley (ca. 1275-1345), a contemporary of Ockham, was a master of arts at Oxford and, like Bradwardine, was both a fellow at Merton and a member of Richard de Bury's household. Like William of Sherwood and Peter of Spain, Burley specialized in logical studies. For additional information on Burley see *CHLMP*, pp. 888-89.

[11] Nielsen, pp. 11-15. For an edition of Sherwood's treatise on syncategorematic

Burley came to the same conclusion as Sherwood in his *De primo et ultimo instanti*, in which he examined the problem of determining beginning- and end-points in various types of continuous entities. Following Sherwood, Burley relied on a logical argument to prove that a point dividing time into two segments cannot be common to both segments. In Nielsen's view, this un-Aristotelian assumption allowed "the logical necessity of attributing a dividing point to only one segment [to] become an attribute of time itself."[12] Thus Sherwood's and Burley's preference for propositional logic forced them to conceive of time as composed of indivisibles. Because these discussions were primarily linguistic, and so did not even address the physical aspects of time which feature so prominently in Aristotle's treatment of beginning and ceasing, it is not entirely clear whether Sherwood and Burley were aware of the implications of their solutions for natural philosophy as a whole. Nevertheless, insights into beginning and ceasing substantially enriched the purely logical approaches which characterized most early medieval studies of time. Even if they did not have Book VIII of the *Physics* in mind when they formulated their arguments, their general knowledge of Aristotelian physics served to make their criticism of previous theories more sophisticated because it allowed them to supplement logical arguments with appropriate concepts from Aristotelian natural philosophy.[13] Although they did not perceive beginning and ceasing as a physical problem, their implicit attitudes about time as a complex problem for both logicians and natural philosophers represent a significant advance in western medieval responses to the subject.

The tendency to consider beginning and ceasing as at least partially a physical question was more pronounced in the writing of Peter of Spain. In his *Tractatus syncategorimatum*, Peter supplemented his assessment of the logical functions of the words *incipere* and *desinere* with an

---

words see "Syncategoremata," ed. J. Reginald O'Donnell, *Mediaeval Studies*, 3 (1941), pp. 46-93. For a translation and analysis of this text see Norman Kretzmann, *William Sherwood: Treatise on Syncategorematic Words* (Minneapolis, Minnesota: University of Minnesota Press, 1968).

[12] Nielsen, p. 16. See also Wilson, pp. 32-33. For an edition of Burley's text see "'De Primo et Ultimo Instanti' des Walter Burley," eds. Herman and Charlotte Shapiro, *Archiv für Geschichte der Philosophie*, 47 (1966), pp. 157-73.

[13] Kretzmann, "Incipit/Desinit," pp. 108-9. Murdoch and Sylla evaluate Burley's position in "The Science of Motion," in *Science in the Middle Ages*, pp. 242-45, and argue that Burley's logical analysis of this problem was an outgrowth of studies on Aristotelian theories of motion. They emphasize Burley's importance in establishing an approach to the study of limits which later scholars such as Richard Kilvington, William Heyetsbury (and, I would argue, Thomas Bradwardine) expanded.

analysis of permanent and successive continua. He considered the
problem of before and after both grammatically as a matter of tense and
physically in terms of the nature of time.[14] Unlike Sherwood and
Burley, Peter proposed a solution that concurred with Aristotle's view of
time and provided a model for Bradwardine to follow in his own early
attempts to understand beginning and ceasing. The characteristic feature
of Peter's analysis was his emphasis on the infinite divisibility of permanent and successive continua. After briefly explaining why *incipere*
and *desinere* should be classified as syncategorematic words, he devoted
a major portion of his discussion to the physical properties of different
kinds of continua. In distinguishing permanent from successive continua he pointed out that

> the being of permanent things is a whole at one and the same time while
> the being of successive things is not a whole at one and the same time but
> only in a succession of parts. . . . It is impossible that more than one time
> occur at one and the same time, . . . [P]ermanent things are naturally prior
> and successive things naturally posterior, since permanent things are the
> cause of successive things. . . . [Moreover,] permanent things are intrins-
> ically limited while successive things are not limited intrinsically but are
> limited by permanent things—for example, a change is limited by a quan-
> tity or quality.[15]

In other words, Peter employed an Aristotelian argument to prove that
continua are limited in different ways depending on how they exist in
time.

These considerations, Peter goes on to say, play an important role in
the assignment of actual limits:

> Thus as regards permanent things the being of which is obtained in an in-
> divisible [instant], one can give the first instant of their being and of their
> non-being afterwards, but one cannot give the last instant of their not being
> beforehand nor of their being. . . . But as regards successive things—being
> of which is not obtained in an instant, one gives neither the first nor the last
> instant of their being but gives the last instant of their not being beforehand
> and their first instant of their not being afterwards. For while they have
> their being in a certain time, they have not being at the limit of that time;
> and just as there is no interval between time and its limit, so there is none
> between their being and their not being.[16]

---

[14] *Ibid.*
[15] From an excerpt from *Tractatus syncategorematum*, translated by Kretzmann,
"Incipit/Desinit," in Appendix A, pp. 122-23.
[16] *Ibid.*, p. 123.

Although permanent continua necessarily exist in time, their temporal limits are relatively unambiguous: one merely follows the Aristotelian principle of affirming the first and last instants of being. Because successive continua run parallel with time, however, one cannot so easily assess first and last instants: if time is a continuous entity, divided into segments by nows, the first and last instants of a time segment cannot properly be considered part of the successive entity. This perspective comes directly from Aristotle's description of continuity in the *Physics*.

Although he recognized the logical dilemmas that could arise from accepting Aristotle's definitions, Peter did not dwell on them. In the tradition of Aristotle himself, in fact, Peter devised a linguistic solution to the problem of beginning and ceasing which accounted for both Aristotelian physics and contemporary logical studies. The vocabulary which Peter used to express his solution became widely known in academic circles and had a particularly strong influence on Bradwardine. His solution takes the form of five rules concerning the meaning and usage of *incipere*:

> Rule One. When the verb 'begins' occurs with permanent things the being of which is obtained at an indivisible [instant], it indicates an assertion of the present and the negation of the past. . . .
>
> Rule Two. When the verb 'begins' occurs with successive things or with permanent things the being of which is not obtained in an instant, it indicates a negation of the present and an assertion of the future, because successive things do not have being at their outset. . . .
>
> Rule Three. When being is added to the verb 'ceases' it indicates a negation of the present and an assertion of the past, no matter what sort of thing it occurs together with. The reason for this is that one cannot give the last instant of a thing's being whether the thing is permanent or successive. . . .
>
> [Rule Four]. Similarly, when the not being of things that are simply permanent is added to the verb 'ceases,' it indicates a negation of the present and an assertion of the past. . . .
>
> [Rule Five]. But when the not being of successive things is added to 'ceases,' it indicates an assertion of the present and a negation of the future, since one does not give the last instant of not being to successive things.[17]

Peter's analysis of beginning and ceasing had direct bearing on Bradwardine's view of time for several reasons. Most obvious, Bradwardine

---

[17] *Ibid.*, pp. 123-24.

adopted Peter's method for assigning limits in almost every respect in his own treatise on beginning and ceasing, to the point of incorporating large portions of Peter's treatise into his own work. Peter's study also encouraged Bradwardine to think about continuity along the Aristotelian lines which already appealed to him and provided a ready-made vocabulary for expressing his own views about continuity. Though it is not itself a mathematical work, the *Tractatus syncategorimatum* stands in the late medieval tradition of applying Aristotelian physics to apparently nonphysical problems and so possibly contributed to the flourishing of mathematical studies among the Mertonians.[18] Most important, Peter's contentions about ceasing in Rule Five reemphasized Aristotle's suggestion that syncategorematic terms might be used to predict the future. Peter did not develop this idea but later thinkers, including Bradwardine, paid this suggestion considerable attention.

Bradwardine's *De incipit et desinit* and his *Geometria speculativa* were both written in the early 1320s and represent some of his first attempts at academic discourse. Because of their mathematical nature, topics involving beginning and ceasing, continuity and infinity attracted his attention as soon as he undertook advanced studies; and, judging from the content of subsequent work, these topics continued to fascinate him even after he shifted his attention to theological inquiry. Nielsen has established that Bradwardine wrote the *De incipit et desinit* in 1323, while he was in the middle of his arts course. The form and content of the text indicate that Bradwardine wrote it shortly after completing the part of the curriculum which concentrated on logic. In fact, according to Nielsen, the word *igitur* in the first sentence of the text suggests that the discussion of beginning and ceasing might have been part of a larger work listing the functions of several syncategorematic words.[19]

One need not look far to find a reason for the survival of this particular section if Nielsen's conjecture about its relation to Ockham's *Summa logicae* is correct. Nielsen argues that Bradwardine presented his position on beginning and ceasing in response to Ockham's treatment of the same subject in the first book of the *Summa logicae*, which Ockham had completed by 1323. In Book II of the *Summa logicae*, which he revised sometime after 1323, Ockham advanced a

---

[18] See Kretzmann, "Incipit/Desinit," p. 121 and Wilson, p. 31.

[19] Nielsen, p. 6. The *De incipit* is a fragment and has no specific title. The first sentence of the fragment (*De incipit*, 1.1, p. 47) reads as follows: "Ad clariorem igitur notitiam istarum duarum dictionum 'incipit' et 'desinit' habendam in primis taliter procedimus."

substantially different opinion on the same topic. Nielsen's analysis of these passages suggests that Ockham not only considerably modified his position on beginning and ceasing after 1323 but did so directly in accordance with Bradwardine's criticisms of his original position.[20] If indeed an arts student was able to persuade Ockham to change his mind on this issue, it might be wise to reconsider the precise nature of their relationship. Most comparisons of Ockham and Bradwardine emphasize Ockham's influence on Bradwardine's theology, especially in the negative sense that Ockham's views prompted a fierce response on Bradwardine's part. Nielsen's research indicates that the connection between the two thinkers was probably much more complex, collegial and mutually stimulating than the conventional interpretation of their interaction has recognized.

The narrow scope and strong reliance on Aristotelian physics in the *De incipit et desinit* indicates that this was a fairly early work. In this treatise Bradwardine set himself a single and limited task: to resolve the problem of assigning limits to permanent and successive things within the context of Aristotle's teaching on the continuum. Because the text probably represents Bradwardine's first serious reflections on the subject, it is not surprising that his approach was conservative. Not only did he stay close to the opinions of Aristotle and Peter of Spain, but he also intentionally confined his discussion specifically to logical questions which did not have a theological dimension. The main theme of the work is the mind's inability to acquire determinate knowledge about future events. Thus the future, from the human perspective, is entirely contingent.[21] Although this position seems contrary to the more deterministic approach which he later took in the *De futuris contingentibus* and in the *De causa Dei*, his conscious decision to consider contingency without reference to God gave him the freedom to avoid aspects of the problem which involve divine causation or prescience. Subsequent discussions of beginning and ceasing in the *De continuo* confirmed Bradwardine's tendency in earlier works to treat logical and physical problems separately from theological ones.[22]

---

[20] Nielsen, pp. 5-6. Because their disagreement concerned an aspect of proportional logic and has no bearing on either man's view of time, it will not be considered here.

[21] *Ibid.*, pp. 3-4.

[22] *Ibid.* Nielsen also suggests that Bradwardine might have written the *De incipit* before his conversion experience (see Introduction), when he was immersed in the study of natural philosophy and convinced of Aristotle's authority. Certainly the narrow scope of the treatise and its relatively unsophisticated style indicate Bradwardine's youth. Yet because Bradwardine never indicated precisely when his conversion experience occurred,

More compelling evidence for the early date of the *De incipit et desinit* is Bradwardine's rather unimaginative analysis of Aristotle and Peter of Spain. His uncritical acceptance of Aristotle's view of time and continuity indicates a basic knowledge of the *Physics* but his arguments do not convey the originality which he demonstrated in reevaluating Aristotle in the *De proportionibus* and the *De continuo*. Even in this presumably early effort, the text is structured as a series of geometric proofs, in spite of its essentially nongeometrical subject. This Euclidean approach to a logical problem reflects Bradwardine's growing interest in mathematics, a feature of his thought which left its mark on all of his writings, including those devoted to theology. It is revealing to note in this context that, even though both his topic and his method were logical, he tried as often as possible in the *De incipit et desinit* to explain his theories in terms of physical concepts such as motion and time and even stated explicitly in the text that he wished to speak as a natural philosopher, not a logician.[23]

Like Peter of Spain, Bradwardine focuses in this text on the thesis that the infinite divisibility of continua seriously complicates the task of assigning limits for particular physical changes. Bradwardine's first two propositions essentially restate Peter's distinctions between permanent and successive continua and he concludes along with Peter that, in the case of permanent continua, one should affirm the first and last instants of being. In the third proposition Bradwardine tries to work out in a series of detailed corollaries how the problem of beginning and ceasing affects the analysis of successive things such as motion, in which a single instant cannot truly constitute being. Thus he asserts, following Aristotle, that it is impossible to determine logically or physically when a motion begins to be, because one would have to isolate the instant at which the motion did not yet exist but would exist immediately afterward.[24] Working out the implications of this proposition for the

---

it is difficult to use this event for dating a text. As Nielsen points out, however, Bradwardine could have written the *De incipit* either before or after his conversion experience because he left theological questions out of consideration.

[23] *De incipit*, 2.3, p. 50: "Quod hec est necessaria 'omnia motus est,' probo sic physice loquendo." See also Nielsen, pp. 24-25. In spite of Bradwardine's remark, his methods in this text were mostly logical. See Murdoch, "Proportional Analysis in Medieval Philosophy: A Case Study," *Synthese*, 40 (1979), 125-26.

[24] *De incipit*, 2.3, p. 51: "Istis prehabitis TERTIA CONCLUSIO est, quod hec propositio est impossibilis 'motus incipit esse.' Istam conclusio probo sic: ista propositio est necessaria 'omnis motus est' igitur sua opposita simpliciter est impossibilis, videlicet 'aliquis motus non est,' et per consequens ista est impossibilis 'motus non est.' Consequentia est bona, ergo ista copulativa est impossibilis 'motus nunc non est et immediate

study of motion is the chief task of the *De incipit et desinit*. To shed
light on this dilemma, Bradwardine devotes the corollaries of the third
proposition to a comparison between successive continua and permanent
continua which are not so seriously affected by the problem of beginning
and ceasing.

Having analyzed at length the problem of assessing beginning- and
end-points for permanent and successive things respectively, Bradwardine turns very briefly in proposition four to the subject of things
which possess being in only one instant, a notion which Burley had first
introduced to the discussion of beginning and ceasing in the 1310s. Not
being entirely convinced that instantaneous things can really exist, however, Bradwardine addresses the issue only perfunctorily.[25] In the final
proposition Bradwardine summarizes his conclusions with a series of
rules, based on Peter of Spain's method for analyzing propositions containing the verbs *incipere* and *desinere*. Bradwardine's entire conception of time in this treatise, in fact, parallels that of Peter of Spain:
time is both the medium in which permanent things exist and also a
successive continuum in its own right which measures and limits other
successive things. In the case of a permanent thing, the infinitely
divisible nature of time makes it impossible to determine the exact moment the thing comes into being or ceases to be: one must choose to
affirm either the first and last instants of being or the last and first instants of non-being. Following Peter, Bradwardine claims that one
should always affirm the first and last instants of being in cases of permanent things. He contends, moreover, that one cannot predict the
future of a permanent thing merely by affirming its beginning in the present. He rejects the logic which expounds the sentence "Socrates begins
to be" as "Socrates is now, therefore Socrates will be" on the grounds
that such an exposition uses the same instant to affirm both Socrates'
present and future state. Thus, on the basis of tense analysis, he questions the assumption made by some grammarians that propositions in the
future tense can reveal the truth about a permanent object.[26] Relying

---

post hoc erit.' Sed ista copulativa—ut prehabitum est—convertitur cum ista propositione
'motus incipere esse,' igitur ista propositio 'motus incipit esse' est impossibilis."
Nielsen, p. 24, refers the reader to Aristotle's assertion in *Physica*, VI, 6.236b34, p. 239:
"Ostenso autem hoc manifestum est quod omne quod movetur necesse motum esse
prius." Trans. Barnes, p. 400: " . . . it is evident that everything in motion must have
been in motion before."

[25] See Nielsen's discussion of instantaneous being, p. 23 and pp. 29-30.

[26] *De incipit*, 2.3.1.1, pp. 55-56: ". . . pro cuius solutione notandum est quod futurum
contingens duplex est, quia quoddam est futurum contingens quod pro illo pro quo est

heavily on Aristotelian physical theory, therefore, Bradwardine concedes
that the future state of permanent things can be predicted but only in a
limited and artificial way. Logical analysis can predict that something
which *is* will continue until it *ceases to be*, but this revelation offers no
concrete information about the actual future state of that thing.

In the case of successive things, Bradwardine contends, again along
Aristotelian lines, that it is impossible to make any true statements about
them except retrospectively.[27] His first argument against predicting the
future of a successive entity relates to Aristotle's initial problem of
designating first and last instants of being. To predict the future state of
a successive thing, such as motion, one would have to know the next
adjacent instant, something which the infinite divisibility of time makes
extremely difficult. If one cannot even designate a beginning-point for a
motion, says Bradwardine, one can hardly be expected to determine
what will follow after it.[28] A more significant obstacle to knowing the
future of a successive thing is that the existence of a successive thing
unfolds itself in time. One cannot fully know something which has not
yet happened and therefore does not exist. Bradwardine refers to
Aristotle's distinction between our perception of what might happen in
the future and the sensible reality of the present. Even our sensible
perception of present motion is suspect, however, since neither the
senses nor the mind can tell us exactly when a motion in the present has
begun. Under these circumstances it is clearly impossible to make
predictions about a future motion which is completely beyond our
experience.[29] Bradwardine does not deny the common experience of

---

verum nullo modo potest esse falsum, et tale futurum contingens est 'nunc futurum contingens,' quod sequitur necessario ex propositione vere et mere de presenti. . . . Per hoc
dico ad argumentum concedendo quod de primis futuris contingentibus potest esse determinata veritas et determinata et distincta scientia sicut de propositionibus mere de
presenti ex quibus talia contingentia sequuntur. De futuris secundis contingentibus nulla
est veritas determinata nec certa scientia et de talibus loquitur Aristoteles in loco sepius
allegato."

[27] Nielsen, pp. 24-25.

[28] *De incipit*, 2.3.1.2.1.1, pp. 57-58: ". . . si ista consequentia sit bona 'Sortes
movetur localiter, ergo Sortes movebitur localiter,' cum illud consequens sit de futuro
contingenti de quo non est aliqua determinata veritas, sequitur etiam quod de isto antece-
dente 'Sortes movetur localiter' non erit aliqua determinata veritas, quia in omni bona
consequentia si consequens sit alicui dubium et antecedens erit eidem dubium. Et si consequens sit indeterminate verum vel falsum, et antecedens erit indeterminate verum vel
falsum. Et per consequens sequitur quod aliqua propositio mere de presenti non erit determinate vera vel falsa."

[29] *Ibid.*, p. 60: "Ad aliud quod dicitur de Aristotele qui ponit motum esse sensibile
commune, hoc ideo dicit non quia sentimus aliquid moveri, sed quia pluribus sensibus

motion or even the human capacity to measure it. He simply rejects the notion that one can know in the present the future state of a successive thing because knowledge of any physical being requires sensory experience, which one cannot obtain for a future event.

The final argument against the possibility of certain knowledge about the future state of successive things contains the treatise's most explicit statement about the nature of time. The basis of Bradwardine's argument is Aristotle's insistence that the successive nature of time makes it impossible to designate an instant in the future before it actually occurs. Such a designation would require the measurement of a motion from outside of time, which violates the definitions of both motion and time.[30] In the subsequent analysis of this problem, Bradwardine develops at length the thesis that the future of successive things lies beyond certain human knowledge because time, space and motion are all interrelated. As parallel successive continua, all three are subject to the ambiguities which result from their infinite divisibility.[31] In other words, Bradwardine implies that one cannot use syncategorematic terms to draw conclusions about the future, for the transition from present to future is a physical not a logical process. As far as Bradwardine is concerned, then, *incipere* and *desinere* are only really useful in affirming the present state of permanent things; their utility in affirming the present state of successive things is limited; and they cannot function at all as true indicators of future states in logical propositions.

When Bradwardine returned to the problem of beginning and ceasing in the *De continuo*, he treated it geometrically, without significant

---

percepimus quod aliquid movebatur. Quia sicut nos non possumus percipere per sensum vel per intellectum quod aliquid movebitur, ita etiam non possumus percipere per sensum vel per intellectum quod aliquid movetur."

[30] *De incipit*, 2.3.1.2.1.2, p. 62: "Ista enim—ut videtur—non stant simul 'nullam spatium immediate post hoc erit pertransitum' quia ista sunt contradictoria, ut patet de se. Sed ista videntur equivalere 'aliquod spatium erit pertransitum immediate post hoc' et 'immediate post hoc aliquod spatium erit pertransitum.' Antecedens prime consequentie patet inductive, videlicet quod nullum spatium erit pertransitum immediate post hoc, quia quocumque spatio dato tempus erit antequam illud spatium erit pertransitum, ut de se patet. Item, immediate post hoc aliquod spatium erit pertransitum, igitur sine medio aliquod spatium erit pertransitum. Et ultra, in nullo tempore aliquod spatium erit pertransitum, ergo in non-tempore aliquod spatium erit pertransitum, igitur motus erit sine tempore. Consequens est impossible, igitur illud ex quo sequitur."

[31] Of course Bradwardine is speaking here only about predicting the future of real beings using *incipit* and *desinit* propositions. He is not concerned with whether time and space are theoretically infinite.

reference to syncategorematic words. Nor did he pay much attention to the question of contingency, presumably because it did not lend itself to mathematical analysis and he had already dealt with that aspect of the subject in the *De futuris contingentibus*. Although it made no reference to contingency, the *De continuo* reconfirmed, and indeed expanded upon, the underlying theory about time which informed Bradwardine's views on beginning and ceasing. In his initial definitions, for example, Bradwardine restated with mathematical precision the Aristotelian position on continuity which governs all statements involving before and after. His seventeenth definition states that "for something to be, to have been, or to be about to be *after* another thing, is the same as to be, to have been, or to be about to be *with a mean* between those things." Definition eighteen says that "for something to be, to have been, or to be about to be *immediately after* another thing, is the same as to be, to have been, or to be about to be *without a mean* [between those things]."[32] The purpose of definition eighteen was to affirm Aristotle's assertion that beginning and ceasing occur in the same instant, or as Bradwardine later expressed the idea in proposition twenty-seven, "every beginning or ending is not measured in time, but in an instant."[33]

Bradwardine then distinguished the beginnings of permanent things, which have first and last instants of being, from successive things, which have first and last instants of non-being. In other words, permanent things are intrinsically bounded while successive things are extrinsically bounded. To say otherwise, one would have to assume that a thing must have both a last instant of non-being and a first instant of being and, consequently, that continua are composed of immediate indivisibles.[34] According to Murdoch, Bradwardine's views about beginning and ceasing had an important function in his overall strategy against the atomists. Bradwardine's success in this enterprise rested on his ability to perceive the inconsistencies of the atomist position and to tailor Aristotelian physical theory to suit the particulars of the debate.[35] By popularizing Bradwardine's criticisms of the atomists, the *De continuo* contributed to the achievement of fourteenth-century philosophers who greatly clarified the nature of continuity through their investigations of successive continua.[36]

---

[32] *De continuo*, p. 2, ll. 5-8; translated by Murdoch in his introduction of the text, p. 176.

[33] *De continuo*, p. 40, ll. 1-2: "Omnis incepto vel destino non mensuratur tempore sed instanti."

[34] See Murdoch, pp. 178-80.

[35] *Ibid.*, pp. 185-86.

[36] *Ibid.* See also Wilson, pp. 51-56. As a mathematician like Bradwardine, William Heytesbury also approached the problem of beginning and ceasing by analyzing

In the *De incipit et desinit* and the *De continuo* Bradwardine
presented a physical rather than a psychological view of time. Even on
those occasions when he admitted the role of human perception in
defining time, he discussed this perception in Aristotelian terms. By
consciously avoiding the issue of divine knowledge he was able to
describe time and motion as successive continua whose natures and
directions are determined by natural law. Such a secular view of time
was extremely useful in his mathematical studies, encouraged his respect
for Aristotle and satisfied his desire to find order in the natural world.
Nevertheless, Bradwardine could not escape from the influence of
contemporary speculation at Oxford about contingency, which called
into question the validity of a human-centered approach to time.
Aristotle himself had addressed the problem of contingency, much in the
same way as he had tried to solve the problem of beginning and ceasing,
and so made an important contribution to an extremely complex debate.
In the *De incipit et desinit* Bradwardine consciously avoided, as
Aristotle had done, any consideration of broader philosophical or
theological implications of contingency. By the fourteenth century,
however, it was impossible to do full justice to the topic of contingency
without taking into account the work of the Christian thinkers who had
transformed contingency from a merely logical problem into a potent
and controversial theological one. Their continuing efforts to establish a
relationship between God's certain knowledge about the future and
human uncertainty led to subsidiary discussions about a wide variety of
difficult theological topics including predestination, free will and divine
causation. Medieval theologians, in fact, made significant progress in
bridging the gap between contingency as a logical problem and the
temporal aspects of God's relationship with creation.

The *De futuris contingentibus* was probably composed about the
same time as the *De incipit et desinit* while Bradwardine was still a
master of arts. It represents one of Bradwardine's first attempts to sort
out the philosophical implications of contingency and to consider
whether and to what extent the future has been predetermined. He had
already concluded in the *De incipit et desinit* that the future seems to be
contingent from the human perspective because we cannot attain certain

---

instantaneous motion, a concept which Burley had suggested and Bradwardine had almost completely ignored. In the process, Heytesbury derived several important theories
regarding motion, continuity and infinity. The works of Heytesbury and Bradwardine
illustrate the strong connection which existed between logic and natural philosophy in
early fourteenth-century Oxford.

knowledge of the future through logical analysis of propositions or observations of nature; but this does not mean that the future is also contingent to God. In the *De futuris contingentibus* Bradwardine explored, perhaps for the first time in his career, certain aspects of the transition from past to future which he later refined in the *De causa Dei*. His initial attempt to resolve the problem of contingency can be seen as a perceptive but somewhat immature response to a complex body of authority ranging from Aristotle's metaphysical works to Ockham's studies of divine causation.

Aristotle's main contribution to the medieval debate about contingency comes from his discussion of truth in Book IX of the *De interpretatione*. The passage which Aristotle devoted to future contingents is, unfortunately, so confusing that neither medieval nor modern scholars have been able to agree on precisely what he was trying to prove about the truth of future events.[37] In his analysis of the passage, Jaakko Hintikka suggests that the source of Aristotle's difficulty with contingency, like his problem with beginning and ceasing, derived from the inability of his physical theory to provide simple, unambiguous answers to questions about the truth of temporally indefinite sentences.[38] Aristotle approached the problem of contingency by distinguishing generally between things that are necessarily true for a given time and those which are only possible. He offered no firm criteria, however, for determining the relative truth of various kinds of statements about the future. Although he admitted that some events might be eternally necessary, he believed that most truths tend to be contingent, claiming that

> not everything is or happens of necessity: some things happen as chance has it, and of the affirmation and negation neither is true rather than the other; with other things it is one rather than the other and as a rule, but still it is possible for the other to happen instead. . . . Clearly, then, it is not necessary that of every affirmation and opposite negation one should be true and the other false. For what holds of things that are does not hold for things that are not but may possibly be or not be.[39]

---

[37] Jaakko Hintikka, "The Once and Future Sea Fight: Aristotle's Discussion of Future Contingents in *De interpretatione 9*," in *Time and Necessity: Studies in Aristotle's Theory of Modality* (Oxford: Clarendon Press, 1973), p. 147. In this essay Hintikka thoroughly explores Aristotle's extensive but rather confusing treatment of the logical implications of contingency. Although it is not possible to cover all of this material, relevant aspects of Aristotle's view of contingency will be treated below.

[38] Hintikka, p. 152.

[39] *De interpretatione vel Periermenias translatio Boethii specimina translationum recentiorum, Aristoteles latinus*, II, 1-2, ed. Laurentius Minio-Paluello (Leiden: E. J.

This rather vague argument suggests that the contingency of an event or thing is based on whether it is necessary both now and in the future. While it is logically necessary that a certain future thing will either be or not be, one cannot prove its future existence or nonexistence in the present. From the human point of view, then, future things are almost entirely contingent. Whereas all true statements about the past are necessary, most future statements must wait for retrospective verification.[40] From the perspective of contingency, then, past and future represent fundamentally different states of time.

Because of its large scope and obvious theological implications, the problem of contingency received much greater attention throughout the middle ages than the more specialized problem of beginning and ceasing. Although he probably had not yet begun his theological studies when he wrote the *De futuris contingentibus*, Bradwardine's philosophical training had advanced enough so that he was prepared to consider more than just the physical and logical aspects of contingency.[41] In developing his own philosophical approach to contingency, Bradwardine was guided by the work of Augustine and Boethius, who came to be, along with Aristotle, one of Bradwardine's favored authorities.

Augustine's approach to contingency appealed to Bradwardine chiefly because it considered contingency as much a physical problem as a theological one. Augustine supplemented Aristotle's view of contingency by paying greater attention to its moral implications and offered an alternative method for defining the problem. Whereas Aristotle concerned himself mostly with the issue of truth in temporally indefinite statements, Augustine considered the human perspective on contingency in future events. In Book V, Chapter 9, of the *City of God*, Augustine presented his own view of contingency through his criticism of Cicero's radically contingent cosmology. According to Augustine, Cicero's major

---

Brill, 1965), IX, 19a19-22; 19a36-b4, pp. 16-18: "... non omnia ex necessitate vel sunt vel fiunt, sed alia quidem utrumlibet et non magis vel adfirmatio vel negatio, alia vero magis quidem in pluribus alterum, sed contingit fieri et alterum, alterum vero minime. . . . Quare manifestum est quoniam non est necesse omnes adfirmationes vel negationes oppositarum hanc quidem veram, illam autem falsam esse; neque enim quemadmodum in his quae sunt se habent etiam in his quae non sunt, possibilium tamen esse aut non esse, sed quemadmodum dictum est." Trans. Barnes, p. 30. For a critical edition of this text, see *Aristoteles latinus* II, 1-2, *De interpretatione vel Periermenias, Translatio Boethii specimina translationum recentiorum*, ed. Laurentius Minio-Paluello (Leiden: E. J. Brill, 1965).

[40] Hintikka, pp. 164-65.

[41] See M. Jean-François Genest's discussion in "Le *De futuris contingentibus* de Thomas Bradwardine," *Recherches augustiniennes*, 14 (1979), p. 253.

error was his unreasonable denial of any kind of foreknowledge or fate, which was due to his fear of rigid predestination. Cicero would much rather reject fate or God altogether than live believing that there is no opportunity for independent will or action. In making this claim, Augustine contended, Cicero incorrectly assumed that human acknowledgement of divine prescience amounts to the surrender of individual freedom.[42]

Augustine subsequently condemned Cicero's assessment of the relationship between the human and the divine will and thus dismissed Cicero's insistence on viewing contingency from the divine perspective. In Augustine's opinion, God's foreknowledge does not interfere with the exercise of human will; on the contrary, God's foreknowledge actually enhances and protects human freedom. As the first efficient cause of every event, God gives to his creatures a world in which they can exercise their wills freely according to their abilities: "their future strength is completely determined and their future achievements utterly assured."[43] Augustine's conception of the will not only preserved both God's prescience and human freedom but also placed the question of contingency in a human context. God's knowledge of the future does not make human knowledge of a particular future event any more certain, except in instances of prophesies, and even here one cannot know exactly how or when God will fulfill them. Augustine's position on contingency was entirely consistent, therefore, with his view of time, which also stressed human perception. God made time so that his creatures would have a sensible reference for ordering their existence and to give them a place in history. Thus time and contingency must always be related to eternal being.[44] In this sense, Augustine's approach to contingency had a metaphysical significance which Aristotle's lacked. Nevertheless, both Aristotle and Augustine emphasized, in different ways, the necessity of separating absolute truth from the human perception of truth.

In the *Consolation of Philosophy* Boethius offered an interpretation of contingency which lay somewhere between Aristotle's and Augustine's. Like Aristotle, Boethius wanted to establish degrees of necessity and was, in fact, much more successful than Aristotle had been in Book IX of the *De interpretatione*. In Boethius' view, the order of

---

[42] *Concerning the City of God against the Pagan*, trans. Henry Bettensen (Harmondsworth, Middlesex: Penguin, 1972), p. 191. Quotation from Cicero, *De fato*, 17.40.

[43] *City of God*, p. 194.

[44] See Jordan, "Time and Contingency," pp. 268-69.

the natural world depends on the absolute necessity of certain events such as the rising and setting of the sun. As for contingent things, Boethius distinguished cases in which the possibility of one outcome is equal to another from cases in which a certain outcome is extremely unlikely but still possible. Boethius also maintained Aristotle's position that a true prediction concerning a future event cannot be considered necessary solely on the grounds that the prediction turns out to be correct: only individual events in time which are always true should be considered necessary.[45]

Through his consideration of the theological aspects of contingency, however, Boethius arrived at a position on the function of will in determining future events which closely resembled Augustine's. In the first place, God is not subject to the same kind of observation of past, present and future that his creatures experience because he is outside of time. God's foreknowledge does not involve the kind of control which Cicero and others have attributed to him. In fact, his influence is of an entirely different order:

> since God abides forever in an eternal present, His knowledge, also transcending all movement of time, dwells in the simplicity of its own changeless present, and, embracing the whole infinite sweep of the past and future, contemplates all that falls within its simple cognition as if it were now taking place. And therefore, if thou wilt carefully consider that immediate presentment whereby it discriminates all things, thou wilt more rightly deem it not foreknowledge as of something future, but knowledge of a moment that never passes. For this cause the name chosen to describe it is not prevision, but providence, because, since utterly removed in nature from things mean and trivial, its outlook embraces all things as from some lofty height. Why then dost thou insist that the things which are surveyed by the Divine eye are involved in necessity, whereas clearly men impose no necessity on the things which they see?[46]

Boethius again echoed Augustine on the question of the human response to contingency. He argued that, while many unexpected events seem to arise from chance, they really occur as the result of "causes [arising] from that inevitable chain of order, which, flowing from the fountainhead of Providence, disposes all things in their due time and place."[47] Moreover, in establishing that order, God has provided for the human

---

[45] Chadwick, *Consolations*, pp. 157-59.

[46] *The Consolation of Philosophy*, trans. H. R. James (London: Elliot Stock, 1897), p. 260-61.

[47] *Ibid.*, p. 228.

will to exercise freedom in choosing future actions. The freedom of a human soul is relative to its capacity to use freedom wisely.[48] So while emphasizing the Aristotelian distinctions between necessity and possibility, Boethius also placed contingency in a broader cosmological context which links human freedom with the obligation to recognize moral and natural order.

Medieval discussions of contingency bear the influence of Aristotle, Augustine and Boethius in varying degrees.[49] Anselm, for example, used Boethius' observation concerning different levels of possibility to draw his own distinctions about necessity. Thus he differentiated between "antecedent" necessity, which is absolute, and "subsequent" necessity, in which God's foreknowledge does not interfere with free choice. In Anselm's view, only the rigid "antecedent" necessity could impair the free exercise of choice.[50] Similarly, Peter Abelard concluded from his reflections on Aristotle's discussion of future contingent sentences that God knows and can reveal contingent truths without enforcing determinism or undermining divine infallibility.[51] Peter Lombard later introduced a more sophisticated approach to contingency which involved the question of whether God can know what he does not know, thus making an initial distinction between that which is necessary and that which is immutable.[52] Robert Grosseteste went on to contrast simple necessity (those things, like mathematical principles, which would be the same regardless of the course of history) and immutable truths, which cannot change once they have been established. Grosseteste's theories about the relationship between past and future

---

[48] *Ibid.*, pp. 231-32.

[49] The material for the following summary is taken from Calvin Normore, "Future Contingents," *CHLMP*, pp. 359-69.

[50] Normore, pp. 359-61, notes that Anselm discussed aspects of antecedent and subsequent necessity in several works, including *Cur Deus homo*, II, 17; *De concordia praescientiae et praedestinationis et gratiae Dei cum libero arbitrio*, Quaestio I; *De concordia*, I, 3; and in his *Incomplete Works*, sometimes called the *Philosophical Fragments*. The standard edition for all of these texts is *Sancti Anselmi Opera Omnia*, ed. Franciscus Salesius Schmitt (Rome: 1938).

[51] Normore, pp. 361-63, cites the following texts in which Abelard discussed aspects of future contingency: *Editio super Aristotelem De Interpretatione*, ed. Mario dal Pra, in *Pietro Abelardo: Scritti di logica* (Florence: La nuova Italia Editrice, 1969), p. 103; *Logica 'Ingredientibus,'* ed. Bernhard Geyer, in *Peter Abaelards philosophischen Schriften* (Münster: Aschendorff, 1919-27), pp. 427 ff.; and *Dialectica*, ed. Lambertus Maris De Rijk, *Wijsgerige teksten en studies*, I (Assen: Van Gorcum, 1970), p. 212.

[52] Normore, p. 363, cites Lombard's *Sentences*, Book I, Distinctions 38-40. For a standard edition of this text see *Libri IV Sententiarum*, ed. Albanus Heysse (Florence: Editiones Collegii S. Bonaventura ad Claras Aquas, Grottaferrata, 1916).

necessity stimulated a heated debate about the modal aspects of contingency which continued well into the fourteenth century.[53]

Thomas Aquinas was the main instigator of that phase of the debate over contingency which most directly influenced Bradwardine. Aquinas fueled the controversy by forcefully reintroducing two Boethian theses: that God's being in the eternal present allows God to know the future without determining it and that God's knowledge that a person will make a particular choice does not detract from the freedom of that choice.[54] Aquinas readily identified the logical dilemma of admitting the necessity of God's eternal knowledge while affirming human free will. To resolve this dilemma, he insisted that the Boethian description of an omniscient, omnipotent and eternal God had to be maintained at all costs. Aquinas drew considerable criticism for this approach, especially among the Franciscan scholars. Duns Scotus, for example, argued against Aquinas that there is an objective difference between past and future which God experiences as much as humans do. For Scotus, contingency derives from God's complete freedom to will the opposite of anything that he wills.[55] Henry of Harclay followed Scotus' lead in questioning Aquinas' theory that God's foreknowledge of an event makes it necessary. Harclay argued instead that God can know future events contingently because God does not have to will them with necessity. Thus, observes Mark Henniger, "Harclay takes the Scotist turn to the problem by grounding the contingency of God's knowledge of future contingents in God's will which freely wills or permits that they do or do not take place."[56] In rejecting Aquinas' logical solution to

---

[53] Normore, pp. 364-66, cites Grosseteste's *De liber arbitrio*, Chapter 6, ed. Ludwig Baur, in *Die philosophischen Werke des Robert Grosseteste, Bischof von Lincoln* (Münster: Aschendorff, 1912). In "Henricus de Harclay," p. 27, Dales makes a connection between Grosseteste's *De finitate motus et temporis* and a tradition of speculation on beginning and ceasing which derived from Maimonides and Boethius of Dacia, and which went on to exercise considerable influence on Bonaventure and Harclay. This observation is important because it indicates both the variety of interpretations of the topic of contingency available to late medieval scholars and because it shows a distinct link between discussions of beginning and ceasing as a physical problem and contingency as a theological one.

[54] Normore, pp. 366-67, cites especially Aquinas' *Summa Theologica*, Book I, Questions 14, 25 and 62. For a standard edition of this work see *Opera Omnia*, ed. S. E. Fretté and P. Maré (Paris: L. Vivès, 1874-89).

[55] Normore, pp. 367-69, cites Duns Scotus' *Lectura* on Lombard's *Sentences*, Book I, Distinctions 39 and 40. For an edition of Scotus' *Lectura* see *Opera Omnia*, ed. Luke Wadding (Paris: L. Vivès, 1891-95).

[56] Mark C. Henniger interprets Harclay's position in "Henry of Harclay's Questions on Divine Prescience and Predestination," *Franciscan Studies*, 40 (1980), p. 176, and

the dilemma of contingency, Scotus and Harclay also rejected the Augustinian and Boethian assumptions on which it was based.

The philosophers who most directly prompted Bradwardine to write the *De futuris contingentibus*, however, were Peter Aureoli and William of Ockham. It was Aureoli who suggested the principles about contingency which Ockham later developed into a sophisticated logical theory of necessity.[57] Bradwardine first challenged this theory in the *De futuris contingentibus*, then expanded his criticism of it much more skillfully in the *De causa Dei*. Aureoli's argument was based on the assumption that a thing which is immutable in a particular state must therefore be necessary in that state. From this premise he tried to prove that a true statement about the future is both immutable and necessary. Aureoli was fully aware of the central dilemma of this thesis: a statement which is true both in the present and at the time of its fulfillment leaves no room for contingency or choice. He therefore softened his original position by expanding the role of contingent statements about the future, which, he claimed, need not be either true or false in the present.[58] In this way he saved the logician from the necessity of verifying future truths in the present, but he put his whole theory in doubt by failing to explain how something could be true about the future but not true in the present. Aureoli left it to others, such as Ockham and Gregory of

---

cites the following from his edition of Question I, paragraph 19, pp. 202-4: "Ista primo contra hoc quod ipse dicit, quod ista est simpliciter necessaria 'Deus scit *a* fore' quia non est contingentia in Deo nec mutatio: illud quod Deus non necessario scit nisi quia vult, si non necessario vult non necessario scit. Ista propositio [est] plana. Sed futurum contingens est hoc: Deus [enim] non scit hoc nisi quia vult hoc vel voluntate efficienti vel voluntate permissiva. Probatio: nam talis veritas non scitur ex natura rei sicut veritas necessaria. Verba gratia, cognoscens diametrum et cognoscens symmetrum, statim ex natura rei scit quod diametrum non est symmetrum. Item cognoscens totum vel partem, ex natura rei statim componit 'totum est maius parte,' quia natura rei hoc sibi determinat necessario. Sed veritas contingens non est huiusmodi. Certum est [quod] 'Socrates est currens' non scitur ex natura Socratis et cursus; unum non determinat sibi alternum. Ergo si scitur, [scitur] ex aliqua alia causa determinate Socratem ad cursum, quae causa contigenter determinat. Sed omnis talis causa ideo causat quia Deus vult vel permittit, ergo nullum tale scitur nisi quia Deus vult vel permittit fieri vel fore. . . . Ergo nihil scit Deus de contingenti nisi quia vult, sed non necessario vult nec necessario permittit; ergo non necessario scit."

[57] For background information, see Tachau's chapter on Aureoli in *Vision and Certitude*, pp. 85-112. Aureoli, d. 1322, was a Franciscan who studied theology at Bologne, Toulouse and Paris. Tachau, pp. 85-86, cautions against the tendency of modern scholarship to skip from Scotus to Ockham without considering Aureoli's significant, original and influential work.

[58] Normore, pp. 369-70.

Rimini, to address the logical difficulties which arose from this new proposal. His use of arguments from Aristotle, Grosseteste and Lombard ensured that his conclusions would be widely publicized, if not precisely followed, throughout the fourteenth and fifteenth centuries.[59]

Ockham's speculations about contingency appear in many of his philosophical writings. In addition to discussions in the *Summa logicae* and the *Quodlibeta*, the *Tractatus de praedestinatione et de praescientia Dei et de futuris contingentibus* provides an extended treatment of Ockham's view of contingency. In the *Tractatus de praedestinatione* Ockham is particularly interested in addressing the question of how the necessity of a statement varies according to whether it refers to a past, present or future time. He also makes a distinction here between the necessity of statements about things which God has predetermined and that of purely logical statements which do not reveal whether God's predestination is involved in them. According to Philotheus Boehner, who has edited the *Tractatus de praedestinatione* and several other of Ockham's works, Ockham conceives of contingency as a fundamentally logical and linguistic problem, although he admits that contingency also has some significant theological ramifications.[60]

The thrust of Ockham's analysis in the *Tractatus de praedestinatione*, reminiscent of treatises on syncategorematic words, was to decide whether verbs such as *praedestinare* and *reprobare* refer primarily to the present or to the future. Because statements about the future cannot be verified as true or false, he argued, one cannot determine whether they are absolutely necessary as one can when the statement is about the past. Even a statement containing the word *praedestinare* or *reprobare* in the past tense, however, still refers to the future until the event in question takes place and can be verified. On the other hand, God knows the truth of every proposition whether it applies to the past or present, in which it is possible for us to share in his knowledge, or to the future, in which it is not. Therefore, there cannot be any proposition which is neither true nor false. Moreover, if a statement about the future is true, it is necessarily true only after the instant in time at which God fulfills the prophecy. Until this instant, the statement could be true but would not

---

[59] *Ibid.*, p. 370.

[60] See Philotheus Boehner, "Ockham's *Tractatus de praedestinatione et de praescientia Dei et de futuris contingentibus* and its Main Problems," in *Collected Articles on Ockham*, ed. Eligius M. Buytaert (St. Bonaventure, New York: The Franciscan Institute, 1958), p. 423. See also Adams's chapter on divine omniscience, human freedom and future contingents in *Ockham*, pp. 1115-1150.

be necessarily true, because an action can only be necessary after it has been completed.[61] Ockham's reasoning is based on the observation that human and divine perceptions of the future are entirely different in character and scope.

Ockham then must explain how it is possible for God to know the future without depriving humanity of its free will. In contrast to many of his predecessors, who placed God outside of time, Ockham credits God with an immediate experience of time which resembles a human one.[62] In the sixth assumption of the *Tractatus de praedestinatione* Ockham maintains that God's capacity to know the future is a logical, not a cosmological, reality:

> It must be held beyond question that God knows with certainty all future contingents—i.e., He knows with certainty which part of the contradiction is true and which false. . . . It is difficult, however, to see how He knows this [with certainty], since one part [of the contradiction] is no more determined to truth than the other. . . . For that reason, I maintain that it is impossible to express clearly the way God knows future contingents. Nevertheless it must be held that He does so, but contingently. . . . Despite [the impossibility of expressing it clearly], the following way [of knowing future contingents] can be ascribed [to God]. Just as the [human] intellect on the basis of one and the same [intuitive] cognition of certain non-complexes can have evident cognition of contradictory contingent propositions such as 'A exists,' 'A does not exist,' in the same way it can be granted that the divine essence is intuitive cognition that is so perfect, so clear, that it is evident cognition of all things past and future, so that it knows which part of a contradiction [involving such things] is true and which part false.[63]

Though more perfect than human knowledge in every respect, God's knowledge of the future is still contingent. By drawing an analogy between human and divine knowledge of contingent events, Ockham suggests that God's experience of the future is comparable to ours: like us, he is waiting for the future to come into being so that his knowledge of the future can be necessitated.

---

[61] Boehner, *The Tractatus praedestinatione et de praescientia Dei et de futuris contingentibus* (St. Bonaventure, New York: The Franciscan Institute, 1945), pp. 49-50.

[62] For example, Adams, pp. 1117-1137, examines at great length Ockham's criticism of Aquinas and Scotus, who insisted (in different ways) that God is timeless in a Boethian sense, despite the logical problem this view presents.

[63] *William Ockham: Predestination, God's Foreknowledge and Future Contingents*, trans. Marilyn McCord Adams and Norman Kretzmann (New York: Appelton-Century-Crofts, 1969), pp. 48-50.

Ockham's discussion of whether God's knowledge of the future can change further emphasizes God's temporality. In Ockham's view, one of God's supreme powers is his capacity to know the truth of changing propositions without changing himself. Moreover, Ockham argues that in certain cases God does not know future events, but his lack of knowledge in no way impairs his perfect understanding of the future:

> [Some contingents] that are future as regards their wording suggest (*implicant*) that present or past things are future. Suppose, for example, that the proposition 'Socrates will sit down at t_1' is asserted after t_1. This suggests that past things are future—viz. that t_1 is future and that sitting down is future. Such a proposition about the future can change from truth to falsity, since before t_1 it was true and after t_1 it is false. And God can *not* know such a future contingent after He *did* know it, as a result of change of things and the passage of time, without any change on His part.[64]

This argument not only firmly places God inside time but also preserves, albeit in a limited way, the contingency of future events at the expense of God's absolute knowledge.

Ockham admitted that he could not easily prove his theories about contingency with human reason alone. He considered faith, rooted in scripture and the saints, to be the best form of verification.[65] This admission did not spare him from the criticism that his conception of divine foreknowledge directly contradicted patristic views. His acknowledged inability to explain his logical theories in terms of the orthodox position on God's relationship to time made Ockham's views on contingency the subject of considerable debate. While he was relatively successful philosophically in placing his theories about contingency in the context of a changing physical universe, he had more trouble in convincing his colleagues of the religious merit of his arguments. At the heart of his difficulty lay his view of time, which seemed to suggest that God experiences time in the same Aristotelian way of motion and change as his creatures experience it.[66]

---

[64] Question II, article III, trans. Adams and Kretzmann, pp. 61-62.

[65] From Book I, Distinction 38 of Ockham's commentary on Lombard's *Sentences*, also called his *Ordinatio*, ed. and trans. Adams and Kretzmann in Appendix I of *William Ockham, Predestination*, p. 90: "This conclusion [concerning God's complete knowledge of future contingents], although it cannot be proved *a priori* by means of the natural reason available to us, nevertheless can be proved by means of the authorities of the Bible and the Saints, which are sufficiently known."

[66] The issue of Ockham's view of time and Bradwardine's reaction to it will be discussed at length below in Chapter Seven. Bradwardine's reaction to some of Ockham's followers will be explored in Chapter Eight.

Bradwardine's chief objective in the *De futuris contingentibus* was to refute the human-centered view of divine time expressed by Ockham and some of his contemporaries. Bradwardine agreed with Ockham that Aristotelian physics provides a good explanation of time as a natural phenomenon but he refused to believe that God shared in any way the human experience of time. Because the *De futuris contingentibus* posited such a rigid separation of God from time and advocated such a firm commitment to the notion of God's absolute prescience, the treatise could give the impression that Bradwardine saw practically no role at all for human free will. Later, in the *De causa Dei*, he would treat the subject of contingency with much greater subtlety and insight. In this first effort, his inexperience in dealing with complex philosophical and theological questions led him to uncompromising positions and exposed his lack of expertise in philosophical inquiry. On the subsidiary issue of whether God causes sin by virtue of his prior knowledge of it, for example, Bradwardine had little to offer beyond an apology for not yet having mastered the problem.[67] Nevertheless the *De futuris contingentibus* demonstrated Bradwardine's general familiarity with the contemporary state of the debate over contingency and offered a reasonable criticism of Ockham's position which was clear and relatively well-developed in spite of its failure to present a satisfactory alternative.

Bradwardine set out in the *De futuris contingentibus* to prove that God has complete foreknowledge of all future contingents by virtue of his eternal nature. In the sixth opinion, Bradwardine defined the temporal basis for his view of contingency, which echoed Boethius' and Anselm's assertion that everything is eternally present to God and therefore God has complete knowledge of every future event.[68] Bradwardine

---

[67] Genest, p. 253. See also *De futuris*, Opinion 7, 20, p. 293, which simply states: "Septima opinio est que ponit quod nihil est in futurum contingens ad utrumlibet, sed omnia que eveniunt necessario eveniunt. Sed ista opinio est tam contra philosophiam quam theologiam, ideo hic illa non reprobantur."

[68] Most of the direct references in the text are to Augustine, Boethius and Anselm. *De futuris*, Opinion 6, 17-18b; 18e; 18h-19; p. 292: "Respondetur pro intencione Anselmi et aliorum diciencum quod omnia sunt Deo presencia: verum est in esse cognito, et consimiliter dicet Philosophus quod anima est quodammodo omnia, scilicet sensibilia omnia comprehendit per sensum et omnia intelligibilia per intellectum, et non excluditur quin aliqua sint futura et quod illa Deus prescit. Nec similiter vult Anselmus dicere quod omnia sunt Deo presencia, scilicet futura. Sed verum est quod hec consequencia non valet: 'omnia sunt sibi presencia in esse cognito, igitur non habet prescienciam'; sed verum est quod bene sequitur 'igitur non habent prescienciam excludendo de illis scienciam.'"

thus stressed the difference between the creature, whose knowledge of the future is necessarily contingent because of his position in time, and God, who knows everything there is to know simultaneously. Bradwardine reinforced his contention that God knows all things in an eternal present by stressing God's immutability. In contrast to Ockham's conception of God, Bradwardine's view did not admit that God experiences change and time. There is no reason to consider the question of whether God can change his mind about the truth of a future statement because God knows eternally the truth of every proposition. Not even God's willingness to respond to his creation, as through answering a prayer, undermines this immutability.[69] Bradwardine then demonstrated in the same way that his view of God is thoroughly consistent with revelations about God's nature in scripture. God's perfect knowledge of the future ensures that his revelations were, are and will be true, whether they come to us through prophecy or through the natural unfolding of events in the created world.[70]

When it came to explaining how human free will could be accommodated in his theory of God's unchanging omniscience, however, Bradwardine had nothing very original to offer. He derived his main argument about free will from Augustine's criticism of the Stoics in Book V of the *City of God*, in which Augustine had claimed that God allows the human will to participate freely in his eternal plan.[71] This and

---

[69] *Ibid.*, p. 294: ". . . si Deus habet prescienciam futurorum contingencium ad utrumlibet, sequitur quod Deus potest velle et promittere oppositum nunc sciti, promissi et voliti ab eo. Consequens est falsum, quia sic Deus potest mutari de scitis, volitis et promissis, quod est contra illud *Malachie* 3° [Malachi 3:6]: 'Ego Dominus et non mutor', et ita sequitur quod non erit si sicut Deus promisit vel voluit fore, igitur Deus mutatur. . . . Sed contra: quia sic sequitur quod contingenter potest scire aliquid fore futurum postquam non fuit futurum et e converso. Consequens est falsum, quia sciencia sua est necessaria preteritorum, ut hujus: 'diluvium fuit,' et idem est apud Deum scire diluvium fuisse et scire ipse fore quando non fuit. Igitur sequitur quod sciencia sua est necessaria futurorum."

[70] See especially *De futuris*, Opinion 8, 24a-25p, pp. 295-98; also Genest's introduction, pp. 263-64.

[71] *Ibid.*, 35j, p. 303: "Confirmatur, quia si Deus velit illum actum stare in voluntate ejus per diem continue et voluntas illius potest tunc illum actum ante finem diei dimittere, sequitur quod Deus non foret omnipotens, quia non potest uti creatura sua ut nunc vult ea uti. Consequens est falsum. Et quod Deus possit velle hominis voluntatem immutabiliter stare per diem vel in eternum, consequencia patet per Augustinum in *Enchiridion* et 5° *De civitate Dei*, c. 10°, ubi arguit conta Stoycos, qui maluerunt negare prescienciam in Deo quam libertatem arbitrii in hominibus. Contra quos dicit Augustinus ibidem quod necessitas et libertas non repugnant in aliquo, quia necesse est Deum velle se esse in vivere in tamen libere, et sic de beatis, et sic potest esse in nobis;

several other similar references to Augustine and Boethius indicate that Bradwardine adopted, essentially uncritically, their conception of the relationship between God's future knowledge and the human will.[72] Bradwardine's definition of divinity, based as it was on the classical and patristic principles of omniscience, immutability, eternity and omnipotence, gave him little choice but to acknowledge God's capacity for complete knowledge of future contingent events.

Bradwardine's youth and relative inexperience with theological matters apparently led him to a rigid and uncompromising position in the *De futuris contingentibus*. The conclusion of the treatise left no room for doubt that he was comforted much more by arguments which demonstrated God's absolute prescience than by those which emphasized free will. Bradwardine was content simply to acknowledge that some kind of free will must be possible because both scripture and Christian writers had affirmed this doctrine. Nor did he show any inclination to define free will so that it was compatible with his deterministic view of necessity. Bradwardine's final word on contingency in the *De futuris contingentibus* was that, while the capacity to know the truth of a future contingent statement is beyond the capacity of human imagination, God, with his absolute power, is not constrained by human weakness.[73]

---

dicit quod necessitas ex natura, ut est illa qua moriemur, repugant libertati arbitrii, sed non illa qua dicitur necesse est hoc esse vel fore universaliter. Et sic concedit quod necessitas aliqua est in voluntate, que non repugnat libertati arbitrii, ut predictum est, igitur merito de demerito." For a standard edition of the *Enchiridion* see *Enchiridion ad Laurentium de Fide et Spe et Caritate*, ed. Ernest Evans, in *Aurelii Augustini Opera*, Part XIII, 2, Volume XLVI of *Corpus Christianorum Series Latina* (Turnholti: Typographi Brepols, 1969), pp. 21-114.

[72] See for example *De futuris*, Opinion 8, 35p, p. 304: "Et sic potest Deus facere, et movere ad faciendum illud quod bonum est fieri omnia instrumenta, et tamen credimus nos facere nostra voluntate et contra voluntatem Dei, et sic peccamus necessario. Et hoc patet in illo processu: 'Ve Assur' (Is., 10:15), ubi dicitur virga et baculus Jude rex Assur; et simul habetur *Enchiridion* c. 25º." (See *Enchiridion*, 25:99 and 26:100-1). Also 44c, p. 313: "Item hoc patet per Augustinium per super *Genesim* [*Contra Gaudentium* 1:30:35], ubi dicitur quod non potuit in superversione Sodome perdere justos cum impiis, quia foret contra justiciam et ideo hoc non potest velle facere, et per consequens non potest hoc facere; sed tamen de potencia absoluta potuit hoc fecisse si voluisset." Also 45g, pp. 314-15: "Similiter Boecius in *De consolacione*, prosa ultima (5:6:36), dicit quod necesse est futura evenire referendo illa ad cognicionem divinam, sed propria natura libera sunt et a nexibus necessitatis absoluta." And again, 47h, p. 316: "Item Anselmus [*De concordia*, 1:2] et Boecius [*Philosophiae consolatio*, 5:6:27-36], ubi supra, distinguunt de necessitate, que est duplex, quedam antecedens et quedam consequens, et dicunt quod in futuro est necessitas consequens et non antecedens."

[73] *De futuris*, Responsio propria ad questionem, 54a, p. 323: "Sed accipiendo contingens ad utrumlibet simpliciter, sic conceditur consequencia et consequens, scilicet quod

Significantly, Bradwardine was not opposed to Aristotle's position on contingency as such; his concern was only to define contingency so that it did not minimize God's nontemporal knowledge of future contingent events.

Bradwardine's early position on contingency, as it was expressed in the *De incipit et desinit* and the *De futuris contingentibus*, was based on the tension which he perceived between two equally compelling temporal theories. As a mathematician and natural philosopher, Bradwardine found Aristotle's definition of time both reasonable and useful; as a Christian philosopher, he was attracted to Augustine's and Boethius' more psychological conception of time, which seemed to offer a better explanation of time's relationship to eternity. In both treatises on contingency Bradwardine exhibited a tendency towards rigid, almost dogmatic, logic, so that he might express his philosophical opinions as mathematically precise truths. Thus his commitment to the thesis that the continuous nature of time prohibits logical predictions about the future was just as strong as his pronouncement that God's perfect foreknowledge repudiates real contingency. At the heart of this apparent contradiction lay Bradwardine's even more fundamental belief that Aristotle's conception of time and other features of the natural world accurately described God's creation. Though he realized that one could never hope to determine God's temporal relationship to his creation using natural philosophy alone, Bradwardine thought that Aristotelian physics allowed the natural philosopher to study the world from the human perspective and in human terms.

These writings on contingency also have much to say about Bradwardine's academic personality in the 1320s. He was at once receptive to the ideas of his thirteenth-century predecessors and defiant in support of the positions which attracted his interest. If Nielsen's assessment of Bradwardine's interaction with Ockham in the *De incipit et desinit* is correct, the *De futuris contingentibus* also clearly indicates Bradwardine's ability as a young scholar to engage in debate with his more

---

nihil est vel erit contingens ad utrumlibet, eo quod nihil est vel erit in eternum nisi quod determinatum ad volitum et prescitum a Deo fore, quia nihil fiet in eternum nisi a potencia ordinata cause superioris vel inferioris. Sed secundum quid fient plura contingencia, quia illa potencia non est plus ordinata ad unam partem contradictionis quam ad aliam, ut est potencia absoluta in utraque causa. Et sic dico de casu et fortuna, quia nihil eveniet in eternum immediate a Deo, vel a Deo creatura mediante, quin fiet a proposito saltem cause superioris, licet plura in istis inferioribus a casu et fortuna secundum quid fiant, et non a proposito cause inferioris; et hoc intendit Philosophus de contingenti equaliter vel utrumlibet, vel de casu et fortuna."

established peers. Although it would be too much to expect complete consistency in his early treatises, Bradwardine's work on contingency, along with his mathematical studies of proportionality and continuity, provide a good indication of his general intellectual outlook. While he did not confine his studies to problems which could be solved easily with mathematics alone, he applied mathematical methods to logical and metaphysical subjects whenever possible. Underlying all of his main positions was the assumption that there is an order in nature which can be understood mathematically, not in the purely symbolic sense of Platonic mathematics, but in the active observation and description of natural phenomena according to Aristotelian physics.

As a concept which has both cosmological and physical significance, time emerged again and again in Bradwardine's early writings, though he did not, so far as we know, devote a separate treatise to the problem of time. In his early treatises the problem of time always arose in the context of proportional velocity, continuity or contingency. While his studies of motion in the *De proportionibus*, the *De continuo* and the *De incipit et desinit* all depend on his Aristotelian understanding of time as a physical concept, however, the *De futuris contingentibus* attempted to confront the much more difficult problem of explaining how human beings can experience contingency in their temporal existence without denying certain knowledge to God. It was the logical dilemma of contingency in a temporal world created by a timeless God which troubled Bradwardine in the *De futuris contingentibus*. Although he tried to resolve the dilemma through recourse to Aristotelian natural philosophy he eventually realized that a purely creature-oriented view of time only partially explains the cosmological significance of the distinction between time and eternity.

In the *De futuris contingentibus* Bradwardine posed challenging questions about time and contingency but found himself unable to answer them. By the time that he wrote the *De causa Dei*, however, he was better able to describe the distinction between time and eternity, to assess the place of time in his own cosmological system and to reconcile Aristotelian physics with Augustinian theology. Bradwardine's mature view of time naturally grew out of his interaction with colleagues in the 1330s. Undoubtedly, the spiritual conversion which he underwent while studying arts intensified his response to academic treatments of time.[74] Certainly, his early speculations about time as a physical and logical concept profoundly informed his approach to God's use of time, which

---

[74] For discussions of this conversion experience, see the Introduction and Chapter Seven.

lies at the center of his attack on the modern Pelagians in the *De causa Dei*. Without an understanding of Bradwardine's mathematical way of thinking and his devotion to an Aristotelian perspective on nature, it is easy to underestimate his ability to balance different cosmologies and conciliate opposing schools of thought in the *De causa Dei*, a work that is generally portrayed as highly polemical. The foregoing discussion of Bradwardine's early explorations of the problem of time offers the necessary background for exploring the cosmology which he presented in the *De causa Dei*.

CHAPTER SEVEN

TIME IN THE *DE CAUSA DEI*

The *De causa Dei* is Bradwardine's longest and most widely read theological work. Although it is as long as or longer than most contemporary sentence commentaries, the *De causa Dei* does not purport to be such; rather, it is a polemical work focused on a single issue: God's role as the first cause in every created act. Bradwardine composed this treatise in order to defend his belief in God's absolute omniscience against the suggestion of some contemporary scholars that there is a logical contradiction between God's complete foreknowledge of an event and the ability of a person participating in that event to make free choices. Despite Bradwardine's derisive reference to the "modern Pelagians" at the beginning of the treatise, the structure of the *De causa Dei* clearly indicates that the target of Bradwardine's polemic was the general concept of possible limitations on God's power, not the specific theories of particular theologians.[1] In this respect, the *De causa Dei* follows the same pattern as Bradwardine's works of natural philosophy. The text consists of a series of axioms and corollaries arranged and tested with Bradwardine's characteristic mathematical precision.

In stating these axioms, Bradwardine made no pretense of originality. Augustine and Anselm had already stated most eloquently Bradwardine's central thesis that God is the first cause of every created act, and Thomas Aquinas had developed it further as both a philosophical and a theological problem in his *Summa theologica*. Bradwardine's contribution was to restate this Augustinian position in language which reflected advances in early fourteenth-century natural philosophy. His

---

[1] Another indirect indication that the *De causa Dei* was directed towards defining a particular theological position rather than attacking certain academic colleagues is the remarkable degree of respect Bradwardine enjoyed in the 1330s and 1340s. Despite the vehemence of his language against "pelagian" notions, Bradwardine's ideas were accepted, discussed, challenged and modified in ways which were appropriate in a collegial setting. I am inclined to think, therefore, that the emphasis previous studies have placed on Bradwardine's personal dislike for Ockham and the "nominalists" is misleading because it focuses too much attention on individual personalities and not enough attention on the academic environment in which Bradwardine and his colleagues shared.

capacity for precise mathematical reasoning, combined with his passionate disdain for the contemporary suggestion that grace need not precede a meritorious act, gave his analysis of the divine causality a special sharpness and urgency. Bradwardine fully appreciated the implications of his view of the first cause for other theological questions, such as contingency, free will, grace, and predestination. Indeed, the burden of the three books of the *De causa Dei* was to illustrate both philosophically and theologically how the human will can be guided at all times by God's will and yet remain free.

The deterministic nature of Bradwardine's arguments made the *De causa Dei* a controversial work when it was published in 1344 and to some extent it remains so even today. It is important to remember, however, that many of Bradwardine's ideas were perfectly consonant with the Augustinian theological tradition and the questions he raised about alternative theologies were both perceptive and valid. Thus one has every reason to expect that there would have been scholarly interest in the work among his academic colleagues. Bradwardine's activities in the 1340s helped to ensure that the *De causa Dei* would reach an even wider and more varied audience. By the late 1330s, he had attracted powerful ecclesiastical patronage and was enjoying the prominence of his positions as chancellor of St. Paul's and chaplain to Edward III. Despite these new responsibilities, Bradwardine was able to maintain close ties with his former colleagues at Merton: he dedicated the *De causa Dei* to the Mertonians, who had urged him to put his complaints against the "modern Pelagians" into writing.[2] Bradwardine's reputation as a learned and saintly man and his strident claims about topics of contemporary interest assured a large readership for the *De causa Dei*, especially in academic circles. Any analysis of this work must consider, therefore, both the context of the academic debate which shaped its contents and the influential position of its author.

Modern readers of the *De causa Dei*, like their medieval counterparts, respond to the polemical tone of the work and sense in it some of the confusion of mid-fourteenth century theological discourse which Bradwardine tried to overcome. Although they all concede the importance of the work, historians disagree strongly about why it was significant. In spite of their different interpretations of Bradwardine's purpose, for example, both Leff and Oberman contend that the *De causa Dei* is almost wholly theological in character. According to Leff, "Bradwardine eschewed philosophy and metaphysics. He was not primarily concerned

---

[2] See Chapter One for a discussion of Bradwardine's dedication of the *De causa Dei*.

with the problems of being or its nature, nor with the scope of human knowledge."[3] After acknowledging the philosophical interest of the text, Oberman also argues that Bradwardine was "first and foremost a theologian, for whom philosophy served as a necessary means for the expression of theological thoughts."[4] Other historians contend, however, that it was Bradwardine's distinctive philosophical outlook which gives the *De causa Dei* its remarkable character. In his assessment of Bradwardine's criticism of the "modern Pelagians," for example, F. C. Copelston portrays Bradwardine as a metaphysician who based his doctrine of grace on the Aristotelian principle that whatever moves is moved by something else; and, as a Christian, Bradwardine merely specified that the first cause of any movement ultimately is God.[5] Unlike Augustine and Boethius, who used a psychological argument to explain how God causes the human will to act predictably and freely, Bradwardine relied firmly on Aristotelian cosmology in his analysis of this problem.[6]

Bradwardine's views of time and eternity provide a good means for assessing the extent to which his theology was shaped by Aristotelian metaphysics. Time, as the continuum which distinguishes limited created being from the eternal perfection of God, has both physical and theological significance in Bradwardine's cosmology. The variety of contexts in which the problem of time arises throughout the *De causa Dei* reveals the importance of time in Bradwardine's attempt to reconcile his Aristotelian natural philosophy with the doctrines of grace and justification which he derived from Augustine. In this chapter, I shall trace Bradwardine's treatment of time under three broad headings—the role of time in creation, the philosophical enigma of time, and the function of time in theological discussions of sin and grace—in order to examine Bradwardine's method of synthesizing Aristotelian natural philosophy with Augustinian theology. This analysis of Bradwardine's view of time in the *De causa Dei* will demonstrate that the problem of time held a central place in Bradwardine's metaphysical system as well as in his conception of God's absolute power because it is the distinction between time and eternity which reveals how God can create an orderly universe and participate in every created motion or act without being constrained by the rules which he has established for his creation.

---

[3] *Bradwardine and the Pelagians*, p. 16.
[4] *Archbishop Thomas Bradwardine*, p. 1.
[5] *A History of Medieval Philosophy* (London: Methuen, 1972), pp. 259-60.
[6] *Ibid.*, p. 258.

Throughout the *De causa Dei*, Bradwardine affirmed the study of God's activity in the world as the proper task of the Christian scholar. As a devoted follower of Aristotle and a gifted natural philosopher in his own right, Bradwardine remained committed even in his theology to the validity of Aristotelian natural philosophy. In the tradition of Aquinas, Bradwardine had advocated in his earlier works the exploration of natural phenomena through human reason. By the time he had begun to conceive of the *De causa Dei*, however, his interest had grown in the long-standing struggle to reconcile reason with faith. Bradwardine's first attempt to integrate his Augustinian-Boethian view of eternity with his Aristotelian view of time culminated in the *De futuris contingentibus*, in which he seemed to rule out the possibility that God and humanity could share a common experience of time. Such nineteenth- and early twentieth-century historians as Lechler, Workman and Laun saw the *De causa Dei* simply as a more mature version of his earlier thesis which posited a radical separation between God and humanity. More recently, this view has been defended and enlarged upon by Leff and Robson, who, like their predecessors, see both Bradwardine and Wyclif as advocates of an extreme predestinarianism.[7] Because he held that God in his absolute power can do anything and insisted that God participates directly in every human act, Bradwardine has been accused both of theological determinism and of drastically diminishing the human capacity for creativity or independence.

If one keeps in mind Bradwardine's Aristotelian outlook on the natural world, however, another interpretation of the *De causa Dei* becomes possible. Bradwardine the scientist wished to find order and rationality in the created universe; and, like all theologians of his age, he looked to God to find the source of that order. In an intellectual environment of intense speculation about what God could or could not do, Bradwardine's approach to God can be seen as optimistic and a positive inducement to all kinds of human endeavor rather than a grim, paralyzing sort of determinism. For Bradwardine, the notion of predestination was in fact a consolation to those who were anxious about the state of their relationship with God: he intended not to frighten people but to reassure them, in the face of disquieting remarks by some theologians that God might intervene in the world without observing his own natural laws or that his knowledge of the future might be altered by acts of human will.[8]

---

[7] See the Introduction for a more thorough explication of these positions.

[8] From a conversation with Dr. Jeremy I. Catto, Oriel College, Oxford, January, 1987. Dr. Catto has suggested that the comforting tone of some passages of the *De causa Dei*

In Bradwardine's opinion, God has created the world in such a way that its orderly development in time in no way restricts his power, in his eternal present, to participate in his creation. On the contrary, God's constant involvement with his creation ensures order and goodness without any threat of divine capriciousness.

The main theses of the three books of the *De causa Dei* give an indication of how Bradwardine envisioned God's activity in the world.[9] In Book I Bradwardine argues that God is the source of every good act: "Grace, which is a habit freely given by God, together with the human will is the proper efficient cause of whatever good and meritorious act man performs."[10] Moreover, although the human will must cooperate in the process of causing a good act, the gift of grace is "naturally prior" to the human will.[11] Book II develops the idea that God has created the human will in such a way that it can freely choose one course of action or another. In this sense, the human will is undetermined and its future is contingent. At the same time, any act of the created will requires God, who in his infinite and perfect knowledge knows what choice will be made, to be its coeffector.[12] In Book III Bradwardine explores the implications of this principle of "antecedent necessity" for the temporal order of creation. Here Bradwardine tries to explain how God's function as first cause influences the past, present and future of every aspect of his creation.[13] All three theses stress the creature's experience of God rather than God's experience of creation: God intervenes in the world and directs its entire development without being changed himself. This perspective is reasonable in light of the fact that philosophers and theologians from antiquity had recognized the human incapacity fully to comprehend God.

Bradwardine's conception of God's relationship to creation rests on the premise that the physical world exists in time and operates according to natural laws established by God. In his view of matter, for example,

---

might have been prompted by Bradwardine's desire to reassure people in the court of Edward III (among others) who did not fully understand contemporary theological debates and were disturbed by them.

[9] Weisheipl, "Ockham and the Mertonians," p. 652.

[10] *De causa Dei*, I, 40, p. 364, A: "Quod gratia, quae est habitus gratis datus a Deo una cum voluntate humana est causa efficiens proprie cuiuslibet boni et meritorij actus sui."

[11] *Ibid.*, I, 41, p. 371, A: "Quod gratia prius naturaliter quam voluntas humana efficiat actus bonos."

[12] *Ibid.*, II, p. 540, B: "Quod cuiuslibet actus voluntatis creatae Deus est necessarius coeffector." See also chapter 29, p. 577, B: "Quod voluntas increata et creata in coefficiendo actum voluntatis creatae, non sunt coaequales, nec coaequaeuae in ordine naturali."

[13] See Weisheipl, "Mertonians," p. 652.

Bradwardine restates the Aristotelian definition of matter as a formless, potential substance which only becomes a real being when a form is added to it. Along with Aquinas, Bradwardine contends that God has created both matter itself and the forms which shape matter into real things.[14] All things, therefore, come into being in accordance with the divine plan. God's love ensures that everything which he creates is good, so that nature itself is fundamentally good.[15] Because God not only gives matter its form but also determines the laws which govern all motion and change, God must be seen as the prime mover in every act.[16]

Bradwardine bases this thesis firmly on the philosophical and logical studies of Aristotle, who had argued that every effect must be caused by an event which precedes it. Therefore, every individual act, and indeed creation as a whole, proceeds from God as the first cause.[17] Bradwardine obviously did not see a contradiction between his belief in God as a direct and primary participant in the world and Aristotelian explanations for how the world actually operates. In fact, Aristotle's initial observation that all effects in the physical world have causes stands as the underlying principle both of Bradwardine's natural philosophy and of his theology.

Although he accepted Aristotle's definition of matter and his theory of causation, Bradwardine could not agree with his conviction that the world is eternal. We have already seen how closely Bradwardine followed Aristotle's conception of time in his works of natural philosophy. There is no reason to suppose that in the *De causa Dei* Bradwardine rejected the Aristotelian principles concerning time's continuity, its infinite divisibility or its relationship to motion after having proven the validity of

---

[14] *De causa Dei*, I, 2, p. 163, A: ". . . Deum est de se potentiale, ipse autem solus actus per se et purus, sicut praemissa testantur. Item omne de se fluxibile et informe, ad hoc quod sigatur stabiliter et formetur, necessario indiget aliqua fixione et forma ipsum immediate sigente atque formante; huiusmodi igitur fixio sive forma, vel est per se fixa seu fixio, formata seu forma, et tunc est Deus, et habetur intentum. . . ." See Leff, pp. 56-57.

[15] *De causa Dei*, I, 26, p. 251, A: "Quod tota vniuersitas rerum est bona, et nulla res per se mala"; and I, 30, p. 271, E: "Quod res voluntariae diuinae prouidentiae legibus gubernantur."

[16] *Ibid.*, I, 4, p. 174, B: "Prima, quod nihil potest quicquam mouere sine Deo idem per se et proprie comouente. Secunda, quod nihil potest quicquam mouere sine Deo immediate idem mouente. Tertia, quod nihil potest quicquam mouere sine Deo idem mouente immediatius alio motore quocunque."

[17] *Ibid.*, p. 174, E: "Pro secundo dicendum quod Philosophus in talibus loquitur, sicut Philosophus naturalis, scilicet de immediatione causae secundae, causae scilicet naturalis; et haec est immediatio secundum quid, quia tantum in genere creatorum; non autem de immediatione simpliciter, quae simpliciter omnem mediam causam priuat."

these features so successfully in his works of natural philosophy. Nevertheless, Bradwardine made it clear in several passages in the *De causa Dei* that the idea of a created world of infinite duration cannot be sustained.[18] Bradwardine contended that none of the classical philosophers, including Plato and Aristotle, had been able to prove that the universe has existed from eternity. Aristotle's theory of causation in fact suggested the contrary, because the motion of the universe must have been caused initially by something. In keeping with the medieval interpretation of Aristotle, Bradwardine attributed to God this initial motion, which began the process of creation.[19]

One of the main goals of the *De causa Dei*, therefore, was to illustrate precisely how all created acts proceed initially from God. The idea of couching the story of creation in myth, as Plato had done in the *Timaeus*, held no appeal for Bradwardine. The truth, Bradwardine contended, should be clear both to natural philosophers and to theologians: because it consists of real being, the universe must have been created; and logic, observation of the natural world and revelation all point to creation by God. Bradwardine did not think speculation on how God created the universe or how he could exercise his absolute power over it was

---

[18] For example, Bradwardine states as a corollary to his first proposition that the created world has to be limited, temporally and spacially, in order to distinguish the mutability of created being from the perfect, infinite simplicity of God. See *De causa Dei*, I, 1, 6, p. 5, A: "Mvtentur credentes Deum non necessario, sed contingenter esse summe perfectum et Deum, ipsumque esse mutabiliem [nouiter] irascibilem, placibilem, tristabilem, laetabilem, atque possibilem, nouiter quacunque alia passione: opinantes quoque quod Deus sit nomen accidentale, et non essentiale simpliciter. Quod autem Deus sit necessario summe perfectus et Deus, ex prima suppositione consequitur euidenter; cum perfectus et melius sit sic esse; quam contingenter, sicut patet ex premisses in ostensione suppositionis illius."

[19] Bradwardine devotes Book I, chapter 1, corollaries 33, 34, 37 and 40 to various aspects of creation in time. See especially *De causa Dei*, I, 1, 34, p. 66, B-C: "Constat autem Philosophis quod prius, et ante accipitur dupliciter ad propositum, scilicet secundum naturam et secundum tempus. Pono igitur contrate Aristoteles et Averroes quod mundus incepit et motus in A instanti, et quod nullum fuit tempus, mutatio, neque successio temporalis, aut aliqua duratio vera mutalibis, aut partibilis, magna, vel parua ante illium primum motum qui sit B. Pono igitur consequenter quod nihil omnino praecessit A prioriate aliqua temporali, sicut nihil praecedit coelum exterius prioriate vel superioritate locali, et quod hoc sit consequens, patet per teipsum 10. ilius 8[i] dicentem; Prius et posterius quomodo erunt, tempore non existente, aut tempus, si non sit motus? et ex alia parte pono, quod Deus aeternus, euisque aeterna sapientia ac voluntas praecessit A prioriate naturae, sicut causa causatum. Cum ergo tu Aristoteles per totum illum processum supponis quod cuiuslibet rei factae non esse praecedit necessario suum esse, et hoc loquendo de praecessione temporali, vt innuis 10. et tu Averroes hoc idem dicis expresse in comment. decimaoctavo quoque decimoquinto ac alijs hoc supponis."

particularly useful, for the human mind cannot grasp the full meaning of creation. This notion lies at the heart of Bradwardine's criticism of his opponents' alternative approaches to God's absolute power. Bradwardine was much more intrigued by the question of how God, despite existing in an eternal present, nonetheless continues to participate actively in the historical development of his creation.

In Book I, chapter 1, of the *De causa Dei*, Bradwardine defends the theses that God is the greatest and most perfect goodness and that every created thing has a definite beginning, concluding along Thomist lines that all things proceed from a first cause which is God.[20] Later, two long corollaries explore the metaphysical and logical reasons for affirming the creation of the world and God's power to direct it.[21] As we might expect from a specialist in natural philosophy, Bradwardine's arguments for creation are particularly effective when he illustrates the difference between God's eternal present and the temporal limits of created being with concrete references to natural phenomena. In corollary 40, for example, Bradwardine embarks on an extensive attack on the physical theory of those philosophers, including Aristotle, Plato, Anaxagoras and Averroes, who persist in claiming that the universe is eternal in spite of irrefutable cosmological evidence to the contrary.[22]

In addition to logical arguments against the eternity of the world, Bradwardine adds the ingenious reasoning that the principles of Euclidean geometry preclude the possibility of a universe limitless in space and time. Bradwardine's understanding of continuity and the problem of beginning and ceasing are crucial in this context; for, as he points out, the majority of classical philosophers, including Democritus, Aristotle and Epicurus, had agreed that permanent continua have external limits.[23]

---

[20] *Ibid.*, I, 1, p. 1, C.

[21] *Ibid.*, I, 1, parts 33-34, pp. 65-71.

[22] *Ibid.*, I, 1, corollary 40, pp. 119-45.

[23] *Ibid.*, I, 40, p. 125, D: "Puto autem quod Democritus primo istam sententiam adinuenit, et Epicurus postea confirmauit, sicut de sententia affirmante cuncta geri fortuito, Lactantius primi institutionum diuinarum aduersus Gentes primo, recitat manifeste, sicut 27. huius primi plenius recitatur. Et haec videtur opinio, quam Aristoteles I. de Coelo et Mundo 76. et post, nitium reprobare. Singula namque minima corpora, qualis videtur minimus puluis terrae, de singulis mundis assumpta, et modo praedicto ad inuicem cumulata, vniuersum locum, situm, spacium, seu vacuum verum vel imaginarium totaliter occuparent. Vbi ergo hospitarentur alia corpora plura incomparabiliter et maiora? quomodo contenarentur illa situ minori, et non totale spatium vniuersum totaliter occuparent? Quomodo etiam cubi illi, partes fili, seu corpora minima de mundis singulis nunc collecta, et sphaerice cumulata non prius occurabunt tantum spacium, quantum modo spacium vniuersum? et quomodo nunc occupant spacium amplius, quam tunc

It is the existence of external limits which allows objects, whether physical or purely mathematical, to be compared.[24] Bradwardine therefore adopts a mathematical argument concerning the external limits of permanent continua to verify the theological truth that God creates and provides spacial and temporal limits for every existing thing.

The question of temporal limits for created things has additional significance for Bradwardine's theology because, in keeping with the Augustinian-Boethian definitions of time and eternity, time distinguishes created being from eternal being. Whether a thing is permanent or successive, it exists in time and therefore has limits. All successive continua such as motion or temperature share the characteristics of finity and infinity: while they are potentially infinite in respect of their divisibility, they do not have limitless duration.[25] By placing his creation within time, God ensures that it remains distinct from himself and has limits. Indeed, Bradwardine goes so far as to say that God cannot create something which is necessary and limitless in itself, for only God can have these qualities.[26]

In spite of its negative wording, this assertion is not meant to restrict God's power in any way. Rather, it serves to emphasize Bradwardine's larger contention that the created world is not only distinct from God but also receives its goodness directly from God. Bradwardine's use of a mathematical argument to disprove the possibility of an eternal universe indicates the extent to which his natural philosophy informed his theological views. It is evident from Corollary 40 that he had no difficulty in reconciling his opinions about continuity, infinity, time and motion with his belief in the supreme power of God. Bradwardine maintained, in

---

fecerunt? Praesertim cum secundum doctrinam Geometrarum certissimam, sphaera sit capacissima figurarum."

[24] *Ibid.*, p. 126, E: "Infinito namque simpliciter maius esse non potest, sed secundum quid tantum, et secundum quid finite."

[25] *Ibid.*, p. 130, D: "Nec potest quis vlterius fingere cauillando, quod tam B quam C secundum quid est infinitum, et secundum quid finitum, sicut secundum sententiam Aristotelis, partes praeterita et futura temporis simpliciter infiniti, quas copulat praesens instans; quia infinitum intensiue quantumlibet modicum remittatur, est simpliciter et omniquaque finitum intensiue: vt patet de caliditate posita infinita intensiue, quae si quantumlibet remittatur, necessario est simpliciter omniquaque finita; Finitur enim superius intrinsece ad certum gradum finitum, et inferius extrinsece ad non esse caliditatis, sicut et quaelibet forma intensibilis terminatur."

[26] *Ibid.*, p. 131, B: "Ideo fortassis dicetur quod Deus non potest facere creataram, quae sit ex se necesse esse et aeterna, quare nec Deum. Sed etsi non possit facere creaturam istas virtutes seu proprietates habere, faciat ipsam habere omnes alias virtutes possibiles creaturae, et quamlibet simpliciter infinite."

fact, that Aristotle and other classical philosophers contributed directly to his proof of the finity of the created world despite their conviction that the world is infinite. In contrast to Bradwardine's former efforts to explain and redefine Aristotelian principles, his discussion of time and eternity in the *De causa Dei* amounts to a self-conscious rejection of certain Aristotelian principles and a thoughtful revision of others.

Bradwardine's profound belief in God the creator led him, in effect, to adopt a cosmology which emphasized the Augustinian and Boethian distinction between divine eternity and the imperfect changeability of the created world. Echoing certain themes from the *Timaeus*, Bradwardine conceived of creation as neither corrupt nor fundamentally evil simply because it changes and exists in time: the very fact that God has made the world and loves it makes it good.[27] Nor did he think that human reason is inadequate to the task of investigating the natural order which God has made.[28] Nevertheless, Bradwardine had to come to terms with the dilemma posed by the central theses of the *De causa Dei*: God is both an active participant in every aspect of creation and yet distinct from it because he is infinite and immutable. In resolving this dilemma Bradwardine returned to the conception of time which he had first developed in the *De futuris contingentibus*.

Bradwardine considered it a matter of primary importance to prove that God is not affected by time but has a kind of being which transcends the temporal order of his creation. One of the first objections Bradwardine made in the *De causa Dei* was directed against those who try to

---

[27] *Ibid.*, I, 26, p. 251, A: "Hic autem in mediastino pro praecedentibus et sequentibus ostendendum, totum vniuersitatem rerum omnium esse bonam, nec esse in ea aliquid quod sit malum. Huius enim oppositum Empedocles, Pictagoras, Manes, Manichaei haeretici dicere videbantur, sicut 18ª pars Corollarij primir docet. Omne sequidem per se volubile et amabile a bono sapiente, est aliquo modo bonum, vt tam Philosophi, quam Theologi partier contestantur: et quaelibet pars mundi est per se volubilis et amabilis a Deo, sicut et per se creabilis, et conseruabilis est ab eo, sicut ex capitulis 2.3.6.8.&9. poterit apparere."

[28] In fact, says Bradwardine, the act of applying reason to the observation of the natural world, as Aristotle had done, is one of the best ways of arriving at an understanding of God's infinite goodness. See, for example, *De causa Dei*, I, 11, p. 198, C-D: "Dicit enim Philosophus 4. Metaph 9. quod hoc est primum principium complexorum, Idem simul inesse, et non inesse eidem, et secundum idem est impossibile; sed ne tanto Philosopho tantillus videar obgarrire, sciendum quod duplex est principium, cognoscendi scilicet et essendi, vel, quoad nos et quoad naturam; Ipse autem loquitur ibi de primo principio cognoscendi, et apud nos tantum, per quod generaliter in omnibus scientijs regulamur, sicut processus textus et comment. satis ostendit. Principium autem complexorum primum simpliciter est de Deo vt puta Deus est, vel Deus scit omnia, vel Deus vult omnia, vel aliquid quicquam tale."

make God more accessible to human experience by likening him to created things. In an impressively thorough repudiation of the polytheism of the ancient world, Bradwardine warned against the error of reducing the manifest greatness of God's creation to pantheism by worshipping as gods such objects as trees, the sun or the moon.[29] Because nature worship was not a widespread practice in mid-fourteenth-century England, one might wonder why he should have given so much attention to it. Part of the explanation lies, of course, in his effort to provide encyclopedic coverage of all challenges to the primacy of divine causality. Although Bradwardine could not have worried seriously about Babylonian, Egyptian or Roman religious practices, he was extremely distressed by the underlying assumption that the world had formed itself out of primordial chaos rather than being created from nothing by God. Bradwardine therefore used the subject of polytheism to make the larger point that God cannot be conceived as "temporal, created or corruptible."[30] It is in this context that Bradwardine laments the human failure, both in ancient times and in his own, to recognize God's transcendence over his creation.[31]

Bradwardine further emphasizes God's distinctiveness by asserting that God remains infinite and eternal despite his capacity to enter into the created world.[32] Bradwardine develops this point most thoroughly in the second chapter of Book I, which demonstrates why God necessarily is the first cause in every human act. In this passage Bradwardine explicitly states his thesis, which he derived from Aristotle, Avicenna and Algazali, that God is the first cause from which all effects proceed. God is not, however, simply a craftsman who, having created the world,

---

[29] *Ibid.*, I, 1, part 13, pp. 8-10.

[30] *Ibid.*, p. 10, A: "Nulla ergo res temporalis, generabilis, corruptibilisue est Deus."

[31] *Ibid.* "O miserabiliter miserabilis, miser homo, si tamen homo, cur non verecundaris naturam irrationalem naturaliter viliorem, ignobiliorem, imperfectiorem et tibi subiectam adorare et colere pro Domine Deo tuo? cuius etenim animus non praeponit Deum suum sibi ipsi, et omnibus alijs in ordine dignitatus. . . ."

[32] This definition of God naturally raises questions about Bradwardine's view of the incarnation, for God must have assumed physical and temporal limits to enter the world in the person of Jesus Christ. Bradwardine's response to this question, in keeping with Augustine's response as he expressed it in *De civitate Dei*, XXI.15, was that God, though changeless and divine, miraculously took on human nature for our redemption. The clear implication of this response is that God has the power to be simultaneously eternal and temporal. Bradwardine argued similarly in *De causa Dei*, I, 1, 35, pp. 72-76, in favor of the possibility of Christ's conception and birth through the Virgin Mary. Bradwardine returned to this point later in *De causa Dei*, III, 42-45, pp. 785-93, where he affirmed God's power to ensure the eternal truth of prophesies made by Jesus and other prophets.

leaves it to operate according to its own mechanisms and by its own energy. Instead, God, as the first cause of every created act, is always directly involved in his creation. Leff observes that Bradwardine uses here the terms of Aristotelian metaphysics to portray God as the "triple cause, formal, efficient and final," of every created act: formal, because he establishes the conditions in which the act will take place; efficient, because he actively participates in every phase of the act; and final, because his participation makes a potential act real and actual.[33]

From a cosmological point of view, God's most mysterious power is his ability to participate so fully in creation and to encompass all creation within himself without being changed, limited or corrupted.[34] Bradwardine draws on a long tradition of metaphysical speculation when he accords to God a perfect, uncreated being. Following Augustine, he

---

[33] Leff, pp. 48-49. Bradwardine compares God's causality to that of an architect who transforms the idea of a house into an actual physical object in *De causa Dei*, I, 2, p. 154, B: "Imaginare itaque in mente Architecti formam domus fabricandae quam solummodo respicit, vt ad eius imitationem domum faciat, et imaginare cum hoc per impossibile ipsius voluntatem ita potentem, quod se sola applicet materiam formandam in domum; et imaginare cum his quod materia domus esset fluida, nec posset permanere in forma recepta in se, si separatetur a forma in mente Architecti, sicut aqua figurata sigillo argenteo, separato sigillo, statim amitteret figuram receptam. Imaginare itaque voluntatem artificis applicantem materiam domus ad formam in mente sua, non solum vt sic formetur in domum, sed quamdiu domus manet in esse domus, vt formaliter in esse seruetur. Eo itaque modo quo forma huiusmodi in mente Architecti esset forma domus, est ars siue sapientia, siue verbum omnipotentis Dei, forma omnium creaturum; Ipsa enim simul est exemplar efficiens, Formans, et in forma data conseruans. Et infra dicit aeternam Dei sapientiam sic esse formam omnium, velut si imagineris figuram sigilli argente vitam et intelligentiam, intelligentem se volentemque figuare ad sui imitationem simultudinem magis minusue expressam ceram fluidam, non potentem per se permanere in aliqua figuratione recepta, ipsaque hac sola voluntate informem et fluidam ceram ad se moueret, sibique applicaret, et sic suam simultudenem aliquantam imprimeret, et impressam seruaret; sic aeterna Patris sapientia est forma omnium."

[34] See, for example, *De causa Dei*, I, 2, p. 147, B-C: "Quare et Chrysostomus istud expondendo, homilia 2ª sic ait; Ferens, inquit, omnia hoc est gubernans; siquidem cadentia et ad nihilum tendentia contenit. Non enim minus est continere mundum quam fecisse; sed si oportet aliquid audacius dicere, adhuc amplius est. Nam in faciendo quidem ex nullis existentibus rerum essentiae productae sunt; In continendo vero, ea quae facta sunt, ne ad nihilum redeant, continentur. Hic ergo dum reguntur, et ad inuicem sibi repugnantia coaptantur, magnum et valde mirabile plurimumaeque virtutis indicium declaratur. Dicitque Augustinus in De diuinitatus Dei essentia, et de inuisibilitate, atque incommutabilitate, 1° sic de Deo; Procul dubio nullus est locus ab eius praesentia absens: Super omnem quippe creaturam praesidet regendo, subtus est omnia sustinendo atque portando, non pondere laboris, sed infatigabili virtute; quoniam nulla creatura ab eo condita per se subsistere valet, nisi ab eo sustinetur qui eam creauit; extra omnio est, sed non exclusus, intra omnia est, sed non conclusus."

attributes great significance to God's response to Moses in the Book of Exodus. In replying "I am who I am," God has offered humanity an insight into his true nature as a simple, perfect and universal being.[35] By his very nature, God cannot be other than distinct from created things, which are changeable, have limits, pass in and out of existence and lack the perfection of the creator. Bradwardine's Platonic interpretation of the passage from Exodus exposes his dependence on Augustine for his view of God. Like Augustine, Bradwardine is able to accept Platonic statements about God's perfection and completeness as well as revelation through scripture, in spite of his preference for Aristotelian natural philosophy. Bradwardine's conception of God as distinct and changeless plays a key role in his solution to the philosophical and theological problem of God's intervention in a changeable but largely rational world.

Bradwardine's statements about time in the *De causa Dei*, therefore, need to be examined primarily in the context of his conception of God's distinctiveness from creation. Bradwardine considers it a mistake to think that time is not in itself a creation or to assume that time is a peculiar sort of indefinite creation with no beginning or end. Rather, time is a created, limited entity which has the special function of providing a frame of reference for all other created entities. No created thing exists which does not exist in time; indeed, time is such a fundamental concept in creation that God alone can exist outside time. If one accepts the premise that God is a perfect being and the first cause of every created act, says Bradwardine, one must also admit that God created the world from nothing and placed his creation within the limits of time. To say otherwise would be to claim the existence of other kinds of pre-temporal beings which share in God's eternity and infinity. Even Aristotle, who thought that the world is eternal, proved through his natural philosophy that the world could not have been made from pre-existing material.[36]

---

[35] *Ibid.*, p. 154, E: "An forte et hoc est quod Deus sciscitanti Moysi nomen eius, velate respondit, Ego sum qui sum, sic dices filijs Israel, Qui est, misit me ad vos. Exod. 3 quasi velit innuere se esse seipsum simpliciter per seipsum, et se etiam esse quodammodo totum ens, essentificando videlicet alia vniuersa."

[36] *Ibid.*, I, 1, part 40, pp. 139-40, E-A: "Ex his omnibus potest cuilibet sobrio non proteruo rationabiliter apparere, mundum nedum habuisse principium temporale, verum et fuisse creatum ex nihilo. Ex qua namque materia fieret praecedente? qualis esset illa, simplex, vel composita; aeterna vel nova? Quare et tu, Aristoteles, multum rationabiliter saepe probas, mundum non fuisse factum ex materia praeiacente? Quid ergo consequentius consequentia naturali, quam concesso mundum habuisse principium temporale, concedere ipsum fuisse creatum ex nihilo consequenter?" See Oberman, pp. 53-54.

God alone, then, is free from the constraints of time; and time, as the medium of creation, assures us of God's eternal, infinite and perfect being. God is able to exist outside time yet still participate in the lives of his creatures because he sees all of his creation from an eternal present. God knows all things simultaneously and eternally, and there is nothing to obscure his vision at any instant of creation: he does not need to wait for his knowledge to be completed or his prophecies fulfilled in time.[37] Bradwardine thus supplements his metaphysical argument about God's relationship to the world through time with an epistemological one.

In Book I, chapter 6, Bradwardine contends that God has complete knowledge of every created thing. Relying on a powerful range of authorities, including Plato, Aristotle, Seneca, Boethius, Augustine and Averroes, Bradwardine develops a complex logical argument in favor of God's eternal knowledge. God's knowledge is necessary for the existence of every created thing, says Bradwardine, because it is God's eternal knowledge of a thing which makes it real. Bradwardine quotes, for example, from Avicenna's commentary on Aristotle's *De anima* that "all things of the earth which are past, present or future have being in the mind of the creator."[38] He goes on to suggest that God's knowledge not only is complete but also exists in God's mind in a perfect and universal form. God's knowledge thus transcends time and the limitations of created being.[39] Having built up an extensive list of authorities in his favor, Bradwardine considers it a simple matter to prove in a brief corollary that God, "both omnipotent and omniscient," has complete knowledge of every created thing, whether it is possible or impossible, whether it can be verified by human reason or only imagined.[40]

---

[37] *Ibid.*, I, 7, p. 189, C: "Deus enim scit omnia simul et semper, non per vices temporum; sicut ipsa scita incipiunt esse, vel desinunt more humano, quoniam apud ipsum non est transmutatio, nec vicissitudinis obumbratio." See Oberman, p. 54.

[38] *Ibid.*, I, 6, p. 183, C: "Quare et Auicenna 4. de Anima 2. dicit, Omnia quae in mundo sunt praeterita, praesentia, et futura, habent esse in sapientia creatoris."

[39] *Ibid.*, E: "Et si ipsi habuerunt scientiam huiusmodi saltem paruam, vel qualemcunque coniecturam tenuissimam, verum tamen, quis nesciens, seu potius insaniens Deum audebit asserere nescium futurorum; cum per primam Suppositionem, tertiam partem, et quartam Corollarij primi huius, necessario consequatur ipsum ea cognoscere perfectius infinite. Amplius autem si Deus secundum praemissa habet scientiam omnium praesentium, praeteritorum, et similiter futurorum, cum scire actualiter et particulariter, distincte et certe sit perfectius, quam scire tantum habitualiter, potentialiter et vniuersaliter, confuse et incerte."

[40] *Ibid.*, p. 184, A: "Quod Deus habet distinctam scientiam omnium, nedum praesentium, praeteritorum et futurorum: verum et omnium possibilium et impossibilium, imaginabilium et cognoscibilium quouismodo, unde et omnisciens, sicut et omnipotens veraciter dici potest."

Bradwardine's strongest statements about the problem of time and eternity come in chapter 51 of Book III, which is devoted entirely to the topic of eternity. Once again drawing on authorities from Plato to Averroes, he contrasts the mutability and limitation of created being with the immutability and infinity of God. Because he is eternal, neither God nor any of his acts can be completely measured in time. In God there is no divisibility; no past, present or future; no succession. God's existence is simple, unified, perfect and simultaneous. The patterns of flux and change which human beings observe in time are part of a created order which is separate from God and does not change him. God sees everything in a single instant.[41] Throughout this passage Bradwardine reveals his continuing interest in the physics of motion and succession by using images of nature to define negatively God's eternal serenity. Bradwardine suggests, in fact, that knowledge of the manifestations of God in nature deeply enriches the understanding of the eternal God. He acknowledges with Plato that it is motion, especially the motion of the heavenly bodies, the constant pattern of night and day, which distinguishes our world of time and change from God's timeless existence.[42] In Bradwardine's view, then, time as a created being has a central place in the natural order which God has made for his creatures. Indeed, time is the divine construct which allows human beings to comprehend God's eternal presence in an ever-changing created world.

---

[41] *Ibid.*, III, 51, p. 826, B-C: "Constat siquidem secundum Philosophorum sententiam, quod mensura debet esse vnigenita et similis mensurato: homo autem mutabilis est, et actiones eius mutabile, quare et mensurantur mensura mutabili, scilicet temporali, ipso videlicet tempore vel instanti: Deus vero, et quaelibet actio eius intrinseca, puto cognito et volutio, immutabilis est omnino, sicut quintum et vicesimum tertium primi docent; quare nec Deus, nec aliqua actio eius intrinseca per se immediate et proprie mensuratur mensura mutabili, scilicet tempore vel instanti, sed mensura immutabili, inuaribili, stabili, et aeterna, seu potius ipsa aeternitate immutabiliter penitus, insuccessibiliter, vniformiter atque stabiliter permanente. In ipsa namque nulla diuisibilitas, nulla maioritas, nulla minoritas, nulla prioritas, nulla posterioritas, nulla mutabilitas, nulla accessio, nulla recessio, nulla successio, nihil praeteritum, nihil futurum, nec vlla penitus differentia successiua, sed indiuisibilis, simplex, vnica, eadem, insuccessibilis, ac instantanea praesentialitas et simultas, sicut ostenditur primo primi, imo superindiuisibilis, supersimplex, superunica, supereadem, superinsuccessibilis, ac superinstantanea praesentialitas et simultas temporalis instantis."

[42] *Ibid.*, p. 827, A-B: "Vnde Plato 1. Timei 9. vtens aeuo pro aeternitate sic ait, Dies et noctes et menses et annos, qui ante coelestem exordinationem non erant, tunc nascente mundo iussit existere, quae omnia partes sunt temporis, nosque haec cum aeuo assignamus eidem solitariae naturae, non recte partes indiuiduae rei singimus. Dicimus enim fuit, est, erit; At illi solum esse competit iuxta veram sui certamque rationem, fuisse vero deinceps et fore non competit; haec quippe geniturae temporis propria. Motus enim sunt, vnus praeeuntis, alter imminentes non aeui sed temporis."

Like Aristotle and Averroes, Bradwardine associates time with motion and implies that time and motion can be used to measure each other. In the context of eternity, however, the concept of time has a much more significant cosmological function, for it is the flux of time itself which gives created things their special character and makes them different from God. To illustrate this point, Bradwardine appropriately chooses a geometrical metaphor to describe God's temporal relationship to his creation: God is a single point on a line; he is a single instant in time. In his eternal present God does not experience any of the effects of time as his creatures do, either physically, as in successive continuity, or psychologically, as in memory.[43] The importance of time in Bradwardine's cosmology, then, is that it establishes the proper scope for the study of nature, while its counterpart, eternity, frees God to participate in his creation without being changed or restricted by it. In Oberman's words, "by his theocentric thinking Bradwardine sees the idea of time as the limiting factor for the creature, characterizing the relation between man and God as an infinite distance, whereas this distance does not exist for God."[44]

We may conclude, therefore, that although Bradwardine did not present a systematic analysis of time in the *De causa Dei*, his view of time had significant bearing on his understanding of creation as it was developed in this treatise. In his other works Bradwardine demonstrated a thorough mastery of Aristotelian natural philosophy and Euclidean geometry. The *De causa Dei* allowed him to display commensurate skill in analyzing other kinds of sources. Plato's *Timaeus*, Augustine's theological works and Boethius' *Consolation of Philosophy* all contributed to Bradwardine's conception of eternity and the relationship of eternity to time in creation. Bradwardine's reading of Anselm, Aquinas and Duns Scotus enhanced his conception of time as a philosophical and theological problem. Throughout the *De causa Dei* Bradwardine suggested that an Aristotelian approach to natural philosophy in no way contradicted the notion of an eternal and limitless creator, so long as one did not try to argue that the world itself is eternal. Bradwardine's remarks about time in the *De causa Dei* indicate that he continued to see time in

---

[43] *Ibid.*, D: "Tempus fluxibile sequitur fluxibilem actionem, scilicet motum coeli; sic aeternitas stabilis sequitur stabilem actionem, scilicet esse Dei, et ab ipsa quodammodo deriuatur, defluit et emanat. Sicut enim punctus fluens lineam, et instans tempus; sic et Deus instans stabilissimus per actum suum veluti quendam fluxum videtur aeternitate causare, et hoc maxime apud cognitionem humanam, quae secundum Philosophum in de memoria et reminiscentia, non sit sine continuo, nec sine ratione temporis atque motus, licet in Deo nullus sit fluxus mutabiliter, aut temporaliter successiuus."

[44] Oberman, p. 54.

Aristotelian terms, as the measure of motion or, more generally, as the successive continuum which embraces all movement and change in created being. Because time is created and therefore has a beginning and an end, its regular, successive nature serves as a frame for all other motions and changes which can be observed in nature. Like Boethius, Bradwardine felt compelled to state that God exists outside the temporal order; otherwise God would be subject to the same forces as created beings and would lose his essential characteristics of infinity, eternity, immutability and omniscience.

By the time he wrote the *De causa Dei*, however, Bradwardine had completed his degree in theology and was thoroughly familiar with the contemporary debates concerning the nature of God's involvement in the world. Thus he fully realized how difficult it is to reconcile logically a conception of God as changeless and eternal with a belief that God participates directly in every aspect of creation. It is almost impossible for the human mind to grasp how God can be simultaneously inside and outside time, how God can prophesy and respond to the petitions of his creatures without himself changing in any way; and yet the educated fourteenth-century Christian was expected to affirm this complex and apparently self-contradictory definition of God. Both scripture and patristic authority demanded it.

As we have already seen, theologians such as Duns Scotus and Ockham tried to solve the problem by proposing alternative cosmologies. They argued in various ways that God, by virtue of his absolute power, has the capacity to change along with his creation in time without losing his qualities of immutability or omniscience.[45] In this way the contingency of at least some acts of the human will could be preserved. Ockham was particularly aware of the dilemma of maintaining God's omniscience while safeguarding human freedom: he ultimately concluded that reason cannot resolve this dilemma and that certain truths about God's essential nature have to be accepted by faith alone.[46]

---

[45] For a full discussion of the implications of the notion of absolute power in late medieval theology and natural philosophy see Edward Grant, "The Condemnation of 1277, God's Absolute Power, and Physical Thought in the Late Middle Ages," *Viator*, 10 (1979), pp. 211-44. Grant attributes the upsurge of speculation on such topics as whether God can undo the past or create more than one world to a response to the condemnations which claimed that Aristotelian natural philosophy restricts the scope of God's power.

[46] Goddu, p. 8, argues that Ockham's tendency to separate natural philosophy and theology stemmed from his deeply held convictions about the necessity of protecting faith from over-zealous reasoning: "For Ockham the issues concerning the relation of

Because Bradwardine refused to admit the possibility of change in God, even to preserve the freedom of the human will, he had to consider an alternative approach to contingency in the *De causa Dei*. His conception of God as distinct from the created world, coupled with his conviction that God participates directly in every human act, made it necessary for him to work out a theory of contingency which respected both positions. Although his treatment of contingency was much more sophisticated in the *De causa Dei* than it had been in the *De futuris contingentibus*, Bradwardine maintained the same thesis in the later work and continued to regard contingency primarily as a philosophical problem. His greater success in the *De causa Dei* is the consequence both of his superior knowledge of the early fourteenth-century debates about contingency and of his readiness, where appropriate, to consider some of the more problematic theological implications of his theory of contingency. In fact, Bradwardine took the same step as Ockham in contending that some mysteries of God's power have to be taken on faith. Nevertheless, in his characteristically optimistic portrayal of the power of human reason, Bradwardine tried to show that faith can serve the pursuit of knowledge: to a certain extent at least, he thought, one can use the same methods to learn about God as one might use to investigate the natural world.[47]

In all of his discussions of contingency Bradwardine attempted to prove that God in his absolute power knows all future contingents but is still able to ensure the freedom of the human will: God "causes the human will to act predictably but freely."[48] Bradwardine shared with Ockham the idea that God in his absolute power can change anything in the universe at will, although they interpreted the significance of this power in different ways. Ockham took what might be called a psychological view of contingency, claiming that because the finite mind cannot reconcile divine foreknowledge with human contingency we must accept contingency as a feature of consciousness and divine

---

faith and reason, theology and science were expressed typically with utter clarity, although the strength of the analogy of science and theology was too strong for him to discard it altogether. But Ockham's characterization of theology as a science was an attempt to restrict theology to a niche safe from questionable metaphysical entities and logical criticisms. . . . By analytical inquiry Ockham demonstrated that philosophy was incompetent to deal with matters of theology, and freed philosophy even further for the examination of the natural world."

[47] Oberman, p. 52.

[48] Copelston, p. 258.

foreknowledge as a matter of faith.[49] Consequently, we must admit that God can act in unpredictable ways. As a metaphysician and natural philosopher, Bradwardine assumed that, although God could act in apparently confusing or unpredictable ways, his constant participation in the activities of creation assures a kind of order which the human mind can observe directly and comprehend. In any event, God's knowledge that an individual will make a particular choice does not make the choice any less free from the human point of view. By emphasizing free will from the human perspective, both Ockham and Bradwardine echoed Augustine. They differed primarily in their approach to the role of divine foreknowledge as a factor in the way that humans make decisions.

In his discussion of late medieval approaches to contingency, Calvin Normore argues that discussions of time and modality almost always made some reference to contingency as well. In the case of Duns Scotus, who helped to focus Bradwardine's attention on God as first cause, contingency relates to the necessity of the past, present and future. Scotus thought that, while the past is necessary because it has already happened, neither the present nor the future are necessary. According to Normore, Scotus contended that "God's knowledge is a single act which never 'passes into the past' and so is as contingent as any present act. God knows what will happen, but he can know otherwise than he knows."[50] Ockham, on the other hand, was convinced that both the past and present are necessary since, once they have happened, they can no longer be changed. Ockham rejected a claim

---

[49] *Ibid.* Bradwardine's opposition to certain younger contemporaries, such as Robert Holcot, Thomas Buckingham and Adam Wodeham, stems from their tendency to go beyond Ockham's rather moderate treatment of the problem of contingency to a much more radical contingency. All three of these theologians used logical and grammatical arguments to safeguard human freedom against rigid determinism. Their main similiarity to Ockham was their use of the concept of God's absolute power to question the capacity of human reason to determine the truth about God and the natural world. Unlike Bradwardine and Ockham, they did not generally try to approach contingency from a cosmological perspective. Thus their opinions shed little light on Bradwardine's use of time as a factor in contingency. Not being a logician and preferring a cosmological approach, Bradwardine dismissed many of their arguments. J. A. Robson suggests, however, in *Wyclif and the Oxford Schools*, pp. 48-49, that Bradwardine may have persuaded Buckingham, a fellow Mertonian, to moderate his approach to contingency. For a fuller treatment of this issue, see Chapter Eight below. For discussions of Holcot's view of contingency, see Normore, pp. 373-74; Streveler, "Robert Holkot's View of Contingency: A Preliminary Account," *Studies in Medieval Culture*, 8-9 (1976), pp. 163-71; Leff, pp. 216-227; and Oberman, pp. 43-46. For Wodeham, see Leff, pp. 241-54, and Oberman, pp. 46-48.

[50] Normore, p. 369.

made originally by Grosseteste that for God to know something he must be in a particular state. Using a linguistic argument, Ockham tried to show that Grosseteste's claim is true only for the human mind because knowing or not knowing a particular thing is the same for God.[51] Ockham took a linguistic approach to the problem, so he paid less attention than Scotus to the issue of transition from past to future. Still, both theologians implicitly acknowledged that God's fundamentally different perception of time is at the heart of human contingency.[52]

In contrast to Scotus and Ockham, Bradwardine approached contingency in the *De causa Dei* in a way that is explicitly temporal. Bradwardine made use of arguments from Grosseteste's *De libero arbitrio*, as well as Anselm's *Cur Deus homo*, to support his theory that God's immutability makes contingency impossible from the divine perspective.[53] Because past, present and future all depend on God's knowledge, which is eternal and absolute, it is inconceivable that he could be subject to any kind of contingency.[54] Indeed, in Bradwardine's opinion, there is no objective difference at all between past and future. God's will simultaneously directs all things which we see modally as past, present and future. Therefore, God is not bound by our perception that a future event finally occurs in time, passes into the past, and can no longer be changed. Because God is free from the temporal limits of succession, he does not have to regard past and future as different. The truth of a past event, like the truth of a future event, is confirmed by God's will alone, which is constant, eternal and unchanging. Though we see the future as contingent and the past as unchangeable, and therefore necessary, God assures the truth and reality of both in his eternal present.[55]

---

[51] *Ibid.*, pp. 372-73.

[52] Both Oberman (p. 54) and Normore (p. 374) emphasize this point.

[53] See *De causa Dei*, III, 50, p. 810, C-D, in which Bradwardine cites his preferred authorities, including Aristotle, Grosseteste, Boethius and Anselm.

[54] *Ibid*, I, 14, p. 209, E: "Si Deus esse desineret, nihil esset praeteritum, nec futurum, verum nec falsum, possibile vel impossibile, necessarium vel contingens, nec etiam posset esse: ex quo et oppositum sequitur euidenter, scilicet ipsum Deum, et sic aliquid praefuisse, esse et fore, et similiter alia posse esse per omnipotentiam Dei magnam. O quam necessarium est hunc esse, quem tam impossibile est desinere vnquam esse, et quod Deum qualitercunque non esse, contradictionem necessarissime continet et importat; et quod necesse esse, videtur maxime proprium nomen Dei." See Normore, pp. 374-75.

[55] *De causa Dei*, III, 52, p. 857, B: "Respondebitur forsitan, quod ex praeteritione rei praeteritae oritur quaedam relatio, qua necesse est simpliciter illam fuisse, quare impossibile est simpliciter illam non fuisse. Sed hoc reprobatum est prius, quando

This thesis is more or less the same as the one which Bradwardine presented in the *De futuris contingentibus* although, as Normore observes, it is developed with much greater skill in the *De causa Dei*. Instead of portraying God's knowledge of everything at once as a static and rigid kind of knowledge, Bradwardine again makes use of a geometrical image to explain how God sees the transition from past to future without changing himself: God is like a point at the center of a circle, and the points moving along its circumference are instants of time. Thus God can see a particular point first as future, then as present, and finally as past in a single observation.[56] This image illustrates God's

---

monstrabatur 'A' non fuisse, nullam contradictionem formaliter implicare. Illam etiam relationem, non est necesse simpliciter esse vel fuisse; Aliquando enim non fuit; quare nec repugnaret formaliter eam nunc non esse; ergo nihil facit necessarium simpliciter. Illa quoque relatio vel est ad Deum, seu ad voluntatem diuinam, vel rem aliquam naturalem seu res aliquas naturales. Primum erat destructum per 30um huius; Secundum stare non potest." Also III, 53, proposition 23, p. 875, D: "Quod cum futura contingentia fiant praesentia, aut in praeteritum dilabuntur, voluntas diuina respectu illorum non desinit esse libera aliqua libertate, seu aliquo modo libertatis intrinsecus, qua vel quo prius fuerat libera, nec incipit esse necessaria aliqua necessitate opposita respectu ipsorum." See also Courtenay, "John of Mirecourt and Gregory of Rimini on Whether God Can Undo the Past," *RTAM*, Part II, 40 (1973), pp. 149-50. In taking this position, of course, Bradwardine found himself at odds with prevailing scholarly opinion. Courtenay analyzes the debate over whether God can undo the past, which reached its climax in Paris in the late 1340s. Although Bradwardine was not directly involved in the Paris condemnations of 1347, the theory that the past is no more necessary than the future was criticized by some theologians as being too deterministic. Courtenay describes Mirecourt's attempt to reach a middle ground between Bradwardine's view that God can freely undo the past and Thomas Buckingham's view that the past cannot be changed even by God. Mirecourt's solution was to argue that God was initially free to make the past in any way he wished, but he cannot change the past once it has occurred (see especially Part II, pp. 147-54). Here, again, the heart of the problem seems to be the difficulty of relating God's experience in his eternal present to the human experience of time. In Bradwardine's view, Mirecourt's solution would affirm his own idea that God can freely act within his creation. When he says that God could alter a past event without contradiction, Bradwardine is stressing that God's will is not temporally limited: even if God "changes his mind," he is not bound by the "before-and-after" which is inherent in change in the created world. Mirecourt reflects sympathy with the philosophical impulse of his age to think that God somehow is able to change through time without impairing his fundamental attribute of immutability. For a more thorough treatment of this particular issue, see also M. Jean-François Genest, "La liberté de Dieu à l'égard du passé selon Pierre Damien et Thomas Bradwardine," *Annuaire de l'école pratique des hautes études*, 85 (1977-78), pp. 391-93.

[56] *De causa Dei*, I, 24, p. 243, D: "Deus autem ex sua infinitissima claritate comprehendit omnes res particulares, et omnes particulas temporis, sicuti sunt, verissime per seipsum: Non enim indiget comparatione vel relatione praeteritorum vel futurorum ad praesens instans, more infirmitatis humanae, sed intelligit omnia simul et

ability to view apparently contingent things without changing and also reinforces Bradwardine's larger contention that God is both distinct from and involved in creation.

Having described in compelling terms God's capacity to observe the transition from future to past in his eternal present, Bradwardine is left with the difficulty of defining the scope of the human will: how can one argue that God has perfect knowledge of every future act without facing the charge of determinism? Bradwardine was not prepared to deny free will, since both scripture and human reason point to the fact that individuals constantly make choices, sometimes with terrible consequences, without conscious awareness of divine encouragement or restraint. Bradwardine, of course, agreed with Boethius that God's eternal knowledge of a future event does not force an individual, living in time, to make predetermined choices. From the human perspective, God's foreknowledge does not presuppose determinism. Whereas in the *De futuris contingentibus*, Bradwardine had been content merely to make this contention and support it with references from relevant authorities, he tried in the *De causa Dei* to define contingency and free will in terms of axioms about God's absolute power over his creation.

Bradwardine based his mature theory of contingency on the principle that God's knowledge is complete and therefore necessary for the reality of his creation. Even free will is "necessary" in the sense that God has created the universe in such a way that human beings are able to exercise their wills freely within it. If God is the first cause of every act, however, he naturally participates in every act of free will; indeed, God is the source of free will. This circumstance is, of course, very difficult to explain. Most of Book III of the *De causa Dei* is devoted to defining the complex relationship between the divine and human wills. Throughout his discussion of free will Bradwardine assumed that, although God permits individuals to use their wills freely, he does not allow them

---

praesentialiter aeque clare; et hoc est, quia non scit per tales propositiones verbales mutabiles, sed per suam essentiam, et propriam voluntatem, quae semper vniformiter, et inuariabiliter omnia repraesentant. Quemadmodum si poneretur visus punctualis quiescens in centro coeli circumuoluti, et videret per extramissione et actiue non passiue, sicut Deus res videt; videret semper vniformiter, sine omni mutatione sui, circumgiratas continue singulas partes coeli, et eandem partem nunc in oriente, nunc in meridie, nunc in occidente: Sic et Deus omni eodem modo ex parte sui intrinsece videt aliquid primo futurum, secundo praesens, tertio vero praeteritum; et hoc est quia non videt patiendo quicquam a visis, seu passiue sed agendo potius seu actiue, sicut superius est ostensum." See Normore, p. 375.

unlimited choices.[57] All of Bradwardine's assertions about contingency and free will are based, moreover, on the assumption that human perceptions of creation are different from God's.[58] While the individual can be guided by God to choose to act in a particular way, he cannot conceive of the choice as being predetermined. Human beings must live in and make choices in a world governed by time: they cannot know with any certainty what will happen in the future and, at any rate, the conviction that God knows the future does not allow them to abnegate their responsibility for their own moral conduct in the present.[59]

It is for this reason that Bradwardine, returning to an idea which he had developed at length the *De incipit et desinit*, strongly denied any possibility of prediction in the *De causa Dei*. In the later work, however, Bradwardine went beyond the relatively simple issue of logical prediction to condemn the use of astrology and the unfounded beliefs in

---

[57] *De causa Dei*, III, 1, p. 637, D-E: "In primis igitur ostendendum, Deum posse necessitare quodammodo omnem voluntatem creatam ad liberum, imo ad liberrimum actum suum, similemque cessationem et vacationem ab actu. Deus enim potest velle voluntatem creatam producere liberum actum suum, et hoc antecedenter, et prius naturaliter voluntate creata; quare et per 10. primi, illa de necessitate obediret, et hoc, quamdiu Deus sic voluerit ipsam velle. . . . Quoniam enim quod Deus vult, non potest non esse, cum vult hominis voluntatem nulla cogi vel prohiberi necessitate ad volendum vel non volendum; et vult effectum sequi voluntatem, tunc necesse est voluntatem esse liberam, et esse quod vult." See Leff, p. 98.

[58] As creator and first cause, God has an understanding of the universe too perfect for created beings to comprehend. See *De causa Dei*, I, 12, p. 201, B: "Quamdiu igitur corpus quod corrumpitur, aggrauat animam, et terrena habitatio deprimit sensum plurima cogitantem, non potest homo intelligere Deum perfecte sicuti est, ipsom et dicente Mosi deprecanti. Non poteris videre faciem meam, non enim videbit homo, et viuet, Exod. 33. Quare secundum Philosophum, 1. Physic. et alibi; Innata est nobis via a notioribus nobis ad notioria naturae, quae sunt simpliciter notioria, a posterioribus siclicet ad priora, et a causatis ad causas. Nomina igitur quibus Deum cognoscimus, non significant ipsum per se essentialiter, et penitus absolute, quoniam a creaturis, et effectibus notioribus nobis transferuntur ad ipsum ignotiorem nobis, licet simpliciter notiorem."

[59] Bradwardine develops at considerable length the connection between necessity and free will in *De causa Dei*, III, chapter 2, pp. 444-48. In a corollary to this chapter Bradwardine makes the point that the human will is free to choose from the possibilities which God makes available to it, p. 448, D-E: "Corollarium, quod non ideo dicitur liberum Arbitrium, quia libere potest velle et nolle quodcunque, sed quia libere potest velle quodcunque obiectum suum volubile, et nolle quodcunque obiectum suum nolubile; sicut si visus esset potentia libera, non ideo tamem posset videre sonam, et visibilia sua tantum. . . . Nec ideo dicitur liberum arbitrium quia libere potest in oppositum cuiuslibet actus sui, vt praemissa demonstrant, sed quia ex rationali arbitrio siue iudicio spontanee illum agit, sicut primum huius ostendit. Nec ideo dicitur liberum arbitrium quia libere potest benefacere et peccare, sicut ex praemissis consequitur euidenter, sed propter causam proximo assignatam."

fortune or fate. Bradwardine devoted three chapters to exploring the classical origins of belief in fate and the occult practices of prediction.[60] He then systematically refuted these beliefs, not only by appealing to scripture and other established theological authorities but also through reference to his own cosmological system. Bradwardine considered it wrong to think that the future will occur in some arbitrary way; but, because the future must unfold according to plan in the mind of God, it is even worse for the human mind pretentiously to try to predict the future. Moreover, since the future is not arbitrary, there is no fate, except in the sense that the divine mind knows what will happen and allows this providence to be fulfilled in time.[61] Bradwardine concluded his arguments against fate with the proposition that all things are governed by laws which are established by divine providence.[62]

This pervasive emphasis on providence in the *De causa Dei* has led twentieth-century historians to examine, and often exaggerate, Bradwardine's cautious approach to contingency. In fact, Bradwardine's treatment of the relationship between contingency and free will is the central issue in Leff's and Oberman's highly influential studies of the *De causa Dei*. Although neither of them examines in detail the philosophical assumptions about time and eternity which support Bradwardine's view of contingency, their approaches to contingency in the *De causa Dei* provide an extremely useful framework for evaluating the connection between Bradwardine's theology and his ideas about time as a physical principle. The following comparison of Leff's and Oberman's interpretations of Bradwardine's view of contingency will serve, therefore, not only to review some of the historiographical issues which have influenced interpretations of Bradwardine's theology for the last three decades but also to suggest opportunities for reevaluating the role of Bradwardine's approach to time in the development of his thesis that God is the first cause of every human act.

Although they differ greatly on many aspects of Bradwardine's theology, both Leff and Oberman agree that, in the case of future contingents, Bradwardine sees no conflict between the necessity of an

---

[60] *De causa Dei*, I, 27-29, pp. 261-271.

[61] *Ibid.*, I, 28, p. 266, D: "Fatum vero inhaerens rebus mobilibus dispositio, per quam prouidentia suis quaeque nectit ordinibus. Prouidentia namque cuncta pariter quamuis diuersa, quamuis infinita complectitur; Fatum vero singula digerit, in motu, locis, formis, ac temporibus distributa, vt haec temporalis ordinis explicatio in diuinae mentis adunata prospectu, prouidentia sit; eadem vero adunatio digesta atque explicata temporibus, Fatum vocetur, quae licet diuersa sint, alterum tamen pendet ex altero."

[62] *Ibid.*, I, 30, p. 271, E: "Quod res voluntariae diuinae prouidentiae legibus gubernantur."

act based on God's foreknowledge and the freedom of an individual to choose that act. Unlike Oberman, however, Leff uses Bradwardine's view of contingency to emphasize Bradwardine's determinism. In Leff's analysis of the problem of contingency, "Bradwardine regards liberty and contingency for God's creatures as relative; as the product of secondary causes they are equally dependent upon God's will as their first cause."[63] For this reason, the divine will is the source of contingency, for God is not only the first cause behind the chosen act, but creator of the world in which the consequences of the act will manifest themselves. Indeed, Bradwardine openly acknowledges that God, having full and absolute knowledge of past, present and future, is able to build the concept of free will into his creation.[64] However, Leff also attributes to Bradwardine the conviction that the future, like God, is immutable:

> Firstly, every act of divine will, past, present and future, must have existed eternally. Secondly, in the same way, all that is about to be, and all that will be, must, of necessity, come to be. Thirdly, that everything, therefore, whether past, present or future, is subject to the same act of creation, and its temporal order bears no relation to the certainty and eternity of its existence in God. The use to which Bradwardine puts these conclusions shows clearly where he departs from tradition: he transforms the eternal instant in God to deny the future any independent existence. Where St. Thomas was content to allow that God saw everything through His own essence which in no way necessitated what He foresaw, Bradwardine changes this neutral intelligence into active approbation: with him, what God sees, He forewills. As a result, the future is as determined as the past and the present: it cannot not come about.[65]

---

[63] Leff, p. 104.

[64] *De causa Dei*, III, p. 685, B-C: "Ponamus igitur simul esse praescientiam Dei, quam sequi necessitas futurarum rerum videtur, et libertatem arbitrij, per quam multa sine vlla necessitate fieri creduntur. . . . Sed si aliquid est futurum sine necessitate, hoc ipsum possit praescire Deus, qui praescit omnia futura; quod autem praescit Deus necessitate futurum est sicut praescitur; necesse est igitur aliquid esse futurum sine necessitate, vel praesciri sine veritate. Nequaquam ergo recte intelligenti nomen, repugnare videntur praescientia, quam sequitur haec necessitas, et libertas arbitrij, a qua remouetur necessitas, quoniam et necesse est, quae Deus praescit, futura esse, et Deus praescit aliquid esse futurum sine omne necessitate." See Leff, p. 104.

[65] Leff, pp. 104-5. Leff cites *De causa Dei*, III, 50, p. 823, A: "Corollarium, quod omnem actum volutionis et cognitionis diuinae praesentem necesse est, necessitate sequente praedicta, semper fuisse, et similiter semper fore; quare et quod omnia, quae praesentialiter sunt, fiunt aut eueniunt, simili necessitate sunt, fiunt et eueniunt in praesenti; et quod omnia quae eueniunt, simili necessitate in futuro; imo et quod omnia quae nunc fiunt, de aliqua necessitate praecedente nunc fiunt; et quod omnia, quae eueniunt, de aliqua necessitate precedente, eueniunt in futuro."

This passage reveals Leff's tendency to interpret Bradwardine's view of the future in theological terms and as a restriction of human freedom without accounting for Bradwardine's Boethian emphasis on God's experience of creation in one eternal present.

Leff then places Bradwardine's determinism in the context of the intellectual radicalism of the late medieval universities. According to Leff, Bradwardine was driven to such an extreme view on future contingents because of his opposition to three contemporary schools of thought. Bradwardine's most obvious opponents were those Stoic and Islamic philosophers who promoted a kind of determinism in which God need not be directly involved in the world. In Leff's view, Bradwardine, whose own conception of God was heavily dependent on Greco-Arabic definitions, was not worried about determinism as such; his chief complaint was that the Stoic and Islamic philosophers made God too impersonal, too far removed from his own creation. Bradwardine also attacked a less unified group of philosophers who went too far in the opposite direction. These thinkers undermined God's omniscience and omnipotence by emphasizing the large scope for free will in human choice. Bradwardine thoroughly rejected any claim that God does not fully know the future, either because he has not yet willed the future or because he can only foresee good and not evil. Even more distressing to Bradwardine was the Pelagian notion that God waits until an act has been completed to assess its merit. Such a position "would remove any order between merit, free actions and reward, denying God's will to be their cause and making the past, present and future all completely contingent and free from necessity."[66]

The third group of opponents angered Bradwardine with their suggestion that since the future, unlike the past and present, does not yet actually exist, it might or might not take place at all. This view not only violated Bradwardine's assumption that the future already exists in the divine mind but also implied that God can change his mind about the future and is therefore mutable. Bradwardine's fierce rebuttal of this point of view suggests to Leff the collapse of Aquinas' moderate balance between contingency and free will in fourteenth-century thought. While Aquinas' metaphysical system allowed God to be the ultimate cause of any human action, it also posited enough of a connection between created being and God to permit a more flexible approach to contingency. Leff argues that fourteenth-century approaches to contingency, on the part of both Bradwardine and of his opponents, so separated created and

---

[66] Leff, pp. 105-6.

uncreated being that philosophers had to favor either free will or necessity. Bradwardine's originality, in Leff's opinion, lies in his ardent and
almost solitary defense of the principle of divine necessity.[67]

At the heart of Bradwardine's argument about future contingents,
says Leff, is his notion that God's will defines future events by making
choices which stand for all eternity. Although God potentially could
have made different choices from the ones which he actually did make,
his ultimate decisions are eternally true: creation is the process of these
decisions coming to fulfillment in time. God cannot subsequently make
a different decision without changing himself; and to change, God would
have to make himself a creature subject to time.[68] Therefore, to say that
God cannot change something that he has willed is not to doubt God's
absolute freedom but to give God's free choices the respect due to them
as eternal truths. According to Leff, Bradwardine locates his opponents'
main error "in confusing this eternity in God with temporal measurements, thereby trying to judge the infinite by finite standards. . . . As a
result, rather than acknowledge the problem of the future, he denies it."[69]

The main weakness of Leff's approach to Bradwardine's view of
contingency is that it underestimates the importance of Bradwardine's
understanding of eternity as both a physical and a theological concept.
Bradwardine's analysis of the role of time in creation not only
acknowledged the problem of the future but, as we have seen, paid it
considerable attention. The image of God as a point in the center of a
circle elegantly conveys Bradwardine's conception of God's relationship
with his temporal creation: God's awareness of past, present and future
in an eternal present ensures the future of the human will without
compelling it to act in a particular way. If we keep this image in mind
when reading the *De causa Dei*, we discover that Bradwardine's purpose
is not to reduce, either explicitly or implicitly, the scope of human action

---

[67] *Ibid.*, pp. 106-7.

[68] *De causa Dei*, III, 52, p. 843, E: "Quod Deus vult, non potest non velle, quia aliter
sua voluntas esset mutabilis."

[69] Leff, p. 108. Leff cites *De causa Dei*, III, 52, p. 841, A-B: "Sic forte in Deo, vbi
non est aliqua temporalis praecessio sed causalis, si respiciatur ipsa Dei natura non in
ratione agendi, et comparetur liberae voluntati hominis nudae ab actu antequam velit,
verum erit dicere, Deus potest non velle quod vult: Si vero respiciatur ipsa diuina natura
in ratione agendi, et comparetur liberae voluntati hominis cum iam actu vult, verum erit
dicere, Deum necesse est velle quod vult, et non velle quod non vult: Impossibile est
enim eum non velle quod vult, vel velle quod non vult. Quam distinctionem facit in
nostro posse et actu prioritas temporalis hanc ibidem facit prioritas causalis et subiecti
super quod redit praedicatio diuersa, diuersa consideratione, sed manifestior est distinctio
vbi comitatur prioritas temporalis."

in the future but to demonstrate how God has incorporated free will eternally into his creation. Bradwardine's temporal theory therefore transforms the problem of the future from a logical one into a cosmological one in which the distinction between time and eternity, not that between past and future, becomes crucial in determining the contingency of a particular event.

One of the chief advantages of Oberman's interpretation of Bradwardine's view of contingency over Leff's is that it takes more into account Bradwardine's ideas about creation, although here again the emphasis is on a theological not a philosophical understanding of contingency. Like Leff, Oberman sees Bradwardine's approach to contingency as a reflection of his conception of eternal and created being. Oberman stresses much more than does Leff Bradwardine's attachment to Christian authority in his treatments of necessity and divine prescience. Oberman reminds us that Bradwardine always worked from the assumption that God is not restricted by time, which only exists for the benefit of his creation. Oberman points out from the start of his analysis of the *De causa Dei* that Bradwardine feels justified in ignoring certain aspects of the problem of future contingency which arise only because of "the imperfect human conceptive faculty."[70] In the words of D. J. B. Hawkins:

> The imaginative difficulty which we have to overcome is the erroneous supposition that He (God) knows actual events as we know them in a temporal series. He knows them as a temporal series, but he does not know them in a temporal series of acts of awareness.[71]

Nevertheless, Bradwardine still had to explain how God can know the outcome of all future events and still give his creatures the freedom of will which scripture promises and human experience seems to require. In Oberman's view, Bradwardine's major task in his discussion of contingency was to explain the relationship between the omniscient divine will and the temporally limited human will.

According to Oberman, Bradwardine, following Bernard of Clairvaux, defined the human will at least partially in terms of the divine will: every rational creature shares with God the capacity to choose freely. The human will is still limited in the sense that it cannot choose from an infinite number of possibilities: it can only choose to accept or

---

[70] Oberman, p. 65.

[71] Quoted by Oberman, p. 65 from *The Essentials of Theism* (London: Sheed and Ward, 1949), p. 123.

refuse a definite possibility that has been presented to it. Bradwardine concurred with Hugh of St. Victor and Peter Lombard that the human will is free not on account of its power to will everything (which belongs only to God) but because it can act spontaneously according to its own powers of judgment. Though the human will is more limited than the divine will, neither will is capricious or arbitrary.[72]

To acknowledge the will's capacity to choose, however, does not necessarily demand acceptance of contingency, because God might pre-determine what the choices will be and know in advance the will's decision. Oberman agrees with Leff that Bradwardine's real difficulty with contingency arose from his unwillingness to diminish in any way God's knowledge of the future or his role as the first cause in every human act. Bradwardine thus came to insist that the will cannot function without grace. He stood in opposition to Ockham and others, who doubted whether grace, as a theological doctrine, and will, as a philo-sophical principle, could be considered together in any coherent treatment of contingency. In Bradwardine's cosmology, however, grace and will come from the same source and must be examined together. Therefore, according to Oberman, Bradwardine always tried to interpret will in terms of grace. In Oberman's view, Bradwardine's insistence on combining a theological starting point with a theocentric approach to contingency has led many to the assumption that he was a rigid determinist.[73]

Oberman notes, however, that Bradwardine's method of synthesizing the views of important authorities with his own profound insights into nature actually contributed to a quite flexible view of human will. Bradwardine maintained throughout the *De causa Dei* his reliance on Christian authority, especially the views of Augustine, Anselm and Thomas Aquinas. All of these theologians had emphasized the impor-tance of grace in guiding the human will and attributed full omniscience to God. Bradwardine was particularly devoted to Anselm, who in his own struggle with the problem of necessity concluded along Boethian lines that God does not really have prescience, but has simple knowl-edge in his eternal present. By eliminating tense from the analysis of God's knowledge, Anselm argued, it is possible to see how the will can remain free in spite of God's knowledge of the future.[74]

---

[72] Oberman, pp. 66-67.

[73] *Ibid.*, p. 70.

[74] *Ibid.*, p. 71. The similarities between Anselm's and Bradwardine's conception of God's eternal knowledge are spelled out most explicitly in Bradwardine's analysis of

Bradwardine also seemed to follow Aquinas almost exactly on two aspects of the question of necessity. Both agreed that the human will lacks the capacity for self-conscious conformity to the divine plan because it cannot envision the final aim. Furthermore, even if God were to reveal the final aim to someone, he would not compel that person to conform to it.[75] According to Oberman, Bradwardine's view of God's role in this process of directing the human will is one in which God "moves man according to his own nature, and freely, and when this is thwarted by sin, He transforms man by His grace."[76] In accepting these positions of Anselm and Aquinas, Bradwardine absorbed virtually the entire Augustinian tradition of defining free will in terms of grace. The combination of Augustine's psychological view of time and his convictions about grace deeply moved Bradwardine, as it had other theologians in the Augustinian tradition.

Nevertheless, Bradwardine was an original thinker and he could not be expected merely to repeat the work of his predecessors. In Oberman's view, the uniqueness of Bradwardine's position on contingency lies in the degree to which he elevated the role of grace in the exercise of human will. Oberman lists four factors which give Bradwardine's approach to contingency its deterministic quality. First, as we have already observed in the discussion of the *De futuris contingentibus*, Bradwardine stressed the vast difference between the divine and human experience of time. He was not very patient with efforts to develop purely psychological or logical explanations for contingency because he saw human lack of knowledge about the future as the inevitable condition of the imperfect human mind. Second, Bradwardine was not satisfied by the conclusions of Anselm and Aquinas, which suggested

---

eternity in *De causa Dei*, III, 51, pp. 826-31. See especially the corollary to Book III, chapter 51, p. 830, D: "Huius autem transumptionis causa est, quia non habemus verbum significans proprie aeternitatis stabilem mansionem, quare necessario cogimur transferre secundum similitudinem qualemcunque verba nostra temporalia secundum differentias quaslibet temporales ad aeternitatem et Deum aeternum, actusque suos intrinsecos coaeternos, quia omni tempori coexistunt, nec vlli tempori defuerunt aut desunt, vel deerunt in futuro. Huic autem testimonium perhibet Anselmus de Concord. 3. Propositum, inquiens, secundum quod vocari sunt Sancti in aeternitate, in qua non est praeteritum vel futurum, sed tantum praesens, immutabile est in aeternitate: non enim fuit aliquid, aut erit aliquid, sed tantum est."

[75] In support of these points, Oberman cites *De causa Dei*, II, 30, pp. 578-97; here Bradwardine explains at great length how God leads the human will without forcing it consciously to follow a particular path.

[76] Oberman, p. 72, says nevertheless that Bradwardine turned the ideas of Anselm and Aquinas in new directions and often away from the orthodox position.

that God's prescience guarantees that what was, is and will be cannot at the same time be what was not, is not and will not be. Bradwardine rejected the notion that God merely protects his creation from internal contradiction in favor of a view which places God in the more active role of directing the events which his creatures perceive in the past, present or future. Third, Bradwardine reinterpreted the Aristotelian theory that potency precedes every act. Bradwardine's predecessors had used this theory to argue that God creates potencies and then allows the will to participate in the process of transition from potency to act. In Bradwardine's view, however, God's use of the process of potency does not mean that he does not know whether or how the act will take place. Finally, Bradwardine stressed the Augustinian argument that the human will does not give up any freedom by following God; indeed, the human will is in its freest state of all when it acts without resistance to the divine will.[77]

Oberman concludes his assessment of Bradwardine's view of necessity by noting that, although Bradwardine expressed his ideas in a rigorous and sometimes extreme form, he did not intend his position on necessity to negate the possibility of free will. In Bradwardine's philosophical and theological system, contingency, not liberty, is the opposite of necessity.[78] Oberman recommends that we approach Bradwardine's theory of necessity from the perspective of Augustine's distinction between "necessitas invita" and "voluntaria":

> The former is the Stoical necessity of fate, the latter the Christian necessity in which God's world dominion is confessed. The statement 'all things that happen, happen of necessity' can accordingly be meant in two ways: as an excuse for guilt with reference to destiny, and as a confession that God performs everything according to his will.[79]

Bradwardine routinely took the latter view and argued throughout the *De causa Dei* that God's will constantly guides the course of creation. Bradwardine's conviction that God's will is necessarily fulfilled reflects his fundamental optimism concerning the natural order, while his emphasis on grace indicates his belief that the human will has a crucial role to play in following God freely and participating in the work of creation. Thus Oberman, like Leff, associates almost all aspects of Bradwardine's view of time and contingency with such theological issues as grace, free will and prescience.

---

[77] *Ibid.*, pp. 73-75.

[78] *Ibid.*, p. 76.

[79] *Ibid.*

The pervasiveness of Leff's and Oberman's theological approach to the *De causa Dei* is confirmed by another major study of Bradwardine's view of contingency. Donald J. McCarthy argues along the lines of Oberman that Bradwardine's approach to the problem of contingency was bound up with his definitions of the nature of God.[80] Like Oberman, McCarthy tries to avoid Leff's verdict of severe determinism by evaluating Bradwardine's conception of the relationship between the divine and human will within the context of grace. Whereas Leff sees Bradwardine's position as a philosophical one dominated by a particular theological outlook, Oberman and McCarthy portray Bradwardine primarily as a theologian with considerable skill in philosophy. McCarthy goes beyond both Leff and Oberman, however, in stressing the metaphysical and cosmological factors which shaped Bradwardine's view of contingency.

McCarthy contends that readers of the *De causa Dei* must take into account not only Bradwardine's sources and conclusions but also the place of the problem of contingency in his theology as a whole. Unlike many of his contemporaries, who were more interested in contingency as a philosophical, grammatical or psychological problem, Bradwardine saw it as a subordinate issue to the more important one of God's participation in the creation through grace. Because he wished more than anything else to prove that God is the first cause of every act, Bradwardine was prepared to minimize the role of free will as a major factor in determining the outcome of an event. Bradwardine did not want to eliminate free choice but he did want to place it firmly under the direction of divine causality. His main task, therefore, was not to examine contingency and free will as distinct doctrines but to devise a theological and philosophical system which allowed "the greatest possible human liberty consistent with the nature of divine willing."[81]

Paying careful attention to Bradwardine's conviction that God's knowledge is perfect and quite different from human knowledge, McCarthy examines Bradwardine's concept of the future. McCarthy cites Bradwardine's remark that God's knowledge of the future is more complete than an astronomer's prediction of an eclipse to illustrate Bradwardine's thinking about the reality of the future: because we have not yet experienced it, the future is not real to us, but this does not mean

---

[80] "Free Choice and Liberty According to Thomas Bradwardine," Dissertation, University of Toronto, 1965.

[81] *Ibid.*, p. 179.

that it is not real for God, who already knows and wills it.[82] Moreover, God not only wills the future to exist but God places future events in the future through the power of his will. God provides whatever being the future has and without God neither past nor future would exist.[83]

According to McCarthy, the Augustinian teaching on eternity and grace, and the work of Anselm and Duns Scotus on divine causality, principally informed these arguments. Bradwardine proved the existence of God by positing that creation is a series of causes, with the primary cause existing in God. Having added all of the other attributes of God which Augustine had included in his vision of God as first cause, Bradwardine was able to explain the function of human will as analogous to God's: in the present a person is free either to do or not do any act of which he is capable. As long as he is in full possession of his reason and is able to make a real decision, the consequence is a free act.[84] God, too, can perform or not perform any act but his omniscience, omnipotence and eternal presentness remove any limitation on his ability to choose. McCarthy therefore concurs with Oberman that Bradwardine's approach to free will is only deterministic from the perspective of God, who, because he has ordained free will as a fundamental feature of rational being, cannot be seen as an unrelenting or unsympathetic controller of human activity.

Although these assessments of Bradwardine's view of contingency recognize implicitly and occasionally even explicitly the crucial role of Bradwardine's conception of eternity and time, none of them approach the *De causa Dei* primarily from the perspective of Bradwardine's natural philosophy. The analysis of various aspects of Bradwardine's view of time in earlier treatises suggests, however, that Bradwardine's approach to time and eternity resulted from his consideration of both philosophical and theological concepts. Indeed, this examination of Bradwardine's mathematical and philosophical treatises has demonstrated that he had an extremely well-developed conception of natural philosophy which could not have failed to influence his theological

---

[82] *Ibid.*, p. 71. See *De causa Dei*, I, 19, p. 226, B: "Neque nonum procedit: Non enim Deus arguitiue tantum, et non intuitiue scit futura, sicut Astrologus calculator inclusus scit eclips in futuram vel praesentem supra horizontem proprium, vel sub illo, per certam demonstationem, non per claram intuitionem; Sed sicut videns Solum, videt eum per speciem eius receptam in oculo, priorem naturaliter visione et causam illius, sine quolibet argumento."

[83] See above, note 54.

[84] McCarthy, p. 3; see also p. 17 for a discussion of Augustine and p. 65 for a discussion of Scotus.

outlook in the *De causa Dei*. He was, in fact, so convinced of the correctness of his views of time and other natural phenomena that he did
not ever attempt to prove them: he considered a relevant citation from
Augustine or Boethius sufficient to verify his theses. Even though the
De causa Dei is not primarily a work of natural philosophy, Bradwardine drew both on Aristotle's doctrine of causality and on his
approaches to natural philosophy to show that created being has an entirely different character from God's eternal being. Support from Plato,
Augustine and Boethius further enhanced Bradwardine's own portrayal
of the distinction between the ever-changing world contained within
temporal limits and the immutable, infinite existence of God. Bradwardine's desire to find order in the natural world, aided by his special
ability to see through the complexities of physical, psychological and
philosophical problems, contributed to his success in examining even
purely theological problems from the perspective of his Aristotelian-
Augustinian cosmology.

The influence of Bradwardine's cosmology on purely theological
matters is nowhere more evident than in his discussion of the two main
theological problems in the *De causa Dei*, sin and predestination. In his
analysis of sin, Bradwardine has to explain why God, who is not only
supremely good but also the first cause of every human act, permits and
indeed seems to cooperate in sin. The problem of predestination involves defining the scope of human responsibility in meritorious acts
and the relationship of human merit to eternal salvation. Bradwardine's
arguments on both subjects are based on his assumption that God sees
his creation in a much simpler and more complete way than his creatures
do. God is both inside creation and distinct from it, like a point in the
center of a circle, while his creatures are restricted both by their
temporal existence and their incomplete knowledge. Although Bradwardine's discussions of sin and predestination add little to our
understanding of his view of time as such, they are worth considering
briefly because they point to some of the limitations of applying an
Aristotelian-Augustinian cosmology to theological problems.

Bradwardine's doctrine of sin depended heavily on a definition of
evil, derived from Neoplatonic philosophers and Augustine, which holds
that evil has no being in itself. Therefore evil, and consequently sin,
represent not positive forces but only the absence of God's goodness.
Augustine had, of course, stressed the non-being of evil in his attack on
the Manicheans, who supposed evil to be a powerful creative force
which actively opposed goodness in the world. By Bradwardine's day,

although the Manichean heresy was no longer considered a serious threat, Augustine's approach had become the basis of the orthodox position on evil and sin. The extensive philosophical and theological debate about evil in the thirteenth and early fourteenth centuries, however, indicates widespread dissatisfaction with conventional explanations for the presence of evil in a divinely created world.[85]

In the face of these debates Bradwardine warmly embraced the Augustinian position for two reasons. First, Augustine's denial of the reality of evil supported Bradwardine's contention that God acts eternally and positively for the good of his creation. Second, Augustine's emphasis on the positive goodness of God strengthened Bradwardine's assumptions about the natural order of creation. Bradwardine was certainly not so naive as to deny the presence or effects of sin, but he relied on Augustine to show that evil and sin had no power to disturb the orderly processes of the created world. Bradwardine maintained throughout the *De causa Dei* that, because God is the first cause and creator of every existing thing, all things must be good in themselves.[86] No action, therefore, is sinful *per se*, only *per accidens*: the same qualities which make homicide and adultery sins are also present in the good acts of natural death and marriage.[87] Sin results from the deliberate choice to act in a way which removes one from God or which causes one to deviate from the course of positive obedience to God's will.

Bradwardine did not agree with Augustine in every respect, however. In Bradwardine's view, the intention behind the act and the degree to which such an act obeys or disobeys God's will mainly determine whether or not it is a sin.[88] Thus, for example, the acts of a child or a

---

[85] For a recent comprehensive study of the problem of evil and sin in late medieval thought see "Philosophy of Mind in Action" and "Ethics," Parts VIII and IX of *CHLMP*, pp. 593-719.

[86] *De causa Dei*, I, 26, p. 251, B: "Omne siquidem per se volubile et amiabile a bono et sapiente, est aliquo modo bonum, vt tam Philosophi, quam Theologi pariter contestantur. . . . Item omnis veritas est bona, quia recta, iusta, et sancta; et omnis essentia est veritas. . . ." See Oberman, p. 124.

[87] *Ibid.*, p. 255, E: "Item si actus adulterij et homicidij per se sint mali, cum actus secundum essentiam similis sit in coniugatis, et non coniugatis, in innocentibus et reis mortis, erit et peccatum in istis." See Oberman, p. 125.

[88] *Ibid.*, II, 2, p. 448, D: "Corollarium, quod non ideo dicitur liberum arbitrium, quia libere potest velle et nolle quodcunque, sed quia libere potest velle quodcunque obiectum suum volubile, et nolle quodcunque obiectum suum nolubile." And *ibid.*, p. 447, B-C: "Et credo quod posset saltem per accidens, si videlicet nolendo et respuendo aliquod paruum bonum posset consequi aliquod maius bonum, vel vitare aliquod maius malum, sicut et potest velle malum. . . ." See Leff, p. 92.

mentally disturbed person cannot be judged in the same way as those of rational adults.[89] By stressing the role of intention in sin, Bradwardine in fact minimizes Augustine's assertion that all sins, whether intentional or unintentional, are reflections of original sin, which plagues the entire human race. Bradwardine's recognition of the role of the will in sin indicates the influence of thirteenth- and fourteenth-century reflections, particularly those of Duns Scotus, on Augustine's doctrine of sin.[90]

Bradwardine's answer to the question of why God permits sin in the first place is rooted both in his metaphysical system and in his understanding of the relationship of the human to the divine will. Because he is the cause of all that exists and does not exist, God must be seen as the cause of sin as well. It follows that God must permit sin as an agent for good and not as an end in itself.[91] The contrast of good and evil makes good more obvious. Simple observation of the natural world reveals that the universe operates on the principle of balancing opposites, as for example in music, humidity, temperature, weight and shape.[92] The integrity of the entire universe depends on the interaction of natural forces in a state of flux. This quality of balance of opposites, which distinguishes ever-changing creation from immutable God, is both good and necessary. So too, then, is the balance of sin and merit.

---

[89] *Ibid.*, II, 3, p. 449, B: "Consequenter autem restat ostendere, quod nulla creatura causa inferior, vel secunda, potest necessitate voluntatem creatum ad rationalem et liberum actum suum, ad meritum proprie vel peccatum. Nam secundum primo huius ostensa, creatura rationalis est liberi arbitrij, et naturaliter libera; Imo et ita libera, sicut creatura irrationalis est naturaliter necessaria; seu necessitabilis siue serua. Sed haec est tam necessitabilis et serua naturaliter quod potest necessitari a causa secunda; ergo et ipsa tam libera quod non potest necessitari ab aliqua causa secunda: Si enim bestia necessitetur ab aliqua causa secunda, necessitabitur a qualibet fortiori; quare nec ab illa, nec ab aliqua fortiori causa secunda necessitabitur voluntas creata, multo magis nec debiliori quacunque."

[90] Leff, p. 58.

[91] *De causa Dei*, I, 12, p. 200, D: "Est etiam causa illius quia, enim bonum est bonum, ideo non est malum, et non e contra; quia non esse malum, penitus nihil ponit, et per consequens nihil causat. Primum ergo principium complexorum nullatenus negatiuum, sed affirmatiuum firmiter arbitrandum." See also I, 34, p. 294, D: "Deus ergo est causa huius veritatis, et non nisi voluntarie. Vult ergo Deus hanc esse veram, Peccatum est."

[92] *Ibid.*, I, 34, pp. 295-96, E-A: "Sic igitur et omnium constitutionem, Coeli, dico, et terrae vndique totius permixtam, maxime contrariorum principiorum vna decorauit harmonia, siccum humido, calidum frigido, graue leui, rectum circulato decorauit: totam terram, et mare, aetherem, atque Solem et Lunam, et totum coelum decorauit vna, quae per omnia transit virtus; ex immixtis et diuersis, ex aere, terra, igne et aqua totum orbem creans et disposens vnius sphaerae superficae; ac maxime contrarias in eo naturas cogens adinuicem concordare, et ex hic ingenians vniuerso salutem." See Leff, p. 60.

Although God does not wish us to sin, he allows us to exercise our wills even if we end up making wrong decisions.[93] Because it is the consequence of free will, sin is part of the fabric of the universe. We utterly mistake God's intentions, and run the risk of attributing to him human goals and understanding, if we equate the existence of sin with the notion that God creates evil for its own sake.

In acknowledging God's active role in creating sin, Bradwardine allowed his cosmological view of God as the first cause of every created act to overshadow his Augustinian conviction that sin represents a turning away from the reality of God's goodness. Bradwardine's positive view of sin put him at odds with tradition and left him open, potentially, to the criticism that his views were unorthodox.[94] That he was never seriously challenged on this point indicates that his opponents understood that his doctrine of sin could not be separated from his conception of God's relationship with creation: to refute Bradwardine's view of sin would require dismantling his entire cosmology. Bradwardine's compelling approach to creation and his fundamentally optimistic view of sin ensured that his ideas would be comforting to his supporters and carefully considered by those who disagreed with him.

Bradwardine's doctrine of predestination, too, is essentially optimistic and based on faith in a God who is both utterly transcendent and immediately personal. Bradwardine's conception of the way in which God decides whom to save is the central feature of his entire argument against the Pelagians, and it is based firmly on the definition of God as eternal and immutable. According to Bradwardine, our temporal experience can give us the incorrect impression that God waits to observe our actions before he decides whether or not we deserve salvation. Justification is actually a completely atemporal phenomenon. Bradwardine therefore questions the accuracy of the metaphor in Psalm 68 that an individual can be erased from the book of life:

> God knows in advance, before the foundation of the world He has predestined all who will reign with His Son in eternal life. Those whom He has enrolled are contained in the book of life. How can they be erased from a book where they were never written? This quotation expresses their hope, that is, they thought themselves to have been entered into the book of life. What does this mean, 'Let them be erased from the book of

---

[93] According to Oberman, p. 129, Bradwardine followed traditional interpretations of the Old Testament, where, for example, God allowed the election of King Nebuchadnezzar as a means for punishing sinners and vindicating the righteous.

[94] Oberman, p. 128.

life'? It is obvious that they were never there to begin with. Thus, therefore, those who had hoped, by reason of their righteousness, that they were written in the book of God, when confronted by their damnation, are made aware that they are 'erased from the book of life,' and they realize that they were never there. The second part of the statement ['Let them not be enrolled with the righteous'] explains the first part. As I have said, 'Let them be erased' is to be understood to refer to their vain hopes. And this can be correctly summarized by saying 'Let them not be enrolled.'[95]

This passage brings into sharp focus Bradwardine's contention that we can only deceive ourselves by assuming that God, like us, is temporal and changeable. Although we must wait until the time of our judgment to know whether we have been saved, God always possesses this knowledge in his eternal present.

Bradwardine makes use of the Aristotelian concept of potency to explain how the will, acting within the temporal limits of creation, fulfills the eternal expectation of God by responding to his grace:

Aristotle shows that power, or capability, is of two kinds, active and passive. Now that which is meant by the quotation, 'He gave them power to become sons of God,' is also asserted in Romans, 'whoever are led by the Spirit of God are sons of God.' God gives men power, that is to say, a rational soul and free will with which man can freely and voluntarily receive grace in the present and glory in the future so that, in both the present and the future, they might become sons of God. Thus in the present, as they are being made sons of God by faith and prevenient grace, which makes them into adopted sons of God, they freely accomplish the pleasing work of sons and so freely persevere in this to such an extent that no one could take away their sonship unless they would permit it.[96]

We must recognize, then, that God is unconstrained in matters of time or power in justifying certain individuals. His decision to save them and his gift of grace amount to the same act, although the human will experiences grace and justification as sequential. Here, as in the case of sin, Bradwardine subordinates the independent function of the human will to the demands of his cosmological system but does not completely undermine it.

Bradwardine relates his doctrines of sin and predestination to his definition of God as first cause of all creation by repeating St. Paul's image of God as a potter:

---

[95] *De causa Dei*, I, 47. Trans. Paul L. Nyhus, in H. A. Oberman, *Forerunners of the Reformation: The Shape of Late Medieval Thought Illustrated by Key Documents* (London: Lutterworth Press, 1966), p. 158. See Saville edition, p. 438, D.

[96] Oberman-Nyhus, p. 154; see Saville edition, p. 437, B-C.

Why do [the Pelagians] not accuse God because He punishes innocent beasts and baptized infants with no small physical pain? Indeed He gave up his own most innocent Son, our Lord Jesus Christ, to a most painful, cruel, and tormenting punishment. But since God is omnipotent, completely free Lord of his whole creation, whose will alone is the most righteous law for all creation—if He should eternally punish the innocent, particularly since he does it for the perfection of the universe, for the profit of others, and for the honor of God Himself, who would presume to dispute with Him, to contradict Him, or ask 'Why do you do this?' I firmly believe, no one! 'Has the potter no right over the clay to make of the same lump one vessel for honor and another for menial use?'[97]

Not only does God have the right to punish certain creatures for the overall good of creation, he can also determine whether a punishment should be merely temporal, eternal or both: "If a man may undergo temporal punishment for the temporal benefit of others, why should he not be punished temporally and eternally for the temporal and eternal benefit of the elect, in order that they might all the more flee from evil and choose the good of the present, that in the future they might have greater joy, deeper love, and higher praise of God?"[98] Thus Bradwardine returns to the basic concept of God's absolute goodness and transcendence to justify divine punishment. In Bradwardine's confident and optimistic view, God's omnipotence and eternal knowledge ensure that creation will proceed in a way which is ultimately good. The human will is obliged to respond to God's love and to refrain as much as possible from willful disobedience; but, if one has faith in God's creation, one need not worry about the philosophical dilemmas surrounding sin and grace.

Even in matters of purely theological interest, therefore, it is difficult to evaluate Bradwardine's thought in isolation from his views about creation, time and eternity. Bradwardine regarded these fundamental concepts as necessary for describing both God's essence and his creative activity. Because Bradwardine not only made metaphysics and logic serve a theological purpose but also used theological principles to support a cosmological system that depends equally on God's will and human perception of creation, the *De causa Dei* cannot be seen exclusively as either a philosophical or a theological work.

Although Bradwardine's main purpose in the *De causa Dei*, to prove that God is the first cause, was, of course, unquestionably theological,

---

[97] *Ibid.*, p. 162; see Saville edition, p. 441, A.
[98] *Ibid.*, p. 161; see Saville edition, p. 440, E.

his interest, as we have seen, was not confined to this issue alone. As a natural philosopher, Bradwardine also wanted to explore the human response to God's creation and the significance of the natural world to man's relationship to God. The *De causa Dei* gives every indication of Bradwardine's confidence in the power of human reason to comprehend the natural world, within the boundaries of our temporal existence, so long as thinkers do not limit God by applying the same standards to him as they would to physical phenomena. For created beings, he argued, temporal and spacial limits are good because they allow us to make comparisons, to measure, to study nature in general. Furthermore, the human mind can even hope to reveal some of God's mystery once it grasps the fact that God is creator of the laws which govern creation but is not himself subject to them. While he did not underestimate the difficulty of obtaining certain knowledge about God, Bradwardine exposed the error of trying to describe God's nature or powers in human terms: hence his impatience with contemporary speculation about God's experience of time, which inevitably tried to temporalize God. In constantly emphasizing the distinction between time and eternity, therefore, Bradwardine presented a view of God which was thoroughly consistent with the whole body of his scientific, metaphysical and religious beliefs.

The preceding examination of Bradwardine's view of time demonstrates that this distinction between time and eternity represents a unifying theme for his most important scientific, philosophical and theological work. For this reason, an understanding of his conception of time can help to answer some of the unresolved questions regarding his thought as a whole. The issue of Bradwardine's determinism, for example, can only be evaluated properly in the context of his particular analysis of the relationship between time and grace. There is no doubt that by the theological standards of his day Bradwardine truly was a determinist: he affirmed that both past and future are equally dependent on God's eternal and unchanging will, and he readily subordinated the scope of the human will to the cause of God's absolute freedom.

Nevertheless, his brand of determinism had a strikingly optimistic, even humanistic tone. Both his objection to logical prediction in his early treatise on beginning and ceasing and his rejection of fate in the *De causa Dei* indicate his belief that the future should be faced confidently and without fear of divine repression. To the human mind, the future provides endless opportunities for choice, for willing cooperation with or conscious disobedience of God's plan for creation. God's participation in our acts, his eternal knowledge of how we will respond and his ability to take all of these responses into account confirm his power to create an orderly universe without restricting human freedom. Moreover, from the human perspective, the future is completely open to the human will: so much so, in fact, that we cannot accurately predict the future, except perhaps in the experimental sense of astronomical observation. Bradwardine considered this juxtaposition of determinism and free will one of the chief mysteries of faith, analogous to the profound cosmological mystery of the juxtaposition of time and eternity.

Those who are inclined to consider Bradwardine a rigid determinist often accuse him, in one way or another, of refusing to recognize contingency as a valid philosophical problem and so reflect their misunderstanding of Bradwardine's cosmological and metaphysical outlook. To be sure, Bradwardine made no attempt to reconcile his view of contingency with contemporary ones which required explanations for how God can be immutable and eternal and yet enjoy a temporal existence. Instead, Bradwardine's most important contribution to the fourteenth-century debate over contingency was to offer an alternative approach, based on a synthesis of Aristotelian, Augustinian, Boethian and Thomist cosmological principles, to the attempts of such theologians as Peter Aureoli, Duns Scotus and Ockham to resolve the problem of contingency logically or grammatically. That Bradwardine approached contingency in a cosmological way, which combined a precise definition of time's relationship to eternity with an Augustinian conception of grace, does not mean that he dismissed everything his contemporaries had to say about the logical problem of time. Bradwardine simply subordinated in his theology purely logical considerations to more metaphysical issues, such as the difference between created and uncreated being and the principle of God as first cause. Therefore, while it cannot be denied that Bradwardine was a determinist, it is equally clear that he used the distinction between time and eternity to ameliorate the consequences of divine determination of human acts.

Bradwardine's method for constructing his alternative approach to the problem of contingency brings us to the related question of the orthodoxy of his synthesis of Aristotelian and Augustinian principles. Oberman portrays Bradwardine as an orthodox conservative who tried to defend his Augustinian views from the radical attacks of such skeptical contemporary theologians as Robert Holcot, Thomas Buckingham and Adam Wodeham. Leff goes even further, claiming that Bradwardine followed his conservative principles with such unyielding rigor that he went well beyond the limits of conventional orthodoxy. Both historians point out that Bradwardine's views about sin and necessity deviated, sometimes markedly, from the dominant perspectives. As in Bradwardine's scientific works, the *De causa Dei* clearly shows that he was not afraid to reevaluate or challenge the opinions of other thinkers, whether they were his own peers, as in the case of Ockham, or revered authorities like Aristotle or Augustine. All of his works which have been examined here reflect, in fact, Bradwardine's ability to redefine and clarify problems by balancing the wisdom of recognized authorities with his own mathematical insight. He freely took what were to him the most convincing aspects of well-established arguments and arranged them axiomatically to produce his own assessments of disputed questions.

Especially in the case of time, Bradwardine showed allegiance to many authorities but subservience to none. His view of time combined Aristotelian definitions of time with the Augustinian-Boethian explanation of its cosmological significance. When he began to explore the theological implications of his cosmology, Bradwardine gathered support from every possible source. Although some conclusions in the *De causa Dei* may appear extreme because of his axiomatic organization of ideas or his uncompromising manner of expression, he based every argument on principles of such wide acceptance that no contemporary seriously challenged either his orthodoxy or his reputation as a gifted thinker. Like other fourteenth-century theologians at Oxford and Paris, Bradwardine took a keen interest in certain ancient philosophical and theological discussions which, on account of the contributions of Aquinas and Duns Scotus in the thirteenth century, had become even more elaborate by the early fourteenth century. Bradwardine shared with Ockham in particular the desire to push the debates about these problems in new directions without sacrificing the commitment to Christian authority. On the issue of time, as we have seen, their main difference was that Bradwardine developed an approach which permitted him to avoid certain aspects of contingency which openly contradicted his cosmology, whereas these very aspects fascinated Ockham and deeply influenced his philosophical system. To the extent that they each achieved major innovations in investigating complicated philosophical and theological problems while remaining faithful to the same body of Christian doctrine, however, both can be seen as "conservative" theologians.

In the introduction to Bradwardine's *Sermo epinicius*, which commemorates the English victory at Crécy, Weisheipl makes the important observation that it is Bradwardine's unique analytical style, not the unconventionality of his opinions, which makes his writing so compelling. Weisheipl contends that the theology of the *De causa Dei* is perfectly in agreement with Thomist teaching about God as the first cause. The impact of the work has been so strong, no less today than in the fourteenth century, because Bradwardine far surpassed his contemporaries in grasping the implications of traditional metaphysics and in conveying his insights to a large audience.[99] His influence and popularity as a thinker are proven by his remarkable success inside and outside of academic circles. His brilliant public career enabled him, in turn, to popularize his essentially traditional views of nature and God among both learned and lay communities. Weisheipl's observation holds as well for Bradwardine's other works. His ideas about geometry, proportionality and continuity also attracted large audiences because they displayed his skill in presenting Euclidean geometry and Aristotelian natural philosophy rationally and in a highly original form. Even his early and relatively immature opinions about beginning and ceasing encouraged his colleagues to reconsider their own views on the subject. In spite of its awkwardness, moreover, the *De futuris contingentibus* demonstrates that Bradwardine was willing even early in his academic career to apply his exceptional analytical talents to a new range of difficult theological questions.

The *De causa Dei* was the product of Bradwardine's attempt to place his well-developed assumptions about the natural world in a broader context and to explain how God uses the physical and spiritual forces which are observed in nature and revealed in scripture to create a unified, balanced and orderly universe. This study of the *De causa Dei* suggests that the distinction between time and eternity, which lies at the heart of both Bradwardine's natural philosophy and his theology, is the point of integration of the entire corpus of his scholarly work. Consequently, no attempt to understand the development of Bradwardine's thought or to assess his role as preserver and transformer of traditional positions can be complete without some reference to his conception of time.

---

[99] "The *Sermo Epinicius*," pp. 295-306.

CHAPTER EIGHT

THE HISTORIOGRAPHICAL SETTING OF BRADWARDINE'S VIEW OF TIME

In this study the physical, philosophical and theological elements of Bradwardine's view of time and eternity have been examined in the context of ancient and medieval approaches to the problem of time. We have traced the development of the large body of speculative literature on this subject from the classical period to the end of the thirteenth century. Texts by philosophers from Plato to John Duns Scotus have reflected both the general importance of the problem of time in the western philosophical tradition and also the complexity and subtlety of the various solutions to the problem of time which have arisen out of scholarly debates. The main conclusion to be drawn from this review is that medieval thinkers inherited an approach to time which tried to balance the poetical cosmology of Plato's *Timaeus* with Aristotle's more concrete natural philosophy. Christian philosophers from Augustine to Aquinas may have reinterpreted Plato's and Aristotle's views of time in light of scripture but they based their assessments of the physical nature of time almost entirely on classical formulations.

This interplay between classical natural philosophy and Christian doctrine provided the foundation for Bradwardine's own views of time as a philosophical and theological concept. In the *De proportionibus*, for example, Bradwardine's axiomatic method of combining Euclidean mathematics and Aristotelian physics allowed him to remain firmly committed to Aristotle without losing the analytical benefits of a more Platonic approach to mathematics. Bradwardine's use of time in his analysis of ratios suggests that he fully accepted Aristotle's definition of time as the number or measure of motion. In the *De continuo*, Bradwardine explicitly defined time as the successive continuum which contains and measures all other continua, whether successive or permanent. The *De continuo* not only reaffirms Bradwardine's commitment to Aristotelian natural philosophy but also presents unambiguously his notion that infinity in the created world is a matter of infinite divisibility, not of infinite duration or dimension. Although he made no attempt in the *De continuo* to compare the continuity of created matter with the infinity or eternity of God, he developed a theory of continuity which is consistent with the cosmology which he later described in the *De causa Dei*.

We have observed, however, the intellectual, and perhaps personal, tension Bradwardine experienced when he tried to reconcile his Aristotelian natural philosophy with his theological convictions. The contrast between his early views on beginning and ceasing and his first speculations about contingency amply illustrates this point. Bradwardine's interest in such topics reflects his growing awareness of the difference between the human perception of time and change, on the one hand, and the divine experience of eternity and immutability, on the other. The *De incipit et desinit*, in which Bradwardine consciously avoided the issue of divine foreknowledge, demonstrates through Aristotelian principles that the future is undetermined and completely unpredictable. In the *De futuris contingentibus* he explored much more cautiously the true relationship between God's knowledge and human perception of the future. By rigidly interpreting the Augustinian-Boethian view of eternity, Bradwardine seems to have denied any possibility of contingency at all, suggesting an almost complete reversal of his opinion in the *De incipit et desinit*.

Finally, we have witnessed in the *De causa Dei* how Bradwardine tried to resolve the apparent paradox between divine omniscience and human free will. Here Bradwardine presented a cosmology which admits no human capacity to attain certain knowledge of the future through logical prediction[1] and which recognizes man's perception of the future as contingent and yet ultimately dependent on the eternal, immutable will of God. By subordinating every created act to God as first cause, Bradwardine placed God at the center of both the physical and the temporal order. Although it was not primarily a work of natural philosophy, the *De causa Dei* was based on a view of time and eternity which enlarged Augustinian notions of eternity and grace with the principles of Aristotelian physics.

This evaluation of Bradwardine's conception of time as a physical, philosophical and theological problem establishes several important

---

[1] Of course Bradwardine admitted that one could have general knowledge about the future but he denied that one could transform general knowledge of the future into certain knowledge through logic or any other means. For example, Bradwardine acknowledged the usefulness of astronomical prediction but he did not think that the prediction of astronomical events in the future constituted certain knowledge of the future because the prediction could only be verified by those events taking place. Similarly, he believed in the truth of divine revelation but he considered it impossible for the human mind to determine how and when a given prophesy might be fulfilled.

points about Bradwardine's thought and fourteenth-century intellectual
life as a whole. First, although Bradwardine was perfectly capable of
distinguishing among the logical, physical, metaphysical and spiritual
aspects of time and eternity, he considered it neither necessary nor
desirable to approach time in a single way. All of his works show his
awareness of the classical and medieval debates about specific topics
such as time, continuity and proportionality, as well as the larger
contemporary debate about the inherent correctness of Aristotelian
natural philosophy. Nowhere does Bradwardine show more clearly his
affinity for the philosophy of Thomas Aquinas than in his multifaceted
treatment of time; in order to reconcile Augustine and Aristotle, both
theologians had to consider the conflicting approaches to time and
eternity which these two authorities present.

Second, Bradwardine's view of time and eternity, in spite of its clear
basis in Aristotelian physics and Euclidean mathematics, helped him to
define the cosmological principles which supported his theological
positions on grace, free will, justification and sin. In fact, his axiomatic
approach to metaphysical problems allowed him to retain and balance
what he considered to be the most convincing aspects of the Aristotelian
and Augustinian-Boethian temporal theories. Bradwardine's approach
allowed him to affirm the accuracy of human observation of change and
motion while acknowledging God's different perspective on creation.
Bradwardine's technical understanding of infinity, continuity, proportionality and limits lent authority to his conception of God as eternal,
immutable, omnipotent and the first cause of every created act.

Third, Bradwardine's treatment of time illustrates one of the most
characteristic features of his analytical method: his ability to refute his
opponents, not by debating every aspect of a problem under discussion
but by systematically eroding the validity of one or two crucial
underlying assumptions. Thus, one of Bradwardine's most effective
challenges to contemporary speculation about contingency, logical
prediction and free will arose directly out of his definition of time as a
created entity, dependent on God for its existence and with no power to
encompass or restrict him. Bradwardine's view of time illustrates,
therefore, how misleading it is to study his natural philosophy and
theology as unrelated features of his thought.

Of course, if this observation is true for Bradwardine, we must suppose it is equally true for his colleagues. Despite his remarkable ability
to apply mathematical analysis to philosophical and theological questions, the scope of his research was established by his membership in a

larger academic community. His achievements cannot be evaluated in isolation from that community. Even in such early treatises as the *Geometria speculativa*, Bradwardine's works addressed questions of great contemporary interest. Whether the topic was physical, philosophical or theological, Bradwardine and his fellow scholars referred to the same body of authority, made use of the same analytical methods and constantly emphasized the orthodoxy of their arguments. For this reason, the dilemma of time's relationship to eternity, unresolved since the classical period, was a recurrent, if implicit, theme in mid-fourteenth-century thought.

Although Ockham and Bradwardine were two of the few thinkers explicitly to examine time as both a physical and theological problem, the issue of time emerged implicitly in a much wider range of late medieval discussions concerning free will, contingency and God's absolute power. Ockham contributed to this discussion by introducing new techniques for evaluating the truth of logical propositions. Bradwardine, as a natural philosopher, helped to focus attention on the cosmological assumptions which theologians must make whenever they try to define the relationship between God and man. Bradwardine's most positive role in these debates was to suggest that no explanation of the operation of human or divine will in the created world is valid if it fails to acknowledge the distinction between God's atemporal existence and the human experience of constant change.

One of the most obvious conclusions to be drawn from the analysis of Bradwardine's view of time is that the place accorded to him in the late medieval academic debates keeps shifting as historians investigate the careers and ideas of the less well-known fourteenth-century thinkers. The current trend in historical analysis of late medieval thought is to step back from the earlier interpretation of fourteenth-century intellectual life as a clear-cut debate between advocates of a radical skepticism and conservative Augustinianism. As William Courtenay has recently observed, we now know more about the complex interchange between major figures such as Ockham and Bradwardine and the hitherto unheard voices of their less politically prominent colleagues.[2] This

---

[2] In "The Reception of Ockham's Thought in Fourteenth-Century England," *From Ockham to Wyclif*, pp. 89-107, Courtenay discusses the contributions of several of these authors, including John of Reading, Robert Graystanes and John Grafton, noting the particular contributions of Katherine Tachau and Hester Gelber in identifying such figures (see Chapter Five, n. 3). For more general insights on the interaction of students and teachers in medieval universities, see also Fletcher, "Inter-Faculty Disputes in Late Medieval Oxford," *From Ockham to Wyclif*, pp. 331-342.

information encourages historians both to continue the search for contributors to late medieval intellectual debates and to reevaluate the ideas of the more established thinkers in light of those discoveries. Better knowledge of the setting allows us to see the participants in the debates more clearly and to consider their responses to philosophical and theological problems with greater respect.[3]

A significant consequence of these new approaches to late medieval intellectual history has been a thorough reevaluation of Ockham's role as an intellectual leader in the early decades of the fourteenth century. While the originality of much of Ockham's thought has never been doubted, he is being portrayed increasingly as a rather conservative Franciscan, who influenced, but certainly did not dominate, those younger scholars whose views were eventually condemned in Paris in 1347.[4] Recent research on such men as Thomas Buckingham, Robert Holcot, Adam Wodeham, John of Mirecourt and Gregory of Rimini underscores the complexity of their thought and provides a better framework for understanding their debates among themselves and with Bradwardine and Richard FitzRalph, their so-called conservative opponents.

In addition to revealing something of the character of Bradwardine's own thought, the study of Bradwardine's view of time as a physical and theological concept can help to elucidate changes in the historical

---

[3] This notion of respect for fourteenth-century approaches to philosophical problems is expressed well by Arthur Stephen McGrade in "Enjoyment at Oxford after Ockham," *From Ockham to Wyclif,* pp. 87-88. McGrade criticizes Gilson's negative and anachronistic portrayal of fourteenth-century theologians because they eschewed metaphysics. Instead, McGrade points out the striking resemblance between fourteenth-century concerns and our own when he states: "Ockham and his nominalist successors were for various reasons critical of Greek speculative metaphysics and its Arab and Christian elaborations, but they did not substitute for the cosmic order of classical metaphysics the rootless rationalistic order of post-enlightenment idealism. Their picture of what we can know of reality apart from God's self-revelation has a more modern look, including a modern uncertainty about what human beings ultimately are, what would ultimately satisfy them, and what ultimately moves the world around them."

[4] The essentially conservative nature of Ockham's thought is an underlying theme in Marilyn McCord Adam's *William Ockham* and in Katherine Tachau's *Vision and Certitude.* This is not to say, of course, that Ockham's views did not have a considerable impact on mid fourteenth-century thought. In this context, see Courtenay and Tachau, "Ockham, Ockhamists, and the English-German Nation at Paris, 1339-1341," *History of the Universities,* 2 (1982), pp. 53-96; J. M. M. H. Thijssen, "Once Again the Ockhamist Statutes of 1339 and 1340: Some New Perspectives," *Vivarium,* 28 (1990), pp. 136-67 and William J. Courtenay, "The Registers of the University of Paris and the Statutes against the Scientia Occamica," *Vivarium,* 29 (1991), pp. 13-49.

analysis of late medieval intellectual life in the last half-century. Because few treatments of Bradwardine's thought have focused specifically on the continuity between his natural philosophy and theology, they usually emphasize the conflict between his positions and those of his so-called opponents. Thus his role in the scholarly debates of the mid-fourteenth century has been somewhat misconstrued: he has been labeled a conservative on account of his opposition to "Ockhamist" assertions about God's absolute power, in spite of his own equally emphatic advocacy of that principle; he has been described as contentious simply for the sake of being contentious, in spite of the evidence that he was well-respected and successful among his peers; and he has been called an "inhumane genius" in spite of his constant acknowledgement of human reason and his unfailing optimism about the goodness of humanity's relationship with God.[5] Moreover, the literature on Bradwardine consistently gives the impression that, although he was an active natural philosopher, his scientific views generated little controversy whereas his theological opinions involved him in a hostile struggle with the nominalists which ended for him only at his death—a view which fails to account for key features of Bradwardine's argumentative style. As we have seen, even his scientific works were clearly polemical and were directed against ideas rather than individual thinkers.[6] The *De causa Dei* indicates that the same observation can be made about Bradwardine's theological views.

One way of understanding the importance of the interrelationship between natural philosophy and theology in late medieval thought is to examine changing perceptions of Bradwardine's role in late medieval debates. The features of the traditional approach to fourteenth-century intellectual life are particularly evident in the studies of Leff and Oberman. Despite their vastly different opinions about the basic direction of Bradwardine's theology, both Leff and Oberman have portrayed Bradwardine as a self-conscious opponent of Ockham and his followers. Their decision to stress theology over natural philosophy leads occasionally to misinterpretations not only of Bradwardine but of Ockham. Recent studies of Ockham have shown that even his most innovative and controversial views about faith and reason depend on his acceptance both of Aristotelian physics and of a Franciscan theological perspective. Bradwardine's work also reveals influences from both natural philosophy and theology.

---

[5] Leff, p. 18. See Introduction, note 3.
[6] Leff, p. 18. See Introduction, note 3.

The tendency among historians to separate the scientific theories of medieval authors from their theological views is, of course, partly a matter of convenience: individual scholars often lack expertise in some of the fields which have bearing on their multidisciplinary approaches to cosmological problems. The reason for focusing attention on Ockham as the leader of a new, skeptical intellectual movement in the early fourteenth century, however, is primarily historiographical. The thesis that Ockham initiated a direct challenge to orthodoxy, one which was checked only temporarily by the Paris condemnations of 1347 and the Great Plague, originated at the end of the nineteenth century and was pursued with vigor for many decades. Its elegance and internal consistency caused it to persist even in the absence of direct evidence either to prove or to disprove it.[7]

One of the most eloquent and influential proponents of the traditional view of the fourteenth-century intellectual climate has been Étienne Gilson, who argued that Ockham almost single-handedly changed the tone of late medieval philosophy. By divorcing faith and reason, says Gilson, Ockham jeopardized the delicate balance between theology and philosophy which his thirteenth-century predecessors had crafted and so brought about the disintegration of scholastic unity:

> The practical effect of [Ockham's] theology was to nullify, in many minds, the effort of what might be called the classical scholasticism of the thirteenth century, including Henry of Ghent and Duns Scotus. Of the rational understanding of faith attempted by Bonaventure, Albert the Great, Thomas Aquinas and their contemporaries, very little, if anything, was left after Ockham. This is the reason why we described Ockhamism as marking the end of the golden age of scholasticism. Faith was intact, but to follow Ockham was to give up any hope of achieving, in this life, a positive philosophical understanding of its intelligible meaning. . . . In this sense, it can be said that the doctrine of Ockham marked a turning point in the history of philosophy as well as of theology. In theology his doctrine was paving the way to the 'positive theology' of the moderns. In philosophy, it was paving the way to modern empiricism. In both cases it really was a *via moderna*: a modern way.[8]

In Gilson's view, then, Ockham transformed the late medieval intellectual community by rejecting completely the philosophical and theological principles which supported the views of his predecessors.

---

[7] Courtenay, "John of Mirecourt and Gregory of Rimini on Whether God Can Undo the Past," Part I, *RTAM*, 39 (1972), p. 231.

[8] *History of Christian Philosophy*, pp. 498-99.

Gilson subsequently described the effect of Ockham's thought on his contemporaries. According to Gilson, Ockham quickly acquired a loyal group of followers who intensified the attack on traditional beliefs. These men came to be known as the "nominalists":

> The expressions 'nominalists' and 'realists' (*nominales, reales*) had been in use as early as the twelfth century. In the thirteenth century, Albert the Great had spoken of the 'nominalists' as of men who placed community in the intellect only. . . . But there have been few nominalists in the thirteenth century. After Ockham, this ancient appellation was used to designate his disciples. Hence a new doctrinal alignment. Despite their constant controversies, Thomists and Scotists were lumped together and made up the class of the 'realists,' or partisans of the 'ancient way' in philosophy and theology (*via antiqua*); the nominalists or terminists (*nominales, terministae*) were also called the moderns (*moderni*), not because they intended to abandon Aristotle, but because they were following a new way (*via moderna*) in interpreting it. . . . On December 29, 1340, some nominalistic theses were prohibited by the [Parisian Faculty of Arts], but these measures no more stopped the spread of Ockhamism than the thirteenth-century interdictions to teach Aristotle had prevented Aristotelianism from invading the mediaeval schools.[9]

This interpretation of Ockham's role in fourteenth-century intellectual life encouraged the notion that there was a single debate between clearly defined parties and suggested that Ockham led his adherents in a blatant attack on traditional views.

In his analysis of nominalism, Gilson equated Ockham's apparent reluctance to accept the possibility of certain knowledge, either of nature or of God, with the principle of skepticism. Gilson portrayed Ockham as at odds generally with all thirteenth-century attempts to reconcile Christian faith with Aristotelian natural philosophy and specifically with Duns Scotus' philosophical refinement of this synthesis:

> The God in whom Ockham believes is Yahweh, who obeys nothing, not even Ideas. Duns Scotus had submitted to the free will of God the choice of essences to be created; instead of letting God be free to choose between essences, Ockham suppresses them. Abélard had made Ideas the privilege of the divine mind; Ockham suppresses universals even in God. It is because there are no universal Ideas in God that there is no universality in things. The so-called Ideas are nothing but the very things producible by God. God needs no Ideas in order to know; by the very fact that God is God, he knows all.[10]

---

[9] *Ibid.*, pp. 499-500.

[10] *Ibid.*, p. 498.

Thus, although protecting himself with the orthodox claim that God, in his absolute power, could do anything, Ockham completely dismantled the rational underpinnings for reconciling faith and reason. In doing so, he negated the work of thirteenth-century theologians whose outstanding achievement had been to demonstrate that such a reconciliation was possible.

According to Gilson, Ockham's rejection of Aristotelian metaphysics further eroded the attempt to reconcile faith and reason. Ockham's approach to knowledge made it impossible for him or his followers to establish either a philosophical basis for faith or even a rational certainty about natural phenomena. In spite of their closeness to modern views of certainty, Ockham's views posed serious and disruptive theological questions in the fourteenth century:

> Like Thomas Aquinas and Duns Scotus, Ockham was first and last a theologian using certain philosophical doctrines in order to elaborate his own understanding of Christian faith. The dissolving influence exercised by his doctrine in the history of mediaeval scholasticism is due to the fact that, professing as he did a radical empiricism in philosophy, he had to reduce the understanding of faith to a bare minimum. An Ockhamist intellect is as badly equipped as possible for metaphysical cognition, and since where there is no metaphysical knowledge theology can expect little help from philosophy, the consequence of Ockhamism was to substitute for the positive collaboration of faith and reason which obtained in the golden age of scholasticism, a new and much looser regime in which the absolute and self-sufficient attitude of faith was only backed by mere philosophical probabilities.[11]

By presenting "Ockhamism" as an anti-Averroist theological reaction, moreover, Gilson stressed Ockham's position as the leader of a group with a well-defined agenda of opposition to thirteenth-century approaches to Aristotle.[12] Although it had more lasting effects than the initial criticisms of Aristotle in the twelfth and thirteenth centuries and displayed a more sophisticated understanding of Aristotelian natural philosophy, Ockham's nominalist school arose, in Gilson's view, from a similar distrust of classical approaches to knowledge.

Gilson's interpretation of Ockham and his followers, though it is an extreme one, provided a model for almost all subsequent discussions of Bradwardine's cosmology. Bradwardine's criticism of the modern Pelagians, who seemed to lack confidence both in the natural order of the

---

[11] *Ibid.*, p. 489.
[12] *Ibid.*, p. 501.

universe and in God's complete knowledge of it, points the reader of the *De causa Dei* to the group of people whom Gilson identified as the "Ockhamists." Not surprisingly, therefore, the standard treatments of Bradwardine's theology routinely have compared Bradwardine to Ockham and his nominalist followers, including Robert Holcot, Thomas Buckingham, Adam Wodeham, Gregory of Rimini and John of Mirecourt. Comparisons have been made because these men have been considered "Ockhamists," sometimes despite the lack of any specific evidence suggesting that the "Ockhamist" label was legitimate. Of course, had they really tried systematically to destroy the Aristotelian foundations of thirteenth-century theology, Bradwardine surely would have opposed them, if only on the grounds that their skepticism undermined the profession of a lively and confident faith. In fact, the attitudes of Bradwardine's contemporaries to Aristotle were varied and complex. Thus comparisons of their views can provide many useful insights into late medieval thought but only so long as we resist the temptation to separate these thinkers into distinct schools.

We have already seen that Ockham, in spite of his real differences from Bradwardine, was perhaps not quite so radical as Gilson and others have made him out to be. Ockham presented his contemporaries with epistemological and logical, rather than purely cosmological, speculations: he was concerned not with what exists but with how we can know about what exists. Nonetheless, his skepticism about the possibility of certain knowledge paralleled Bradwardine's own concerns on this issue and his method for expressing this uncertainty was analogous to Bradwardine's sharp division between the characteristics of created and divine being. Moreover, both theologians accepted the fundamental truth of Aristotelian natural philosophy and both based their theology on the conviction that God, in his absolute power, can do anything. Indeed, in certain respects, Bradwardine pushed this point farther than Ockham.

Similar observations could be made concerning Bradwardine's relationship with the "Ockhamists." Gilson, Leff and Oberman have all maintained that Ockham had followers who together represented the radical challenge which Bradwardine tried to combat in the *De causa Dei*. Because they expressed some of the logical skepticism about knowledge which Ockham had introduced in his philosophical works, these scholars could easily be identified as the modern Pelagians whose notions so distressed Bradwardine. In order to evaluate the extent to which these men actually opposed Bradwardine, historians have focused on their divergent opinions about the nature of God's absolute power.

The usual assumption is that, in following Ockham's conception of God's absolute power, the "Ockhamists" developed a theological perspective that undermined the balance of faith and reason advocated by Augustine and Aquinas. Little attention has been paid to the greater likelihood that Bradwardine disagreed with the "Ockhamists" in direct proportion to their acceptance of a cosmology which temporalized God and made the future contingent not only to humanity but to God.

According to Leff, for example, the "Ockhamist" insistence that God's absolute power allows him to do anything calls into question the necessity of an orderly, predictable universe. Although God, through his ordained powers, gives the impression of rationality, he is not compelled always to act according to these powers. God's absolute power is an attribute "outside all space and time and not directed to any specific universe, or to sustaining any fixed order."[13] This conception of God's absolute power is, in Leff's view, the source of skepticism throughout the whole nominalist movement because

> it combined [the] three features of mutability, possibility and indeterminacy, and applied them to God and revelation. Its central theme was that nothing was impossible for God in His absolute power; and in removing the bar of impossibility, it opened the way to neutrality and indeterminacy. Neutrality was expressed in the refusal to limit God so that any course was as likely as another in his infinite freedom; accordingly, the sceptics refused to limit themselves in what could be said about Him; it enabled them to join the blasphemous to the devotional, to make black part of white, to consider the impossible as possible, all in the name of His freedom. . . . As a result, God was as he willed; His attributes dissolved before the blaze of His omnipotence, making him unknowable not only in the wider and accepted sense, but in those traits which were virtually the precondition of belief. His goodness, perfection, mercy, justice and wisdom all faded from man's vision as beyond his ken. He could be known only by His ability ever to do differently than He had done. God, therefore, lost his certainty; He became identified with infinite possibility rather than with any fixed and ascertainable order. Hence anything could be posited of Him, for His *potentia absoluta* substituted speculation for understanding.[14]

The implications of Ockham's theory for explaining God's relation to the created world are so extreme, says Leff, that Bradwardine had no choice but to refute them.

---

[13] *Bradwardine and the Pelagians*, p. 131.
[14] *Ibid.*, pp. 131-32.

The comparisons which have been made in this study between Ockham's and Bradwardine's treatments of time have indicated that the views of Ockham advanced by Gilson and Leff have somewhat exaggerated the extremity of Ockham's philosophical and theological perspectives. We have seen that Ockham never advocated so rigorous a skepticism that it rendered God and the natural order totally incomprehensible; he merely pointed out that the human tools of propositional logic and philosophical analysis can only partially explain how and why God exercises his absolute power as he does. This reevaluation of Ockham's thought obviously raises serious questions about the interpretation of the work of his followers. If Ockham cannot be accused of excessive or radical skepticism, how, then, do we evaluate the writings of those thinkers whose ideas have been associated with his? In other words, to what extent did the "Ockhamists" deviate from Ockham's essentially moderate position, and to what extent did they advocate the view of God ascribed to them by Gilson and Leff? More important for our understanding of Bradwardine's thought, how did the ideas of the "Ockhamists" influence Bradwardine's arguments concerning time, contingency, grace and free will? Although it would be inappropriate to attempt here a comprehensive analysis of the entire group of scholars commonly referred to as the "Ockhamists," I shall try to address some aspects of the question of Bradwardine's relationship to his contemporaries through two examples of academic interaction in which the issue of time is explicitly present. Thomas Buckingham and Robert Holcot are the two "Ockhamists" most often associated with Bradwardine. Not only did all three move in the same circles, but there is good evidence of mutual influence in both philosophical and theological matters. By briefly comparing their opinions about God's absolute power, natural justice and grace, I hope both to show the complexity of academic interaction in the mid-fourteenth century and to emphasize the role of cosmological differences, particularly those involving time, in late medieval scholarly debate.

Bradwardine's interactions with Thomas Buckingham indicate that Buckingham moderated his somewhat extreme skepticism after considering Bradwardine's complaints against the modern Pelagians, although he remained convinced that Bradwardine's approach to contingency was too deterministic. A slightly younger contemporary of Bradwardine's, Buckingham was born at the turn of the fourteenth century and was a fellow at Merton from 1324 to 1340. Gifted both as a natural philosopher and as a theologian, Buckingham would certainly have had direct contact with so prominent a Mertonian as Bradwardine. In his sentence commentary, completed in the mid 1330s, Buckingham took a great interest in contemporary speculation about the importance of grace in determining the merit of an act. Buckingham's opinion that God, in his absolute power, could create a sinless individual without having to provide him with justifying grace, led him into conflict with both Bradwardine and Richard FitzRalph. Buckingham's assertions about grace corroborated the conventional teaching that unbaptized infants are unjustified even though they are too young to act meritoriously or without grace; nevertheless, the assumptions about God's absolute power, which Buckingham used to support this thesis, raised doubts about his overall orthodoxy.[15] In probing the question of God's capacity to contravene the natural order established by his ordained powers, Buckingham took the potentially dangerous step of undermining the importance of grace.

According to Leff, in fact, Buckingham pushed the "Ockhamist" approach to God's absolute power so far that his theology was only barely orthodox. The doctrine of God's absolute power enabled him to challenge the orthodox position on contingency in two dangerous ways: first, by denying the necessity of grace for a meritorious act; and second, by describing God's knowledge of the future as fully contingent. Instead of stressing God's constant involvement in the world and participation in human acts, Buckingham contended that God has provided human beings with a kind of "natural justice" which allows them to perform good acts without grace. Because one could therefore do good without the constant intervention of God, one could postulate that salvation might be attained without the benefit of created grace. Buckingham even went so far as to suggest that this "natural justice" empowers the human will to reject sin of its own accord.[16]

Buckingham claimed that he placed such a strong emphasis on human freedom only in order to ensure the absolute freedom of God. Leff has suggested, however, that Buckingham's real concern was to safeguard the freedom of the human will and to disguise the radical nature of his views by maintaining the widely accepted view that human freedom depends on and resembles divine freedom. It is perhaps more likely that Buckingham overemphasized the analogy between human and divine freedom on account of his legitimate concern about the restrictions which God's ordained powers might have on his absolute power.

[15] Robson, pp. 41-43.
[16] Leff, pp. 228-30.

Therefore, although Buckingham did not wish to deny the reality of God's ordained power, he struggled with the question of how God could be truly free if he must participate in the world according to his ordained powers. In his early thought, at least, Buckingham expressed views about grace and necessity which appeared to his contemporaries to stress too much the correspondence between human and divine freedom. Bradwardine, in particular, criticized Buckingham's underestimation of the importance of created grace, though his belief in God's absolute freedom equalled or even surpassed Buckingham's.

Buckingham's view of contingency suggests that his cosmology prevented him from accepting Bradwardine's solution to the problem of free will. Leff claims that Buckingham's radical view of contingency reflects better than any other issue Buckingham's extreme skepticism:

> In essence the problem is how to reconcile God's eternal knowledge of everything with man's freedom to act contingently; that is, if God knows all from eternity how can men act freely without either making His knowledge mutable or their actions determined? It is a problem which arises only when there is a break between God's will and His operations in the world; with no hierarchy between God and men, there can, in the circumstances, be only two alternatives, if freedom for the future is to be preserved: either God, while knowing the general shape of things to come, foregoes, in the interests of freedom, any foreknowledge of their details; or His knowledge of these particulars must be contingent, as subject to change as they themselves are. . . . Buckingham . . . chooses the second way and makes God's foreknowledge of the future as contingent as the contingents He knows.[17]

In following this line of argument, says Leff, Buckingham willingly sacrificed two attributes of God, omniscience and immutability, in order to preserve both God's absolute power and the freedom of the human will. Although Buckingham did not deny that God has complete knowledge of all future contingent events, he stated much more openly than Ockham ever had the implication of this contingency for creation: God knows all of the possibilities of the future but he waits to see which possibilities will be realized. To ensure that the future remained contingent, therefore, Buckingham qualified God's foreknowledge, making it a knowledge of potentiality, not of actuality.   By emphasizing these themes, Leff has attempted to portray Buckingham as a theologian for whom conventional explanations of God's powers and ways of acting in his creation are unnecessarily deterministic and therefore misleading.

---

[17] *Ibid.*, p. 234.

Robson argues that Buckingham responded decisively to the unfavor-able reaction that his sentence commentary received in the academic community.   According to Robson, Bradwardine had an especially strong influence on Buckingham, not only because Bradwardine was a highly respected figure in Buckingham's own circle but because they were both interested in the same kinds of philosophical and theological problems.[18] Although Buckingham continued to maintain that the future is in an absolute sense more contingent than the past, because the future still holds the possibility of change, he tried in his later works to find a middle ground between determinism and skepticism.   In his *Quaestiones*, for example, Buckingham reevaluated Bradwardine's criticism of his view of antecedent necessity:

> In a necessary consequence, if the antecedent is not in the free control of the person concerned, then neither is the consequence; and if the con-sequence is under his control so is the antecedent; and the rules brought with authorities and arguments against my second, third, ninth and tenth conclusions have (I hope) been fully refuted to the understanding of those who uttered them. But to what has been said here a certain doctor objects, by proving that whoever has free control over a consequence is also in control of whatever follows from it and whatever is necessarily antecedent. And he says that he understands this only of any antecedent which is not absolutely impossible: and it is his 13th conclusion.[19]

This passage indicates that Bradwardine and Buckingham had a fundamental disagreement about the temporal nature of created acts. Whereas Bradwardine continually affirmed both the past and the future as equally necessary because they exist simultaneously in God's mind, Buckingham insisted on temporal variations in necessity. Even for God, he argued, the past is more necessary than the future because it has lost its contingency.

Although Buckingham conceded that his earlier opinions about grace might have been too extreme, he was not prepared to give up his temporal approach to contingency.[20] Nevertheless, as Robson points

---

[18] Robson, p. 32. In "Anselm and Thomas of Buckingham: An Examination of the *Questiones super Sententias*," *Anselm Studies*, 1 (1983), pp. 231-49, Arthur A. Lee points out that, like Bradwardine, Buckingham's scholarly interest in issues of predestination and contingency was an outgrowth of his genuine Christian faith. His respectful but critical reading of Anselm emphasizes the common theological thread which tied Buckingham and Bradwardine together.

[19] Robson, p. 53, quotes and translates this passage from Buckingham's *Quaestiones*, New College, Oxford MS 134, Fo. 327r[a]. See *De causa Dei*, III, 5, corollary 13, p. 657, E.

[20] Robson, p. 52.

out, Buckingham denied in his *Quaestiones* that the past and future are so contingent that God would arbitrarily change or destroy conditions which are necessary for faith and so gently chastised Bradwardine for misrepresenting his position:

> Likewise the Reverend Doctor, arguing in opposition to this conclusion, says that unless we admit antecedent necessity, we must admit it possible for the whole of God's church to fall, collapse and perish, for the whole vessel of Peter to suffer shipwreck and drowning, for all Christ's faith before the Day of Judgement to be defective and shattered (and even that all the articles of faith concerning the future should be, and should always have been, false and erroneous); that Christ should have lied and all the Saints, Apostles, Martyrs and Confessors who formerly lived in this faith should have been deceived.[21]

Robson, calls this passage a "caricature of the alternative to rigid determinism,"[22] and depicts Buckingham as a moderate theologian trying to find a compromise between restrictive determinism and arbitrary contingency. Buckingham affirmed his orthodoxy by refusing to go too far in either direction. To this extent, he followed Ockham in balancing the necessary truth of God's revelation with seemingly irrefutable sensory evidence that the future contains many possibilities while the past can no longer be changed. Buckingham and Bradwardine were in conflict over this issue because they had fundamentally different conceptions of time. Buckingham was unwilling to accord to God an eternity and simultaneity which completely remove him from the human experience of time; consequently, his view of necessity was ambiguous. Bradwardine, as we have already seen, sacrificed some of the full range of human freedom to avoid this very ambiguity.

Buckingham's and Bradwardine's disagreement concerning God's experience of time manifested itself in different interpretations of God's essential attributes. While they both gave the highest affirmation to God's absolute power, Buckingham stressed God's freedom to change his mind in a temporal way, whereas Bradwardine viewed God's freedom, unlike human freedom, as an entirely atemporal reality. Though wishing to remain orthodox, Buckingham could not relinquish his conviction that divine and human freedom share certain characteristics:

> To the argument alleged by the Master and Reverend Doctor, that unless we admit antecedent necessity in all acts of the will, we must admit the

---

[21] Robson, p. 52.
[22] Robson, p. 58.

possibility of the whole church being destroyed, and so forth: in reply, I wish to know whether God is free to change his ordinances; and if he is, whether he cannot by his free will effect and fulfill all those things here named. . . . For I think that the created will has liberty of contradiction, and no man has the power to destroy Holy Church. . . . And I know that, as logic demands, [I must affirm] the co-operation, grace, predestination, and prescience of God, which I shall not deny. Nor like the Fool shall I deny his existence, nor like Pelagius do I wish to exalt my will as master and God's as mere handmaid. But I wish to attribute to God, as first agent, every good we have and to declare that we are in many things his free instruments, not coerced, and also fit to be rewarded out of his abundant mercy for which, as I am bound, I return all the thanks I can.[23]

Nothing in this statement contradicted Bradwardine's positions about God as first cause or the freedom of the human will to respond to the infinitely divine will. In fact, Buckingham's language clearly indicates that he was responding directly to the criticisms which Bradwardine had outlined in the *De causa Dei*. Buckingham openly acknowledged that God is the first cause of created acts. His differences from Bradwardine arose mostly from the question of how God "changes his mind": for Buckingham, the change could occur temporally, so that the future could be seen as at least somewhat contingent; for Bradwardine, any change in the divine plan would be atemporal and entirely independent of human perceptions of change in time.

Buckingham's disagreement with Bradwardine over the temporal basis of necessity should not be exaggerated, however. There is little doubt that Buckingham would have been sensitive to the charge of "Pelagianism" and expressed his opinions accordingly, although he continued to distinguish between the necessity of the past and the contingency of the future. Leff would have us believe that Buckingham and Bradwardine stood so far apart on this issue that they both strayed perilously close to heresy: that Buckingham, in his extreme interpretation of "Ockhamist" principles, provoked Bradwardine into an equally extreme form of determinism. What Leff fails to take into account in his analysis of Buckingham is the positive influence of academic dialogue. While it is true that Buckingham's temporal approach to contingency resembled Ockham's, he neither slavishly followed Ockham nor altered his cosmology in favor of Bradwardine's when he was alerted to some of Ockham's errors.[24] Robson has shown that communication between

---

[23] Fo. 338r^b-v^a of *Quaestiones*, trans. Robson, p. 58. See above, note 18.

[24] For the subtle differences between Buckingham's and Ockham's views on God's

Buckingham and Bradwardine led to reconsideration and refinement on Buckingham's part, just as, we may suppose, Buckingham's initial response to the problem provided a useful target for Bradwardine's analysis of the problem of contingency. The fact that they did not ultimately agree on every issue does not diminish the value of their attempts to work out their views in an environment of debate and critical reflection. Bradwardine's exchange with Buckingham, far from suggesting bitterness, radicalism and despair over the collapse of an old way of thinking, reflects the capacity of mid-fourteenth-century thinkers to collaborate on new solutions to difficult problems.[25]

Another contemporary of Bradwardine who has been regularly included in the list of "Ockhamists" was Robert Holcot. Holcot was a Dominican who combined study and lecturing at Oxford with an active career of public preaching. In addition, he wrote on a variety of philosophical and theological topics of contemporary interest. Indeed, Oberman has called Holcot a "proto-humanist" due to his avid interests

---

capacity to undo the past, see, for example, Adams, *William Ockham*, pp. 1225-27.

[25] In "Thomas Buckingham's *Ostensio meriti liberae actionis*, Conclusions 1-15: 'De contingentia futurorum et arbitrii libertate': An Edition and Study" (Dissertation, University of Toronto, 1979), Bartholemew Ruben de la Torre examines Bradwardine's interaction with Buckingham on the issue of future contingents. De la Torre suggests that parts of Buckingham's sentence commentary and the first part of the *Ostensio Meriti Liberae Actionis* were direct replies to the *De causa Dei*. Buckingham, who might have been Bradwardine's student, rejected Bradwardine's definition of antecedent necessity and tried to find a "Catholic middle way" between extreme determinism and the indeterminacy advocated by Cicero and, to a lesser extent, by Pelagius (p. 89). De La Torre's analysis of the *De Contingentia Futurorum et Arbitrii Libertate* supports Robson's conclusions about Buckingham's relationship to Bradwardine but does so without substantial reference to Bradwardine's view of time. De La Torre is not specific about the actual dating of Buckingham's writing as compared to the *De causa Dei*. He reports, however (p. 185), a discovery made by Zenon Kaluza that Bradwardine and Buckingham probably did not have a public debate over contingency in Paris which Leff, Oberman and Robson believed had taken place. In "La preténdu discussion parisienne de Thomas de Bradwardine avec Thomas de Buckingham: témoinage de Thomas de Cracovie," *RTAM*, 43 (1976), pp. 209-36, Kaluza demonstrates that Thomas of Cracow, the supposed witness to the debate, could not in fact have witnessed it since he was born eleven years after the deaths of Bradwardine and Buckingham. Kaluza argues instead that Thomas of Cracow was the owner of a manuscript (MS Paris Bib. Nat. Lat. 16409) written by Stephen of Chaumont who had summarized Bradwardine's and Buckingham's differences on future contingents. According to Kaluza, a misreading of the manuscript in the early twentieth century gave historians the idea that a public debate had taken place in Paris, when in fact the communication between Bradwardine and Buckingham occurred in England over a period of several years. Moreover, while this communication indicates disagreement on several points, it does not suggest the personal antagonism which is usually associated with the Paris debate.

in classics and moral theology.[26]   Although he was a friar, Holcot's career paralleled Bradwardine's remarkably closely. Both arrived at Oxford in the 1320s, taught and wrote in the 1330s and early 1340s and spent the last years of their lives away from the universities, though Holcot retired from an active academic career at the same time that Bradwardine was enjoying his most active period of public service. Both died in 1349. More important than these coincidental comparisons, both Bradwardine and Holcot belonged for a time to Richard de Bury's household, which ensures that they were at least reasonably well known to each other. Unlike the Mertonians in Bishop Bury's circle, Holcot did not specialize in natural philosophy. He shared with Bradwardine the distinction, however, of publishing several books which were immediately popular and widely read.[27]   Given his Dominican training, Holcot showed an unusual enthusiasm for many of Ockham's ideas, particularly in the area of logic. Like Ockham, Holcot was fascinated by the problem of reconciling matters of faith with the philosophical constraints of Aristotelian logic.[28] Holcot also took part in discussions about contingency and necessity. He has generally been considered an opponent of Bradwardine's determinism, though historians have disagreed as to the nature and extent of his criticism. Gilson and Leff have portrayed Holcot primarily as an "Ockhamist," whereas Oberman has stressed the more original features of his attack on deterministic theology.

Those historians who emphasize Holcot's ties to Ockham point to Holcot's "nominalistic" tendency to separate faith and reason. According to Gilson, for example, Holcot tried to prove in his sentence commentary that faith and natural philosophy require two separate logical systems, because Aristotelian logic is ineffective for examining a theological mystery such as the Trinity. Holcot's reliance on the concept of God's absolute power to prove that one cannot apply the same analytical methods both to natural philosophy and theology indicates to Gilson that Holcot was deeply influenced by Ockham's teaching about contingency, prediction, natural order and sin.[29] Leff goes even farther than Gilson in identifying Holcot as a follower of Ockham and an inevitable opponent of Bradwardine. Indeed, says Leff, Holcot made himself the main target of Bradwardine's attack on Pelagianism by fully

---

[26] *Forerunners*, p. 133.
[27] Pantin, pp. 144-45.
[28] *History of Christian Philosophy*, pp. 500-1.
[29] *Ibid.*

exploring the implications of Ockham's extreme skepticism. For Leff, Holcot is the quintessential "Ockhamist":

> Robert Holcot well illustrates how fruitfully Ockham provided for his followers along the path of scepticism. He takes up many of the same positions that Ockham held; and he also extends them. Despite his fulsome qualifications to everything, it is not hard to discern the same trait of doubt that moulded Ockham's views. With room for everything, there is hardly room for God; possibility once again dissolves the stable order that Bradwardine proclaims; and men can do all that God can will. Thus, on the one hand, there is divine causality; on the other divine indeterminacy. Holcot's view represents the application to which the latter outlook can be put. As the almost exact contemporary of Bradwardine, he indicates the attitude against which Bradwardine had to contend, and the effect of Ockham's teaching upon thinkers of his generation.[30]

Thus Leff sees Holcot as a leading participant in a well-defined and well-integrated school of thought against which Bradwardine desperately battled.

Like Gilson, moreover, Leff stresses Holcot's use of the principle of God's absolute power, the favored "Ockhamist" method for deferring the charge of heresy. As with Buckingham, Leff underlines Holcot's belief in the inherent goodness of natural human powers, which permits the will to recognize and sometimes even perform good acts without the necessity of created grace. All of these concepts, says Leff, come more or less directly from Ockham. Holcot deviates from Ockham only in the direction of even greater skepticism, as when he denies that the human will need do anything to attain merit, because merit depends on God's will alone.[31]

According to Leff, Holcot's approach to contingency also reflects his tendency towards further skepticism. Holcot accepts Ockham's logical explanation of contingency and his assumption that the future is mutable in order to prove that God cannot know future contingents. Because revelation must be true, God's knowledge of revealed truths must be necessary and complete. Therefore, because God cannot have both complete and incomplete knowledge, it must be the case that he knows revealed truth with certainty and has no certain knowledge of contingent truths. In Leff's view, Holcot uses revelation as "the sign that God cannot know future contingents: in his desire to prevent God's word from being fallible he has chosen the other alternative of limiting his

---

[30] Leff, pp. 216-17.
[31] *Ibid.*, pp. 218-19.

knowledge. . . . As a result, revelation has been transformed: it is now no longer the eternal sign of God's foreknowledge, but of its limitations."[32]

Although Oberman also considers Holcot sympathetic to many of Ockham's positions, he portrays Holcot as a more complex figure. Oberman admits that Holcot and Bradwardine disagreed on certain fundamental theological issues, but he does not think "Ockhamist" doctrines were the only source of the conflict. In fact, Oberman maintains, Holcot supported several of Bradwardine's ideas and sometimes departed significantly from Ockham: he did not simply intensify "Ockhamist" views.[33] By comparing Holcot's and Bradwardine's positions on grace and will, Oberman is able to demonstrate, as Robson demonstrated for Buckingham, both Holcot's independence from "Ockhamism" and his positive contributions to a process of fruitful academic discussion.

Oberman cites Holcot's popular *Commentary on the Wisdom of Solomon* to indicate precisely where Holcot deviated from Bradwardine on the issue of grace. Whereas Bradwardine risks the charges of determinism and unnecessary restriction of the innate human capacity for good in order to assure God's primacy, Holcot tries very hard to preserve the integrity of the human will in the process of justification. Holcot wishes to define merit in such a way that intrinsic human worth is not ignored. Thus he distinguishes between the natural value of an action and its contracted value:

> Now if we understand man's merit according to the first interpretation, the natural goodness of our works does not earn eternal life fully (*de condigno*) but only partially (*de congruo*), since it is appropriate (*congruens*) that if man has done all that he can with his finite resources God should reward him with His infinite resources. But according to the second understanding of merit we can say that our works are fully worthy of eternal life, not because of any merit inherent in the acts themselves but because of grace, since our Lord has established that he who does good works in a state of grace shall receive eternal life.[34]

At this level Holcot appears to be in agreement with Bradwardine. Both accept the necessity of grace for transforming a human act, which is neither good nor bad in itself, into a meritorious one. They agree, moreover, that it is the direct activity of God which ensures a meritorious act.

---

[32] *Ibid.*, p. 226.

[33] Oberman, *Archbishop Thomas Bradwardine*, pp. 45-46.

[34] *Super Libros Sapientiae*, Chapter III, Lecture 35, ed. Heinrich Gran (Hagenau: 1494), trans. Nyhus, in *Forerunners*, p. 143.

Their differences become more apparent, however, when Holcot begins to discuss the precise way in which grace is received. Not only does Holcot claim that "whoever prepares himself to accept grace necessarily receives it," but he implies that God's capacity to give grace can be limited by circumstances:

> it may be said that there is a distinction between compulsory necessity and unfailing necessity [that is, consistency]. With God compulsory necessity has no place, but an unfailing necessity is appropriate to God because of His promise, that is, His Covenant, or established law. This is not an absolute, but rather a conditional necessity. According to God's established law the pilgrim who does whatever he can to dispose himself for grace always receives grace. However, if He should choose to, God could deviate from His law for someone other than the pilgrim or the devil. Then, however much a person [with whom God has not made His Covenant] might dispose himself for grace, he would not receive it. Man's disposition does not require the giving of grace except by congruency, because grace surpasses every natural act; it is impossible for man to fully merit (*de condigno*) through any natural act.[35]

Bradwardine would agree with the final sentiments of this passage but would take exception to the limiting language Holcot employs to define God's scope in giving grace. In Bradwardine's opinion, grace and act are inseparable because God causes and sanctifies the act all at once; Holcot, who has a different view of God's experience of time, sees the process of act and grace as sequential and temporal.

Although Oberman focuses on grace, not the problem of time and eternity, he argues convincingly that the disagreement between Bradwardine and Holcot cannot be conceived simply along the traditional lines of "Ockhamism" versus Augustinian determinism. Holcot shared some of Ockham's views about the nature of God's absolute power and future contingency but he differed with Ockham in his understanding of grace and justification. Oberman's account of the exchange between Holcot and Bradwardine emphasizes themes which were of common interest to a large number of scholars. Instead of searching for the "Ockhamist" source of all Holcot's opinions, Oberman acknowledges the originality of both theologians as well as their dependence on the work of predecessors and contemporaries from various philosophical and theological traditions.

More recent interpretations of Holcot bear out this notion of subtlety and complexity of scholarly interaction in the mid-fourteenth century.

---

[35] Chapter XII, Lecture 145, in *Forerunners*, p. 149.

Historians observe, for example, that Holcot accepted Ockham's logical approach to contingency and note Holcot's ability to adjust Ockham's views to support his own particular interests. Although they do not describe it in such terms, most historians recognize that the conflict between Holcot and Bradwardine had to do with a basic difference in their conception of God's activity in the world. While Bradwardine and Holcot arrived at similar conclusions about grace and God's absolute power, they disagreed about the essential characteristics of the God who dispenses that grace and wields that power.

Furthermore, as Ockham's views increasingly come to be regarded as conventional, it becomes more difficult to distinguish fourteenth-century theologians on the basis of their skepticism.[36] Because Ockham, Bradwardine, Buckingham and Holcot identified many of the same problems and applied to them the analytical methods of their common education, they perhaps had more in common than the standard interpretation of late medieval philosophical trends recognized.[37] Although Holcot's place in the scholarly debates of the mid-fourteenth century has not yet been fully worked out, it is safe to assume that he, like Buckingham and Ockham, possessed the ability to assess the ideas of others and to incorporate them into new perspectives.

The examples of Thomas Buckingham and Robert Holcot indicate that it is no easy matter to explain the complexities of late fourteenth-century intellectual life in terms of a clear-cut division either between conservatives and radicals or between Augustinians and Ockhamists. Much more work remains to be done on the less well-known participants in fourteenth-century academic discussions at Oxford and at Paris, who also contributed to the rich and varied intellectual life of this period.

---

[36] In "Philosophical Scepticism in England in the Mid-Fourteenth Century," *Vivarium*, 21 (1983), pp. 56-7, Leonard Kennedy challenges the definitions of skepticism commonly used by many historians of the late medieval period and suggests that mid-fourteenth-century theologians in England were more skeptical philosophically, if not theologically, than recent studies of their work indicate.

[37] In "Robert Holkot on Future Contingencies: A Preliminary Account," p. 168, Streveler contends that the Augustinian-Boethian solution was actually very similar to the nominalist one, because the definition of an eternal idea in the Augustinian-Boethian tradition corresponds very well to the late medieval definition of a proposition as a statement which is always true. If Streveler is correct, it might be possible to identify points of agreement between late medieval thinkers on matters which seem on the surface to be controversial. Again, the main distinction between an eternal idea and a proposition depends not on the definition of a proposition as such but on the different approaches medieval natural philosophers and logicians took to the temporal factors which affect the truth of propositions.

Although fourteenth-century thinkers considered the same problems and looked to the same authorities as their predecessors, their innovations in logic and natural philosophy helped to push theological speculation, the most revered subject for human reason, in new directions and into new controversies. The closeness of the academic community in training, patronage and belief made lively intercourse inevitable, particularly at Oxford, where the absence of any serious complaints of heresy stimulated a relatively uninhibited exchange of ideas. The multidisciplinary skills of many of the Oxford fellows significantly enriched debates about both traditional and novel topics.

As a highly respected member of late medieval academic circles, both as a natural philosopher and as a theologian, Bradwardine epitomizes the vibrancy and multidisciplinary nature of scholarly debates in that period. His mastery of many types of learning and his productive interactions with colleagues and students reflect the eagerness with which fourteenth-century scholars approached long-standing philosophical and theological problems in new ways. If the thirteenth century was the age of synthesis of Aristotelian natural philosophy and Christian doctrine, the fourteenth century represents an age of exploration of the implications of that synthesis. Occasionally, studies culminated in expressions of uncertainty about the value of using traditional methods to solve complex cosmological and theological questions: hence the charge of skepticism. If we look beyond the obvious lines of debate, however, we can also discern their optimism and confidence about the relationship between God and his creation which characterized the speculation of this period. Bradwardine's treatments of time and eternity and his critical responses to his contemporaries clearly indicate that skepticism in the mid-fourteenth century was not the consequence of anxiety about God's sovereignty or the rationality of the created world; rather, its source was dissatisfaction with traditional analytical methods which were inadequate to the needs of increasingly sophisticated scientific and theological investigations.

This examination of Bradwardine's view of time concurs with other recent studies which suggest that fourteenth-century thought cannot be accurately portrayed by emphasizing individual personalities, well-organized intellectual alliances, pervasive skepticism or the breakdown of thirteenth-century syntheses. Instead, the complex interaction of scholars is the most striking feature of the period. William Courtenay describes the fourteenth century as a time when "methods and topics

were generally more important than individual thinkers."[38]   Bradwardine's scholarly achievements, seen in this context of criticism and
debate, reflect his skill in correcting others' methods, contributing original perceptions based on his special knowledge of mathematics and
natural philosophy, and redefining cosmological problems in a way
which combined the traditional authority of Aristotle, Augustine and
Boethius with fresh interpretations.

Bradwardine's elegant treatment of the problem of time was so tied
up with his cosmology that it could not be accepted by those who proposed alternative cosmologies. By ignoring aspects of the problem
which were paramount to others, he was unable to convince all of his
contemporaries that his approach was the correct one. Nevertheless, the
state of the debate about time in the mid-fourteenth century, with Bradwardine so skillfully defending a view accepted from Plato through
Aquinas while others built on an equally long tradition of criticism of
this view, provides a great insight into the interests and abilities, the
prejudices and limitations, of the entire age. The discussions about time
were neither universally optimistic nor completely pessimistic but they
exhibited an intense desire to understand God and how God acts in the
world. As a physical, metaphysical, logical and cosmological concept,
time afforded many different avenues for investigation. Bradwardine's
training in both natural philosophy and theology put him in a position to
understand the various aspects of time as well as any of his contemporaries. Even today many aspects of the problem of time remain
unsolved but the work of Bradwardine and his colleagues shows how
much can be accomplished when such a complex issue engages the interest of a talented, diverse and well-integrated academic community.

---

[38] Courtenay, "Recent Work on Fourteenth-Century Oxford Thought," p. 232.

BIBLIOGRAPHY

PRIMARY SOURCES

Albertus Magnus. *Alberti Magni Opera Omni.* 38 Vols. Ed. A. Borgnet. Paris: L. Vivès, 1890-99.

Anselm. *Sancti Anselmi Opera Omnia.* Ed. Franciscus Salesius Schmitt. Rome: 1938; rpt. Stuttgart-Bad Constatti: F. Frommann Verlag, 1968.

Aristotle. *The Complete Works of Aristotle: The Revised Oxford Translation.* 2 Vols. Ed. Jonathan Barnes. Princeton, New Jersey: Princeton University Press, 1985.

—. *De generatione et corruptione translatio vetus, Aristoteles latinus,* IX. Ed. Joanna Judycka. Leiden: E. J. Brill, 1986.

—. *De interpretatione vel Periermenias translatio Boethii specimina translationum recentiorum, Aristoteles latinus,* II, 1-2. Ed. Laurentius Minio-Paluello. Leiden: E. J. Brill, 1965.

—. *Physica: translatio Vaticana.* Ed. Augustinius Mansion. In *Series: Aristoteles Latinus,* VII, 2. *Corpus philosophorum medii aevi.* Bruges: Desclée de Brouwer, 1957.

—. *Physica: translatio vetus.* In *Aristoteles latinus,* VII 1, *Fasciculus secundus, Corpus philosophorum medii aevi.* Eds. Fernand Bossier and Jozef Brams. Leiden: E. J. Brill, 1990.

Augustine. *Concerning the City of God against the Pagans.* Trans. Henry Bettensen. Harmondsworth, Middlesex, England: Penguin, 1972.

—. *Augustine's Confessions.* Trans. Henry Chadwick. New York: Oxford University Press, 1991.

—. *The Confessions of Augustine.* Ed. John Gibb. Cambridge: Cambridge University Press, 1908.

—. *The Confessions of Augustine.* Eds. John Gibb and William Montgomery. Cambridge: Cambridge University Press, 1927.

—. *Confessions.* Trans. Richard Sidney Pine-Coffin. Harmondsworth, Middlesex, England: Penguin, 1961.

—. *Enchiridion ad Laurentium de Fide et Spe et Caritate.* Ed. Ernest Evans. In *Aurelii Augustini Opera,* Part XIII, 2. *Corpus christianiorum series latina,* XCVI. Turnholti: Typographi Brepols, 1969, pp. 21-114.

—. *Sancti Augustini confessionum libri XII.* Ed. Lucas Verheijen. Volume 27 of *Sancti Augustini opera in corpus christianorum series latina.* Turnholti: Brepols, 1981.

—. *Sancti Aurelii Augustini Confessionum libri XIII.* Ed. Martinus Skutella. Stuttgart: Teubner, 1969.

—. *Sancti Aurelii Augustini episcopi de civitate dei libri XXII.* Ed. Bernardus Dombart and Alphonsus Kalb. In *Bibliotheca scriptorum Graecorum et Romanorum Teuberniana,* Vol. I. Stuttgart: Teubner, 1981.

Averroes. *Commentary on the Physics*. In Vol. IV of *Aristotelis Opera cum Averrois Commentarius*. Venice: Juntas, 1562-1574.

Boethius. *Anicii Manlii Severini Boethii philosophiae consolatio*. Ed. Ludouicus Bieler. In *Corpus christianorum, series latina*, Vol. 94. Turnholti: Typographi Brepols Editores Pontifici, 1957.

—. *The Consolation of Philosophy*. Trans. Henry Rosher James. London: Elliot Stock, 1897.

—. *The Consolation of Philosophy*. Ed. Edward Kennard Rand. In *Boethius: The Theological Tractates and the Consolation of Philosophy*. Eds. Hugh Fraser Stewart, Edward Kennard Rand and S. J. Tester. London: Heinemann, 1973.

Boethius of Dacia. "Die Opuscula De summo bono sive de vita philosophi und De sompniis des Boetius von Dacia." *AHDLMA*, 6 (1931), pp. 287-317.

Garlandus Compotista. *Dialecta*. Ed. Lambertus Maria De Rijk. Assen: Van Gorcum, 1959.

Geoffrey Chaucer. *The Riverside Chaucer*. Ed. Larry D. Benson. 3rd ed. Boston, Massachusetts: Houghton Mifflin, 1987.

Henry of Harclay. *Quaestio de infinito et continuo*. MS Tortosa Cated. 88; MS Firenze Naz. II.II. 281.

—. "Henricus de Harclay. Quaestio 'utrum mundus potuit fuisse ab aeterno.'" Ed. Richard C. Dales. *AHDLMA* 50 (1983), pp. 223-55.

Hugh of St. Victor. *The Didascalicon of Hugh of St. Victor: A Medieval Guide to the Arts*. Ed. and trans. Jerome Taylor. New York: Columbia University Press, 1961.

John Duns Scotus. *Opera omnia, iussu et auctoritate Pacifici M. Perantoni. Studio et cura commissionis Scotisticae as fidem codicum edita*. 17 Volumes. Ed. Charles Balic. Civitas Vatican: Typis Polyglottis Vaticanis, 1950-66.

—. *Opera Omnia*. Ed. Luke Wadding. Paris: L. Vivès, 1891-1895.

Moses Maimonides. *The Guide of the Perplexed*. Trans. Shlomo Pines. Chicago: University of Chigago Press, 1963.

Peter Abelard. *Dialectica*. Ed. Lambertus Maria De Rijk. *Wijsgerige teksten en studies*, I. Assen: Van Gorcum, 1970.

—. *Editio super Aristotelem De Interpretatione*. Ed. Mario dal Pra. In *Pietro Abelardo: Scritti di logica*. Florence: La nuovo Italia, 1969.

—. *Peter Abaelards philosophische Schriften*. Ed. Bernhard Geyer. Münster: Aschendorff, 1933.

Peter Lombard. *Libri IV Sententiarum*. Ed. Albanus Heysse. Florence: Editiones Collegii S. Bonaventura ad Claras Aquas, Grottaferrata, 1916.

Peter of Spain. Excerpt from *Tractatus Syncategorematum* on "incipit" and "desinit." Ed. and trans. Norman Kretzmann. Appendix A of "Incipit/Desinit" in *MTSM*, pp. 122-28.

Plato. *Plato: Timaeus and Critias*. Trans. Alfred Edward Taylor. London: Methuen, 1929.

—. *The Republic of Plato*. Trans. Francis MacDonald Cornford. Oxford: Clarendon Press, 1961.

—. *The Timaeus of Plato Translated with a Running Commentary*. Trans. Francis MacDonald Cornford. New York: Humanities Press, 1952.

Plotinus. *Plotinus*. Trans. Arthur Hilary Armstrong. 6 Vols. London: Heinemann, 1967.

Robert Grosseteste. *Commentarius in VIII Physicorum Aristotelis; fontibus manu scriptes nunc primum in lucem*. Ed. Richard C. Dales. *Studies in Medieval Thought*. Boulder, Colorado: University of Colorado Press, 1963.

—. *Commentarius in Posteriorum analyticorum libros.* Ed. Pietro Rossi. Unione Accademica Nazionale Corpus Philosophorum Medii Aevi. Testi e Studi, II. Florence: L. S. Olschki, 1981.

—. *Concerning Lines, Angles, and Figures.* Trans. David C. Lindberg. In *Sourcebook in Medieval Science.* Ed. Edward Grant. Cambridge, Massachusetts: Harvard University Press, 1974, pp. 385-88.

—. *Die philosophischen Werke des Robert Grosseteste, Bischof von Lincoln.* Ed. Ludwig Baur. *Beiträge zur Geschichte der Philosophie und Theologie des Mittelalters,* IX. Münster: Aschendorff, 1912.

Robert Holcot. *Super Libros Sapientiae.* Ed. Heinrich Gran. Hagenau: 1494.

Roger Bacon. *The Opus Majus of Roger Bacon.* Ed. John Henry Bridges. Oxford: Clarendon Press, 1897-1900.

Simplicius. *In Aristotelis Categorias Commentarii.* Ed. Carolus Kalbfleish. Berlin: G. Reimeri, 1907.

Thomas Aquinas. *Opera Omnia.* 34 Vols. Eds. S. E. Fretté and P. Maré. Paris: L. Vivès, 1874-89.

—. *St. Thomas Aquinas: Philosophical Texts.* Trans. Thomas Gilby. London: Oxford University Press, 1951.

Thomas Bradwardine. "Bradwardine (?) on Ockham's Doctrine of Consequences: An Edition." Ed. Niels Jorgen Green-Pedersen. *Cahiers de l'Institute du moyen âge grec et latin,* 42 (1982), pp. 85-150.

—. *De causa Dei contra Pelagium et de virtute causarum a suos Mertonenses, libri tres.* Ed. Henry Saville. London: Ex Officina Nortoniana apud Ioannem Billium, 1618.

—. "Le *De futuris contingentibus* de Thomas Bradwardine." Ed. M. Jean-François Genest. *Recherches augustiniennes,* 14 (1979), pp. 249-336.

—. "Geometry and the Continuum in the Fourteenth Century: A Philosophical Analysis of Thomas Bradwardine's 'Tractatus de Continuo.'" Ed. John Emery Murdoch. Diss. University of Wisconsin 1957.

—. "The *Geometria speculativa* of Thomas Bradwardine: Text with Critical Edition." Ed. A. G. Molland. Diss. University of Cambridge 1967.

—. "An Intriguing Fourteenth-Century Document: Thomas Bradwardine's *De arte memorativa.*" Ed. Hüner Gillmeister. *Archiv für das Studium des neueren Sprachen und Literaturen,* 220 (1983), pp. 111-14.

—. "Thomas Bradwardine's Treatise on 'incipit' and 'desinit': Edition and Introduction." Ed. Lauge Olaf Nielsen. *Cahiers de l'Institute du moyen âge grec et latin,* 42 (1982), pp. 1-83.

—. *Thomas of Bradwardine, His Tractatus de Proportionibus: Its Significance for the Development of Mathematical Physics.* Ed. H. Lamar Crosby. Madison, Wisconsin: University of Wisconsin Press, 1955.

Thomas Buckingham *Quaestiones.* New College, Oxford MS 134, fos. 322-441.

—. "Thomas Buckingham's *Ostensio Meriti Liberae Actionis*: Conclusions 1 to 15: 'De Contingentia Futurorum et Arbitrii Libertate': An Edition and Study." Ed. Bartholemew Ruben De La Torre. Diss. University of Toronto 1979.

Walter Burley. "'De Primo et Ultimo Instanti' des Walter Burley." Eds. Hermann and Charlotte Shapiro. *Archiv für Geschichte der Philosophie,* 47 (1966), pp. 157-73.

William of Ockham. *The De Sacramento Altaris of William of Ockham.* Ed. and trans. Thomas Bruce Birch. Burlington, Iowa: The Lutheran Literacy Board, 1930.

—. *Expositio aurea et admonum utilis super artem veterem edita . . . cum quaestionibus Alberti parvi de Saxonia.* Bononiae: 1496.

—. *Expositio in libros I-III Physicorum Aristotelis.* Eds. V. Richter and G. Liebold. In *Guillelmi de Ockham Opera philosophica et theologica ad fidem codicum manuscriptorum edita.* St. Bonaventure, New York: Franciscan Institute of St. Bonaventure University, 1985.

—. "On Possibility and God." Trans. Allan B. Wolter. In *Medieval Philosophy from St. Augustine to Nicholas of Cusa.* Eds. John F. Wippel and Allan B. Wolter. New York: Macmillan, 1969, pp. 445-454.

—. *Ordinatio (Sent. I), Dist. 43.* Ed. Allan B. Wolter. *Franziskanische Studien,* 32 (1950), pp. 92-96.

—. *Philosophia Naturalis Guilelmi Ockham.* Ed. Bonaventura Theulo. Rome: Typis I. B. Robletti, 1637.

—. *Quaestiones in libros physicorum.* MS Paris Bib. Nat. Lat. 17841.

—. *The Tractatus de praedestinatione et de praescientia Dei et de futuris contingentibus.* Ed. Philotheus Boehner. St. Bonventure, New York: The Franciscan Institute, 1945.

—. *The Tractatus de successivis Attributed to William of Ockham.* Ed. Philotheus Boehner. St. Bonaventure, New York: The Franciscan Institute, 1944.

—. *Venerabilis Inceptoris Guillelmi de Ockham Summa Logica.* Eds. Philotheus Boehner, Gedeon Gál and Stephanus Brown. St. Bonaventure, New York: The Franciscan Institute, 1974.

—. *William Ockham: Predestination, God's Foreknowledge and Future Contingents.* Ed. and trans. Marilyn McCord Adams and Norman Kretzmann. New York: Appleton-Century-Crofts, 1969.

William Sherwood. "Syncategoremata." Ed. J. Reginald O'Donnell. *Mediaeval Studies,* 3 (1941), pp. 46-93

—. *Treatise on Syncategorematic Words.* Ed. and trans. Norman Kretzmann. Minneapolis, Minnesota: University of Minnesota Press, 1968.

SECONDARY SOURCES

Adams, Marilyn McCord. *William Ockham.* Notre Dame, Indiana: University of Notre Dame Press, 1987.

Anderson, James F. "Time and the Possibility of an Eternal World." *Thomist,* 15 (1932), pp. 136-61.

Ariotti, P. E. "The Concept of Time in Western Antiquity." In *The Study of Time,* Vol. II. Eds. J. T. Fraser and N. Lawrence. New York: Springer-Verlag, 1975, pp. 69-80.

Baron, Salo Wittmayer, ed. *Essays on Maimonides: An Octocentennial Volume.* New York: Columbia University Press, 1941.

Berlinger, Rudolph. "Le temps et l'homme chez saint Augustin." *L'année théologique augustinienne,* 13 (1953), pp. 260-79.

Bettoni, Efrem. *Duns Scotus: The Basic Principles of his Philosophy.* Ed. and trans. Bernardine Bonansea. Westport, Connecticut: Greenwood Press, 1978.

Bodewig, Ewald. "Zahl und Kontinuum in der Philosophie des hl. Thomas." *Divus Thomas,* 13 (1935), pp. 57-77.

Boehner, Philotheus. "Ockham's *Tractatus de praedestinatione et de praescientia Dei et de futuris contingentibus* and its Main Problems." In *Collected Articles on Ockham.*

Ed. Eligius M. Buytaert. St. Bonaventure, New York: The Franciscan Institute, 1958, pp. 420-41.

Brown, Stephen F. and Stephen Dumont. "The Univocity of the Concept of Being in the Fourteenth Century, III: An Early Scotist." *Mediaeval Studies*, 51 (1989), pp. 1-129.

Callahan, John F. *Four Views of Time in Ancient Philosophy*. Cambridge, Massachusetts: Harvard University Press, 1948.

Callus, Daniel A. "Robert Grosseteste as Scholar." In *Robert Grosseteste, Scholar and Bishop*. Ed. Daniel A. Callus. Oxford: Clarendon Press, 1955, pp. 1-69.

Catto, Jeremy I. ed. *The Early Oxford Schools*. Volume I of *The History of the University of Oxford*. Ed. T. H. Aston. Oxford: Clarendon Press, 1984.

Chadwick, Henry. *The Consolations of Music, Logic, Theology and Philosophy*. Oxford: Clarendon Press, 1981.

Chaix-Ruy, Jules. "Le problème du temps dans les 'Confessions' et dans 'La cité de Dieu.'" *Giornale di metafisica*, 9 (1954), 464-77.

—. *Saint Augustin: temps et histoire*. Paris: Études augustiniennes, 1956.

Chenu, Marie Dominique. *St. Thomas d'Aquin et la théologie*. Bourges: L'imprimerie Tardy, 1959.

Clagett, Marshall. *The Science of Mechanics in the Middle Ages*. Madison, Wisconsin: University of Wisconsin Press, 1959.

Clark, Gordon H. "The Theory of Time in Plotinus." *Philosophical Review*, 53 (1944), pp. 337-58.

Copelston, Frederick Charles. *Aquinas*. Hammondsworth, Middelsex, England: Penguin, 1965.

—. *A History of Medieval Philosophy*. London: Methuen, 1972.

Corish, D. "The Beginning of the Beginning in Western Thought." In *The Study of Time*, Vol. IV. Eds. J. T. Fraser, N. Lawrence and D. Park. New York: Springer Verlag, 1981, pp. 34-45.

Courtenay, William J. "John of Mirecourt and Gregory of Rimini on Whether God Can Undo the Past." *RTAM*, 39 (1972), pp. 224-56; 40 (1973), pp. 147-74.

—. "Recent Work on Fourteenth-Century Oxford Thought." *History of Education Quarterly*, Spring-Summer (1985), pp. 227-32.

—. "The Reception of Ockham's Thought in Fourteenth-Century England." In *From Ockham to Wyclif*. Eds. Anne Hudson and Michael Wilks. Oxford: Basil Blackwell, 1987, pp. 89-107.

—. "The Registers of the University of Paris and the Statutes against the Scientia Occamica." *Vivarium*, 29 (1991), pp. 13-49.

—. "The Role of English Thought in the Transformation of University Education in the Late Middle Ages." In *Rebirth, Reform and Resilience: Universities in Transition, 1300-1700*. Ed. James M. Kittelson and Pamela J. Transue. Columbus, Ohio: Ohio University Press, 1984, pp. 103-62.

—. *Schools and Scholars in Fourteenth-Century England*. Princeton, New Jersey: Princeton University Press, 1987.

Courtenay, William J. and Katherine H. Tachau. "Ockham, Ockhamists, and the English-German Nation at Paris, 1339-1341." *History of the Universities*, 2 (1982), pp. 53-96.

Crombie, Alistair Cameron. *Augustine to Galileo*. London: Heinemann, 1959.

—. *Robert Grosseteste and the Origins of Experimental Science*. Oxford: Clarendon Press, 1953.

Cushman, Robert E. "Greek and Christian Views of Time." *Journal of Religion*, 33 (1953), pp. 254-65.

Dales, Richard C. "Henry of Harclay on the Infinite." *Journal of the History of Ideas*, 45 (1984), pp. 295-301.

—. "Maimonides and Boethius of Dacia on the Eternity of the World." *The New Scholasticism*, 56 (1982), pp. 306-19.

—. *Medieval Discussions of the Eternity of the World.* New York: E. J. Brill, 1990.

Dales, Richard C. and Omar Argerame, eds. *Medieval Latin Texts on the Eternity of the World.* New York: E. J. Brill, 1991.

d'Alverny, Marie Therèse. "Translations and Translators." In *Renaissance and Renewal in the Twelfth Century.* Eds. Robert E. Benson and Giles Constable. Oxford: Clarendon Press, 1982, pp. 421-62.

De Blic, J. "Les arguments de saint Augustin contre l'éternité du monde." *Mélanges de science religieuse*, 2 (1945), pp. 33-44.

De la Torre, Bartholemew Ruben. "Thomas Buckingham's *Ostensio meriti liberae actionis*, Conclusions 1-15: 'De contingentia futurorum et arbitrii libertate': An Edition and Study." Diss. University of Toronto 1979.

Dienstag, Jacob I. *Studies in Maimonides and Saint Thomas Aquinas.* New York: KTAV, 1975.

Drake, Stillman. "Medieval Ratio Theory of Compound Medicines in the Origins of Bradwardine's Rule." *Isis*, 64 (1973), pp. 67-77.

Dronke, Peter, ed. *A History of Twelfth-Century Western Philosophy.* Cambridge: Cambridge University Press, 1988.

Dumont, Stephen. "The Univocity of the Concept of Being in the Fourteenth Century: John Duns Scotus and William of Alnwick." *Mediaeval Studies*, 49 (1987), pp. 1-75.

—. "The Univocity of the Concept of Being in the Fourteenth Century, II: The *De ente* of Peter Thomae." *Mediaeval Studies*, 50 (1988), pp. 186-256.

Etzkorn, Girard J. "Codex Merton 284: Evidence of Ockham's Early Influence at Oxford." In *From Ockham to Wyclif.* Eds. Anne Hudson and Michael Wilks. Oxford: Basil Blackwell, 1987, pp. 31-42.

Evans, Gillian R. *Anselm.* Wilton, Connecticut: Morehouse-Barlow, 1989.

—. "Time and Eternity: Boethian and Augustinian Sources of the Thought of the Late Eleventh and Early Twelfth Centuries." *Classical Folia*, 31 (1977), pp. 105-18.

Fakhry, Majid. *A History of Islamic Philosophy.* New York: Columbia University Press, 1970.

Fleming, Brian. "Thomas Bradwardine: Oxford Scholar, Royal Servant and Archbishop of Canterbury." Thesis. Université catholique de Louvain 1964.

Fletcher, John M. "Interfaculty Disputes in Late Medieval Oxford." In *From Ockham to Wyclif.* Eds. Anne Hudson and Michael Wilks. Oxford: Basil Blackwell, 1987.

Gauthier, René Antonin. *Ibn Rochd (Averroes).* Paris: Presses Universitaires de France, 1948.

—. "Notes sur les débuts (1225-1240) du premier 'averroisme.'" *Revue des sciences philosophiques et théologiques*, 66 (1982), pp. 321-74.

Gelber, Hester. "The Fallacy of Accident and the *dictum de omni*: Late Medieval Controversy over a Reciprocal Pair." *Vivarium*, 25 (1987), pp. 110-45.

Genest, M. Jean-François. "La liberté de Dieu à l'égard du passé selon Pierre Damien et Thomas Bradwardine." *Annuaire de l'école pratique des hautes études*, 85 (1977-78), pp. 391-93.

Genest, M. Jean-François and Katherine H. Tachau. "Le lecture de Thomas Bradwardine sur les Sentences." *AHDLMA*, 56 (1990), pp. 301-306.

Gibson, Margaret, ed. *Boethius: His Life, Thought and Influence.* Oxford: Basil Blackwell, 1981.

Gilson, Étienne. *The Christian Philosophy of Saint Augustine.* Trans. L. E. M. Lynch. London: Victor Gollancz, 1961.

—. *The Christian Philosophy of St. Thomas Aquinas.* Trans. L. K. Shook. London: Victor Gollancz, 1961.

—. *History of Christian Philosophy in the Middle Ages.* London: Sheed and Ward, 1955.

—. *Jean Duns Scot.* Paris: J. Vrin, 1952.

Goddu, André. *The Physics of William of Ockham.* Leiden: E. J. Brill, 1984.

Goldman, Eliezer. "Rationality and Revelation in Maimonides' Thought." In *Maimonides and Philosophy.* Eds. Shlomo Pines and Yirmiyahu Yovel. Boston, Massachusetts: Martinus Nijhoff, 1986, pp. 15-23.

Grant, Edward. "Bradwardine and Galileo: Equality of Velocities in the Void." *Archive for the History of Exact Sciences,* 2 (1965), pp. 344-64.

—. "The Condemnation of 1277, God's Absolute Power, and Physical Thought in the Late Middle Ages." *Viator,* 10 (1979), pp. 211-44.

—. "Science and the Medieval University." In *Rebirth, Reform and Resilience: Universities in Transition, 1300-1700.* Eds. James M. Kittelson and Pamela J. Transue. Columbus, Ohio: Ohio University Press, 1984, pp. 68-102.

Gunn, Alexander J. *The Problem of Time: An Historical and Critical Study.* London: Allen and Unwin, 1929.

Hahn, Sebastian. *Thomas Bradwardine und seine Lehre von der menschlichen Willensfreiheit.* Münster: Aschendorff, 1904.

Harris, Charles Reginald Schiller. *Duns Scotus.* 2 Vols. New York: Humanities Press, 1959.

Harrison, Anne. "Blasius of Parma's Critique of Bradwardine's 'Tractatus de proportionibus.'" In *Scienza e filosofia all'Università di Padova nel Quattrocento.* Ed. A. Poppi. Centro per la storia dell'Università di Padova I. Trieste: Edizione Lint, 1983, pp. 19-69.

Hausheer, Herman. "St. Augustine's Conception of Time." *Philosophical Review,* 46 (1937), pp. 503-12.

Hawkins, Denis John Bernard. *The Essentials of Theism.* London: Sheed and Ward, 1949.

Henniger, Mark C. "Henry of Harclay's Questions on Divine Prescience and Predestination." *Franciscan Studies,* 40 (1980), pp. 167-243.

Heschel, Abraham Joshua. *Maimonides: A Biography.* Trans. Joachim Neugroschel. New York: Farrar, Straus, Giroux, 1982.

Hintikka, Jaakko. *Time and Necessity: Studies in Aristotle's Theory of Modality.* Oxford: Clarendon Press, 1973.

Hudson, Anne and Michael Wilks, eds. *From Ockham to Wyclif.* Studies in Church History, Subsidia 5. Oxford: Basil Blackwell, 1897.

Ivry, Alfred I. "Neoplatonic Currents in Maimonides' Thought." In *Perspectives on Maimonides.* Ed. Joel L. Kraemer. New York: Oxford University Press, 1991, pp. 115-40.

Jordan, Robert. "Time and Contingency in St. Augustine." *Review of Metaphysics,* 8 (1955), pp. 394-417.

Kaluza, Zenon. "L'oeuvre théologique de Nicolas Aston." *AHDLMA,* 45 (1978), pp. 45-82.

—. "La prétendu discussion parisienne de Thomas de Bradwardine avec Thomas de Buckingham: témoinage de Thomas de Cracovie." *RTAM,* 43 (1976), pp. 209-36.

—. "Le problème du 'Deum non esse' chez Étienne du Chaumont, Nicolas Aston et Thomas Bradwardine." *Mediaevalia Philosophia Polonorum,* 24 (1979), pp. 3-19.

Kane, G. Stanley. *Anselm's Doctrine of Freedom and the Will.* New York: Edwin Mellen, 1981.

Kennedy, Leonard A. "Oxford Philosophers and the Existence of God." *RTAM*, 52 (1985), pp. 194-208.

—. "Philosophical Scepticism in England in the Mid-Fourteenth Century." *Vivarium*, 21 (1983), pp. 35-57.

Kenny, Anthony. "Divine Foreknowledge and Human Freedom." In *Aquinas: A Collection of Critical Essays*. Ed. Anthony Kenny. London: Macmillan, 1969, pp. 255-70.

—. *The God of the Philosophers*. Oxford: Clarendon Press, 1979.

Kibre, Pearl and Nancy G. Siraisi. "The Institutional Setting: The Universities." In *Science in the Middle Ages*. Ed. David C. Lindberg. Chicago: University of Chicago Press, 1978, pp. 120-44.

Kittelson, James M. and Pamela J. Transue. *Rebirth, Reform and Resilience: Universities in Transition, 1300-1700*. Columbus, Ohio: Ohio State University Press, 1984.

Kluxen, Wolfgang. "Maimonides and Latin Scholasticism." In *Maimonides and Philosophy*. Eds. Shlomo Pines and Yirmiyahu Yovel. Boston, Massachusetts: Martinus Nijhoff, 1986, pp. 224-32.

Kneale, William Calvert. "Time and Eternity in Theology." *Proceedings of the Aristotelian Society*, 60 (1960-61), pp. 87-108.

Kovach, Francis J. and Robert W. Shahan, eds. *Albert the Great*. Norman, Oklahoma: University of Oklahoma Press, 1980.

Kraemer, Joel L., ed. *Perspectives on Maimonides*. New York: Oxford University Press, 1991.

Kretzmann, Norman. "Incipit/Desinit." In *MTSM*, pp. 101-36.

Kretzmann, Norman, ed. *Infinity and Continuity in Ancient and Medieval Philosophy*. London: Cornell University Press, 1982.

Kretzmann, Norman, Anthony Kenny and Jan Pinborg, eds. *The Cambridge History of Later Medieval Philosophy*. Cambridge: Cambridge University Press, 1982.

Lacey, Hugh M. "Empiricism and Augustine's Problems about Time." In *Augustine: A Collection of Critical Essays*. Ed. Robert Austin Markus. New York: Doubleday, 1972, pp. 280-308.

Laun, Justin Ferdinand. "Die Prädestination bei Wiclif und Bradwardin." In *Imago Dei*. Ed. H. Bornkamm. Giessen: Alfred Töpelmann, 1923, pp. 63-84.

—. "Recherches sur Thomas Bradwardin, précurseur de Wyclif." *Revue d'histoire et de philosophie religieuse*, 9 (1929), pp. 217-33.

—. "Thomas von Bradwardin, der Schüler Augustins und Lehrer Wiclifs." *Zeitschrift für Kirchengeschichte*, 47 (New Series 10) (1928), pp. 333-56.

Leaman, Oliver. *An Introduction to Medieval Islamic Philosophy*. Cambridge: Cambridge University Press, 1985.

Lechler, Gotthard. *John Wycliffe and his English Precursors*. Trans. P. Lorimer. London: The Religious Tract Society, 1878.

Leclercq, Jean. "The Experience of Time and its Interpretation in the Late Middle Ages." *Studies in Medieval Culture*, 8-9 (1976), pp. 137-50.

Lee, Arthur A. "Anselm and Thomas of Buckingham: An Examination of the *Questiones super Sententias*." *Anselm Studies*, 1 (1983), pp. 231-49.

Leff, Gordon. *Bradwardine and the Pelagians*. Cambridge Studies in Medieval Life and Thought, Series 2, Number 5. Cambridge: Cambridge University Press, 1957.

—. *Gregory of Rimini: Tradition and Innovation in Fourteenth-Century Thought*. Manchester: Manchester University Press, 1961.

—. *William of Ockham: The Metamorphosis of Scholastic Discourse.* Manchester: Manchester University Press, 1975.

Lindberg, David C. "On the Applicability of Mathematics to Nature: Roger Bacon and his Predecessors." *British Journal for the History of Science,* 15 (1982), pp. 3-25.

—. *The European Scientific Tradition in Philosophical, Religious and Institutional Context, 600 B.C. to A.D. 1450.* Chicago: University of Chicago Press, 1992.

—. *Theories of Vision from Al-kindi to Kepler.* Chicago: University of Chicago Press, 1976.

—. "The Transmission of Greek and Arabic Learning in the West." In *Science in the Middle Ages.* Ed. David C. Lindberg. Chicago: University of Chicago Press, 1978.

Lindberg, David C., ed. *Science in the Middle Ages.* Chicago: University of Chicago Press, 1978.

Lloyd, A. C. "The Later Neoplatonists." In *The Cambridge History of Later Greek and Early Medieval Philosophy.* Ed. Arthur Hilary Armstrong. Cambridge: Cambridge University Press, 1967, pp. 272-325.

Machamer, Peter K. and Robert G. Turnbull, eds. *Motion and Time, Space and Matter: Interrelations in the History of Philosophy and Science.* Columbus, Ohio: Ohio State University Press, 1976.

Maier, Anneliese. *Ausgehendes Mittelalter: Gesammelte Aufsätze zur Geistesgeschichte des 14. Jahrhunderts.* 2 Vols. Rome: Storia e letteratura, 1967.

—. "Die Subjectivierung der Zeit in der scholastischen Philosophie." *Philosophia Naturalis,* 1 (1951), pp. 361-98.

—. *Die Vorläufer Galileis in 14. Jahrhundert.* Rome: Storia e letteratura, 1966.

—. *Zwischen Philosophie und Mechanik: Studien zur Naturphilosophie der Spätscholastik.* Rome: Storia e letteratura, 1958.

Malino, Jonathan W. "Aristotle on Eternity: Does Maimonides Have a Reply?" In *Maimonides and Philosophy.* Eds. Shlomo Pines and Yirmiyahu Yovel. Boston, Massachusetts: Martinus Nijhoff, 1986.

Mansion, Augustin. "La théorie aristotélicienne du temps chez les péripatéticiens médiévaux: Averroès, Albert le Grand, Thomas d'Aquin." *Revue néo-scholastique,* 32 (1934), pp. 275-307.

Marcolino, Venicio. "Der Augustinertheologie an der Universität Paris." In *Gregor von Rimini. Werk und Wirkung bis zur Reformation.* Ed. Heiko A. Oberman. New York: W. de Gruyter, 1981, pp. 127-94.

Maréchal, Joseph. "Lettres sur le problème du temps chez saint Augustin et sur le problème de la philosophie catholique." In *Mélanges Joseph Maréchal,* Vol. I. Paris: Desclée, De Brouwer et Cie, 1950, pp. 261-69.

Marenbon, John. *Later Medieval Philosophy (1150-1350): An Introduction.* New York: Routledge and Kegan Paul, 1987.

McCarthy, Donald J. "Free Choice and Liberty According to Thomas Bradwardine." Diss. University of Toronto 1965.

McEvoy, James. "La connaissance intellectuelle selon Robert Grosseteste." *Revue philosophique de Louvain,* 75 (1977), pp. 26-29.

—. *The Philosophy of Robert Grosseteste.* Oxford: Clarendon Press, 1982.

—. "St. Augustine's Account of Time and Wittgenstein's Criticisms." *Review of Metaphysics,* 37 (1984), pp. 547-77.

McGrade, Arthur Stephen. "Enjoyment at Oxford after Ockham." In *From Ockham to Wyclif.* Eds. Anne Hudson and Michael Wilks. Oxford: Basil Blackwell, 1987, pp. 63-88.

McGrath, Alister E. "The Anti-Pelagian Structure of 'Nominalist' Doctrines of Justification." *Ephemerides Theologicae Lovanienses*, 57 (1981), pp. 107-19.

——. "Forerunners of the Reformation." *Harvard Theological Report*, 75 (1982), pp. 219-42.

McMullin, Ernan, ed. *The Concept of Matter in Greek and Medieval Philosophy.* Notre Dame, Indiana: University of Notre Dame Press, 1965.

McVaugh, Michael. "Arnold of Villanova and Bradwardine's Law." *Isis*, 58 (1967), pp. 56-64.

Merlan, Philip. *From Platonism to Neoplatonism.* The Hague: Martinus Nijhoff, 1975.

Miller, F. D. "Aristotle Against the Atomists." In *Infinity and Continuity in Ancient and Medieval Thought.* Ed. Norman Kretzmann. London: Cornell University Press, 1982, pp. 87-111.

Molland, A. G. "An Examination of Bradwardine's Geometry." *Archive for the History of Exact Sciences*, 19 (1978), pp. 113-75.

——. "The Geometrical Background to the 'Merton School': An Exploration into the Application of Mathematics to Natural Philosophy in the Fourteenth Century." *British Journal for the History of Science*, 4 (1968), pp. 108-25.

Moody, Ernest A. "Empiricism and Metaphysics in Medieval Philosophy." In *SMPSL*, pp. 287-304.

——. "Galileo and Avempace." *Journal of the History of Ideas*, 12 (1951), pp. 163-93; 375-422.

——. "Laws of Motion in Medieval Physics." In *SMPSL*, pp. 189-201.

——. *The Logic of William of Ockham.* New York: Russell and Russell, 1965.

——. "William of Ockham." In *SMPSL*, pp. 409-39.

Moreau, M. "Mémoire et durée." *Revue des études augustiniennes*, 1 (1955), pp. 239-50.

Multhauf, Robert P. "The Science of Matter." In *Science in the Middle Ages.* Ed. David C. Lindberg. Chicago: University of Chicago Press, 1978, pp. 369-90.

Murdoch, John Emery. "The Analytic Character of Late Medieval Learning: Natural Philosophy Without Nature." In *Approaches to Nature in the Middle Ages.* Ed. Lawrence D. Roberts. Binghamton, New York: Center for Medieval and Early Renaissance Studies, 1982, pp. 171-213.

——. "Atomism and Motion in the Fourteenth Century." In *Transformation and Tradition in the Sciences: Essays in Honor of I. Bernard Cohen.* Ed. Everett Mendelsohn. Cambridge: Cambridge University Press, 1984, pp. 45-66.

——. "From Social to Intellectual Factors: An Aspect of the Unitary Character of Late Medieval Learning." In *The Cultural Context of Medieval Learning.* Eds. John Emery Murdoch and Edith Dudley Sylla. Boston, Massachusetts: D. Reidel, 1975, pp. 271-348.

——. "Infinity and Continuity." In *CHLMP*, pp. 564-91.

——. "The Medieval Language of Proportions: Elements of the Interaction with Greek Foundations and the Development of New Mathematical Techniques." In *Scientific Change.* Ed. Alistair Cameron Crombie. London: Heinemann, 1963, pp. 237-71.

——. "Proportional Analysis in Natural Philosophy: A Case Study." *Synthese*, 40 (1979), pp. 117-46.

——. "Superposition, Congruence and Continuity in the Middle Ages." In *L'Aventure de la science: Mélanges Alexandre Koyré*, Vol. I. Histoire de la pensée, Vol. XII. Paris: École pratique des hautes études, 1964, pp. 416-41.

Murdoch, John Emery and Edith Dudley Sylla. "The Science of Motion." In *Science in the Middle Ages.* Ed. David C. Lindberg. Chicago: University of Chicago Press, 1978, pp. 206-64.

Normore, Calvin. "Future Contingents." In *CHLMP*, pp. 358-81.

Oberman, Heiko A. *Archbishop Thomas Bradwardine, A Fourteenth-Century Augustinian: A Study of his Theology in its Historical Context*. Utrecht: Kemink and Zoon, 1958.

—. *Forerunners of the Reformation: The Shape of Late Medieval Thought Illustrated by Key Documents*. Translations by Paul L. Nyhus. London: Lutterworth Press, 1966.

—. "Thomas Bradwardine: un précurseur du Luther?" *Revue d'histoire et de philosophie religieuse*, 40 (1960), pp. 146-51.

Owen, G. E. L. "Aristotle on Time." In *MTSM*, pp. 3-27.

Pantin, William Abel. *The English Church in the Fourteenth Century*. Cambridge: Cambridge University Press, 1955.

Panofsky, Erwin. *Studies in Iconology*. New York: Harper and Row, 1939.

Pines, Shlomo and Yirmiyahu Yovel, eds. *Maimonides and Philosophy*. Boston, Massachusetts: Martinus Nijhoff, 1986.

Puig, Joseph. "Maimonides and Averroes on the First Mover." In *Maimonides and Philosophy*. Eds. Shlomo Pines and Yirmiyahu Yovel. Boston, Massachusetts: Martinus Nijhoff, 1986.

Quinn, John M. "The Concept of Time in Albert the Great." In *Albert the Great*. Eds. Francis J. Kovach and Robert W. Shahan. Norman, Oklahoma: University of Oklahoma Press, 1980, pp. 21-48.

—. *The Doctrine of Time in St. Thomas: Some Aspects and Applications. An Abstract of a Dissertation*. Washington, D. C.: The Catholic University of America Press, 1960.

Reiss, Edmund. *Boethius*. Boston, Massachusetts: Twayne, 1982.

Rist, John M. "Augustine on Free Will and Predestination." In *Augustine: A Collection of Critical Essays*. Ed. Robert Austin Markus. New York: Doubleday, 1972, pp. 218-52.

Roberts, Lawrence D., ed. *Approaches to Nature in the Middle Ages*. Binghamton, New York: Center for Medieval and Early Renaissance Studies, 1982.

Robson, John Adam. *Wyclif and the Oxford Schools*. Cambridge: Cambridge University Press, 1961.

Rouré, Marie Louise. "La problématique des propositions insolubles au XIII siècle - William Shyreswood, Walter Burleigh et Thomas Bradwardine." *AHDLMA*, 37 (1970-71), pp. 205-326.

Rowe, William L. "Augustine on Foreknowledge and Free Will." In *Augustine: A Collection of Critical Essays*. Ed. Robert Austin Markus. New York: Doubleday, 1972, pp. 209-17.

Rowland, Beryl. "Bishop Bradwardine on the Artificial Memory." *Journal of the Warburg and Courtauld Institutes*, 41 (1978), pp. 307-12.

Sambursky, Samuel and Shlomo Pines. *The Concept of Time in Late Neo-Platonism*. Jerusalem: The Israel Academy of Science and Humanities, 1971.

Sarnowsky, Jürgen. "Natural Philosophy at Oxford and Paris in the Mid-Fourteenth Century." In *From Ockham to Wyclif*. Eds. Anne Hudson and Michael Wilks. Oxford: Basil Blackwell, 1987, pp. 125-34.

Schrödinger, Edwin. *Nature and the Greeks*. Cambridge: Cambridge University Press, 1954.

Schwamm, Hermann. *Das göttliche Vorherwissen bei Duns Scotus und seinen ersten Anhängern. Philosophie und Grenzwissenschaften*, V. Innsbruck: Felizian Rauch, 1934.

Serene, Eileen F. "Robert Grosseteste on Induction and Demonstrative Science." *Synthese*, 40 (1979), pp. 97-115.

Shapiro, Herman. *Motion, Time and Space According to William of Ockham*. St. Bonaventure, New York: The Franciscan Institute, 1957.

Sirat, Colette. *La philosophie juive au moyen âge selon les textes manuscrit et imprimés*. Paris: Editions de Centre National de la Recherche Scientifique, 1983, pp. 179-232.

Smith, Vincent Edward. *St. Thomas on the Object of Geometry*. Milwaukee, Wisconsin: Marquette University Press, 1954.

Sorabji, Richard. *Time, Creation and the Continuum: Theories in Antiquity and the Early Middle Ages*. London: Duckworth, 1983.

Southern, Richard William. *Robert Grosseteste: The Growth of an English Mind in Medieval Europe*. Oxford: Clarendon Press, 1986.

—. *Saint Anselm: A Portrait in a Landscape*. Cambridge: Cambridge University Press, 1990.

Spade, Paul Vincent. "*Insolubilia* and Bradwardine's Theory of Signification." *Annuaire de l'école pratique des hautes études*, 85 (1977-78), pp. 391-93.

Stannard, Jerry. "Natural History." In *Science in the Middle Ages*. Ed. David C. Lindberg. Chicago: University of Chicago Press, 1978, pp. 429-560.

Streveler, Paul A. "Anselm on Future Contingencies: A Critical Analysis of the *De concordia*." *Anselm Studies*, 1 (1983), pp. 165-73.

—. "Robert Holkot on Future Contingencies: A Preliminary Account." *Studies in Medieval Culture*, 8-9 (1976), pp. 163-71.

Stump, Eleonore and Norman Kretzmann. "Eternity." *Journal of Philosophy*, 78 (1981), pp. 429-58.

Sweeney, Leo. *Infinity in the Presocratics: A Bibliographical and Philosophical Study*. The Hague: Martinus Nijhoff, 1972.

—. "The Meaning of *Esse* in Albert the Great's Texts on Creation in *Summa de creaturis* and *Scripta super sententias*." In *Albert the Great*. Eds. Francis J. Kovach and Robert W. Shahan. Norman, Oklahoma: University of Oklahoma Press, 1980, pp. 65-96.

Sylla, Edith Dudley. "Compounding Ratios: Bradwardine, Oresme, and the First Edition of Newton's *Principia*." In *Transformation and Tradition in the Sciences: Essays in Honor of I. Bernard Cohen*. Ed. Everett Mendelsohn. Cambridge: Cambridge University Press, 1984, pp. 11-43.

Tachau, Katherine H. "The Influence of Richard Campsall on Fourteenth-Century Thought." In *From Ockham to Wyclif*. Eds. Anne Hudson and Michael Wilks. Oxford: Basil Blackwell, 1987, pp. 109-24.

—. "The Problem of *species in medio* at Oxford in the Generation after Ockham." *Mediaeval Studies*, 44 (1982), pp. 394-443.

—. *Vision and Certitude in the Age of Ockham: Optics, Epistemology and the Foundation of Semantics 1250-1345*. New York: E. J. Brill, 1988.

Talbot, Charles H. "Medicine." In *Science in the Middle Ages*. Ed. David C. Lindberg. Chicago: University of Chicago Press, 1978, pp. 391-428.

Thijssen, J. M. M. H. "Burdian on Mathematics." *Vivarium*, 23 (1985), pp. 55-78.

—. "Once Again the Ockhamist Statutes of 1339 and 1340: Some New Perspectives." *Vivarium*, 28 (1990), pp. 136-67.

—. "Roger Bacon (1214-1292/97): A Neglected Source in the Medieval Continuum Debate." *Archives internationales d'histoire des sciences* 34 (1984), pp. 25-34.

Vajda, Georges. *Introduction à la pensée juive du moyen âge*. Paris: J. Vrin, 1947.

Vignaux, Paul. *De saint Anselm à Luther*. Paris: J. Vrin, 1976.

Viscovini, Graziella Frederice. "Due commenti anonimi al 'Tractatus proportionum' di Tommaso Bradwardine." *Rinascimento*, Series 2, 19 (1979), pp. 231-33.

Wallace, William A. "The Philosophical Setting of Medieval Science." In *Science in the Middle Ages*. Ed. David C. Lindberg. Chicago: University of Chicago Press, 1978, pp. 91-119.

Wallis, R. T. *Neo-Platonism*. London: Duckworth, 1972.

Walsh, Katherine. *A Fourteenth-Century Scholar and Primate: Richard FitzRalph in Oxford, Avignon and Armagh*. Oxford: Clarendon Press, 1981.

Weisheipl, James A., ed. *Albertus Magnus and the Sciences: Commemorative Essays 1980*. Toronto: Pontifical Institute of Mediaeval Studies, 1980.

Weisheipl, James A. "The Curriculum of the Faculty of Arts at Oxford in the Early Fourteenth Century." *Mediaeval Studies*, 26 (1964), pp. 143-85.

—. *The Development of Physical Theory in the Middle Ages*. New York: Sheed and Ward, 1959.

—. *Friar Thomas d'Aquino: His Life, Thought and Works*. Oxford: Basil Blackwell, 1975.

—. "The Interpretation of Aristotle's Physics and the Science of Motion." In *CHLMP*, pp. 521-36.

—. "Matter in Fourteenth-Century Science." In *The Concept of Matter in Greek and Medieval Philosophy*. Ed. Ernan McMullin. Notre Dame, Indiana: University of Notre Dame Press, 1965, pp. 147-69.

—. "Ockham and the Mertonians." In *The History of the University of Oxford*, Vol. I. Ed. Jeremy I. Catto. Oxford: Clarendon Press, 1984, pp. 607-58.

—. "Ockham and Some Mertonians." *Mediaeval Studies*, 30 (1968), pp. 163-213.

—. "Repertorium Mertonense." *Mediaeval Studies*, 31 (1969), pp. 174-224.

Weisheipl, James A. and Heiko A. Oberman. "The *Sermo Epinicius* Ascribed to Thomas Bradwardine (1346)." *AHDLMA*, 26 (1958), pp. 295-329.

Wilson, Curtis. *William Heytesbury: Medieval Logic and the Rise of Mathematical Physics*. Madison, Wisconsin: University of Wisconsin Press, 1960.

Wissink, J. B. M., ed. *The Eternity of the World in the Thought of Thomas Aquinas and his Contemporaries*. New York: E. J. Brill, 1990.

Wolter, Allan Bernard. *The Philosophy of John Duns Scotus*. Ed. Marilyn McCord Adams. Ithaca, New York: Cornell University Press, 1990.

Workman, Herbert B. *John Wyclif: A Study of the English Medieval Church*. Oxford: Clarendon Press, 1926.

Zawirski, Zygmunt. *L'Évolution de la notion du temps*. Cracow: Librairc Gebethner et Wolff, 1936.

INDEXES

INDEX OF PERSONS AND PLACES

INDEX OF SUBJECTS

250INDEXES

omnipotence 116, 154, 161, 171-173,
178, 180, 181ff, 186, 190, 197, 203,
210, 211, 213, 216, 217ff, 226ff
omniscience: See foreknowledge

Pelagianism 6, 11, 164-167, 190, 201,
203, 216, 217, 219, 224, 226-227
physics 8, 9, 11, 45, 59, 64, 66, 74-76,
79-81, 84, 87, 89, 98, 100-101, 103,
116, 117, 123, 133, 142, 143, 146,
162, 179, 198, 204, 208-210, 232
Platonic philosophy 77, 79-81, 83, 84,
88, 99, 103, 177
predestination 3, 7-9, 11, 132, 151, 156-
160, 166, 168, 186-187, 198, 201-
203, 224
prediction 133, 135, 145, 148, 187-188,
196, 204-205, 209, 210, 226
pre-Socratic philosophy 11, 14, 16-17
proportionality 73ff, 76-78, 84ff, 87,
92ff, 97-98, 129, 163, 207, 210
psychology 29, 31-32, 35, 37, 38, 43,
49, 56, 59, 60, 63, 64, 132, 148, 162,
167, 180, 182, 194, 196, 198
Pythagoreans 16, 19, 20, 23, 43, 129

ratio 85ff, 208
realism 83ff, 114-116, 215
Reformation 7

sin 167, 198-203, 206, 210, 226

skepticism 211, 213, 217ff, 230n, 231
space 15, 17, 19, 21-22, 50, 52, 63, 67,
75, 84, 106-107, 112, 127, 128, 146,
172-173, 204, 218
Stoics 190, 195
succession 34, 88-89, 105-106, 118ff,
125ff, 132-133, 135, 142ff, 148, 173,
179, 180-181, 184, 208
syncategorematic words 136-139, 141ff,
146, 147, 156

time 2, 11, 15, 46-47, 75-76, 100ff,
132ff, 150ff, 173, 174, 177, 182ff,
188, 191-192, 194, 202-209, 218,
232; Abelard's view 42-43; Albertus
Magnus' view 47ff; Anselm's view
41-42; Aquinas' view 59ff; Aristotle's
view 21ff, 26-27, 34, 50, 88-89, 168;
Augustine's view 29ff; Averroes'
view 47ff; Boethius' view 37ff;
Bradwardine's view 93ff, 99, 113,
126ff, 145ff, 159ff, 167, 177ff, 179ff,
209-212; Buckingham's view 222ff;
Duns Scotus' view 67ff; Grosseteste's
view 66ff; Holcot's view 229-230;
Maimonides' view 50; Ockham's
view 118ff; Peter of Spain's view
139ff; Plato's view 17ff, 43; Plotinus'
view 25ff

Studies in the History
of Christian Thought

EDITED BY HEIKO A. OBERMAN

50. HOENEN, M. J. F. M. *Marsilius of Inghen.* Divine Knowledge in Late Medieval Thought. 1993
51. O'MALLEY, J. W., IZBICKI, T. M. and CHRISTIANSON, G. (eds.) *Humanity and Divinity in Renaissance and Reformation.* Essays in Honor of Charles Trinkaus. 1993
52. REEVE, A. (ed.) and SCREECH, M. A. (introd.) *Erasmus' Annotations on the New Testament.* Galatians to the Apocalypse. 1993
53. STUMP, Ph. H. *The Reforms of the Council of Constance (1414-1418).* 1994
54. GIAKALIS, A. *Images of the Divine.* The Theology of Icons at the Seventh Ecumenical Council. With a Foreword by Henry Chadwick. 1994
55. NELLEN, H. J. M. and RABBIE, E. *Hugo Grotius – Theologian.* Essays in Honour of G. H. M. Posthumus Meyjes. 1994
56. TRIGG, J. D. *Baptism in the Theology of Martin Luther.* 1994
57. JANSE, W. *Albert Hardenberg als Theologe.* Profil eines Bucer-Schülers. 1994
58. ASSELT, W.J. VAN. *The Covenant Theology of Johannes Cocceius (1603-1669).* An Examination of its Structure. *In preparation*
59. SCHOOR, R.J.M. VAN DE. *The Irenical Theology of Théophile Brachet de La Milletière (1588-1665).* 1995
60. STREHLE, S. *The Catholic Roots of the Protestant Gospel.* Encounter between the Middle Ages and the Reformation. 1995
61. BROWN, M.L. *Donne and the Politics of Conscience in Early Modern England.* 1995
62. SCREECH, M.A. (ed.). *Richard Mocket, Warden of All Souls College, Oxford, Doctrina et Politia Ecclesiae Anglicanae.* An Anglican Summa. Facsimile with Variants of the Text of 1617. Edited with an Introduction. 1995
63. SNOEK, G.J.C. *Medieval Piety from Relics to the Eucharist.* 1995
64. PIXTON, P.B. *The German Episcopacy and the Implementation of the Decrees of the Fourth Lateran Council, 1216-1245.* Watchmen on the Tower. 1995
65. DOLNIKOWSKI, E.W. *Thomas Bradwardine: A View of Time and a Vision of Eternity in Fourteenth-Century Thought.* 1995

Prospectus available on request

E. J. BRILL — P.O.B. 9000 — 2300 PA LEIDEN — THE NETHERLANDS

only studies through secondary sources
    Averroes
    Maimonides

confused re Scotus
    de rerum primicio by Scotus?

118 good example of total confusion

get Nielsen incipit & desunit & comparue
            Burley!

162   exactness (review)
223   Buckingham vs Bradwardine on God's relation to time
225n Kaluza - NBreview

176 house as or fluid
178   G knows possible & impossible

* 183   Scotus God is never past so always
                contingent (past necessary)
            Ockham present is necessary

185   for Bradwardine God can undo the past
                            God sees rotation
                                185-86
197 phil & theol.

224 dialogue

171 tu
tr 14